P9-DFN-226

PASTOR, CHURCH & LAW

VOLUME THREE

Employment Law

RICHARD R. HAMMAR
J.D., LL.M., CPA

YOUR CHURCH

CHRISTIANITY TODAY
INTERNATIONAL

ISBN-10: 0-917463-35-8
ISBN-13: 978-0-917463-35-8

Published by Your Church Resources
Christianity Today International
465 Gundersen Drive
Carol Stream, IL 60188
(630) 260-6200
www.ChristianityToday.com
www.YourChurch.net
www.ChurchLawToday.com

Edited by: Marian V. Liautaud
Cover design by: Dean Renninger
Interior design by: Mary Bellus

Printed in the United States of America

This publication is designed to provide accurate and authoritative information in regard to the subject matter covered. It is sold with the understanding that the publisher is not engaged in rendering legal, accounting, or other professional service. If legal advice or other expert assistance is required, the services of a competent professional person should be sought. *From a Declaration of Principles jointly adopted by a Committee of the American Bar Association and a Committee of Publishers and Associations.*

To my beloved wife Christine,
and our children, Rachel, Ryan, Abe, and Holly

PASTOR, CHURCH & LAW
Volume Three

TABLE OF CONTENTS
Chapter 8

Preface

The employer-employee relationship is heavily regulated by state and federal law. For example, many employers must withhold federal income taxes and Social Security taxes from wages paid to employees; pay unemployment taxes, obtain workers compensation insurance, refrain from numerous forms of discrimination in the selection and retention of employees, pay the minimum wage and overtime compensation, and comply with federal immigration requirements in the hiring of new employees. In addition, employers may be sued for violating non-discrimination laws or for wrongfully dismissing employees.

Do any of these legal obligations apply to churches? After all, most churches are employers. In addition to a minister, they may employ a secretary, custodian, bookkeeper, music director, counselor, or business administrator. As an employer, is a church subject to the same legal obligations that apply to secular employers? That is the question addressed in this book. Unfortunately, there is no simple answer. Federal immigration reporting requirements clearly apply to church employers. And many states treat churches no differently than secular employers for purposes of workers compensation. This means that they may have to obtain insurance to provide payments to injured employees.

On the other hand, there is much confusion concerning the application of various federal employment and civil rights laws to religious organizations. For example, are churches subject to Title VII of the Civil Rights Act of 1964, which prohibits discrimination in employment on the basis of race, color, national origin, sex, or religion? Are churches subject to federal law banning discrimination in employment decisions based on the age or disability of an employee or applicant for employment? Can the employees of religious organizations organize labor unions? Must churches pay the minimum wage and overtime compensation to their employees? All of these questions, along with several others, are addressed in this third volume of *Pastor, Church & Law, 4th Edition.*

The increasingly regulatory character of government is seen nowhere more clearly than in the context of the employer-employee relationship. Churches must be aware that some of the laws that pertain to this relationship may apply to them, and that First Amendment's guaranty of religious freedom may not provide any protection.

The importance of employment laws and regulations to churches is underscored by surveys conducted each year by Richard Hammar of all published litigation in all federal courts and in all state appellate courts. The results of this research are summarized in Table 8-1. The important thing to note is that employment-related litigation was the most common reason that religious organizations were in court in four of the six years examined. This dramatically demonstrates the importance of this book.

Table 8-1 **Litigation Involving Religious Organizations**

2000	2001	2002	2003	2004	2005
employment [18%]	employment [19%]	employment [14%]	property [12%]	employment [13.8%]	sexual acts [15.9%]
personal injury [14%]	personal injury [12%]	zoning [13%]	employment [11%]	property [13.1%]	employment [15.1%]
property [14%]	property [9%]	personal injury [12%]	personal injury [11%]	zoning [13.1%]	property [14.6%]
zoning [12%]	sexual acts [6%]	sexual acts [12%]	sexual acts [11%]	sexual acts [12.4%]	zoning [11.1%]

by Richard Hammar, or in other volumes in this series, as noted by Table 8-2. All of these resources are available from YOUR CHURCH RESOURCES (Christianity Today International).

Table 8-2 **Employment-Related Topics Addressed in Other YOUR CHURCH Publications**

issue	where addressed
the distinction between employee and self-employed status	Church & Clergy Tax Guide, Chapter 2
sources of taxable income	Church & Clergy Tax Guide, Chapter 4
fringe benefits	Church & Clergy Tax Guide, Chapters 4-5
business expenses	Church & Clergy Tax Guide, Chapter 7
retirement plans	Church & Clergy Tax Guide, Chapter 10
payroll tax reporting requirements	Church & Clergy Tax Guide, Chapter 11
unemployment benefits	Church & Clergy Tax Guide, Chapter 12
salary surveys	Compensation Handbook for Church Staff
compensation planning	Compensation Handbook for Church Staff
works made for hire	The Church Guide to Copyright Law
negligent hiring, negligent supervision, and negligent retention	Volume 4, Chapter 10, Pastor, Church & Law, 4th edition
the "ministerial exception" to employment laws	Volume 4, Chapter 10, Pastor, Church & Law, 4th edition
application of the Occupational Safety and Health Act (OSHA) to church employees	Volume 4, Chapter 9, Pastor, Church & Law, 4th edition

Selection of Employees

Legal Briefs

Churches don't generally think of themselves as employers. And yet, in reality, most churches are employers. In addition to a minister, they may also employ a secretary, custodian, bookkeeper, music director, counselor, or business administrator. So as an employer, is the church subject to the same legal obligations that apply to secular employers? Do you know what employer-employee issues are protected by the First Amendment guaranty of religious freedom, and which ones are not? Never has it been more important to know your church's legal responsibility towards your employees than now. Why? Because employment-related issues land churches in court more than any other area of litigation. (See Table 8-1)

"...employment-related litigation was the most common reason that religious organizations were in court in four of the six years examined."

Avoiding employment litigation begins with the selection of employees. Here's a quick look at what you need to know about hiring new employees at your church:

New Hire Reporting—Employers, including churches, must report all new hires to a designated state agency. (See Table 8-3 for details on what, where and how to report new hires in your state.)

This agency then matches information against its own child support records to locate parents and enforce existing child support orders. Once these matches are done, the information is sent to the "National Directory of New Hires" so other states can compare the information with their own child support records. The information also will be shared with state welfare and unemployment agencies to route out unemployment benefits fraud.

Employment Eligibility Verification—Employers are required by law to confirm the identity of all new hires and their eligibility to work by completing an I-9 form. This is to verify that employees are either American citizens or aliens legally authorized to work in this country. Churches are subject to this requirement.

Unlike tax forms, I-9 forms are not filed with the U.S. government. Employers are required to maintain I-9 records in their own files for three years after the date of hire or one year after the date the employee's employment is terminated, whichever is later. Federal agencies are authorized to request an inspection of your I-9 forms at any time. Typically, they will give employers several days' notice to pull documents out of storage for inspection.

Immigration—Federal immigration law regulates the admission, status, and employability of foreign citizens in this country, and imposes requirements on employers who seek to hire immigrants. This is a growing issue in churches, and federal requirements generally apply to religious organizations.

New Hire Reporting

Key Point 8-02> *Employers must provide a designated state agency with information about every new hire as a result of federal legislation that seeks to facilitate the enforcement of child support orders and reduce fraud in welfare programs. The "new hire reporting law" does not exempt religious organizations.*

In 1996 Congress enacted the Personal Responsibility and Work Opportunity Reconciliation Act, popularly known as the "welfare reform" bill.[1] The Act has many provisions designed to reduce welfare payments and address welfare fraud. One of these provisions requires employers to report all "new hires" to a designated state agency. The purpose of this requirement is to locate "deadbeat dads" who avoid their child support obligations by changing jobs and their place of residence. Forcing these persons to honor their support obligations will enable many women to go off welfare. Another purpose of the new law is to reduce fraudulent unemployment benefits payments to persons who are working.

Technically, states are not required to mandate new hire reporting. But, if they fail to do so, they will forfeit federal funding under certain programs. To date, all states have enacted legislation mandating new hire reporting, and the laws of all 50 states are summarized in Table 8-3.

1. Church Coverage

The new hire reporting requirements apply to all "employers." The Act uses the same definition of "employer" as is contained in section 3401(d) of the Internal Revenue Code. This section defines an employer as "the person for whom an individual performs or performed any service, of whatever nature, as the employee of such person." This definition contains no exception for religious organizations. There is no exception for "small" employers having only one or two employees. Note that the reporting requirement only pertains to *new hires*, as defined by state law. This generally will be any employee hired after a date specified by state law.

2. How It Works

When employers (including churches) report new hire information to their designated state agency, the agency will match the information against its own child support records to locate parents and enforce existing child support orders. Once these matches are done, the information is sent to the "National Directory of New Hires" so other states can compare the information with their own child support records. The information also will be shared with state welfare and unemployment agencies, to detect and prevent fraudulent or erroneous payments.

The federal welfare reform legislation requires that employers include the following six items of information in their new hire reports:

- employee's name
- employee's address

---

[1] 42 U.S.C. § 653a.

- employee's Social Security number
- employer's name
- employer's address
- employer's federal employer identification number (EIN)

Most of this information is contained on the W-4 form ("withholding allowance certificate") completed by each new employee at the time of hire, and as a result most states allow employers to comply with the reporting requirements by sending copies of each new W-4 form completed by a newly hired employee.

Although most states require only the six basic "data elements," some states require or request additional data. See Table 8-3 for the requirements in each state.

> The employer's federal identification number is inserted on line 10 of Form W-4 only when the form is sent to the IRS. Since this happens infrequently, the employer's identification number generally does not appear on the form. So, for an employer to use W-4 forms to comply with the new hire reporting requirements, it must manually insert its federal employer identification number (EIN) on line 10. The employer's name and address also may need to be manually inserted on line 8.

> Some states ask employers to voluntarily report additional information, such as date of hire, or medical insurance information. A summary of each state's law is contained in Table 8-3.

The deadline for filing a report is specified by state law. However, it may not be later than 20 days after an employee is hired.

New hire reports should be sent to the State Directory of New Hires (SDNH) in the state where the employee works. Federal law identifies three methods for submitting new hire information: (1) first class mail, (2) magnetic tapes, or (3) electronically. For employer convenience, most states offer additional options such as fax, e-mail, phone, and website transmissions. Table 8-3 lists the transmission options in each state.

> If your church hires new employees infrequently, the easiest way to comply with the reporting obligation may be to use the state reporting form. Simply complete one form with your federal employer identification number, name, and address, and then make several copies. This way, you will only need to add an employee's name, address, and Social Security number when a new employee is hired.

In some states, employers can report new hires by leaving a voice message on a special voice response system.

> Be sure to check with your designated state agency to find out what reporting options are available in your state. Telephone numbers for all state agencies are included in Table 8-3. Use the option that is easiest for you.

▶ *Does your church use a payroll reporting service? If so, it may be automatically making the new hire reports for you. Check to be sure.*

3. Penalties

The federal welfare reform law prohibits states from assessing a penalty in excess of $25 for each failure to report a new hire. However, states may impose a penalty of up to $500 if an employer and employee "conspire" to avoid the reporting requirements, or agree to submit a false report.

4. Employees in More than One State

Some denominational agencies and parachurch ministries have employees in more than one state. How do they comply with the new hire reporting rules? They may report newly hired employees to the state in which the employees are working; or, they may select one state to receive all new hire reports. If one state is selected, the employer must submit new hire reports electronically or by magnetic tape. The employer should check with the designated state agency to discuss the technical requirements for such a report.

Key Point> *"One state" reporting requires new hire information to be reported twice a month, not less than 12, nor more than 16, days apart.*

Key Point> *A multistate employer that elects to report all new hire information to one state must inform the Secretary of the United States Department of Health and Human Services of its decision by faxing or mailing the notification to: U.S. Department of Health and Human Services, Office of Child Support Enforcement, Multistate Employer Registration, Box 509, Randallstown, MD 21133. The fax number is (410) 277-9325. You also can electronically submit a Multistate Employer Notification form via the Internet. The form can be found on the Office of Child Support Enforcement website.*

Table 8-3 **Complying with the New Hire Reporting Requirement: A State-by-State Summary**

Note: *Explanation of codes used in this table: A (W-4 information, including employee's name, address, Social Security number, plus the employer's name, address, and employer identification number); B (state employer identification number); C (date of hire); D (date of birth); E (salary); F (employer contact person and phone number); G (medical insurance information); H (first day of work); I (an indication if the person is a new hire, a rehire, or refused a job offer); J (state of hire); K (gender); L (medical insurance availability); M (occupation); N (income); O (employee's phone number); P (employee's drivers license number). Code letters in brackets (e.g., [D]) refer to information that may voluntarily be reported by an employer, but which is not required by law. Be sure to check with your designated state agency for the most up-to-date information.*

state	what to report	when to report (days after hire)	method of transmission	telephone assistance
AL	A,F,H,I	7	mail, fax, magnetic tape, cartridge tape, Internet upload, website	334-353-8491
AK	A,[B,C,D]	20	mail, fax, magnetic tape, cartridge tape, CD, diskette	907-269-6685
AZ	A	20	phone, mail, fax, magnetic tape, cartridge tape, diskette, website, FTP, EFT	602-340-0555

state	what to report	when to report (days after hire)	method of transmission	telephone assistance
AR	A,[C,D,J]	20	mail, fax, magnetic tape, cartridge tape, diskette, website	501-376-2125
CA	A,[C,D]	20	mail, fax, magnetic tape, diskette, website	916-657-0529
CO	A	20	mail, fax, magnetic tape, cartridge tape, diskette, website	800-696-1468
CT	A,C,[B,F]	20	mail, fax, magnetic tape, cartridge tape, website	860-263-6310
DE	A	20	mail, fax, e-mail, magnetic tape, cartridge tape, diskette	302-326-6024 ext. 188
DC	A,[C,D,F,K]	20	phone, fax, mail, magnetic tape, cartridge tape, diskette,	877-846-9523
FL	A,C,[B,D]	20	phone, fax, mail, magnetic tape, cartridge tape, diskette, website, FTP	888-854-4791
GA	A,C,D,F,I,[G]	10	phone, fax, mail, magnetic tape, cartridge tape, diskette, website, FTP	888-541-0469
HI	A,C	20	mail, fax, magnetic tape, cartridge tape, diskette	808-692-7029
ID	A,B,C	20	mail, fax, diskette, website, e-mail	800-627-3880
IL	A[C]	20	mail, fax, magnetic tape, cartridge tape, diskette, website, e-mail	800-327-4473
IN	A,C,[D,G,J]	20	mail, fax, magnetic tape, cartridge tape, diskette, website, e-mail, FTP, EFT	866-879-0198
IA	A,C,D,G	15	mail, fax, magnetic tape, cartridge tape	515-281-5331
KS	A,J	20	mail, fax, magnetic tape, cartridge tape	888-219-7801
KY	A,[B,C,D,F, G,J]	20	mail, fax, magnetic tape, diskette, website, Internet upload	800-817-2262
LA	A,L,[C]	20	phone, mail, fax, magnetic tape, cartridge tape, diskette, website, FTP, e-mail	888-223-1461
ME	A,B,C,D, [G,L,M,N]	7	phone, mail, fax, magnetic tape, diskette, website, e-mail	800-845-5808

state	what to report	when to report (days after hire)	method of transmission	telephone assistance
MD	A,B,C,G,M, [D,F,K]	20	mail, fax, magnetic tape, cartridge tape, diskette, website, e-mail	410-281-6000
MA	A,C	14	mail, fax, website	617-626-4154
MI	A,[C,D,O]	20	mail, fax, magnetic tape, cartridge tape, diskette, website, e-mail, FTP	800-524-9846
MN	A[C,D,F,I]	20	phone, mail, fax, magnetic tape, cartridge tape, website, FTP, EFT, diskette	800-672-4473
MS	A,B,C,[D,J,K]	15	mail, fax, magnetic tape, cartridge tape, diskette, website, e-mail, CD	800-241-1330
MO	A,C	20	mail, fax, magnetic tape, cartridge tape	800-585-9234
MT	A,B,C,F, [D,G,J,N]	20	phone, mail, fax, diskette, e-mail	888-866-0327
NE	A,[C,D,F,G,J]	20	mail, fax, magnetic tape, cartridge tape, diskette, website	888-256-0293
NV	A,[B,C,D,J]	20	mail, fax, magnetic tape, cartridge tape, diskette	888-639-7241
NH	A,B,F,[C,J]	20	mail, fax, magnetic tape, diskette	888-803-4485
NJ	A,[C,D,K]	20	phone, mail, fax, magnetic tape, cartridge tape, diskette, website, e-mail	888-624-6339
NM	A,[C,D,F,G,J]	20	phone, mail, fax, magnetic tape, cartridge tape, diskette, website, FTP	888-878-1607
NY	A,[C]	20	mail, fax, magnetic tape, cartridge tape, diskette	800-972-1233
NC	A,B,[C,D,F]	20	mail, fax, magnetic tape, cartridge tape, diskette, website	888-514-4568
ND	A,[B,C,D]	20	mail, fax, magnetic tape, cartridge tape, diskette, e-mail, EFT	800-755-8530
OH	A,C,D,[K]	20	mail, fax, magnetic tape, cartridge tape, diskette, e-mail, EFT	800-208-8887

state	what to report	when to report (days after hire)	method of transmission	telephone assistance
OK	A,C,[B,D,G,L,M]	20	mail, fax, magnetic tape, cartridge tape, diskette, website	800-317-3785
OR	A,[B,C,D,F]	20	mail, fax, cartridge tape, diskette, CD, FTP	503-986-6053
PA	A,C,F,[D]	20	mail, fax, cartridge tape, diskette, website, e-mail, FTP	888-724-4737
RI	A,G,[C,D,J]	14	phone, mail, fax, magnetic tape, cartridge tape, diskette, website	888-870-6461
SC	A,[C,D,F]	20	mail, fax, magnetic tape, cartridge tape, diskette, website	800-768-5858
SD	A,[C,D,J]	20	phone, mail, fax, cartridge tape, diskette, website	888-827-6078
TN	A,C,[D,G,J,K]	20	phone, mail, fax, magnetic tape, cartridge tape, diskette, website	888-827-2280
TX	A,[B,C,D,F,J,M]	20	phone, mail, fax, diskette, website, FTP, magnetic tape, cartridge tape, DTS, CD	888-839-4473
UT	A,[C,D]	20	phone, mail, fax, magnetic tape, cartridge tape, diskette, website	801-526-4361
VT	A,C	20	mail, fax, magnetic tape, cartridge tape, diskette, website, EFT	802-241-2194
VA	A,[B,C,D,F,J]	20	phone, mail, fax, magnetic tape, cartridge tape, diskette, website, modem, FTP	800-979-9014
WA	A,D	20	mail, fax, magnetic tape, cartridge tape, diskette, website	800-562-0479
WV	A,[C,D]	14	phone, mail, fax, diskette, website	800-835-4683
WI	A,[C,D,J]	20	phone, mail, fax, magnetic tape, cartridge tape, diskette, website	888-300-4473
WY	A,[C,D,F,G]	20	mail, fax, magnetic tape, cartridge tape, diskette, website, FTP	800-970-9258

Employment Eligibility Verification

§ 8-03

Key Point 8-03> *Employers are required by law to confirm the identity, and eligibility to work, of all new hires. This is done by having each new hire complete Immigration and Naturalization Service Form I-9. Churches are subject to this requirement.*

Key Point> *One federal court ruled that churches can be forced to comply with the immigration reporting requirements even if compliance would violate their religious convictions.[2]*

DID YOU KNOW?

Every employer in the United States is required to confirm the identity of all new employees and verify that they are either American citizens or aliens legally authorized to work in this country. These rules, enacted by Congress in the Immigration Reform and Control Act of 1986 as a means of stemming the tide of illegal immigration, represent one of the most comprehensive reporting schemes ever adopted by the federal government.[3] Religious organizations are subject to the new rules.

The Immigration Reform and Control Act made all U.S. employers responsible to verify the employment eligibility and identity of all employees hired to work in the United States after November 6, 1986. To implement the law, employers are required to complete Employment Eligibility Verification forms (Form I-9) for all employees, including U.S. citizens. Every U.S. employer must have a Form I-9 in its files for each new employee, unless:

- the employee was hired before November 7, 1986, and has been continuously employed by the same employer.
- Form I-9 need not be completed for those individuals:
- providing domestic services in a private household that are *sporadic, irregular,* or *intermittent;*
- providing services for the employer as an independent contractor (i.e. carry on independent business, contract to do a piece of work according to their own

---

[2] American Friends Service Committee v. Thornburgh, 718 F. Supp. 820 (C.D. Cal. 1989).

[3] 8 U.S.C. § 1324a.

means and methods and are subject to control only as to results for whom the employer **does not** set work hours or provide necessary tools to do the job, or whom the employer does not have authority to hire and fire); and

• providing services for the employer, under a contract, subcontract, or exchange entered into after November 6, 1986. (In such cases, the contractor is the employer for I-9 purposes; for example, a temporary employment agency.)

Unlike tax forms, I-9 forms are not filed with the U.S. government. The requirement is for employers to maintain I-9 records in their own files for three years after the date of hire or one year after the date the employee's employment is terminated, whichever is later. This means that I-9 forms need to be retained for all current employees, as well as terminated employees whose records remain within the retention period.

Key Point> *U.S. immigration law does not prohibit storage of a private employer's I-9 records in employee personnel files.*

Discrimination

The law protects certain individuals from unfair immigration-related employment practices, including refusal to employ based on a future expiration date of a current employment authorization document. The U.S. government entity charged with oversight of the laws protecting against unfair immigration-related employment practices is the Office of Special Counsel for Immigration Related Unfair Employment Practices, which is part of the Civil Rights Division of the U.S. Department of Justice.

Employee's responsibilities

A new employee must complete Section 1 of a Form I-9 no later than close of business on his or her first day of work. The employee's signature makes him or her responsible for the accuracy of the information provided. The employer is responsible for ensuring that the employee completes Section 1 in full. No documentation from the employee is required to substantiate Section 1 information provided by the employee.

Employer's responsibilities

The employer is responsible for ensuring completion of the entire form. No later than close of business on the employee's third day of employment services, the employer must complete Section 2 of the Form I-9. The employer must review documentation presented by the employee and record document information of the form. Proper documentation establishes both that the employee is authorized to work in the U.S. and that the employee who presents the employment authorization document is the person to whom it was issued. The employer should supply to the employee the official list of acceptable documents for

"An employer should not continue to employ someone who cannot present documentation that meets the requirements."

establishing identity and work eligibility. The employer may accept any List A document, establishing both identity and work eligibility, or combination of a List B document (establishing identity) and List C document (establishing work eligibility), that the employee chooses from the list to present (the documentation presented is not required to substantiate information provided in Section 1). The employer must examine the document(s) and accept them if they reasonably appear to be genuine and to relate to the employee who presents them. Requesting more or different documentation than the minimum necessary to meet this requirement may constitute an unfair immigration-related employment practice. If the documentation presented by an employee does not reasonably appear to be genuine or relate to the employee who presents them, employers must refuse acceptance and ask for other documentation from the list of acceptable documents that meets the requirements. An employer should not continue to employ someone who cannot present documentation that meets the requirements.

Authenticating documents

Employers are not required to be document experts. If an employee presents a document that appears legitimate but is in fact not genuine– or is genuine but does not belong to the person who presented it, the employer will not be held responsible for accepting these documents. As long as the document reasonably appears to be genuine or to relate to the person presenting it, this is the standard the government uses in assessing an employer's liability for hiring an ineligible employee. Employers can request assistance from the nearest Immigration field office if they are uncertain of a document's genuineness.

It occasionally happens that an employer learns that an employee whose documentation appeared to be in order for Form I-9 purposes is not actually authorized to work. In such cases, the employer should question the employee and provide another opportunity for review of proper Form I-9 documentation. If the employee is unable under such circumstances to provide satisfactory documentation, employment should be discontinued (alien employees who question the employer's determination may be referred to an Immigration field office for assistance).

False documentation includes documents that are counterfeit or those that belong to someone other than the employee who presented them. It occasionally happens that an employee who initially presented false documentation to gain employment subsequently obtains proper work authorization and presents documentation of this work authorization. In such a case, U.S. immigration law does not require the employer to terminate the employee's services. However, an employer's personnel policies regarding provision of false information to the employer may apply. The employer should correct the relevant information on the Form I-9.

D I D   Y O U   K N O W ?

There are two separate and unrelated photocopy issues relating to the Form I-9. First, an employer can accept only the original documents (not necessarily the first document of its kind ever issued to the employee, but an actual document issued by the issuing authority), with the single exception of a certified photocopy of a birth certificate. Second, it is permissible (but not required) for an employer to attach photocopies of this documentation to each employee's Form I-9. Where this practice is undertaken by an employer, it must be consistently applied to every employee, without regard to citizenship or national origin.

Green cards

The terms *Resident Alien Card*, *Permanent Resident Card*, *Alien Registration Receipt Card*, and *Form I-551* all refer to documentation issued to an alien who has been granted permanent residence in the United States. Once granted, this status is permanent. However, the document that an alien carries as proof of this status may expire. Starting with the "pink" version of the Resident Alien Card (the "white" version does not bear an expiration date), and including the new technology Permanent Resident Cards, these documents are valid for either two years (conditional residents) or ten years (permanent residents). When these cards expire, the alien cardholders must obtain new cards. An expired card cannot be used to satisfy Form I-9 requirements for new employment. Expiration dates do not affect current employment, since employers are neither required nor permitted to re-verify the employment authorization of aliens who have presented one of these cards to satisfy I-9 requirements (this is true for conditional residents as well as permanent residents). Even if unexpired, "green cards" must appear genuine and establish identity of the cardholder.

Social Security cards

The Social Security Administration (SSA) currently issues SSA numbers and cards to aliens only if they can present documentation of current employment authorization in the U.S. Aliens such as lawful permanent residents, refugees, and asylees are issued unrestricted SSA cards that are undistinguishable from those issued to U.S. citizens.

Note the status of the following documents in satisfying the I-9 requirements:

- SSA card states "Valid only with INS (or DHS) Authorization." These cards are issued to aliens who present proof of temporary work authorization. They do not satisfy the Form I-9 requirements.

- SSA card states "Not Valid for Employment." These cards are issued to aliens who have a valid non-work reason for needing a Social Security number (e.g., federal benefits, state public assistance benefits), but are not authorized to work in the U.S.

- IRS-issued "Individual Taxpayer Identification Numbers" (ITINs). These numbers are issued to aliens dealing with tax issues (e.g., reporting unearned income such as savings account interest, investment income, royalties, scholarships, etc.). An ITIN card does not qualify as employment eligibility verification on Form I-9.

Retention of I-9 forms

All of an employer's current employees (unless exempt) must have Forms I-9 on file. A retention date can only be determined at the time an employee is terminated. It is determined by calculating and comparing two dates. To calculate date A, the employer should add three years to the hire date. To calculate date B, the employer should add one year to the termination date. Whichever of the two dates is later in time is the date until which that employee's Form I-9 must remain in the employer's employment eligibility verification files.

Official inspection of I-9 records

Upon request, all Forms I-9 subject to the retention requirement must be made available in their original form or on microfilm or microfiche to an authorized official of the Bureau of Immigration and Customs Enforcement, Department of Labor, and/or the Justice Department's Office of Special Counsel for Unfair Immigration-Related Employment Practices. The official will give employers at least 3 days advance notice before the inspection. Original documents (as opposed to photocopies) may be requested.

Immigration

§ 8-04

Key Point 8-04> *Federal immigration law regulates the admission, status, and employability of foreign citizens in this country, and imposes requirements on employers who seek to hire such persons. These requirements generally apply to religious organizations.*

Churches are increasingly hiring foreign nationals as employees and independent contractors. Consider the following examples.

Case Studies

- *Paul is a citizen of a foreign country where he is employed as a pastor. Paul is in the United States on a visitor's visa. He speaks in a church, and an offering is collected for him. The offering amounts to $700. The church treasurer is not sure how to han-*

dle this payment. Should she issue Paul a 1099 form? Does she need to withhold federal income taxes and Social Security taxes?

• Mary is a citizen of a foreign country, and speaks very little English. A church hires her as a custodian. The church treasurer is not sure how to report her income. He is wondering if he should issue her a W-2, and if taxes need to be withheld.

• Joe is a pastor in a foreign country. While traveling in the United States on a visitor's visa, he frequently attends a church that consists mostly of former residents of his native country. The church would like Joe to become a full-time associate pastor.

These examples illustrate the importance of church leaders being familiar with the application of immigration and federal tax law to current or prospective workers who are not citizens of the United States. Unfortunately, immigration law is complex and poorly understood. And, few attorneys specialize in this area of law.

1. Immigration Basics

visas—in general

What is a visa? Are foreign citizens required to have a visa to enter the U.S.? Must they have a visa to work for a church as either an employee or independent contractor?

Citizens of most foreign countries need a visa to enter the United States. A visa does *not* permit entry into the U.S., but rather indicates that the visa holder's application has been reviewed by a U.S. consular officer at an American embassy or consulate, and that the officer has determined that the individual is eligible to enter the country for a specific purpose. Consular affairs are the responsibility of the U.S. Department of State.

A visa allows the holder to travel to the United States as far as the port of entry (airport or land border crossing) and ask the immigration officer to allow entry into the country. Only the immigration officer has the authority to permit entry into the United States. He or she decides how long the person can stay for any particular visit. Immigration matters are the responsibility of the U.S. Citizenship and Immigration Services (USCIS), a bureau of the U.S. Department of Homeland Security. The former Immigration and Naturalization Service (INS) no longer exists.

There are two categories of U.S. visas—immigrant and nonimmigrant. *Immigrant visas* are for people who intend to live permanently in the U.S. *Nonimmigrant visas* are for people with permanent residence outside the U.S. but who wish to be in the U.S. on a temporary basis for tourism, medical treatment, business, temporary work, or study. Both kinds of visas are described below.

immigrant visas

An *immigrant* is a foreign national who has been granted the privilege of living and working permanently in the United States. Applicants must go through a multi-step process to become an immigrant. In most cases, the United States Citizenship and Immigration Service (USCIS) must first approve an immigrant petition that usually is filed by an employer or relative. Then, an immigrant visa number must be available even if the applicant is already in the United States (some exceptions apply). After that, if the applicant is already in the United States, he or she may apply to adjust to permanent resident status. Persons who are outside the United States will be notified to go to the local U.S. consulate to complete the processing for an immigrant visa.

Immigrants to the United States are divided into two categories: (1) those who may obtain permanent residence status without numerical limitation (this includes immediate relatives and previous lawful permanent residents), and (2) those subject to an annual limitation. The latter category is further divided into the following groups:

Family-sponsored. Certain relatives of U.S. citizens or permanent residents may receive all of the visas not used by immediate relatives, but no less than 226,000 visas per year.

Employment-based. A total minimum of 140,000 immigrant visas yearly are available for this category which is divided into five preference groups: (1) persons of extraordinary ability in the sciences, arts, education, business, or athletics; outstanding professors and researchers; and certain multinational executives and managers (the EB-1 visa); (2) professionals holding advanced degrees, and persons of exceptional ability in the sciences, arts, and business (the EB-2 visa); (3) professionals holding baccalaureate degrees, skilled workers with at least two years experience, and other workers whose skills are in short supply in the United States (the EB-3 visa); (4) certain religious workers, ministers of religion, certain international organization employees and their immediate family members, and qualified, recommended current and former U.S. government employees (the EB-4 visa); (5) persons who create employment for at least ten unrelated persons by investing capital in a new commercial enterprise in the United States (the EB-5 visa). Note that most of these visas require the U.S. employer to *complete a labor certification request* (Form ETA 750) for the applicant, and submit it to the U.S. Department of Labor's Employment and Training Administration. The Department of Labor must either grant or deny the certification request.

Lottery. The diversity lottery makes available a maximum of 55,000 immigrant visa numbers annually to persons selected at random from countries with low rates of immigration to the United States.

Certain applicants such as priority workers, investors, certain special immigrants, and diversity immigrants can petition for an immigration visa on their own behalf. All others must have a relative or potential employer petition for them.

Key Point> *Most visitors to the United States enter the country as tourists. With the introduction of visa-free travel to citizens of 27 countries, it is now possible for many travelers to enter the United States without a visa under the Visa Waiver Program (VWP) if they meet several requirements. One requirement is that the length of stay in the United States cannot exceed 90 days.*

green cards

Persons whose applications for immigrant visas are approved become *lawful permanent residents* of the U.S. and generally may live and work in this country indefinitely. As proof of their status and eligibility to work they are issued a Permanent Resident Card, also known as a "green card," or "Form I-551."

▶ *Green cards are not green, but they used to be and the name has persisted.*

▶ *An immigrant visa is not evidence of eligibility to work. An immigrant also must obtain a green card ("Permanent Resident Card").*

work permits

Applicants for adjustment to permanent resident status from some other status are eligible to apply for a *work permit* while their cases are pending. USCIS Form I-765 is used to apply for a work permit. Persons do not need to apply for a work permit once they adjust to permanent resident status. Legal permanent residents will receive a Permanent Resident Card (green card) that will prove that they have a right to live and work in the United States permanently.

Key Point> *Anyone traveling to the United States with the intention of working there temporarily must obtain a nonimmigrant work visa. Persons entering the United States on a visitor or business visa are not permitted to work.*

nonimmigrant visas

The Immigration and Nationality Act provides several categories of nonimmigrant visas for a person who wishes to work temporarily in the United States. There are annual numerical limits on some classifications. The most relevant classifications for church leaders include the following:

B-1. Temporary visitor for business.

H-1B. Applies to persons in a specialty occupation which requires the theoretical and practical application of a body of highly specialized knowledge requiring completion of a specific course of higher education. This classification requires a labor attestation issued by the Secretary of Labor.

H-2B. Applies to temporary or seasonal nonagricultural workers. This classification requires a temporary labor certification issued by the Secretary of Labor.

R-1. Temporary religious workers. Religious ministers or workers may qualify for the religious worker classification "R" visa if, for the two years immediately preceding the time of application, they have been a member of a religious denomination which has a bona fide nonprofit religious organization in the United States. Bona fide religious organizations in the United States must have tax exempt status as an organization described in section 501(c)(3) of the federal tax code.

> ## DID YOU KNOW?
>
> The continuing threat of terrorism in the U.S. has resulted in much greater scrutiny of religious workers' visa applications by the USCIS. Some of the terrorists involved in the September 11 terrorist attacks were allegedly in the U.S. on religious workers visas.

religious activities and the B-1 visa

Some religious workers enter the United States with a B-1 visa. B-1 visas permit certain forms of employment, as noted below:

(1) Missionary work. Persons who are performing missionary work on behalf of a religious denomination may be eligible for a B-1 visa, provided they will receive no salary or compensation from the United States other than an allowance or other reimbursement for expenses incidental to their stay, and the work they are to perform in the United States will not involve the selling of articles or the solicitation or acceptance of donations.

(2) Evangelical tours. Persons coming to the United States to engage in an evangelical tour, and who do not plan to take an appointment with any one church, may be eligible for a B-1 visa provided they will receive no compensation from a U.S. source, other than the offerings contributed at each evangelical meeting.

(3) Preaching. Persons who will be preaching in the United States for a temporary period, or will be exchanging pulpits with their U.S. counterpart, may be eligible for a B-1 visa provided they will continue to be reimbursed by their church in their home country and will receive no salary from the host church in the United States.

(4) Voluntary service program. Persons who will participate in a voluntary service program which benefits a U.S. local community, and who establish that they are a member of, and have a commitment to, a particular recognized religious or nonprofit charitable organization, may be eligible for a B-1 visa if the work to be performed is traditionally done by volunteer charity workers; no salary or remuneration is received from a U.S. source, other than an allowance or other reimbursement for expenses incidental to their stay in the United States; and they will not engage in the selling of articles or the solicitation and acceptance of donations. A voluntary service program is an organized project conducted by a recognized religious or nonprofit charitable organization to provide assistance to the poor or the needy, or to further a religious or charitable cause.

Note that travelers who qualify for a B-1 visa may also be eligible to travel visa free under the visa waiver program (described above).

2. Working for Compensation

In general, foreign nationals cannot perform services for compensation in the United States unless they meet one of the following conditions:

The foreign national is a lawful permanent resident (any category of immigrant visa) and holds a Permanent Resident Card ("green card"). Such persons generally can live and work permanently in the United States without limitation.

The foreign national has a nonimmigrant temporary work visa that permits certain kinds of work for a specified period of time.

Unless a foreign worker meets one of these conditions, he or she generally is not legally permitted to perform work for compensation in the United States. The most common *nonimmigrant* visas are summarized below

B-1 business visitor

Business visitors generally are not permitted to perform work in the United States for compensation. Some religious workers enter the United States with a B-1 visa. The United States Bureau of Citizenship and Immigration Services (USCIS) has ruled that B-1 visas permit certain forms of employment by religious workers, as noted below:

Missionary work. Persons who are performing missionary work on behalf of a religious denomination may be eligible for a B-1 visa, provided they will receive no salary or compensation from the United States other than an allowance or other reimbursement for expenses incidental to their stay, and the work they are to perform in the United States will not involve the selling of articles or the solicitation or acceptance of donations.

Evangelical tours. Persons coming to the United States to engage in an evangelical tour, and who do not plan to take an appointment with any one church, may be eligible for a B-1 visa provided they will receive no compensation from a U.S. source, other than the offerings contributed at each evangelical meeting.

Preaching. Persons who will be preaching in the United States for a temporary period, or will be exchanging pulpits with their U.S. counterpart, may be eligible for a B-1 visa provided they will continue to be reimbursed by their church in their home country and will receive no salary from the host church in the United States.

Voluntary service program. Persons who will participate in a voluntary service program which benefits a U.S. local community, and who establish that they are a member of, and have a commitment to, a particular recognized religious or nonprofit charitable organization, may be eligible for a B-1 visa if the work to be performed is traditionally done by volunteer charity workers; no salary or remuneration is received from a U.S. source, other than an allowance or other reimbursement for expenses incidental to their stay in the United States; and they will not engage in the selling of articles or the solicitation and acceptance of donations. A voluntary service program is an organized project conducted by a recognized religious or nonprofit charitable organization to provide assistance to the poor or the needy, or to further a religious or charitable cause.

Note that travelers who qualify for a B-1 visa may also be eligible to travel visa free under the visa waiver program. (This subject is developed more fully in *Church Treasurer Alert*, August 2004. Go to **www.churchlawtoday.com** for subscription information).

B-2 tourist visitor

Tourist visitors generally are not permitted to perform work in the United States for compensation.

F-1 academic student

A nonresident alien admitted to the United States as a student generally is not permitted to work for compensation or to engage in business while in the United States. In some cases, a student admitted to the United States with an F-1 visa is granted permission to work, and it is so noted on the student's copy of Immigration Form I-94 (Arrival-Departure Record).

USCIS permits on-campus work for students in F-1 status if it does not displace a U.S. resident. On-campus work means work performed on the school's premises. On-campus work includes work performed at an off-campus location that is educationally affiliated with the school. On-campus work under the terms of a scholarship, fellowship, or assistantship is considered part of the academic program of a student taking a full course of study and is permitted by the USCIS.

Employment due to severe economic necessity and for optional practical training is sometimes permitted for students in F-1 status. Students granted permission to work due to severe economic necessity or for optional practical training will be issued Form I-688B or Form I-766 by USCIS.

It is possible for a student holding an F-1 visa to change to an R-1 visa if a religious organization submits a Form I-129 to the USCIS. The R-1 visa is described below.

M-1 vocational student

People who wish to pursue full-time vocational studies are usually admitted to the United States on an M-1 nonimmigrant visa. The M-1 category includes students in vocational or other nonacademic programs, other than language training.

Students in M-1 status who have completed a course of study can accept employment or practical training for up to six months and must have a Form I-688B or Form I-766 issued by USCIS. In all other cases, any services performed by a nonresident alien student are not considered as performed to carry out the purpose for which the student was admitted to the United States.

Persons holding an M-1 visa may not accept employment in the United States. However, they may apply for practical training after they complete their studies. If approved, they will be allowed to have one month of practical training for every four months of study they have completed. They are limited to six months total practical training time. Vocational students must apply to the USCIS for authorization to work under these limited circumstances (Form 538).

H-1B specialty occupation

The H-1B is a nonimmigrant classification used by an alien who will be employed temporarily in a specialty occupation. A specialty occupation requires theoretical and practical application of a body of specialized knowledge along with at least a bachelor's degree or its equivalent. For example, architecture, engineering, mathematics, physical sciences, social sciences, medicine and health, education, business specialties, accounting, law, theology, and the arts are specialty occupations. Current law limits to 65,000 the number of aliens who may be issued a visa or otherwise provided H-1B status in 2004. The numerical limitation was temporarily raised to 195,000 in 2001, 2002 and 2003.

H-1B status requires a sponsoring U.S. employer. The employer must file a labor condition application (LCA) with the Department of Labor attesting to several items, including payment of prevailing wages for the position, and the working conditions offered. The employer must then file the certified LCA with a Form I-129. Based on the USCIS petition approval, the alien may apply for the H-1B visa, admission, or a change of nonimmigrant status.

Under current law, an alien can be in H-1B status for a maximum period of six years at a time. After that time an alien must remain outside the United States for one year before another H-1B petition can be approved.

H-1B aliens may only work for the petitioning U.S. employer and only in the H-1B activities described in the petition. The petitioning U.S. employer may place the H-1B worker on the worksite of another employer if Department of Labor rules are followed. H-1B aliens may work for more than one U.S. employer, but must have a Form I-129 petition approved by each employer.

As long as the employer-employee relationship exists, an H-1B alien is still "in status" even though not currently performing the authorized services. An H-1B alien may work in full or part-time employment and remain in status.

An H-1B alien can take steps toward Lawful Permanent Resident status without affecting H-1B status. This is known as "dual intent" and has been recognized in the immigration law since passage of the Immigration Act of 1990.

R-1 religious worker

Key Point > *At the time of publication of this text, U.S. Citizenship and Immigration Services (USCIS) had proposed significant revisions to its regulations pertaining to the nonimmigrant (R-1) religious worker visa. Currently, nonimmigrants may request a religious worker visa at a consular post or a port-of-entry without any prior stateside review of the petition. One of the key proposed changes to the regulations includes a petition requirement that will allow USCIS to verify the legitimacy of the petitioner and the job offer before a visa is issued or the worker is admitted into the United States. The proposed revisions also would reduce the initial period of admission for a nonimmigrant from three years to one, giving the agency an opportunity to review whether or not the terms of the visa have been met during the initial year before extending the worker's stay in the United States. USCIS is also proposing to add new definitions, or amend current ones, to better describe the statutory eligibility criteria.*

An R-1 visa authorizes a foreign national to live and work in the United States on a temporary basis to:

- carry on the vocation of a minister of the religious denomination, or

- work in a professional capacity in a religious vocation or occupation or organization within the denomination, or

- work in a religious vocation or occupation for an organization within the denomination, or for a bona fide organization which is affiliated with the religious denomination

A minister is someone who is authorized by a recognized denomination to conduct religious worship and perform other duties usually performed by members of the clergy such as administering the sacraments. The term *religious worker* does not apply to lay preachers.

A religious vocation means a calling to religious life, evidenced by the demonstration of a lifelong commitment, such as taking vows. Examples include nuns, monks, and religious brothers and sisters. A religious occupation means a habitual engagement in an activity which relates to a traditional religious function. Examples include liturgical workers, religious instructors or cantors, catechists, workers in religious hospitals, missionaries, religious translators, or religious broadcasters. It does not include janitors, maintenance workers, clerks, fund raisers, solicitors of donations, or similar occupations.

Applicants may qualify for the R-1 visa if, for the two years immediately preceding the time of application, they have been a member of a religious denomination which has a bona fide nonprofit religious organization in the United States. Bona fide religious organizations in the United States must have tax exempt status as an organization described in section 501(c)(3) of the federal tax code.

The U.S.-based religious organization that wants to employ the applicant must submit the application for an R-1 visa. Form I-129 is used for this purpose. The I-129 petition must be filed with:

- A written statement from an authorized official of the religious organization that will be employing the alien establishing (1) that the alien has been a member of the denomination for the required two years; (2) a description of the proposed position, and that the alien is qualified for the position; (3) the arrangements, if any, for salary, benefits, and other compensation; (4) the name and location of the place the alien will provide the services; (5) the organization's affiliation with the denomination.

- Evidence showing that the religious organization or any affiliate which will engage the alien's services is a bona fide nonprofit, religious organization in the U.S. and is exempt from taxation in accordance with section 501(c)(3) of the Internal Revenue Code of 1986.

The initial admission period for ministers and religious workers entering the United States in R-1 status is limited to three years. Employers must file an I-129 petition with the USCIS to request an extension. Extensions may be granted for a total stay not to exceed five years.

Negligent Selection   § 8-05

One of the most significant legal risks facing churches is negligent selection. The term *negligence* means carelessness or a failure to exercise reasonable care. *Negligent selection*, then, means carelessness or a failure to exercise reasonable care in the selection of a worker. Negligent selection claims can arise any time that a church's failure to exercise reasonable care in the selection of an employee or volunteer leads to a foreseeable injury. This topic is addressed fully in Chapter 10 (Volume 4) of *Pastor, Church & Law*, 4th edition.

PART TWO

Compensation and Benefits

Legal Briefs

Churches need to be aware of several legal and tax issues related to the wages and benefits they provide for their employees. Here are the critical points you need to know in Part 2:

Workers compensation—Workers compensation laws were enacted in all 50 states to give injured workers a quicker, less costly, and more certain recovery than was possible by suing an employer directly for negligence. In exchange for such benefits, employees give up the right to sue an employer directly if they've gotten sick or been injured on the job.

> "If you have not procured workers compensation insurance, your church may be exposed to uninsured risk..."

Workers compensation laws only cover injuries and illnesses suffered by *employees* on the job. The term *employee* generally is defined very broadly to effectuate the objectives of the workers compensation law. As a result, persons whom a church may deem self-employed for income tax purposes may be deemed employees for purposes of the workers compensation law.

Generally, a church is not subject to any penalties if it knowingly hires and compensates a person who is receiving workers compensation benefits. It is the employee, and not the employer, who may be required to return benefits paid while he or she is earning wages from a job.

If you have not procured workers compensation insurance, your church may be exposed to uninsured risk for injuries sustained by employees in the course of their employment. Even if your church has general liability insurance, this ordinarily will not cover a workers compensation-related claim.

Fair Labor Standards Act—The federal Fair Labor Standards Act (FLSA) generally requires covered employers to pay their employees at least the federal minimum wage, plus overtime premium pay of one and a half times the regular rate of pay for all hours worked over 40 hours in a workweek. However, the FLSA includes a number of exemptions from the minimum wage and overtime requirements. These exemptions have created considerable confusion over the years regarding who is, and who is not, exempt. This chapter explains the application of the FLSA, and its exemptions, to church staff.

Introduction

There are several legal and tax issues associated with the compensation and benefits a church pays to its employees. This chapter will address workers compensation, the minimum wage, and overtime pay. Several other issues are addressed in other books by Richard Hammar, as summarized in Table 8-4.

Table 8-4 **Compensation-Related Topics Addressed in Other YOUR CHURCH Publications**

issue	where addressed
sources of taxable income	Church & Clergy Tax Guide, Chapter 4
fringe benefits	Church & Clergy Tax Guide, Chapters 4-5
business expenses	Church & Clergy Tax Guide, Chapter 7
retirement plans	Church & Clergy Tax Guide, Chapter 10
payroll tax reporting requirements	Church & Clergy Tax Guide, Chapter 11
unemployment benefits	Church & Clergy Tax Guide, Chapter 12
salary surveys	Compensation Handbook for Church Staff
compensation planning	Compensation Handbook for Church Staff
works made for hire	Volume 4, Chapter 9, *Pastor, Church & Law*, 4th edition

Workers Compensation

Workers compensation laws have been enacted in all 50 states. These laws provide compensation to employees as a result of job-related injuries and illnesses. The amount of compensation is determined by law and generally is based upon the nature and extent of the employee's disability. In exchange for such benefits, employees give up the right to sue an employer directly. Fault is irrelevant under workers compensation laws. As one court has observed, "workmen's compensation, like the gentle rain from heaven, falls on the just and unjust alike." [4] The only inquiries are (1) did an employment relationship exist; (2) did the injury occur during the course of employment; and (3) what were the nature and extent of the injuries?

Workers compensation laws are founded on the premise that job-related injuries and illnesses are inevitable and should be allocated between the employer and the consumer as a cost of doing business. This is accomplished, in most cases, by the employer purchasing insurance to cover the costs of workers compensation benefits, with the cost of such insurance being passed on to consumers through price adjustments.[5] As a result, the ultimate cost of an employee's work-related injury or illness is borne by the consumers of the product or service that the employee was hired to produce.

---

[4] Thomas v. Certified Refrigerators, Inc., 221 N.W.2d 378 (Mich. 1974).

[5] Gunter v. Mersereau, 491 P.2d 1205 (Ore. 1971).

Treatment of Churches   § 8-07.1

Key Point 8-07 > *All states have enacted workers compensation laws to provide benefits to employees who are injured or become ill in the course of their employment. Benefits generally are financed through insurance premiums paid by employers. Workers compensation laws were enacted to give injured workers a quicker, less costly, and more certain recovery than was possible by suing an employer directly for negligence. Prior to the general acceptance of workers compensation statutes in the early part of the twentieth century, injured employees were often unsuccessful in collecting damages from their employers. When they did collect, the awards were sometimes so high that they threatened the solvency of the employer. In every case, the costs to the injured employee of suing an employer were high. Churches are subject to workers compensation laws in most states.*

Some state workers compensation laws contain one or more of the following religious exemptions:

- Employees of religious organizations are exempted from mandatory coverage.

- Ministers are exempted from the definition of covered employee.

- Employees are exempted from coverage who are members of a religious sect that is doctrinally opposed to the acceptance of public insurance benefits.

In addition, some states exempt activities not carried on for monetary gain, or exempt any employer having fewer than a specified number of employees. These definitions are summarized in Table 8-5.

Are churches exempt from workers compensation laws that contain no specific exemption for churches, nonprofit organizations, or organizations employing less than a specified number of employees? Although few courts have considered the question, the prevailing view is that religious organizations are subject to workers compensation laws unless specifically exempted.[6] One court stated the rule as follows:

> The fact that [a religious organization] is a purely charitable enterprise does not of itself release [it] from the obligations of our workers compensation act, which, unlike the acts of some states, does not except charitable or religious institutions, as such, from its operation, nor exclude their employees from its benefits. Where the relationship of employer and employee actually exists between a charitable institution and an injured workman, the latter is entitled to the benefits of our act, otherwise not.[7]

---

[6] Roman Catholic Archbishop v. Industrial Accident Commission, 230 P. 1 (Cal. App. 1924); Gardner v. Trustees of Main St. Methodist Episcopal Church, 250 N.W. 740 (Iowa App. 1933); Meyers v. Southwest Region Conference Assoc., 88 So.2d 381 (La. App. 1956); Schneider v. Salvation Army, 14 N.W.2d 467 (Minn. App. 1944); Victory Baptist Temple v. Industrial Commission, 442 N.E.2d 819 (Ohio App. 1982), *cert. denied* 459 U.S. 1086 (1982).

[7] Schneider v. Salvation Army, 14 N.W.2d 467, 468 (Minn. App. 1944). *See also* Hope v. Barnes Hospital, 55 S.W.2d 319 (Mo. App. 1932).

A federal court in Ohio rejected the claim that subjecting churches to workers compensation laws violates their constitutional rights.[8] A church argued that the state of Ohio, through its workers compensation system, had "assumed lordship over the church in direct contravention to the biblical principle that Jesus is 'head over all things to the church' (Eph. 1:22) and that 'in all things [Christ] might have preeminence' (Col. 1:18)." In addition, the church argued that "it would be a sin to contribute to workers compensation out of church funds designated for biblical purposes and that tithe and offering money . . . belongs to God." The court concluded that these allegations were "sufficient to allege infringement of [the church's] religious beliefs." However, "the mere fact that a religious practice is burdened by a governmental program does not mean that an exemption accommodating the practice must be granted," since "the state may justify a limitation on religious liberty by showing that it is essential to accomplish an overriding governmental interest."

The court concluded that a state's interest in assuring the efficient administration and financial soundness of the workers compensation fund, and in protecting the interests of injured workers, amounted to a compelling interest that overrode the church's religious beliefs. The court noted that the Ohio law did exempt clergy from coverage under the workers compensation, and this limited exemption sought "to obviate excessive interference with the religious ministry of churches." Also rejected was the church's claim that the workers compensation program would impermissibly "entangle" government and church, since other courts had upheld even greater reporting requirements as constitutionally permissible. The court observed that exempting churches from coverage under the workers compensation law would force injured workers to sue churches in the civil courts, "an even more undesirable result from a scriptural standpoint."

An Ohio state appeals court, in upholding the coverage of church employees under a state workers compensation law, observed:

> The workers compensation law has been characterized by the broadest possible coverage with frequent amendments to insure that no class of employers or employees was unintentionally excluded. If the legislature had intended to exclude religious institutions, it had ample opportunity to do so. We believe that the legislature intended for employees of religious institutions to come under the protections of the [law].[9]

The court rejected the church's claim that subjecting it to the workers compensation law violated the constitutional guaranty of religious freedom. It relied on a 1982 decision of the United States Supreme Court rejecting the claim of Amish employers that their constitutional rights were violated by subjecting them to Social Security taxes.[10] The Supreme Court had agreed that the religious beliefs and practices of Amish employers were burdened by the Social Security tax, but it concluded that "because the broad public interest in maintaining a sound tax

---

8   South Ridge Baptist Church v. Industrial Commission, 676 F. Supp. 799 (S.D. Ohio 1987).

9   Victory Baptist Temple v. Industrial Commission, 442 N.E.2d 819 (Ohio 1982), *cert. denied* 459 U.S. 1086 (1982). *But see* NLRB v. Catholic Bishop of Chicago, 440 U.S. 490 (1979).

10   United States v. Lee, 455 U.S. 252 (1982).

system is of such a high order, religious belief in conflict with the payment of taxes affords no basis for resisting the tax." The Ohio court concluded:

> The state has an "overriding governmental interest" in compensating workers and their dependents for death, occupational disease, and injury arising out of and occurring during the course of employment. To accomplish this purpose, the state has enacted comprehensive legislation creating a system that requires support by mandatory contributions by covered employers. Widespread voluntary coverage would undermine the soundness of the program and be difficult, if not impossible, to administer with a myriad of exceptions flowing from a wide variety of religious beliefs. The assessments imposed on employers to support the system are uniformly applicable to all, except as the [legislature] provides explicitly otherwise. Thus, we find no constitutionally required exemption for [a church] from the operation of the Workers Compensation Act.[11]

This same rationale has been articulated by many of the courts finding that churches are covered by workers compensation laws. As one commentator has observed: "The basic reason . . . is straightforward. It is that the compensation act expressly covers all employers, then specifically exempts such employers as it wants to exempt, so that if charitable [or religious] employers are not expressly exempted the only possible conclusion is that they are covered."[12]

In 1979, the United States Supreme Court ruled that in determining whether or not the National Labor Relations Board (NLRB) could assert jurisdiction over parochial school teachers, the courts must first ask whether an assertion of jurisdiction would give rise to serious constitutional questions under the First Amendment.[13] If serious constitutional questions would arise, then the agency cannot assert jurisdiction over religious institutions without demonstrating an "affirmative intentions of the Congress clearly expressed" to confer such jurisdiction. This same analysis should apply to the application of workers compensation laws to churches that are opposed, on the basis of doctrinal considerations, to coverage. Few state workers compensation laws expressly include churches among the employers who are covered, and so there is no "affirmative intention of [the legislature] clearly expressed" to cover churches. This argument has never been addressed by any court.

Some have maintained that workers compensation laws were intended to apply only to commercial businesses and should not be extended to non-business activities such as the operation of a church. Many courts have rejected this reasoning as a basis for exempting charitable organizations from workers compensation laws, largely on the ground that the term *business* is so broad that it encompasses charitable activities.[14] One court has observed: "It is well to remember that in His earthly career the Head of the Christian Church seriously declared, 'I must be about my Father's business.' Wherefore does not church activity qualify as

---

[11] 442 N.E.2d at 822.

[12] A. LARSON, THE LAW OF WORKMEN'S COMPENSATION § 50.42 (1998) [hereinafter referred to as LARSON].

[13] NLRB v. Catholic Bishop of Chicago, 440 U.S. 490 (1979). *See* note 154, *infra*, and accompanying text.

[14] LARSON, *supra* note 12, at §§ 50.20-20.25.

business? This term has such recognition apart from pecuniary gain."[15] Another court, in holding that a church is engaged in a "business" subject to the state's workers compensation law when constructing a new sanctuary, observed: "The business of a church is not strictly confined to charitable purposes, spiritual uplift, and the saving of souls. Such, no doubt, is the ultimate object and purpose of all church associations; but it is a matter of common knowledge that, in order to attain such ends, it is also necessary to construct and maintain houses of worship in which the business of the church is carried on."[16]

The court also noted that a church could be a *business* under a state workers compensation law since there was no requirement that a business be "profitseeking."

> Pecuniary = of or
> pertaining to money

Q If a church is not exempt from workers compensation law, what is the effect of its failure to obtain workers compensation insurance?

A Most workers compensation laws are compulsory. The employer has no prerogative to remain outside the system. In a "compulsory" jurisdiction, a covered employer that fails to obtain workers compensation insurance will ordinarily be subject to a direct action by an injured employee, or may be treated as a "self-insurer" and accordingly be liable for the damages prescribed by the workers compensation law.[17] A few states permit employers to elect coverage under workers compensation law. To coerce employers into electing coverage, these states impose various legal disabilities upon employers that do not elect coverage.

Workers compensation laws only cover injuries and illnesses suffered by *employees* on the job. The term *employee* generally is defined very broadly to effectuate the objectives of the workers compensation law.[18] As a result, persons whom a church may deem self-employed for income tax purposes may be deemed employees for purposes of the workers compensation law. In some cases, however, a court may conclude that a particular worker in fact is self-employed and accordingly not covered by the workers compensation law.

Case Studies

• *A South Carolina state appeals court ruled that a construction company president who donated his labor in constructing a new church was not eligible for workers compensa-*

---

[15] Tepesch v. Johnson, 296 N.W. 740, 745 (Iowa App. 1941). *See also* Hope v. Barnes Hospital, 55 S.W.2d 319, 321 (Mo. App. 1932) ("[T]here is nothing about the act as a whole which discloses a legislative purpose to have limited its application solely to industries and businesses within the ordinary sense of the word.").

[16] Greenway Baptist Church v. Industrial Commission, 636 P.2d 1264, 1267 (Ariz. App. 1981).

[17] Larson, *supra* note 12, at §§ 67.21-67.29.

[18] Mill Street Church of Christ v. Hogan, 785 S.W.2d 263 (Ky. App. 1990).

tion benefits following an injury on the job.[19] *The court noted that workers compensation benefits are available only to "employees," and that state law defined the term* employee *as one who works for wages under a written or oral contract of hire. The injured worker in this case "donated his labor in the construction of the church. There is no evidence he was paid wages or had a right to demand payment. There is also no evidence [that he] entered into a tithing agreement with [the church] so that his work could be considered as a credit toward his tithe obligation. We find no evidence of an employment relationship between [him and the church]. He was not hired by [the church] and he was not performing any paid service for [the church]." As a result, the court concluded that the worker "was a volunteer and not an employee" under the state workers compensation law. Accordingly, the church, through its workers compensation insurance carrier, was not obligated to pay benefits to the injured worker.*

D I D   Y O U   K N O W ?

Churches are subject to workers compensation laws in most states. Yet, many churches have not procured workers compensation insurance. This may expose them to an uninsured risk for injuries sustained by employees in the course of their employment. Churches should review their liability insurance policies to ascertain what, if any, coverage exists for injured employees. Often, general liability policies exclude the insured's employees on the assumption that they are covered under a workers compensation policy. This can create a dangerous gap in coverage.

Q   Is a homeless person who is paid $5 per hour by a church for performing miscellaneous services as part of a "charitable work program" an employee covered by state workers compensation law?

A   Yes, concluded a California appeals court. A church operated a charitable program for homeless or transient persons. Sometimes, the church made small payments directly to needy individuals. In other cases, when persons "wished to maintain their dignity and asked to do work," the church would attempt to find work for them to do (generally at a rate of $5 per hour). Most persons worked at most a day. However, one individual worked for nearly 4 weeks, performing a variety of tasks including roofing, gardening, digging, drywall work, painting, and laying a carpet. This individual sustained serious injuries when he fell off a ladder while doing roofing work. The victim later asserted that he had been an "employee" of the church and accordingly was entitled to workers compensation benefits. The church vigorously rejected

---

[19] McCreery v. Covenant Presbyterian Church, 383 S.E.2d 264 (S.C. App. 1989).

this position, claiming that the victim was a volunteer who was paid an "honorarium" for participating in the church's charitable work program. A state agency ruled in favor of the church, noting that private charities should not be discouraged from providing aid by requiring them to pay workers compensation. The agency noted that "in fact, [the church] has apparently discontinued its benevolence fund program due to the litigation and liability issues raised in this case." The victim appealed, and a state appeals court concluded that he was an employee of the church, and as such was entitled to workers compensation benefits. The court concluded: "[The victim] worked shoulder to shoulder with covered employees, did the same work, received wages, and ran the same risks.... He worked at a set hourly rate, for cash wages.... They were hourly wages, indistinguishable in any way from the wages paid to any laborer, except that they were probably considered below the prevailing wage rate for the kind of work done."[20]

Case Studies

• *An Alabama court ruled that a church custodian was entitled to workers compensation benefits as a result of an injury she suffered on the job since the church "regularly employed" five or more persons as required to trigger coverage under the state workers compensation law.[21] A church hired a woman as a custodian. The custodian was injured when she slipped and fell while stripping a floor at the church. She later filed a claim for workers compensation benefits, which a court denied on the ground that the church employed fewer than five persons. The Alabama workers compensation law specifies that it does not apply " to an employer who regularly employs less than five employees in any one business." At the time of the injury the church had six paid staff members—its pastor, music director, a pianist, an organist, and a youth director. The church treated the pianist, organist, and youth director as independent contractors, issued them 1099 forms, and withheld no federal taxes. The custodian appealed the denial of workers compensation benefits. She asserted that she and the other staff members at the church were employees rather than independent contractors, and so the "five employee" requirement was met. A state appeals court concluded that the church was paid compensation to six staff positions, and that all were employees thereby triggering workers compensation benefits. It noted that the evidence that some of the six staff members were independent contractors rather than employees was inadequate. This case demonstrates that churches cannot avoid workers compensation coverage by treating workers as independent contractors who in reality are employees.*

• *The Delaware Superior Court ruled that workers compensation was the sole remedy available to a teenage counselor at a church camp who was sexually molested by an older counselor, and so the teenage counselor could not sue the church camp for damages based on negligent hiring or negligent supervision.[22] The court noted that the state workers compensation law specifies that "every employer and employee, adult and*

[20] Hoppmann v. Workers Compensation Appeals Board, 277 Cal. Rptr. 116 (Cal. App. 1991).

[21] Gordon v. West Weaver Baptist Church, 2000 WL 1134589 (Ala. App. 2000).

[22] Murdoch v. Camp Arrowhead Church Camp, 2003 WL 21526993 (Del. Super. 2003).

minor, shall be bound by the [workers' compensation statute] to pay and to accept compensation for personal injury or death by accident arising out of and in the course of employment, regardless of the question of negligence and to the exclusion of all other rights and remedies." Based on this language, the victim's lawsuit had to be dismissed if the camp and church could prove that (1) she was an employee, (2) she suffered a personal injury, and (3) the injury arose in the course of employment. Under these circumstances, workers compensation would be the counselor's sole remedy and her negligence claim would have to be dismissed. The court concluded that all three requirements were met, and so the counselor's sole remedy was workers compensation. This case suggests that a church employee who is a victim of sexual misconduct in the course of employment cannot sue his or her employing church based on negligence or any other "common law" theory of liability. The employee's sole remedy is workers compensation. However, note that this defense may be unavailable to a church that fails to secure workers compensation insurance.

• A Pennsylvania court ruled that the widow of a man who suffered a heart attack as a result of stress he experienced while working at a church was entitled to workers compensation benefits.[23] A man suffered a heart attack while performing repairs at a church, and his heart attack eventually led to his death. The deceased worker's widow filed a claim for workers compensation, in which she requested compensation for her husband's death plus an additional $256,000 to reimburse Medicare for monies it expended for medical care of the worker following the accident. A workers compensation judge ruled that the widow had proven that her husband's activities at work substantially contributed to his heart attack, and therefore she was entitled to benefits. This case demonstrates an important principle. While most church leaders continue to believe that churches are "exempt" from state workers compensation laws, the opposite is often the case. Failure to purchase workers compensation insurance can result in a significant uninsured risk, as this case illustrates. In the case of a fatality, the damages can be in the hundreds of thousands of dollars.

> "Failure to purchase workers compensation insurance can result in a significant uninsured risk."

Compensating Employees Who Are Receiving Workers Compensation Benefits

§ 8-07.2

Key Point 8-07.2> *Employees who accept employment while receiving workers compensation benefits may be committing fraud. This can have serious consequences for the employee, including criminal prosecution and repayment of benefits paid while engaged in gainful employment.*

Some churches employ a pastor, or lay employee, who is receiving workers compensation benefits. In such a case the employee may be committing fraud by engaging in compensated employment. This can have serious consequences,

---

[23] Merva v. Workers' Compensation Appeal Board, 784 A.2d 222 (Pa. App. 2001).

including charges of fraud, and repayment of benefits paid while engaged in gainful employment.

▶ *Church leaders should consider asking employees at the time of hire if they are receiving workers compensation benefits. If they are, verify that the employee is legally permitted to pursue compensated employment. This will help to reduce the church's risk of liability for paying wages to such a person.*

Case Studies

• *The Ohio Supreme Court ruled that an employee of a manufacturing company who was injured on the job and awarded workers compensation benefits was engaging in fraud by accepting compensation for performing services as pastor of a church.[24] The employee was injured while working for a secular employer, and he received a workers compensation award based on "permanent total disability." Several years later, his former employer learned that for nearly 15 years following his "injury" he had been earning a weekly salary of $600 as a pastor. A state agency later issued an order terminating his benefits, charging him with fraud, and ordering him to repay all benefits he had received. The state supreme court affirmed this order.*

• *The Tennessee Supreme Court ruled that a person's entitlement to workers compensation benefits based on "total disability" was not affected by the receipt of $215 each week for services performed as a music minister at his church.[25] The court noted that the minister's physicians testified that there was no manual work that he could do, and that he could only perform non-manual work for short periods. It concluded that the only reason that he received income from his church "was due to the generosity of the church, not because he was employable in the open labor market. . . . The evidence in this case supports a finding that the combination of limitations and other factors rendered him unemployable in the open market and therefore totally disabled" despite the income paid to him by his church. This ruling suggests that in rare cases a person who is receiving workers compensation or Social Security benefits based on total disability may be able to receive compensation for performing limited services on behalf of a church so long as (1) the person meets the definition of "totally disabled" under applicable law, and (2) the compensation paid by the church "is due to the generosity of the church, not because the person was employable in the open labor market."*

• *A Louisiana court upheld the denial of workers compensation benefits to an injured worker who had been seen performing compensated services for a church.[26] The court noted that under Louisiana law a forfeiture of workers compensation benefits is proper when: (1) there is a false statement or representation, (2) that is willfully made, and (3) that is made for the purpose of obtaining workers compensation benefits. The court concluded that each of these elements was met. It relied, in part, on the surveillance videotape showing the person working at a church despite the fact that his workers compensation benefits were based on his claim that he was unable to perform compensated*

---

[24] State v. Pride Cast Metals, Inc., 764 N.E.2d 1021 (Ohio 2002).

[25] Cage v. Yasuda Fire & Marine Insurance Company, 2005 WL 1412135 (Tenn. 2005).

[26] Cajun Rental & Services v. Hebert, 918 So.2d 605 (La. App. 2005).

work. Upon being asked if he had ever provided "work of any kind" for the church, he explained that he thought he "did some volunteer work for them there." The court concluded that the statement that he had performed no work for wages was willful and was made for the purpose of affecting workers' compensation benefits.

Generally, a church is not subject to any penalties if it knowingly hires and compensates a person who is receiving workers compensation benefits. It is the employee, and not the employer, who may be required to return benefits paid while he or she is earning wages from a job. Still, it is a "best practice" for churches to consider the following precautions:

- If a church employee or independent contractor is receiving workers compensation benefits, be sure the person is legally permitted to perform compensated employment before allowing him or her to continue working.

- If a church employee or independent contractor is receiving workers compensation benefits, be sure the employee complies with any "notification" requirements prescribed by state law. Persons receiving workers compensation benefits may be required to notify a state agency if there is any improvement in their condition, or if they perform compensated employment. Failure to do so may make the recipient legally obligated to return some or all of the workers compensation benefits that were paid.

- Note that an injured employee or independent contractor is performing "compensated employment" (which may jeopardize eligibility for workers compensation benefits) if he or she is receiving compensation for performing services. The fact that the amount of compensation is small may be irrelevant. And, the employee cannot avoid disqualification by characterizing church compensation as "love gifts."

- If your church has at least 15 employees, and is engaged in commerce, then you are subject to the Americans with Disabilities Act. This Act generally prohibits covered employers from discriminating in employment decisions on the basis of the disability of a person who is able to perform the essential functions of a job with or without reasonable accommodation by the employer. There are exceptions. For example, churches are permitted to discriminate on the basis of religion in their employment decisions. Many states have their own disability laws, and some of these laws apply to employers with fewer than 15 employees (and none requires interstate commerce).

Dismissing Employees for Filing a Workers Compensation Claim

§ 8-07.3

Key Point 8-07.3> *In many states employers can be sued for dismissing or in any way discriminating against an employee who files a workers compensation claim.*

Table 8-5 **Application of Workers Compensation Laws to Religious Employers**

Note: All laws are subject to change. To determine the current text of any statute, you should visit a library, contact a workers compensation office in your state, check the website maintained by your state department of labor, or consult with an attorney.

state	minimum number of employees to be subject to workers compensation law	exemption of employees of churches and other religious organizations
Alabama	5	none
Alaska	1	none
Arizona	1	none
Arkansas	3	Employment means every employment in the state in which three (3) or more employees are regularly employed by the same employer in the course of business except . . . a person performing services for any nonprofit religious, charitable, or relief organization. *Ark. Code 11-9-102*
California	1	"Employee" excludes the following . . . any person performing services in return for aid or sustenance only, received from any religious, charitable, or relief organization. *Cal. Labor Code 3352*
Colorado	1	The workers compensation law is not intended to apply to employees of eleemosynary [of or relating to charity], charitable, fraternal, religious, or social employers who are elected or appointed to serve in an advisory capacity and receive an annual salary or an amount not in excess of seven hundred fifty dollars and are not otherwise subject to the "Workers' Compensation Act of Colorado." *Colo. Stat. 8-40-302*
Connecticut	1	none
Delaware	1	none
D.C.	1	none
Florida	4	none
Georgia	3	none

state	minimum number of employees to be subject to workers compensation law	exemption of employees of churches and other religious organizations
Hawaii	1	"Employment" does not include the following service: (1) Service for a religious, charitable, educational, or nonprofit organization if performed in a voluntary or unpaid capacity; (2) Service for a religious, charitable, educational, or nonprofit organization if performed by a recipient of aid therefrom and the service is incidental to or in return for the aid received; (3) Service for a school, college, university, college club, fraternity, or sorority if performed by a student who is enrolled and regularly attending classes and in return for board, lodging, or tuition furnished, in whole or in part; (4) Service performed by a duly ordained, commissioned, or licensed minister, priest, or rabbi of a church in the exercise of the minister's, priest's, or rabbi's ministry or by a member of a religious order in the exercise of nonsecular duties required by the order. "Religious, charitable, educational, or nonprofit organization" means a corporation, unincorporated association, or foundation organized and operated exclusively for religious, charitable, or educational purposes, no part of the net earnings of which inure to the benefit of any private shareholder or individual. *Hawaii Stats. 386-1*
Idaho	1	none
Illinois	1	none
Indiana	1	none
Iowa	1	none
Kansas	1	"Employment" does include persons employed by educational, religious and charitable organizations, but only to the extent and during the periods that they are paid wages by such organizations. *Kansas Stats. 44-508*
Kentucky	1	The workers compensation law does not apply to persons performing services in return for aid or sustenance only, received from any religious or charitable organization. *Ky. Stats. 342.650*
Louisiana	1	The workers compensation law does not apply to uncompensated officers and uncompensated members of the board of directors of bona fide, nonprofit organizations which are charitable, educational, religious, social, civic or fraternal in nature. *La. Stats. 23:1046*
Maine	1	none
Maryland	1	An individual is not a covered employee while performing a service only for aid or sustenance from a charitable or religious organization. *Md. Code 9-235*

state	minimum number of employees to be subject to workers compensation law	exemption of employees of churches and other religious organizations
Massachusetts	1	none
Michigan	3	none
Minnesota	1	none
Mississippi	5	The term "employer" does not include nonprofit charitable, fraternal, cultural, or religious corporations or associations, that have in service five (5) or more workers or operatives regularly in the same business or in or about the same establishment under any contract of hire, express or implied. *Miss. Code 71-3-5*
Missouri	5	Volunteers of a tax-exempt organization which operates under the standards of Section 501(c)(3) of the federal Internal Revenue Code, where such volunteers are not paid wages, but provide services purely on a charitable and voluntary basis. *Mo. Stat. 287.090.1*
Montana	1	Unless an employer elects to be covered, the workers compensation law does not apply to service performed by an ordained, commissioned, or licensed minister of a church in the exercise of the church's ministry or by a member of a religious order in the exercise of duties required by the order. *Mont. Stats. 39-71-401*
Nebraska	1	none
Nevada	1	Covered employees do not include any clergyman, rabbi or lay reader in the service of a church, or any person occupying a similar position with respect to any other religion. *Nev. Stats. 616A.110*
New Hampshire	1	none
New Jersey	1	none
New Mexico	3	none
New York	1	The workers compensation law applies to "all other employments, except persons engaged in a teaching or non-manual capacity in or for a religious, charitable or educational institution . . . not hereinbefore enumerated, carried on by any person, firm or corporation in which there are engaged or employed one or more employees regularly, in the same business or in or about the same establishment either upon the premises or at the plant or away from the plant of the employer, under any contract of hire, express or implied, oral or written . . . unless the employer has elected to bring such employees under the law . . . .A duly ordained, commissioned or licensed minister, priest or rabbi, a sexton, a christian science reader, or a member of a religious order, shall not be deemed to be employed or engaged in employment under the terms of this section. Recipients of charitable aid from a religious or charitable institution who perform work in or for the institution which is incidental to or in return for the aid conferred, and not under any express contract of hire, shall not be deemed to be employed or engaged in employment under the terms of this section.

state	minimum number of employees to be subject to workers compensation law	exemption of employees of churches and other religious organizations
New York	1	All persons who are members of a supervised amateur athletic activity operated on a nonprofit basis shall not be deemed to be employed or engaged in employment under the terms of this section, provided that said members are not also otherwise engaged or employed by any person, firm or corporation participating in said athletic activity. The terms 'religious, charitable or educational institution' mean a corporation, unincorporated association, community chest, fund or foundation organized and operated exclusively for religious, charitable or educational purposes, no part of the net earnings of which inure to the benefit of any private shareholder or individual." *Workers Compensation Law section 3*
North Carolina	3	none
North Dakota	1	The workers compensation law does not apply to the clergy and employees of religious organizations engaged in the operation, maintenance, and conduct of the place of members of worship. *ND Stat. 65-01-02*
Ohio	1	The workers compensation law does not apply to a duly ordained, commissioned, or licensed minister or assistant or associate minister of a church in the exercise of ministry. *Ohio Rev. Code 4123.01* An employer who is a member of a recognized religious sect or division of a recognized religious sect and who is an adherent of established tenets or teachings of that sect or division by reason of which the employer is conscientiously opposed to benefits to employers and employees from any public or private insurance that makes payment in the event of death, disability, impairment, old age, or retirement or makes payments toward the cost of, or provides services in connection with the payment for, medical services, including the benefits from any insurance system established by the "Social Security Act," may apply to the administrator of workers compensation to be excepted from payment of premiums and other charges assessed under the workers compensation law, or if the employer is a self-insuring employer, from payment of direct compensation and benefits to and assessments required by the workers compensation law. *Ohio Rev. Code 4123.15*
Oklahoma	1	none
Oregon	1	The workers compensation law does not apply to a person performing services primarily for board and lodging received from any religious, charitable or relief organization; or a person performing services on a volunteer basis for a nonprofit, religious, charitable or relief organization, whether or not such person receives meals or lodging or nominal reimbursements or vouchers for meals, lodging or expenses. *Ore. Stats. 656.027*

state	minimum number of employees to be subject to workers compensation law	exemption of employees of churches and other religious organizations
Pennsylvania	1	An employer may file an application with the Department of Labor and Industry to be excepted from the provisions of the workers compensation law in respect to certain employees. The application shall include a written waiver by the employee of all benefits under the act and an affidavit by the employee that he is a member of a recognized religious sect or division thereof and is an adherent of established tenets or teachings of such sect or division by reason of which he is conscientiously opposed to acceptance of the benefits of any public or private insurance which makes payments in the event of death, disability, old age or retirement or makes payments toward the cost of, or provides services for medical bills (including the benefits of any insurance system established by the Federal Social Security Act). *77 Pa. Stats. 484*
Rhode Island	1	none
South Carolina	4	none
South Dakota	1	Every duly elected or appointed executive officer of a corporation, other than a charitable, religious, educational, or other nonprofit corporation, shall be an employee of such corporation under this title. *SD Stats. 62-1-7* Notwithstanding any other provision of this title, any charitable, religious, educational, or other nonprofit corporation which has accepted the provisions of this title may cause any duly elected or appointed executive officer to be an employee of such corporation under this title by specifically including such executive officer among those to whom such corporation secures the payment of compensation . . . and such executive officer shall remain an employee of such corporation under this title while the payment of compensation is so secured. *SD Stats. 62-1-8*
Tennessee	5	none
Texas	1	none
Utah	1	none
Vermont	1	none
Virginia	3	none
Washington	1	Mandatory coverage of all employees under the workers compensation law does not apply to any person performing services in return for aid or sustenance only, received from any religious or charitable organization. *Rev. Code Wash. 51.12.020*

state	minimum number of employees to be subject to workers compensation law	exemption of employees of churches and other religious organizations
West Virginia	1	Churches are not required to subscribe to the state workers compensation fund, but may elect to do so. Whenever there are churches in a circuit which employ one individual clergyman and the payments to the clergyman from the churches constitute his or her full salary, such circuit or group of churches may elect to be considered a single employer for the purpose of premium payment into the workers compensation fund. *W. Va. Code 23-2-1*
Wisconsin	3	An employer may file with the department an application for exemption from the duty to pay compensation under the workers compensation law with respect to any employee who signs a waiver of all benefits under the law, and an affidavit that he or she is a member of a recognized religious sect and that, as a result of the employee's adherence to the established tenets or teachings of the religious sect, the employee is conscientiously opposed to accepting the benefits of any public or private insurance that makes payments in the event of death, disability, old age or retirement, or that makes payments toward the cost of or provides medical care, including any benefits provided under the federal Social Security act. *Wis. Stat. 102.28*
Wyoming	1	none

Fair Labor Standards Act   § 8-08

In 1938 Congress enacted the Fair Labor Standards Act to protect employees engaged in interstate commerce from substandard wages and excessive working hours. The Act achieves its purpose by prescribing a maximum workweek of 40 hours for an employee engaged in commerce, unless the employee is paid at the rate of one and one half times the regular rate of compensation for all hours worked over 40, and by prescribing a minimum wage for all employees engaged in interstate commerce. The Act also requires equal pay for equal work regardless of gender, and restricts the employment of underage children.

The Act initially covered only those employees "engaged in commerce or in the production of goods for commerce." Congress greatly expanded the Act's coverage in 1961 by amending the Act to cover "enterprises" as well as individual employees. The Act now provides that employers must pay the minimum wage and overtime compensation not only to employees actually engaged in commerce or in the production of goods for commerce, but also to any employee "employed in an enterprise engaged in commerce or in the production of goods for commerce."

In summary, for the minimum wage and overtime compensation require-ments to apply to a particular worker, the following two requirements must be satisfied: (1) the worker must either be (a) engaged directly in commerce or in the production of goods for commerce, or (b) employed by an enterprise engaged in commerce or in the production of goods for commerce, and (2) the worker must be an employee.

The more important of these terms are discussed in the following para-graphs, along with pertinent exemptions.

Enterprises

§ 8-08.1

Key Point 8-08.1 >*The Fair Labor Standards Act mandates that employers pay the minimum wage, and overtime compensation, to employees who work for an enterprise engaged in commerce. There is no exception for religious organizations, but there are exceptions for certain classifications of employees.*

The Act defines an *enterprise* as "the related activities performed . . . by any person or persons for a common business purpose." The United States Supreme Court has noted that this definition *excludes* most religious and charitable organ-izations to the extent that they are not operating for profit and are not pursuing a "business purpose."[27] On the other hand, religious and charitable organizations will be deemed to be an "enterprise" subject to the minimum wage and overtime compensation requirements if they are engaged in commercial or business activ-ities.

In 1966, Congress amended the Act to include within the definition of "enterprise" any "preschool, elementary or secondary school, or an institution of higher education (regardless of whether or not such . . . institution or school is public or private or operated for profit or not for profit)." The Act now provides that schools and preschools, even those operated by churches, are "deemed to be activities performed for a common business purpose."

The fact that a church school or preschool is now deemed to be an "enter-prise" does not end the analysis. As noted above, the enterprise must be "engaged in commerce or in the production of goods for commerce," and the worker must be an employee. The Act defines the term *enterprise engaged in commerce or in the production of goods for commerce* to include an enterprise that:

(1) "has employees engaged in commerce or in the production of goods for commerce, or that has employees handling, selling, or otherwise working on goods or materials that have been moved in or produced for com-merce by any person, *and* is an enterprise whose annual gross volume of sales made or business done is not less than $500,000"; *or*

(2) "is engaged in the operation of a . . . preschool, elementary or secondary school, or an institution of higher education (regardless of whether or not

---

[27] Tony & Susan Alamo Foundation v. Secretary of Labor, 471 U.S. 290 (1985).

such . . . institution or school is public or private or operated for profit or not for profit)."

According to this language, church-operated schools and preschools are deemed to be "enterprises engaged in commerce or in the production of goods for commerce." A "fact sheet" published by the Department of Labor states:

The amendments to the FLSA specifically extended FLSA coverage to preschools as covered "enterprises," regardless of whether public or private or operated for profit or not for profit, and without regard to the annual dollar volume of the business. As a result, all such enterprises are required to comply with applicable provisions of the FLSA.

Daycare centers and preschools provide custodial, educational, or developmental services to preschool age children to prepare them to enter elementary school grades. This includes nursery schools, kindergartens, head start programs, and any similar facility primarily engaged in the care and protection of preschool age children. Individuals who care for children in their home are not considered daycare centers unless they have employees to assist them with the care of the children.

This language leaves no doubt that the Department of Labor interprets the term *preschool* to include a church-operated child care facility even if the facility is primarily a custodial rather than an educational institution.

preschools

The Act applies to any "enterprise engaged in commerce or in the production of goods for commerce," and specifically includes church-operated preschools within this definition.

Case Studies

• *A federal district court in South Carolina ruled that church-operated preschools are subject to the Act's minimum wage and overtime pay requirements.*[28] *However, the court concluded that the term preschool suggests a facility that imparts education in an institutional setting, and that this term did not include child care centers that are primarily custodial in nature. The court observed: "A facility operating only as a nursery for babies and small children, such as that portion of [the church's] operation designated as a child care center would not, in the opinion of this court, be considered imparting education." The court rejected the conclusion of the Department of Labor in its Publication 1364 that the term "preschool" included child care facilities. The court concluded: "The [church's] operation of the child care center is primarily designed to provide custodial care which is suitable to the age of the child. This is typical child care which is found in the home and, in the opinion of this court, is not intended by Congress to be within the meaning of 'preschool.' It is not education in an institutional setting." However, the court did conclude that the church's kindergarten was a preschool, and that its employees were entitled to the minimum wage and overtime pay.*

---

[28] Marshall v. First Baptist Church, 23 Wage & Hour Cases (BNA) 386 (D.S.C. 1977).

• A federal district court in Texas ruled that a church had to provide information to the government in an investigation concerning the alleged failure of the church to pay the minimum wage to its child care workers.[29] The church argued that its operation of a day care center was an integral part of the ministry of the church itself and therefore the subjecting of that center to minimum wage laws violated the constitutional guaranty of religious freedom. The church maintained that its daycare employees were church members who had received a divine call to Christian education and believed that it was their right and duty to serve God by working for minimal compensation. In rejecting the church's position, the court observed that "there is apparently no explicit exemption in the Fair Labor Standards Act for churches or church-related schools. The Court can find none and [the church] has not suggested any. Indeed, the Act specifically defines a covered enterprise to include a preschool, even if it be private and operated on a nonprofit basis." The court then strongly suggested that workers at a church-operated preschool would be covered by the Act. It quoted with approval from an earlier federal appeals court decision noting that "neither the Supreme Court nor this court has held that the employment relationship between a church and all of its employees is a matter of purely ecclesiastical concern." Further, with respect to the church's claim that all of its preschool workers were engaged in "ministry," the Court observed: "While religious organizations may designate persons as ministers for their religious purposes free from any governmental interference, bestowal of such a designation does not control their extra-religious legal status."

A few other federal courts have ruled on the application of the minimum wage requirements to workers at secular child care facilities.

One court concluded that preschools are covered by the Act, and that the word *preschool* includes child care facilities that are primarily custodial in nature.[30] The child care facility in question was open from 6:00 AM to 6:00 PM, Monday through Friday and accepted children ranging in age from infancy to 12 years, with most children being three to five years of age. Children were accepted on a regular, occasional, or drop-in basis and charges were based on weekly, daily, or hourly periods. Most of the children were brought to the facility by working parents. The center was in a one-story building located within a fenced yard. One room was used as an office and another contained kitchen facilities. The other rooms were equipped with cribs, cots, tables, chairs, pictures, television, and a great variety of toys, books, and games. Playground equipment was in the yard. The center posted a schedule of activities, generally designating time periods for breakfast, morning activities, lunch, naps, snacks, and outdoor play. Occasionally children were taken on field trips. Children of school age were transported from the center to their school and back. The center employed no certified teachers and had no written lesson plans, achievement records, or progress reports.

The center claimed that it was not covered by the minimum wage requirements since it was a purely custodial child care facility rather than a preschool with a primarily educational function. In rejecting this distinction, the court referred to the opinion of a noted expert in child development, who had testified for the government and emphasized the opportunities for learning in child care

---

[29] Donovan v. Central Baptist Church, 25 Wage & Hour Cases (BNA) 815 (S.D. Tex. 1982).

[30] United States v. Elledge, 614 F.2d 247 (10th Cir. 1980).

facilities. The expert testified that children learn from exposure to books, art, and music and from interaction with other children and with adults from outside the family, and that their learning process cannot be formalized because of limited attention spans. The expert defined "preschool" as a facility in which several children unrelated are supervised by adults and in which there are opportunities for learning. She stated that the term *preschool* produces confusion and professional discontent because it simply means "before school" but that professional consensus recognizes that institutions for the care of preschool aged children are generally educational in nature because they provide appropriate learning opportunities for preschool age children in a group setting with adult supervision. The court noted that this is the approach taken by the Department of Labor, and it concluded that it was reasonable. Accordingly, the court concluded that "[a]pplication of the Fair Labor Standards Act may not be avoided by the assertion of primary emphasis on custody and the rejection of the undenied learning opportunities afforded to the children." The court further observed that the Act "was passed for humanitarian and remedial purposes" and accordingly that it "must be liberally construed to apply to the furthest reaches consistent with congressional direction."

A few other courts, while agreeing that secular preschools are automatically covered under the Act, have concluded that the term *preschool* does not include child care facilities that are primarily custodial in nature and that are not licensed or regulated under state law.[31]

schools

As noted above, the Fair Labor Standards Act's minimum wage and overtime pay requirements apply to the employees of any "enterprise engaged in commerce or in the production of goods for commerce." The Act specifically includes church-operated schools within this definition. The coverage of church-operated schools under the Act was affirmed by a federal appeals court in an important decision.[32]

The court concluded that a church-operated school violated the Act by paying employees less than the minimum wage and by paying women less than men for comparable work (the Act requires that males and females be paid equally for the same work). The church agreed that it paid women less than men, and that it did not pay some workers the minimum wage. However, it asserted that (1) the school was not covered by the Fair Labor Standards Act, (2) school employees were "ministers" and therefore excluded from coverage under the Act, and (3) applying the Act to the church's school would violate the constitutional guaranty of religious freedom.

A trial court rejected the church's arguments, and ordered it to distribute $177,680 among those female teachers who had been paid less than men, and $16,818 among those workers who had not received the minimum wage. The church appealed, and a federal appeals court upheld the trial court's decision in favor of the government. In rejecting the church's claim that the Fair Labor

---

[31] Marshall v. Rosemont, 584 F.2d 319 (9th Cir. 1978).

[32] Dole v. Shenandoah Baptist Church, 899 F.2d 1389 (4th Cir. 1990).

Standards Act did not apply to a church-operated school, the court noted that the Act was amended in 1966 to specifically cover nonprofit, private schools. The court also rejected without explanation the church's claim that its school employees were really church employees and therefore exempt from the Act. The church had demonstrated that the school was "inextricably intertwined" with the church, that the church and school shared a common building and a common payroll account, and that school employees must subscribe to the church's statement of faith. The court also rejected the church's claim that its school employees were exempt from the Act because they were "ministers" who considered teaching at the school "their personal ministry." It noted that they "perform no sacerdotal functions, neither do they serve as church governors. They belong to no clearly delineated religious order." Further, "the exemption of these teachers would create an exception capable of swallowing up the rule"— since it would mean that all teachers at church-operated schools would be exempt (contrary to the intent of the 1966 amendment to the Act that was designed to include them).

> Sacerdotal = priestly

The court rejected the church's claim that its constitutional right of religious freedom would be violated by subjecting its school employees to the minimum wage and "equal pay" provisions of the Act. The church claimed that its "head of household" salary supplements (paid to males) "was based on a sincerely-held belief derived from the Bible," and that employee wages should be fixed by the church acting under divine guidance rather than by the government. The court acknowledged that the church might suffer a burden on the practice of its religion, but it insisted that any burden would be limited. It observed that although the church's head of household salary supplement (for males) "was grounded on a biblical passage, church members testified that the Bible does not mandate a pay differential based on sex. They also testified that no [church] doctrine prevents [the school] from paying women as much as men or from paying the minimum wage. Indeed, the school now complies with the Fair Labor Standards Act . . . ." This limited burden on the church's religious beliefs was outweighed by the government's compelling interest in ensuring that workers receive the minimum wage. The court observed that school employees whose religious convictions were violated by the school's coverage under the Act could simply return a portion of their compensation back to the church. Or, they could volunteer their services to the school.

This ruling indicates that church-operated primary and elementary schools in the fourth federal circuit (which includes the states of Maryland, North Carolina, South Carolina, Virginia, and West Virginia) must comply with the Fair Labor Standards Act's "equal pay" and minimum wage provisions. It is likely that other federal appeals courts will agree with this ruling, meaning that church-operated schools in other states should assume that their employees are protected by the Act. However, note that this ruling only applies to church-operated primary and secondary schools. It does *not* apply to churches themselves.

Other federal courts have concluded that church-operated schools are covered by the Act.[33]

---

[33] *See, e.g.,* Equal Employment Opportunity Commission v. Fremont Christian School, 781 F.2d 1362 (9th Cir. 1986).

Case Studies

• A federal district court in Indiana ruled that the "Equal Pay Act" (a part of the Fair Labor Standards Act) applies to a church-operated school.[34] A Baptist church operated a private school. The federal Equal Employment Opportunity Commission ("EEOC") sued the church for alleged violations of the Equal Pay Act. The EEOC alleged that the church unlawfully paid higher wages and benefits to male teachers than to a class of female teachers performing equal work, and further that the church unlawfully reduced the male teachers' wages in an attempt to comply with the Equal Pay Act. The church claimed that Congress did not intend for the Fair Labor Standards Act, or the Equal Pay Act, to apply to churches or church-operated schools, and therefore neither the EEOC nor the federal court had "jurisdiction over the church." The court noted that the Fair Labor Standards Act does specifically apply to church-operated schools. It "explicitly includes schools (public or private) and other not for profit organizations within the definition of 'enterprises' subject to that statute."

• A federal appeals court concluded that the federal minimum wage law applied to the staff of a church-operated school.[35] A church in Little Rock, Arkansas, operated an elementary and secondary school utilizing a self-study program that taught all subjects from a biblical point of view. The school was an integral part of the church. Each class had a supervisor assisted by a classroom "monitor." Both worked with the children but did not conduct formal classroom instruction. Supervisors graded papers, answered students' questions, conducted prayer, and counseled the students. Monitors performed duties equivalent to teachers' aides in the public schools. The school required that all supervisors and monitors be "born again" Christians. Supervisors received compensation of $125 per week ($3.29 per hour for a 38-hour week), while monitors received $100 per week ($2.63 per hour for a 38-hour week). The Department of Labor charged the church with violating the federal minimum wage law (Fair Labor Standards Act), and sought back wages of some $23,000 for 18 current and former supervisors and monitors. A federal district court upheld the government's position, and the church appealed. A federal appeals court agreed that the federal minimum wage law applied to the school's employees, and it upheld the award of back pay. It emphasized that the minimum wage law specifically applies to church-operated school employees, and it rejected the suggestion that the supervisors and monitors were exempt from coverage on the ground that they are "ministers."

• A federal district court in Ohio ruled that a church-operated school was subject to the Equal Pay Act (a part of the Fair Labor Standards Act).[36] The school, consisting of instruction from preschool through secondary levels, was operated by four Church of Christ congregations. The school adopted a policy of paying its teachers who qualified as a "head of household" an additional allowance of $1,500 per year. A "head of household" was defined as a teacher who was married with dependent children. The sponsoring churches adhered to the conviction that the Bible places the responsibility of the "head of a family" on the husband. Accordingly, the head of household allowance was not paid to a female unless her husband was either absent or unable to work. The Equal

---

[34] Equal Employment Opportunity Commission v. First Baptist Church, 56 Fair Empl. Prac. Cases (BNA) 1132 (N.D. Ind. 1991). The court rejected the church's argument that the Supreme Court's "Catholic Bishop" test supported its position. This test is discussed in section 8-12.6 of this chapter.

[35] DeArment v. Harvey, 932 F.2d 721 (8th Cir. 1991).

[36] E.E.O.C. v. Tree of Life Christian Schools, 751 F. Supp. 700 (S.D. Ohio 1990).

Employment Opportunity Commission ("EEOC") charged the school with violating the Equal Pay Act, and demanded that all employees be paid the head of household allowance (regardless of gender). The EEOC also ordered the school to pay "back pay" of $132,000 to female employees who had been denied the allowance in the past. The school maintained that (1) the Equal Pay Act did not apply since the school's alleged discrimination was not based on gender (but rather adherence to a religious principle), (2) the teachers were "ministers" and as such were not subject to the Act, and (3) application of the Act to the school employees violated the First Amendment guaranty of religious freedom. The court rejected all of the school's defenses, and ruled in favor of the EEOC. The court began its opinion by noting that the provisions of the Equal Pay Act specifically apply to the employees of church-operated schools. The court then rejected each of the school's three defenses. In rejecting the school's first argument, the court insisted that the school's "head of household" allowance policy was in fact based on gender "albeit as a means of giving witness to a religious belief that men and women occupy different family roles." In rejecting the school's second argument, the court acknowledged that the teachers and administrators viewed themselves as teachers of the Christian faith who considered their work religious ministry and a religious calling. The court responded to this perception by noting that the school's "designation of these persons as 'ministers' for religious purposes does not determine their extra-religious legal status. There is no indication that any of the teachers are ordained ministers of the churches, nor do they perform sacerdotal functions. Although it appears undisputed that the principles of the Christian faith pervade the school's educational activities, this alone would not make a teacher or administrator a 'minister' for purposes of exempting that person from the [Fair Labor Standards Act's] definition of 'employee.'" In rejecting the school's third argument, the court concluded that "the compelling interests underlying the Equal Pay Act substantially outweigh its minimal impact on [the school's] religious beliefs . . . . [The school] remains free to practice its religious beliefs in ways that do not unlawfully discriminate in its wage scales on the basis of gender. Accordingly, the court finds the [school's] free exercise argument is without merit." In support of its decision, the court noted that while the school insisted that the Bible makes a distinction between the familial roles of men and women, "it concedes that the Bible does not mandate that men must be paid more than women for identical tasks."

DID YOU KNOW?

For a worker to be entitled to the minimum wage and overtime compensation, he or she must be an "employee." The Act defines the term *employee* as "any individual employed by an employer," and adds that an employee includes a person who is "suffered or permitted" to work.[37]

---

[37] 29 U.S.C. §§ 203(e) and 203(g).

Individual Coverage

§ 8-08.2

Key Point 8-08.2> *The Fair Labor Standards Act mandates that employers pay the minimum wage, and overtime compensation, to employees who are engaged in commerce or in the production of goods for commerce. There is no exception for religious organizations, but there are exceptions for certain classifications of employees.*

Even when there is no enterprise coverage, employees are protected by the FLSA if their work regularly involves them in commerce between states ("interstate commerce"). The FLSA covers individual workers who are "engaged in commerce or in the production of goods for commerce."

Examples of employees who are involved in interstate commerce include those who produce goods (such as a secretary typing letters in an office) that will be sent out-of-state, regularly make telephone calls to persons located in other states, handle records of interstate transactions, travel to other states on their jobs, and do janitorial work in buildings where goods are produced for shipment outside the state.

The Department of Labor Field Operations Handbook describes individual coverage as follows:

> Individual coverage depends on the nature of the particular employee's work. An employee is covered on an individual basis in each workweek in which he or she performs any work constituting engagement in interstate or foreign commerce . . . . As a practical matter [the Wage and Hour Division of the Department of Labor] does not assert individual coverage over an employee who is ordinarily engaged in employment which is not so covered but who may on isolated occasions spend an insubstantial amount of time performing individually covered work. However, this rule is not applicable in any workweek in which an employee spends a substantial amount of time doing individually covered work. If, in viewing the employment over a more extended period, it is apparent that the pattern of individual coverage is regular and recurrent, the employee involved is so covered in each workweek in which he does such work, regardless of whether the amount of time spent in this work is substantial or insubstantial.
>
> It is not possible to establish precise guidelines to be followed in determining whether an employee who is not otherwise covered on an individual basis spends an insubstantial amount of time on isolated occasions in the performance of individually covered work. In view of the remedial purposes of the Act, the application of this rule is limited to circumstances where the time consumed by an employee in doing such covered work is obviously trivial, and the incidence of this covered work is so infrequent and out-of-pattern that it would be unrealistic to assert individual coverage solely on such grounds. This must be decided on the facts in a particular case.[38]

The Department of Labor Field Operations Handbook addresses the individual coverage of several categories of employees under the FLSA. The only one relevant to church staff would be "clerical" employees. Section 11c00 of the Field

---

[38] Field Operations Handbook § 11a01.

Operations Handbook states:

> Office and clerical employees who are engaged in the sending and receiving of out-of-state remittances, letters, bills, contracts, etc. or whose work involves the regular and recurrent use of the interstate mails, telephone, telegraph, and similar agencies of communication across state lines, are engaged in interstate commerce. . . . Those who not only transmit, but also prepare letters, bills, contracts, and other papers which are sent out of the state, are actually engaged in the production of goods for interstate commerce.

Regulations adopted by the Department of Labor state:

> The Act makes no distinction as to the percentage, volume, or amount of activities of either the employee or the employer which constitute engaging in commerce or in the production of goods for commerce. However, an employee whose in-commerce or production activities are isolated, sporadic, or occasional and involve only insubstantial amounts of goods will not be considered "engaged in commerce or in the production of goods for commerce" by virtue of that fact alone. The law is settled that every employee whose activities in commerce or in the production of goods for commerce, even though small in amount are regular and recurring, is considered "engaged in commerce or in the production of goods for commerce".[39]

Federal Court Rulings

§ 8-08.3

Key Point 8-08.3 > *Several federal courts have addressed the coverage of church employees under the Fair Labor Standards Act.*

The Fair Labor Standards Act does not specifically exempt religious organizations from its provisions, and many courts have ruled that the Act covers the employees of such organizations.

One court held that the Act applied to the employees of a religious denomination's publishing plant even though the plant was organized "to glorify God, publish the full Gospel to every nation, and promote the Christian religion by spreading religious knowledge."[40] The court observed that the amount of goods sent outside the state where they are produced does not have to be large in order to subject the producer to the provisions of the Act, since the shipment in commerce of "any" goods produced by employees employed in violation of the Act's overtime and minimum wage requirements is prohibited. The plant's interstate shipments were more than sufficient, concluded the court, to involve its employees in interstate commerce. In rejecting the plant's claim that it was engaged in religion and that religion is not commerce, the court observed:

> If we grant that religion itself is not commerce, it still does not follow that a corporation organized for religious purposes may not engage in "commerce" as defined in the Fair Labor Standards Act, that is, by engaging in "trade, commerce, transportation,

---

[39] 29 C.F.R. 779.109.

[40] Mitchell v. Pilgrim Holiness Church Corp., 210 F.2d 879 (7th Cir. 1944).

transmission, or communication among the several states." By engaging in the printing business, as this defendant did, we think it was clearly engaged in "commerce" with the meaning of the Act.[41]

The court also rejected the plant's claim that its First Amendment right to freely exercise its religion would be violated by subjecting it to the provisions of the Act. The court noted that First Amendment rights are not without limit but may be restricted by the state if it has a sufficiently compelling interest. The objectives underlying the Fair Labor Standards Act, concluded the court, were sufficiently compelling to override a religious organization's First Amendment rights under the circumstances of the present case.

In a related case, another court observed that "organizations affecting commerce may not escape coverage of social legislation by showing that they were created for fraternal or religious purposes."[42]

In 1985, the United States Supreme Court unanimously ruled that the Fair Labor Standards Acts applied to some 300 "associates" who performed commercial work for a religious organization in exchange for lodging, food, transportation, and medical care.[43] The foundation engaged in several commercial enterprises, including advertising, landscaping, service stations, restaurants, manufacture and sale of candy and clothing, record keeping, construction, plumbing, sand and gravel, electrical contracting, hog farms, feed and farm supplies, real estate development, and freight hauling. Most of the associates who performed such activities were former "derelicts, drug addicts, and criminals" who had been evangelized by the foundation.

The Court observed that the Act would apply to the foundation's commercial activities if two conditions were satisfied: (1) the activities comprised an enterprise engaged in commerce, and (2) the associates were "employees." The Court concluded that both conditions were satisfied, and therefore the foundation's associates were entitled to the protections of the Act. In finding the foundation's commercial activities to be an enterprise engaged in commerce, the Court observed that "[t]he statute contains no express or implied exception for commercial activities conducted by religious or other nonprofit organizations, and the agency charged with its enforcement has consistently interpreted the statute to reach such businesses." The Court rejected the foundation's assertion that its exemption from federal income taxation constituted governmental recognition of its status as a nonprofit religious and educational organization rather than a commercial one.

As to the second condition, the Court concluded that the foundation's associates were employees despite the foundation's characterization of them as "volunteers" who worked without any expectation of compensation in any form. The Court acknowledged that an individual who "without promise or expectation of compensation, but solely for his personal purpose or pleasure, [works] in activities carried on by other persons either for their pleasure or profit" is not an employee. However, it noted that the Act defines *wages* to include in kind benefits such as

---

[41] *Id.* at 882.

[42] McClure v. Salvation Army, 460 F.2d 553, 557 (5th Cir. 1972).

[43] Tony and Susan Alamo Foundation v. Secretary of Labor, 471 U.S. 290 (1985).

food, lodging, and medical care, and that the associates clearly were compensated employees under this definition. In response to the testimony of several associates that they expected no compensation for their labors and that they considered their work to be "ministry," the Court held that "economic reality" rather than the views of the associates was determinative, and that under this test the associates were employees since they "must have expected to receive in kind benefits—and expected them in exchange for their services."

The Court rejected the foundation's claim that payment of wages to its associates would violate their right to freely exercise their religion. The Court noted that "[i]t is virtually self evident that the free exercise of religion clause does not require an exemption from a governmental program unless, at a minimum, inclusion in the program actually burdens the claimant's freedom to exercise religious rights." Since the foundation in fact compensated the associates by providing them with noncash benefits including food and lodging, the Court saw no merit in the associates' assertion that receipt of compensation would violate their religious rights.

The Court emphasized that if a religious organization could engage in a commercial activity in direct competition with ordinary commercial enterprises and remain exempt from the provisions of the Act, it would be free to pay substandard wages and thereby would realize an unfair advantage over its commercial competitors that would jeopardize the right of potentially large numbers of workers to receive minimum wage jobs. The Court also noted that there was no reason "to fear that . . . coverage of the foundation's business activities will lead to coverage of volunteers who drive the elderly to church, serve church suppers, or help remodel a church home for the needy," since none of these activities is commercial in nature and those who perform such services ordinarily do so without any expectation of either cash or inkind compensation.

A few courts have concluded that the Salvation Army, though a religious organization, is an employer engaged in an industry affecting commerce.[44] However, one federal court ruled that a transient lodge operated by the Salvation Army was not subject to the Act, even though the Salvation Army as a whole was engaged in commerce.[45] The court based this conclusion on the fact that the transient home was not a commercial operation, and the transients were required to perform only incidental services (e.g., making their beds, raking leaves).

Case Study

- *A federal court in North Carolina ruled that a church-operated vocational training program was in violation of federal child labor law.[46] The church used children as young as 11 years of age to work as laborers on a variety of construction projects. The children performed several tasks including remodeling, carpentry, concrete and masonry work, framing, and hanging sheet rock. Children under 16 years of age were not paid for their services, although they generally worked 8 hours each day. The church attempted to avoid the minimum wage, overtime pay, and child labor provisions of the Fair Labor Standards Act*

---

[44] *See, e.g.,* McClure v. Salvation Army, 460 F.2d 553 (5th Cir. 1972).

[45] Wagner v. Salvation Army, 660 F. Supp. 466 (E.D. Tenn. 1986).

[46] Reich v. Shiloh True Light Church of Christ, 895 F. Supp. 799 (W.D.N.C. 1995).

by claiming that the children under age 16 were "vocational trainees" or students rather than employees (the Act applies only to employees). The federal Department of Labor asserted that the children were employees, and that the church had violated the Act. A federal court agreed. The court began its opinion by stressing that the Act applies to all employees employed by an enterprise engaged in commerce, and that the term "employee" is very broadly defined as anyone who is "suffered or permitted to work." The court noted that "a broader or more comprehensive" definition would be difficult to articulate. It also pointed out that the "economic realities" of a position must be considered in deciding whether or not a worker is an employee. The court conceded that in some cases a trainee will not be an employee; but the test to be applied in such cases is whether the trainee or the employer is the "primary beneficiary" of the trainee's labor. If the employer is the primary beneficiary, then the trainee is an employee. The court ruled that this test was met. It conceded that "there is nothing in the federal statutes . . . that prevents church members from arranging for some instruction of their children in vocational pursuits." However, "When the means adopted to serve that end consist of employing children in commercial enterprises that compete with other enterprises fully subject to the labor laws . . . the religious beliefs of the church members cannot immunize the employers from enforcement of the federal statutes. . . . The sectarian purposes of the church members may be served by other means, but their service cannot be sought by putting children to productive work at power saw tables and on brick masons' scaffolding, in violation of the nation's labor laws. Were we confronted merely with violations involving older children or merely with excess hours in non-hazardous environments, this might have been a different case. In the case before us, however, the interest of the United States in prohibiting the employment of children in industrial environments must prevail."

Two federal court rulings contain an extensive analysis of the application of the Fair Labor Standards Act to religious organizations. These cases are helpful in understanding this important question, and they are summarized below.

Case 1. Bowrin v. Catholic Guardian Society, 417 F.Supp.2d 449 (S.D.N.Y. 2006)

A church-affiliated nonprofit organization operated residential programs for mentally disabled persons and foster children. Nine employees (the "plaintiffs") sued their employer in federal court claiming that it had failed to pay them overtime compensation for hours worked in excess of 40 per week.

The court noted that an employer is subject to the FLSA's overtime pay requirements in either of the following two situations: (1) the employee individually is "engaged in commerce or in the production of goods for commerce," or (2) the employer is an enterprise "engaged in commerce or in the production of goods for commerce," regardless of whether the individual employee was so engaged. The court noted that under the FLSA's individual coverage provision, any employee "engaged in commerce or in the production of goods for commerce" is covered by the Act whether or not his or her employer is an enterprise engaged in commerce.

The plaintiffs conceded that they had not been "engaged in the production of goods for commerce," and so "the issue of individual coverage turns on whether the plaintiffs were or are engaged in commerce."

Department of Labor regulations specify that employees are engaged in commerce "when they are performing work involving or related to the movement of persons or things (whether tangibles or intangibles, and including information and intelligence)" between states.[47] As a result, an employee is engaged in commerce "when regularly using the mails and telephone for interstate communication, or when regularly traveling across state lines while working." However, Department of Labor regulations also specify:

> This does not mean that any use by an employee of the mails and other channels of communication is sufficient to establish coverage. But if the employee, as a *regular and recurrent* part of his duties, uses such instrumentalities in obtaining or communicating information or in sending or receiving written reports or messages, or orders for goods or services, or plans or other documents across state lines, he comes within the scope of the act as an employee directly engaged in the work of "communication" between the state and places outside the state.

The court concluded, based on this language, that when an employee's interstate activities "are *de minimis,* or not regular or recurring, as a practical matter neither courts nor the Department of Labor consider the employee covered under the FLSA." It cited the following examples:

• Sporadic or occasional shipments of insubstantial amounts of goods are insufficient to bring an employee within the coverage of the FLSA.[48]

• Four trips out-of-state by one employee on work-related activities over the course of 19 months were "sporadic to say the least," while frequent trips out-of-state and consistent use of the mails to send correspondence out-of-state was sufficient for another employee to be covered by the FLSA.[49]

• An employee's use of the phone and mails to accomplish 14 to 30 major purchases from out-of-state vendors between 1992 and 1997 were considered sufficient to find coverage under the FLSA.[50]

The court conceded that "there is not a clear standard for determining when an individual employee's interstate activities tip the scale and becomes substantial for purposes of determining coverage." It noted that an official publication of the Department of Labor, Wage and Hour Division (WHD), states that the WHD does not assert individual coverage where an employee spends "insubstantial amount of time" "on isolated occasions" performing covered work.[51] The publication acknowledges that "it is not possible to establish precise guidelines to be followed" on the question of whether individually covered work is insubstantial and isolated. However, it goes on to clarify that

> in view of the remedial purposes of the FLSA, the application of this [*de minimis* or "insubstantial amount"] rule is limited to circumstances where the time consumed by an

---

[47] 29 C.F.R. § 779.103.

[48] Remmers v. Egor, 332 F.2d 103 (2d Cir. 1964).

[49] Isaacson v. Penn Cmty. Servs., 1970 WL 794 (D.S.C. 1970).

[50] Boekemeier v. Fourth Universalist Society, 86 F.Supp.2d 280 (S.D.N.Y. 2000).

[51] Field Operations Handbook § 11a01(a).

employee in doing such covered work is obviously trivial, and the incidence of this covered work is so infrequent and out-of-pattern that it would be unrealistic to assert individual coverage solely on such grounds. This must be decided on the facts in a particular case.

Department of Labor regulations provide the following clarification regarding out-of-state travel:

Employees who are *regularly engaged* in traveling across state lines in the performance of their duties (as distinguished from merely going to and from their homes or lodgings in commuting to a work place) are engaged in commerce and covered by the act. On the other hand, it is equally plain that an employee who, in *isolated or sporadic instances*, happens to cross a state line in the course of his employment, which is otherwise intrastate in character, is not, for that sole reason, covered by the FLSA. Doubtful questions arising in the area between the two extremes must be resolved on the basis of the facts in each individual case.[52]

the nine plaintiffs

The court noted that "whether the plaintiffs are covered for work done . . . will require an analysis of their alleged interstate activities to determine (1) whether those activities are of the type covered by the Act, and (2) whether these are performed frequently enough to give rise to coverage under the Act." It observed:

The court agrees with the employer's position that distributing personal mail and phone cards to residents in the home, and picking up personal calls for residents that originate out-of-state, do not constitute the type of use of the mails or channels of interstate commerce sufficient to trigger coverage under the Act. As discussed above, the Department of Labor does not consider "*any* use by an employee of the mails and other channels of communication" to implicate individual coverage. *29 C.F.R. § 776.10 (emphasis added)*. Rather, individual coverage may exist when that "use" is "regular and recurrent" and performed to obtain or communicate information, or to order goods or services across state lines. Although neither the substance nor volume criteria triggering individual coverage under the FLSA are well defined, typically it is the use of the interstate mails and placement of out-of-state phone calls occurring in the course of conducting an organization's clerical or administrative business that appear to trigger individual coverage, if "regular and recurrent" and a "substantial part" of the employee's work. *Field Operations Handbook § 11n01*. It is undisputed that plaintiffs' handling of mail and receipt of telephone calls occurred only in the context of distributing mail and relaying calls and messages to residents. Employees cannot be considered to be "using" the mails simply because they physically touch letters that have arrived from out-of-state for residents in the homes. Nor does answering calls that happen to originate from out-of-state constitute "use" of the channels of interstate commerce. As a matter of common sense, these types of activities do not require an employee to be "directly engaged in the work of 'communication' between the state and places outside the state." *29 C.F.R. § 776.10*.

However, the court did find the employees' trips to other states for shopping and recreation with residents of the homes to be interstate activities "that may bring

---

an employee within the scope of individual coverage," since "traveling across state lines in connection with one's duties clearly implicates coverage under the Act" so long as the travel is neither infrequent nor *de minimis*.

The court concluded that two of the nine plaintiffs were covered under the FLSA because the home in which they worked qualified as an "enterprise." The court then addressed the individual coverage of the remaining seven employees. Its conclusions are summarized in the following table.

employee	duties	conclusion
1	Drove residents to another state to go shopping on two occasions. She also distributed mail to the residents three to four times a week.	Not covered by FLSA, so not entitled to overtime pay.
2	Over the course of two years made five trips out-of-state on recreational or shopping excursions with residents. Received phone calls from out-of-state approximately two times a month for two years, and six or seven times in the most recent year.	Not covered by FLSA, so not entitled to overtime pay. The court found five trips over two years to be *de minimis*.
3	The employee made four trips to other states with residents for recreation, plus another trip to another state to attend a week-long training seminar.	Not covered by FLSA, so not entitled to overtime pay.
4	The employee transported residents to another state two to four times per month to shop. The employer disputed the remainder of her alleged interstate activities, including the receipt of out-of-state telephone calls, and her handling of mail within the home.	"Two to four trips per month out-of-state to shop with residents are frequent enough to bring this employee under FLSA coverage. The disputed activity with respect to phone calls and mail are not considered in determining whether she is covered on an individual basis."
5	This employee traveled to another state for shopping on one occasion, and at least twice for recreation with the residents. She answers the phone and sometimes places calls as part of her job.	Not covered by FLSA, so not entitled to overtime pay.
6	No interstate activity alleged.	Not covered by FLSA, so not entitled to overtime pay.
7	This employee traveled once a week to a neighboring state to shop for food and other items for residents and the home.	"Weekly trips to [a neighboring state] are regular and recurrent enough to bring her under the Act's coverage."

liquidated damages

The court ruled that the employer was required to pay "liquidated damages" in addition to unpaid overtime compensation. According to the FLSA, employers that fail to pay overtime compensation may be obligated to pay not only the unpaid overtime compensation but also "an additional equal amount as liquidated damages." However, an employer will not be required to pay liquidated damages if it can demonstrate that it had "reasonable grounds" for believing that it was not obligated to pay overtime compensation. The court cautioned that this defense required evidence "of at least an honest intention to ascertain what the Act requires and to comply with it. The employer must show more than that it did not purposefully violate the provisions of the FLSA to establish that it acted in good faith." The court ruled that the employer was not entitled to this defense, and accordingly assessed liquidated damages in addition to back overtime pay.

statute of limitations

An employer who has violated the FLSA must pay unpaid wages for two years from the filing of a lawsuit, unless the employer has "willfully" violated the Act, in which case unpaid wages are due for three years. The court concluded that the special three-year rule did not apply in this case since there was no evidence that the employer "*knew* it was violating the FLSA." While the employer may not have "taken sufficient steps to ensure compliance with the FLSA," it did "make some effort to ascertain whether it was entitled to an exemption."

application of the FLSA to religious employers

The court rejected the employer's suggestion that it was exempt from FLSA since it was a religious organization. It noted that Department of Labor, Wage and Hour Division, "clearly recognizes that individual employees of nonprofit organizations who do not engage in substantial competition with other businesses may be covered on an individual basis." It quoted from a Department of Labor publication: "Employees of educational, eleemosynary, or nonprofit organizations may be covered on an individual basis . . . . Employees, such as office and clerical personnel, whose work involves the regular use of the interstate mails, telegraph, telephone, and similar instrumentalities for communication across state lines are actually engaged in interstate commerce."[53]

> Eleemosynary = dependent on or supported by charity

Case 2. Boekemeier v. Fourth Universalist Society, 86 F.Supp.2d 280 (S.D.N.Y. 2000)

A church in New York City supplemented its income by leasing its facilities and property on a short and long-term basis to individuals and organizations. In soliciting customers to rent its facilities, the church performed monthly mass mailings, issued press releases and placed advertisements in magazines and on the Internet. About half of the groups that rented space from the church for special events were from a state other than New York.

The church's total income for each fiscal year from 1993 to 1996 surpassed $500,000. This income came from the following categories:

(1) rental income

(2) contributions (contributions that qualify as tax-deductible charitable contributions)

(3) investment income (revenue derived from dividends and interest received as a result of investments made by the church)

---

[53] Field Operations Handbook § 11n01.

(4) special events income (revenue derived from the coin-operated soda machine on the church's premises, any fund-raising events conducted by the church, and any letter writing campaigns or other special fund-raising efforts conducted by the staff of the church)

(5) miscellaneous income (credits from merchants, adjustments to reflect outstanding checks which never were negotiated, and income derived from meals served at the church)

(6) gain on sale of investments (revenue from the sale of securities owned by the church)

(7) social action committee income (contributions received by the church's social action committee)

(8) insurance proceeds derived from any claim made on a church insurance policy

The following table reflects the amount of income attributable to each such category for the fiscal years in question:

income source	1994	1995	1996
rental income	$467,912	$481,427	$451,973
contributions	57,289	41,444	50,690
investment income	6,319	6,512	7,008
special events	12,087	8,511	9,069
miscellaneous	3,024	6,718	2,406
gain on investments	18,850	(8,982)	(1,437)
social action com.	1,123	600	200
insurance proceeds	15,520	0	0

The church placed the money it received from its rental activities, contributions, and other sources of income into a single, unrestricted fund, and from that fund paid its employees' salaries and other expenses.

the plaintiff

A man ("Ralph") began employment with the church in 1990 as an "Assistant Building Engineer." His job responsibilities included custodial and maintenance work, assisting the church's short and long-term tenants, and purchasing equipment and cleaning and maintenance supplies.

Ralph purchased custodial supplies and other equipment from five out-of state-vendors. The majority of such purchases were for custodial supplies, but on separate occasions Ralph also purchased a refrigerator, electronics equipment, and a computer from these vendors. Ralph also claimed to have purchased materials from a supplier of plumbing parts from California.

Ralph and the church agreed that he made between one and four purchases of custodial supplies from out-of-state vendors in 1992; between three and six such purchases in 1993; between three and four such purchases in 1994; between one and four such purchases in 1995; between two and six such purchases in 1996; and between four and six such purchases in 1997. In other words, Ralph made a total of between fourteen and thirty such out-of-state purchases between 1992 and 1997.

Also as part of his regular duties, on an average of twice per month, Ralph showed church facilities to potential short-term tenants for special events like weddings and meetings. He further worked directly with some short-term tenants to set up for their special events, both in advance and at the time of their rentals, and at times suggested how such tenants might accomplish what they were trying to do. In addition, Ralph generally was available during special events to help in case any problems arose and to clean up after the event. For example, Ralph performed custodial and maintenance tasks for a preparatory school that met on church premises during the entire time that he was employed by the church. He also performed custodial and "set-up" tasks for the National Broadcasting Company ("NBC") in connection with its use of the church as a "control center" during the broadcast of the 1997 Macy's Thanksgiving Day Parade.

Throughout his employment, Ralph was paid an annual salary that did not vary according to the number of hours he worked. His days and hours of work changed several times during the course of his employment, but he had regularly scheduled hours and was expected to and did work additional hours. At all such times, Ralph received "compensatory time" for working excess hours rather than receiving any additional monetary compensation. The allocation of compensatory time to Ralph was governed by a "compensatory time policy" set forth in the church's personnel manual. The personnel manual provided that employees of the church were entitled to straight compensatory time for work in excess of 35 hours per week if the employee obtained the prior approval of the Director of Management and Marketing or the senior minister. An employee could be credited for compensatory time without prior approval if the employee's supervisor approved the overtime and either an emergency existed or the supervisor submitted a written explanation of why additional hours were needed. The personnel manual made no mention of how compensation time would be treated at an employee's termination.

The church kept no records of the number of hours Ralph worked, and as a matter of church policy, no full-time employees completed time sheets. However, Ralph maintained personal records showing time worked on weekends and at special events. The church presented no evidence to contradict the information contained in Ralph's records.

While Ralph did not always follow church policy in obtaining compensatory time, he did inform the church's Director of Management and Marketing of the amount of compensatory time that they owed during his employment, and the church never denied credit for any such time.

Ralph claimed that the church board knew that church employees were "potentially" covered by the overtime pay requirements of the Fair Labor Standards Act. As proof, he pointed to an excerpt in the board's minutes under the heading "Concerns of the Board," which expressed concern over "overtime and compensatory time as it applies to hourly staff and to management." In addition, in 1996 the church treasurer warned a staff member that the church needed to "limit" its income-producing activities so as not to exceed $500,000 per year.

Ralph sued the church and the church board members individually, claiming that they had violated the Fair Labor Standards Act by not paying him overtime compensation while he was employed by the church.

enterprise coverage

The court began its opinion by noting that in order to prove Ralph was entitled to overtime wages, he "must demonstrate either that the church was an enterprise subject to the requirements of the FLSA or, alternatively, that Ralph was himself engaged in commerce as the FLSA defines these terms."

As noted above, employees who are "employed by an enterprise engaged in commerce or in the production of goods for commerce" that has "annual gross sales" or "business done" of $500,000 or more are entitled to overtime pay and the minimum wage unless specifically exempted. The church conceded that it would meet the definition of an "enterprise" engaged in commerce if it met the $500,000 annual gross sales or "business done" requirement. The court agreed with this conclusion, noting that "Ralph's handling of janitorial goods that have moved in commerce and the church's employment of several individuals involved in an extensive advertising campaign to solicit interstate special event renters are more than sufficient to invoke enterprise coverage should the church meet the [Act's] gross dollar volume requirement."

In order for Ralph to be entitled to overtime pay on the basis of the church's status as an enterprise engaged in commerce, the church must have annual gross sales or "business done" of at least $500,000. Did the church's revenue, described above, meet this requirement? The court noted that the "church's gross income for each fiscal year between 1994 and 1996 exceeded $500,000." However, it pointed out that

> enterprise coverage will apply . . . only to the extent the business done by the relevant enterprise exceeds $500,000 for any of these years. Given its nonprofit charitable status, the church generally would not be considered an enterprise under the Act. However, the Act is applicable to its activities insofar as they "serve the general public in competition with ordinary commercial enterprises." *Tony and Susan Alamo Foundation v. Secretary of Labor,* 471 U.S. 290 (1985). As the church's rental activities are in direct competition with other short and long-term commercial landlords and special event locations, they are clearly commercial under the standard articulated by [the Supreme Court in the *Alamo* decision].

The church argued that only the funds from its rental activity should be calculated into the gross business done of the enterprise because it serves as the sole commercial business in which the church is engaged. And, since its rental income did not exceed the $500,000 threshold in any year, it did not meet the enterprise test, and Ralph was not entitled to overtime pay.

Ralph, on the other hand, argued that aside from moneys received from contributions, all of the church's sources of income should be included in the calculation of its gross annual sales. Ralph noted that the church commingled all of its income in one fund, and that money from this fund was used by the church to support all of its operations, including the payment of employees and expenses related to its rental activities.

The court interpreted the $500,000 requirement to include only the following categories of church income:

(1) income from the operation of a "business," such as rental income;

(2) income from special events, such as revenue from a coin-operated soda machine on the church's premises, fund-raising events conducted by the church, and letter-writing campaigns or other special fund-raising efforts conducted by the staff of the church; and

(3) other sources of income that are "sufficiently related to the church's business income" to warrant inclusion in the gross volume amount.

individual coverage

Even if a worker's employer does not meet the "enterprise" test, the worker may be covered by the FLSA's minimum wage and overtime protections if he or she is "engaged in commerce" or "engaged in the production of goods for commerce." Ralph agreed that he did not participate in the production of goods for commerce, so individual coverage depended on the extent to which he was "engaged in commerce."

The court noted that for an employee to be engaged in commerce, "a substantial part of the employee's work must be related to interstate commerce." Further, the test "is not whether the employee's activities affect or indirectly relate to interstate commerce but whether they are actually in or so closely related to the movement of the commerce as to be a part of it."

The court noted that Ralph's purchases "were made from five different vendors, and included not only custodial supplies but also other important items to the church like a computer, electronic equipment and a refrigerator. Additionally . . . Ralph made between 14 and 30 such purchases over the course of his employment. Moreover . . . the church's Director of Management and Marketing has estimated that Ralph made 'dozens' of purchases from only one of these vendors, and that it was a 'normal part' of his duties to place orders with such vendors." The court concluded that "such recurrent and frequent purchases of goods from out-of-state vendors are more than sufficient to trigger the protection of the FLSA."

damages

The court noted that under the Fair Labor Standards Act an employee is due "back wages" for two years from the filing of his action, unless the employer "willfully" violates the Act, in which case back wages are due for three years. A violation is "willful" only if the employer "shows a reckless disregard for the provisions of the Act." The court noted that "willfulness cannot be found on the basis of mere negligence or on a completely good faith but incorrect assumption that a pay plan complied with the FLSA in all respects."

In addition, the Act provides that an employer that has violated overtime pay or minimum wage provisions shall be liable not only for back wages but also "an additional amount as liquidated damages" unless "the employer shows . . . that the act or omission giving rise to such action was in good faith and that he had reasonable grounds for believing that his act or omission was not a violation of the [Act]."

Ralph insisted that the church's violation of the overtime pay protections of the Fair Labor Standards Act was willful and that its violation was not in good faith, making Ralph eligible for both a three-year damage limitations period and liquidated damages. In support of these contentions, Ralph noted that the church board's minutes contain the statement "overtime and compensatory time as it applies to hourly staff and to management" under the heading "Concerns of the Board." In addition, Ralph contended that the church's Director of Management and Marketing was warned by the church treasurer that the church needed to limit its income-producing activities to not more than $500,000 per year. The church disagreed. The court concluded that the church might have acted willfully, but that further proof was needed. It ordered this issue to be determined by a jury.

The court then addressed the proper method for calculating Ralph's damages. The church claimed that Ralph was entitled to overtime compensation *only for the weeks he actually performed work in interstate commerce*. Ralph countered that he was entitled to overtime compensation for every week of overtime he worked because defendants did not keep records detailing the type of work that he performed. The court agreed with Ralph and ruled that he was entitled to overtime pay whenever he worked overtime since his employer failed to keep records of the time he spent specifically working in interstate commerce. It observed, "An employer who has not kept the records required by [the Act] cannot be heard to complain that there is no evidence of the precise amount of time worked in interstate commerce, including overtime so worked." The court also referred to a Department of Labor opinion stating that if an employer wishes to pay overtime to an employee only for duties performed in interstate commerce, "the employer's records must clearly show this delineation in duties performed and wages paid." *U.S. Department of Labor, Wage and Hour Division, Opinion WH-230 (1993).*

Department of Labor Opinion Letters
§ 8-08.4

Key Point 8-08.4> *The United States Department of Labor has issued several opinion letters addressing coverage of church employees under the Fair Labor Standards Act.*

The United States Department of Labor has issued three "opinion letters" that directly address the application of the FLSA to church employees. These opinion letters are summarized below:

Opinion Letter FLSA2005-12NA (September 23, 2005)

A church employed a person in a full-time salaried position who also works a second job for the church as an hourly employee. It was the church's position that no employee of the church was engaged in interstate or commercial activities, and that the church did not receive financial support through any commercial ventures.

The Opinion Letter concluded that the church was not subject to "enterprise" coverage under the FLSA:

> Enterprise coverage does not apply to a private, nonprofit enterprise where the eleemosynary, religious or educational activities of the nonprofit enterprise are not in substantial competition with other businesses, unless it is operated in conjunction with a hospital, a residential care facility, a school or a commercial enterprise operated for a business purpose. . . . It appears that the local church you represent satisfies none of these tests and, thus, is not covered on an enterprise basis. Further . . . enterprise coverage is not applicable to employees engaged exclusively in the operation of a church or synagogue since their activities are not performed for a business purpose within the meaning of FLSA.

The Opinion Letter noted that employees of enterprises not covered under the FLSA may still be individually covered by the FLSA "in any workweek in which they are engaged in interstate commerce, the production of goods for commerce or activities closely related and directly essential to the production of goods for commerce. Examples of such interstate commerce activities include making/receiving interstate telephone calls, shipping materials to another state and transporting persons or property to another state."

The Opinion Letter further clarified:

> As a practical matter, the Wage and Hour Division will not assert that an employee who on isolated occasions spends an insubstantial amount of time performing individually covered work is individually covered by the FLSA. As stated in Field Operations Handbook 11a01, individual coverage will not be asserted for employees who occasionally devote insubstantial amounts of time to:
>
> - Receiving/making interstate phone calls;
> - Receiving/sending interstate mail or electronic communications;
> - Making bookkeeping entries related to interstate commerce.

The church asked the Department of Labor how to calculate overtime for an employee simultaneously holding a salaried position and an hourly position. The duties of the employee's salaried position were food preparation, while the duties of the hourly position were janitorial. The work of both positions was conducted in the church building. The Opinion Letter concludes:

> Employees of a church are individually covered under FLSA where they regularly and recurrently use the telephone, telegraph, or the mails for interstate communication or

receive, prepare, or send written material across state lines. . . . Generally, custodians would not be covered under FLSA on an individual basis unless they regularly clean offices of the church where goods are regularly produced for shipment across state lines. A cook in a church would not be covered on an individual basis unless the employee is ordering, receiving or preparing goods that are moving or will move in interstate commerce. Therefore, because the employee in question does not engage in these interstate activities, the employee would not be individually subject to the FLSA. In light of all of the above information, it is our opinion that the church and the culinary and janitorial employees within it are not covered by the FLSA.

Key Point > *This Opinion Letter specifically referenced the following two Opinion Letters dated November 4, 1983. and July 23, 1975. This demonstrates that the Department of Labor still considers these earlier Opinion Letters to be correct interpretations of the FLSA.*

Opinion Letter, November 4, 1983

A synagogue asked the Department of Labor for an opinion regarding the application of the FLSA to custodians and a cook. The custodians' duties included set-up work for meetings, keeping the premises cleaned and repaired, and cutting the grass and serving food for various functions. The synagogue also employed a cook who prepared food following certain religious services and activities. The other employees of the synagogue were a rabbi, secretary, and part-time religious school teachers.

The Department of Labor concluded that it was not presented with enough information to enable it to make a ruling on the application of the FLSA to the synagogue staff. However, it did provide the following information to assist the synagogue in reaching an informed decision:

FLSA applies to employees *individually* engaged in interstate commerce or in the production of goods for interstate commerce and to all employees in certain enterprises which are so engaged. Employees of a church or synagogue are individually covered under FLSA where they regularly and recurrently use the telephone, telegraph, or the mails for interstate communication or receive, prepare, or send written material across state lines. Individual coverage will not be asserted, however, for office and clerical employees of a church or synagogue who only occasionally or sporadically devote negligible amounts of time to writing interstate letters or otherwise handle interstate mail or make bookkeeping entries related to interstate transactions. Generally, custodians would not be covered under FLSA on an individual basis unless the employees regularly clean offices of the church or synagogue where goods are regularly produced for shipment across state lines. A cook in a church or synagogue would not be covered on an individual basis unless the employee is ordering, receiving or preparing goods that are moving or will move in interstate commerce.

Whether or not enterprise coverage applies to the operations of a nonprofit religious organization, such as a church or synagogue, depends on several factors. Generally, enterprise coverage is not applicable to employees engaged exclusively in the operation of a church or synagogue since their activities are not performed for a "business purpose" within the meaning of FLSA. However, where the nonprofit religious organization employs employees in connection with the operation of the type of institutions described in sections 3(r) and 3(s) of the FLSA [pertaining to hospitals, elementary and secondary schools, preschools, residential care institutions, and institutions of higher education, all of which are presumed to be "enterprises" whose employees are all covered by FLSA regardless of annual gross income] they will be covered on an enterprise basis, since such activities have, by statute, been declared to be performed for a business purpose.

Additionally, activities of a religious organization may be performed for a "business purpose" where, for example, they engaged in ordinary commercial activities, such as operating a printing and publishing plant. In such cases, employees employed in these business activities may be individually covered under FLSA if they are engaged in commerce or the production of goods for commerce, or on an enterprise basis . . . if the business has employees engaged in commerce or in the production of goods for commerce or employees handling, selling, or otherwise working on goods or materials that have been moved in or produced for commerce by any person, and the enterprise has an annual dollar volume of sales made or business done of not less than [$500,000] exclusive of excise taxes at the retail level which are separately stated. Contributions, pledges, donations, and other funds raised through activities such as raffles and games that are in furtherance of the educational, eleemosynary and religious activities of a nonprofit organization are not included in computing the annual dollar volume of business done of the enterprise.

Individuals who volunteer their services, usually on a part-time basis, to a church or synagogue not as employees or in contemplation of pay are not considered to be employees within the meaning of FLSA. For example, persons who volunteer their services as lectors, cantors, ushers or choir members would not be considered employees. Likewise, persons who volunteer to answer telephones, serve as doorkeepers, or perform general clerical or administrative functions would not be employees. However, in situations where the understanding is that the person will work for wages there will be an employment relationship. On the other hand, a bookkeeper could not be treated as an unpaid volunteer bookkeeper for the employing institution in the same workweek in which he or she is also an employee.

Persons such as priests, ministers, monks, nuns, lay brothers, deacons and other members of religious orders or communities who serve pursuant to their religious obligations in the schools, hospitals, and other institutions operated by their church or religious order or community shall not be considered to be "employees."

This Department of Labor Opinion Letter contains a number of important clarifications. Consider the following:

- **Individual coverage.** Church employees are individually covered under FLSA, even if their employing church is not an "enterprise," if they "regularly and recurrently use the telephone, telegraph, or the mails for interstate communication or receive, prepare, or send written material across state lines."

- **Occasional or sporadic tasks.** Individual coverage will not be asserted "for office and clerical employees of a church who only occasionally or sporadically devote negligible amounts of time to writing interstate letters or otherwise handle interstate mail or make bookkeeping entries related to interstate transactions."

- **Custodians.** Church custodians are not covered under FLSA on an individual basis unless they "regularly clean offices of the church where goods are regularly produced for shipment across state lines."

- **Cooks.** A cook employed by a church is not covered on an individual basis unless he or she is "ordering, receiving or preparing goods that are moving or will move in interstate commerce."

- **Enterprise coverage.** The FLSA defines an *enterprise* as "the related activities performed . . . by any person or persons for a common business purpose." The United States Supreme Court has noted that this definition excludes most religious and charitable organizations to the extent that they are not operating for profit and are not pursuing a "business purpose." However, some religious organizations will satisfy the definition of an enterprise if they have annual sales revenue of $500,000 or more. The Opinion Letter cites a printing plant as one example. However, contributions, pledges, donations, and other funds raised through activities such as raffles and games that are in furtherance of a church's exempt purposes are not included in computing the annual dollar volume of business done by the enterprise.

- **Church-operated hospitals and schools.** The FLSA specifies that hospitals, elementary and secondary schools, preschools, residential care institutions, and institutions of higher education are presumed to be "enterprises" whose employees are all covered by FLSA regardless of annual gross income, since such employment is specifically designated by the FLSA as being for a business purpose. However, persons such as priests, ministers, monks, nuns, lay brothers, deacons and other members of religious orders or communities who serve pursuant to their religious obligations in the schools, hospitals, and other institutions operated by their church or religious order or community shall not be considered to be "employees."

- **Volunteers.** Individuals who volunteer their services, usually on a part-time basis, to a church "not as employees or in contemplation of pay are not considered to be employees within the meaning of FLSA." For example, persons who volunteer their services as lectors, cantors, ushers or choir members would not be considered employees. Likewise, persons who volunteer to answer telephones, serve as doorkeepers, or perform general clerical or administrative functions would not be employees. However, in situations where the understanding is that the person will work for wages there will be an employment relationship.

- **Can employees be treated as volunteers?** The Opinion Letter concludes that "a bookkeeper could not be treated as an unpaid volunteer bookkeeper for the employing institution in the same workweek in which he or she is also an employee."

Opinion Letter, July 23, 1975

This Opinion Letter addressed the question of "the application of the provisions of the Fair Labor Standards Act to a secretary employed by a local church." The Opinion Letter concludes:

> This Act applies to employees individually engaged in or producing goods for interstate commerce and to employees of certain enterprises so engaged.
>
> Church employees would be individually covered under the Act where they regularly and recurrently use the telephone, telegraph or mails for interstate communications or receive, prepare or send material across state lines. We would not, however, assert individual coverage for office or clerical employees of a church, such as the secretary, who only occasionally or sporadically devote negligible amounts of time to such interstate transactions. Additionally, coverage would not be applicable to church employees, such as a janitor, engaged exclusively in the operation of the church since their activities are not performed for a business purpose.

Exemptions

§ 8-08.5

Key Point 8-08.5> *The Fair Labor Standards Act exempts employees employed in an executive, administrative, or professional capacity from the minimum wage and overtime pay provisions. To be covered by one of these exemptions, an employee must perform specified duties, and be paid a salary in excess of a specified amount.*

The FLSA requires covered employers to pay their employees at least the federal minimum wage, and overtime premium pay of one and a half times the regular rate of pay for all hours worked over 40 hours in a workweek. However, the FLSA includes a number of exemptions from the minimum wage and overtime requirements, including "any employee employed in a bona fide executive, administrative, or professional capacity . . . as such terms are defined from time to time by [Department of Labor] regulations."

These exemptions are summarized below.

A. Executive employees

DOL regulations[54] define an exempt "executive" employee as any employee who is:

(1) compensated on a salary basis at a rate of not less than $455 per week ($23,660 per year);

(2) whose primary duty is management of the enterprise in which the employee is employed or of a customarily recognized department or subdivision thereof;

---

[54] 29 C.F.R. §§ 541.100 *et seq.*

(3) who customarily and regularly directs the work of two or more other employees; and

(4) who has the authority to hire or fire other employees or whose suggestions and recommendations as to the hiring, firing, advancement, promotion or any other change of status of other employees are given particular weight.

This definition includes the following key terms that are more fully defined by the regulations, as noted in the following paragraphs:

- salary basis (including board and lodging provided by the employer)
- primary duty
- management
- customarily and regularly
- two or more employees
- particular weight

"salary basis"

Exempt employees (not covered by the minimum wage and overtime pay rules) must be paid on a "salary basis" of at least $455 per week. Being paid on a "salary basis" means an employee regularly receives a predetermined amount of compensation each pay period on a weekly, or less frequent, basis. The predetermined amount cannot be reduced because of variations in the quality or quantity of the employee's work. Subject to exceptions noted below, exempt employees must receive the full salary for any week in which they perform any work, regardless of the number of days or hours worked.

Deductions from pay are permissible when an exempt employee

- is absent from work for one or more full days for personal reasons other than sickness or disability
- for absences of one or more full days due to sickness or disability if the deduction is made in accordance with a bona fide policy of providing compensation for salary lost due to illness
- to offset amounts employees receive as jury or witness fees, or for military pay
- for penalties imposed in good faith for infractions of safety rules of major significance
- for unpaid disciplinary suspensions of one or more full days imposed in good faith for workplace conduct rule infractions

Also, an employer is not required to pay the full salary in the initial or terminal week of employment, or for weeks in which an exempt employee takes unpaid leave under the Family and Medical Leave Act.

An employer will lose the exemption if it has an "actual practice" of making improper deductions from salary. The exemption is lost during the time period in which the improper deductions were made for employees in the same job classi-fication working for the same managers responsible for the actual improper deductions. Employees in different job classifications or who work for different managers do not lose their status as exempt employees. Factors to consider when determining whether an employer has an actual practice of making improper deductions include, but are not limited to:

- the number of improper deductions, particularly as compared to the number of employee infractions warranting deductions

- the time period during which the employer made improper deductions

- the number and geographic location of both the employees whose salary was improperly reduced and the managers responsible

- whether the employer has a clearly communicated policy permitting or prohibiting improper deductions

Isolated or inadvertent improper deductions will not result in loss of the exemption if the employer reimburses the employee for the improper deductions.

If an employer (1) has a clearly communicated policy prohibiting improper deductions and including a complaint mechanism, (2) reimburses employees for any improper deductions, and (3) makes a good faith commitment to comply in the future, the employer will not lose the exemption for any employees unless the employer willfully violates the policy by continuing the improper deductions after receiving employee complaints.

Key Point > *Administrative, professional and computer employees may be paid on a "fee basis" rather than on a salary basis. If the employee is paid an agreed sum for a single job, regardless of the time required for its completion, the employee will be considered to be paid on a "fee basis." A fee payment is generally paid for a unique job, rather than for a series of jobs repeated a number of times and for which identical payments repeatedly are made. To determine whether the fee payment meets the minimum salary level requirement, the test is to consider the time worked on the job and determine whether the payment is at a rate that would amount to at least $455 per week if the employee worked 40 hours. For example, a person paid $250 for a project that took 20 hours to complete meets the minimum salary requirement since the rate would yield $500 if 40 hours were worked.*

Key Point > *A church cannot make a nonexempt employee exempt by paying him or her a salary.*

board and lodging

The final regulations specify that an exempt employee must earn the minimum salary amount ($455 per week) "exclusive of board, lodging or other facilities." The regulations state that "the costs incurred by an employer to provide an employee with board, lodging or other facilities may not count towards the minimum salary amount required for exemption. Such separate transactions are not prohibited between employers and their exempt employees, but the costs to employers associated with such transactions may not be considered when determining if an employee has received the full required minimum salary payment."

The final regulations define the term "other facilities" to include items similar to board and lodging, such as meals furnished by the employer; housing furnished for dwelling purposes; and transportation furnished to employees for ordinary commuting between their homes and work.

Case Studies

• *A church owns a parsonage that in the past was used as the residence for the church's senior pastor. When the senior pastor purchased a home a few years ago, the church allowed a non-minister employee to reside in the parsonage. The annual rental value of the parsonage is $12,000. This amount is not considered in deciding if the employee is paid on a salary basis of at least $455 per week ($23,660 per year).*

• *A youth pastor is paid an annual salary of $20,000 by his church. In addition, he is permitted to live in a church-owned parsonage. The parsonage has an annual rental value of $15,000. This amount is not considered in deciding if the youth pastor is paid on a salary basis of at least $455 per week ($23,660 per year).*

• *A youth pastor is paid an annual salary of $20,000, and in addition is paid an annual housing allowance of $12,000 that he uses to rent a home for his family. Is a housing allowance considered in deciding if the youth pastor is paid on a salary basis of at least $455 per week ($23,660 per year)? The final regulations do not address this issue directly, but they do state that the value of "board" and "housing furnished for dwelling purposes" are not included. These terms may be interpreted broadly to include compensation that is provided to a minister to provide housing in lieu of a parsonage, meaning that the youth pastor in this example would not meet the $23,660 threshold for exempt status. This conclusion seems to be consistent with the purpose of the law to make the minimum wage and overtime pay protections of the Fair Labor Standards Act available to as many employees as possible. Note two additional considerations. First, the final regulations specify that "there are some workers, such as . . . clergy, who are statutorily exempt or whose exempt status is not affected by the increased salary requirement in the final rule," and that "clergy and religious workers are not covered by the FLSA." This language indicates that the position of the DOL is that clergy are not subject to the minimum wage and overtime pay requirements of the FLSA no matter how little they earn. Second, as noted in Section 8-08.7, two federal appeals courts have ruled that the so-called "ministerial exception" prohibits the DOL from applying the FLSA to ministers.*

• *A church allows a staff member to commute between her home and the church in a church-owned vehicle. The value of this benefit is not considered in deciding if the employee is paid on a salary basis of at least $455 per week ($23,660 per year).*

"primary duty"

The final regulations define "primary duty" to mean the principal, main, major or most important duty that the employee performs. Determination of an employee's primary duty must be based on all the facts in a particular case, with the major emphasis on the character of the employee's job as a whole.

"management"

The final regulations clarify that "management" includes, but is not limited to, activities such as

- interviewing, selecting, and training of employees
- setting and adjusting their rates of pay and hours of work
- directing the work of employees
- maintaining production or sales records for use in supervision or control
- appraising employees' productivity and efficiency for the purpose of recommending promotions or other changes in status
- handling employee complaints and grievances
- disciplining employees
- planning the work
- determining the techniques to be used
- apportioning the work among the employees
- determining the type of materials, supplies, machinery, equipment or tools to be used or merchandise to be bought, stocked and sold
- controlling the flow and distribution of materials or merchandise and supplies
- providing for the safety and security of the employees or the property
- planning and controlling the budget
- monitoring or implementing legal compliance measure.

"customarily and regularly"

The phrase "customarily and regularly" means greater than occasional but less than constant; it includes work normally done every workweek, but does not include isolated or one-time tasks.

"two or more employees"

The phrase "two or more other employees" means two full-time employees or their equivalent. For example, one full-time and two half-time employees are equivalent to two full-time employees. The supervision can be distributed among two, three or more employees, but each such employee must customarily and regularly direct the work of two or more other full-time employees or the equivalent. For example, a department with five full-time nonexempt workers may have up to two exempt supervisors if each supervisor directs the work of two of those workers.

"particular weight"

Factors to be considered in determining whether an employee's recommendations as to hiring, firing, advancement, promotion or any other change of status are given "particular weight" include, but are not limited to, whether it is part of the employee's job duties to make such recommendations, and the frequency with which such recommendations are made, requested, and relied upon. Generally, an executive's recommendations must pertain to employees whom the executive customarily and regularly directs. It does not include occasional suggestions. An employee's recommendations may still be deemed to have "particular weight" even if a higher level manager's recommendation has more importance and even if the employee does not have authority to make the ultimate decision as to the employee's change in status.

B. Administrative employees

The DOL regulations[55] define an exempt "administrative" employee as any employee who is:

(1) compensated on a salary or fee basis at a rate of not less than $455 per week ($23,660 per year), exclusive of board, lodging or other facilities;

(2) whose primary duty is the performance of office or non-manual work directly related to the management or general business operations of the employer or the employer's customers; and

(3) whose primary duty includes the exercise of discretion and independent judgment with respect to matters of significance.

Note that the final regulations eliminated the "position of responsibility" test contained in the 2003 proposed regulations. The DOL concluded (after reviewing thousands of public comments) that the "position of responsibility" standard "does little to bring clarity and certainty to the administrative exemption." As a result, the "position of responsibility" requirement and its definition as "work of substantial importance" or "work requiring a high level of skill or training" were deleted. Instead, the final regulations require that exempt administrative employees exercise "discretion and independent judgment with respect to matters of significance." The final regulations contain two independent, yet related, requirements for the administrative exemption. First, the employee must have a primary duty of performing office or non-manual work "directly related to management or general business operations." This requirement refers to the type of work performed by the employee. Second, the employee's primary duty must include "the exercise of discretion and independent judgment with respect to matters of significance."

This definition includes several key terms that are more fully defined by the regulations. The terms "salary basis" and "primary duty" are fully explained in the discussion of exempt "executive" employees (see above). Those definitions apply equally to administrative employees. Other key terms include:

- directly related to management and general business operations
- employer's customers
- discretion and independent judgment
- matters of significance

---

[55] 29 C.F.R. §§ 541.200 *et seq.*

"directly related to management or general business operations"

To meet the "directly related to management or general business operations" requirement, an employee must perform work directly related to assisting with the running or servicing of the business. Work "directly related to management or general business operations" includes, but is not limited to, work in functional areas such as

- tax
- finance
- accounting
- budgeting
- auditing
- insurance
- quality control
- purchasing
- procurement
- advertising
- marketing
- research
- safety and health
- personnel management
- human resources
- employee benefits
- labor relations
- public relations
- government relations
- computer network, Internet and database administration
- legal and regulatory compliance

Many of these functions have no direct application to church employees, but they provide an excellent overview of the level of activity required to be "directly related to management or general business operations." The final regulations provide the following additional information that will be useful in evaluating whether church staff positions qualify for the "administrative employee" exemption:

An employee who leads a team of other employees assigned to complete major projects for the employer (such as purchasing, selling or closing all or part of the business, negotiating a real estate transaction or a collective bargaining agreement, or designing and implementing productivity improvements) generally meets the duties requirements for the administrative exemption, even if the employee does not have direct supervisory responsibility over the other employees on the team.

An executive assistant or administrative assistant to a business owner or senior executive of a large business generally meets the duties requirements for the administrative exemption if such employee, without specific instructions or prescribed procedures, has been delegated authority regarding matters of significance.

Human resources managers who formulate, interpret or implement employment policies and management consultants who study the operations of a business and propose changes in organization generally meet the duties requirements for the administrative exemption. However, personnel clerks who "screen" applicants to obtain data regarding their minimum qualifications and fitness for employment generally do not meet the duties requirements for the administrative exemption. Such personnel clerks typically will reject all applicants who do not meet minimum standards for the particular job or for employment by the company. The minimum standards are usually set by the exempt human resources manager or other company officials, and the decision to hire from the group of qualified applicants who do meet the minimum standards is similarly made by the exempt human resources manager or other company officials. Thus, when the interviewing and screening functions are performed by the human resources manager or personnel manager who makes the hiring decision or makes recommendations for hiring from the pool of qualified applicants, such duties constitute exempt work, even though routine, because this work is directly and closely related to the employee's exempt functions.

"employer's customers"

An employee may qualify for the administrative exemption if the employee's primary duty is the performance of work directly related to the management or general business operations of the employer's customers. As a result, employees acting as advisors or consultants to their employer's clients or customers may be exempt.

"discretion and independent judgment"

In general, the exercise of discretion and independent judgment involves the comparison and the evaluation of possible courses of conduct and acting or making a decision after the various possibilities have been considered. The term must be applied in the light of all the facts involved in the employee's particular employment situation, and implies that the employee has authority to make an independent choice, free from immediate direction or supervision. Factors to consider include, but are not limited to:

- whether the employee has authority to formulate, affect, interpret, or implement management policies or operating practices

- whether the employee carries out major assignments in conducting the operations of the business

- whether the employee performs work that affects business operations to a substantial degree

- whether the employee has authority to commit the employer in matters that have significant financial impact

• whether the employee has authority to waive or deviate from established policies and procedures without prior approval

The fact that an employee's decisions are revised or reversed after review does not mean that the employee is not exercising discretion and independent judgment. The exercise of discretion and independent judgment must be more than the use of skill in applying well-established techniques, procedures or specific standards described in manuals or other sources.

The regulations provide the following additional clarification:

The exercise of discretion and independent judgment must be more than the use of skill in applying well-established techniques, procedures or specific standards described in manuals or other sources. The exercise of discretion and independent judgment also does not include clerical or secretarial work, recording or tabulating data, or performing other mechanical, repetitive, recurrent or routine work. An employee who simply tabulates data is not exempt, even if labeled as a "statistician."[56]

"matters of significance"

The term "matters of significance" refers to the level of importance or consequence of the work performed. An employee does not exercise discretion and independent judgment with respect to matters of significance merely because the employer will experience financial losses if the employee fails to perform the job properly. Similarly, an employee who operates very expensive equipment does not exercise discretion and independent judgment with respect to matters of significance merely because improper performance of the employee's duties may cause serious financial loss to the employer.

Case Studies

• A church wants to avoid the FLSA overtime pay requirements for its custodian (who often works more than 40 hours per week) and so it pays her an annual salary of $15,000 instead of an hourly wage. This common technique will not work under either prior law or the final regulations that took effect in August 2004. First, the custodian receives a salary of less than $23,660 per year. With few exceptions, no employee who is paid a salary of less than $23,660 can be treated as exempt from the FLSA overtime pay requirement. Second, the custodian does not meet the current definition of an exempt "administrative" employee since her primary duty is not the performance of office or non-manual work related to the management or general business operations of the employer and her primary duty does not include the exercise of discretion and independent judgment with respect to matters of significance. The final regulations state: "The exercise of discretion and independent judgment must be more than the use of skill in applying well-established techniques, procedures or specific standards described in manuals or other sources. The exercise of discretion and independent judgment also does not include clerical or secretarial work, recording or tabulating data, or performing other mechanical, repetitive, recurrent or routine work. An employee who simply tabulates data is not exempt, even if labeled as a "statistician."

---

[56] 29 C.F.R. §§ 541.202 *et seq.*

• *Same facts as the previous case study, except that the church increases the custodian's salary to $25,000 in order to avoid the overtime pay requirement. This will not work. While the salary test is met, the custodian still does not meet the "duties" requirement summarized in the previous case study.*

• *A church treasurer has heard about the new DOL definitions of exempt "administrative" employees. He would like the church secretary to be an exempt employee because she works so many hours of overtime. He tells the senior pastor that if the secretary is paid a salary of at least $23,660, then the church can treat the secretary as an exempt administrative employee and avoid having to pay overtime. This advice is probably incorrect. It is possible in some cases that a secretary will meet the new definition of an administrative employee, or even an executive employee, but this will not be true in most cases. The final regulations specify that an administrative employee is one whose primary duty is performing "office or non-manual work directly related to the management or general business operations of the employer or the employer's customers," and whose primary duty includes the exercise of discretion and independent judgment with respect to matters of significance. The final regulations state: "The exercise of discretion and independent judgment must be more than the use of skill in applying well-established techniques, procedures or specific standards described in manuals or other sources. The exercise of discretion and independent judgment also does not include clerical or secretarial work, recording or tabulating data, or performing other mechanical, repetitive, recurrent or routine work. An employee who simply tabulates data is not exempt, even if labeled as a "statistician." Most secretaries will not meet this test and so they would be nonexempt workers under the new rules. This means that they are legally entitled to overtime pay for all hours worked in excess of 40 during the same week.*

• *The senior pastor of a large church has an administrative assistant who without instructions or prescribed procedures has been delegated the authority to arrange meetings, handle callers, and answer correspondence. The assistant is paid an annual salary of $30,000. The assistant would qualify as an exempt administrative employee under the new regulations. The regulations give the following case of an exempt administrative employee: "An executive or administrative assistant to a chief executive of a business if such employee, without specific instructions or prescribed procedures, has been delegated authority to arrange meetings, handle callers and answer correspondence."*

"educational establishments and administrative functions"

The administrative exemption is also available to employees compensated on a salary or fee basis at a rate not less than $455 a week and whose primary duty is performing administrative functions directly related to academic instruction or training in an educational establishment. Academic administrative functions include operations directly in the field of education, and do not include jobs relating to areas outside the educational field. Employees engaged in academic administrative functions include:

• the superintendent or other head of an elementary or secondary school system, and any assistants responsible for administration of such matters as curriculum, quality and methods of instructing, measuring and testing the learning potential and achievement of students, establishing and maintaining academic and grading standards, and other aspects of the teaching program

- the principal and any vice-principals responsible for the operation of an elementary or secondary school department heads in institutions of higher education responsible for the various subject matter departments

- academic counselors and other employees with similar responsibilities

The term "educational establishment" means an elementary or secondary school system, an institution of higher education or other educational institution. The FLSA defines elementary and secondary schools as those day or residential schools that provide elementary or secondary education, as determined under state law. Under the laws of most states, such education includes the curriculums in grades 1 through 12; under many it includes also the introductory programs in kindergarten. Such education in some states may also include nursery school programs in elementary education. Factors relevant in determining whether post-secondary career programs are educational institutions include whether the school is licensed by a state agency responsible for the state's educational system or accredited by a nationally recognized accrediting organization for career schools. Also, for purposes of the exemption, no distinction is drawn between public and private schools, or between those operated for profit and those that are not for profit.

Case Studies

- *A church wants to avoid the FLSA overtime pay requirements for its custodian (who often works more than 40 hours per week) and so it pays her an annual salary of $15,000 instead of an hourly wage. This common technique will not work under either the current or former definitions of "exempt employee," for two reasons. First, the custodian earns less than $23,660 per year; and second, the custodian does not satisfy the new "duties" test since her primary duty is not the performance of office or non-manual work directly related to the management or general business operations of the employer or the employer's customers, and her primary duty does not include the exercise of discretion and independent judgment with respect to matters of significance.*

- *Same facts as the previous case study, except that the church increases the custodian's salary to $25,000 in order to avoid the overtime pay requirement. This will not work. While the salary test is met, the custodian still does not meet the "duties" requirement summarized in the previous example.*

- *The senior pastor of a large church has an administrative assistant who without instructions or prescribed procedures has been delegated the authority to arrange meetings, handle callers, and answer correspondence. The assistant is paid an annual salary of $30,000. The assistant would qualify as an exempt administrative employee under the final regulations. The regulations give the following example of an exempt administrative employee: "An executive or administrative assistant to a chief executive of a business if such employee, without specific instructions or prescribed procedures, has been delegated authority to arrange meetings, handle callers and answer correspondence."*

C. Professional employees

DOL regulations[57] define an exempt "professional" employee as follows:

(1) an employee who is compensated on a salary or fee basis at a rate of not less than $455 per week ($23,660 per year), exclusive of board, lodging or other facilities;

(2) whose primary duty must be the performance of work requiring advanced knowledge, defined as work which is predominantly intellectual in character and which includes work requiring the consistent exercise of discretion and judgment;

(3) the advanced knowledge must be in a field of science or learning; and

(4) the advanced knowledge must be customarily acquired by a prolonged course of specialized intellectual instruction.

This definition includes several key terms that are more fully defined by the regulations. The terms "salary basis" and "primary duty" are fully explained in the discussion of exempt "executive" employees (see above). Those definitions apply equally to professional employees. Other key terms include:

- work requiring advanced knowledge

- field of science or learning

- customarily acquired by a prolonged course of specialized intellectual instruction

work requiring advanced knowledge

"Work requiring advanced knowledge" means work which is predominantly intellectual in character, and which includes work requiring the consistent exercise of discretion and judgment. Professional work is therefore distinguished from work involving routine mental, manual, mechanical or physical work. A professional employee generally uses the advanced knowledge to analyze, interpret or make deductions from varying facts or circumstances. Advanced knowledge cannot be attained at the high school level.

field of science or learning

Fields of science or learning include law, medicine, *theology*, accounting, actuarial computation, engineering, architecture, teaching, various types of physical, chemical and biological sciences, pharmacy and other occupations that have a recognized professional status and are distinguishable from the mechanical arts or skilled trades where the knowledge could be of a fairly advanced type, but is not in a field of science or learning.

---

[57] 29 C.F.R. §§ 541.300 *et seq.*

customarily acquired by a prolonged course of specialized intellectual instruction

The learned professional exemption is restricted to professions where specialized academic training is a standard prerequisite for entrance into the profession. The best evidence of meeting this requirement is having the appropriate academic degree. However, the word "customarily" means the exemption may be available to employees in such professions who have substantially the same knowledge level and perform substantially the same work as the degreed employees, but who attained the advanced knowledge through a combination of work experience and intellectual instruction.

Key Point > *This exemption does not apply to occupations in which most employees acquire their skill by experience rather than by advanced specialized intellectual instruction.*

computer employees

Computer systems analysts, computer programmers, software engineers or other similarly skilled workers in the computer field are eligible for exemption as professionals. Employees who qualify for this exemption are highly skilled in computer systems analysis, programming, software engineering or similar computer functions. Because job titles vary widely and change quickly in the computer industry, job titles do not determine the applicability of this exemption. To qualify for the computer occupations exemption, the following tests must be met:

(1) the employee must be compensated *either* on a salary or fee basis at a rate not less than $455 per week *or*, if compensated on an hourly basis, at a rate not less than $27.63 an hour;

(2) the employee must be employed as a computer systems analyst, computer programmer, software engineer or other similarly skilled worker in the computer field performing the duties described below;

(3) the employee's primary duty must consist of: (1) the application of systems analysis techniques and procedures, including consulting with users, to determine hardware, software or system functional specifications; (2) the design, development, documentation, analysis, creation, testing or modification of computer systems or programs, including prototypes, based on and related to user or system design specifications; (3) the design, documentation, testing, creation or modification of computer programs related to machine operating systems; or (4) a combination of the aforementioned duties, the performance of which requires the same level of skills.

The computer employee exemption does not include employees engaged in the manufacture or repair of computer hardware and related equipment. Employees whose work is highly dependent upon, or facilitated by, the use of computers and computer software programs (e.g., engineers, drafters and others skilled in computer-aided design software), but who are not primarily engaged in computer systems analysis and programming or other similarly skilled computer-related occupations identified in the primary duties test described above, are also not exempt under the computer employee exemption.

creative professionals

The regulations create an exemption for "creative professionals" if the following conditions are met:

- the employee must be compensated on a salary or fee basis at a rate not less than $455 per week;

- the employee's primary duty must be the performance of work requiring invention, imagination, originality or talent in a recognized field of artistic or creative endeavor.

This definition includes a few key terms that are more fully defined by the regulations. The terms "salary basis" and "primary duty" are fully explained in the discussion of exempt "executive" employees (see above). Those definitions apply equally to creative professional employees. Other key terms include:

invention, imagination, originality or talent

This requirement distinguishes the creative professions from work that primarily depends on intelligence, diligence and accuracy. Exemption as a creative professional depends on the extent of the invention, imagination, originality or talent exercised by the employee. Whether the exemption applies, therefore, must be determined on a case-by-case basis. The requirements are generally met by actors, musicians, composers, soloists, certain painters, writers, cartoonists, essayists, novelists, and others as set forth in the regulations. Journalists may satisfy the duties requirements for the creative professional exemption if their primary duty is work requiring invention, imagination, originality or talent. Journalists are not exempt creative professionals if they only collect, organize and record information that is routine or already public, or if they do not contribute a unique interpretation or analysis to a news product.

recognized field of artistic or creative endeavor

This includes such fields as, for example, music, writing, acting and the graphic arts.

teachers

Teachers are exempt if their primary duty is teaching, tutoring, instructing or lecturing in the activity of imparting knowledge, and if they are employed and engaged in this activity as a teacher in an educational establishment. Exempt teachers include, but are not limited to, regular academic teachers; kindergarten or nursery school teachers; teachers of gifted or disabled children; teachers of skilled and semi-skilled trades and occupations; and vocal or instrumental music teachers.

Key Point > *The salary and salary basis requirements do not apply to bona fide teachers. They are considered professional employees regardless of the form or amount of compensation they are paid.*

The final regulations state:

The possession of an elementary or secondary teacher's certificate provides a clear means of identifying the individuals contemplated as being within the scope of the exemption for teaching professionals. Teachers who possess a teaching certificate qualify for the exemption regardless of the terminology (*e.g.,* permanent, conditional, standard, provisional, temporary, emergency, or unlimited) used by the state to refer to different kinds of certificates. *However, private schools and public schools are not uniform in requiring a certificate for employment as an elementary or secondary school teacher, and a teacher's certificate is not generally necessary for employment in institutions of higher education or other educational establishments. Therefore, a teacher who is not certified may be considered for exemption, provided that such individual is employed as a teacher by the employing school or school system.*[58]

Case Studies

• *A church-operated elementary and secondary school employs several full-time teachers. Some are state certified, but others are not. Most are paid an annual salary of less than $22,100. Are any of these teachers exempt employees under the proposed regulations? The answer is yes. The regulations provide that teachers are exempt whether or not they are state-certified or licensed, and regardless of the amount of their salary.*

highly compensated employees

Highly compensated employees performing office or non-manual work and paid total annual compensation of $100,000 or more (which must include at least $455 per week paid on a salary or fee basis) are exempt from the FLSA if they customarily and regularly perform at least one of the duties of an exempt executive, administrative or professional employee identified in the standard tests for exemption.

Ministers $ 8-08.6

Key Point 8-08.6> *Ministers who are employed to perform ministerial services, and who are paid a salary that meets or exceeds the "salary test," are professional employees exempt from the provisions of the Fair Labor Standards Act. Ministers not compensated on a salary basis, or who earn a salary below the salary test, may not be covered by the Act. Department of Labor regulations suggest that the Act does not apply to any ministers, and a few federal courts have ruled that the so-called ministerial exception prevents the application of the Act to ministers.*

---

[58] 29 C.F.R. §§ 541.303 (emphasis added).

Q How does the FLSA treat ministers?

A Professional employees are exempt from FLSA, and this would include ministers so long as they meet the minimum salary test ($455/week).

Q What about ministers who earn less than $455/week, or who are not paid on a salary basis?

A They technically do not meet the definition of an exempt professional employee, but can churches be compelled to pay these ministers overtime pay consistently with the First Amendment guaranty of religious freedom? This is an unresolved question. Note the following considerations:

(1) The official "economic report" accompanying the final DOL overtime regulations contains the following statements:

- "Most employees earning less than $455 per week ($23,660 annually) who are exempt under the existing regulations will be entitled to overtime pay under the final regulations (there are some workers, such as teachers, doctors, lawyers, and clergy, who are statutorily exempt or whose exempt status is not affected by the increased salary requirement in the final rule)."

- "Clergy and religious workers are not covered by the FLSA."

- "The Department excluded [in making its coverage predictions] the 14.9 million workers not covered by the FLSA, such as the self-employed and unpaid volunteers, and the clergy and religious workers."

- "Of the 499 occupation codes in the CPS [current population survey] . . . two are assigned to clergy and religious workers (codes 176 and 177) who are not covered by the FLSA . . . ."

In addition, Table 3-1 in the final regulations lists "clergy and religious workers" as one of six categories of "Occupations Exempt from FLSA's Overtime Provisions." This same conclusion is repeated in this same report.

This language suggests that the official position of the Department of Labor is that clergy are not subject to the minimum wage and overtime pay requirements of the FLSA no matter how little they earn.

(2) Two federal courts have specifically ruled that the FLSA does not apply to ministers due to the so-called "ministerial exception." These cases are summarized below. It should be noted that

these cases are binding precedent only in the states of Maryland, North Carolina, South Carolina, Virginia, Washington, and West Virginia. They are persuasive, but not binding, precedent in other states. Therefore, in other states this issue has not definitely been resolved by the courts. However, the final Department of Labor regulations (quoted above) provide some basis for concluding that the FLSA minimum wage and overtime pay requirements do not apply to ministers. Church leaders wanting a definitive answer in a particular case should consult with an attorney.

Case 1. Alcazar v. Corporation of Catholic Archbishop of Seattle, 2006 WL 3791370 (W.D. Wash. 2006)

A federal court in Washington ruled that the "ministerial exception" prevented it from resolving several claims brought by seminary students against a religious organization, including violation of a state minimum wage law.

The court noted that the First Amendment guaranty of religious freedom has created a "ministerial exception" to employment laws, and that this exception prohibits a court from "inquiring into the decisions of a religious organization concerning the hiring, firing, promotion, rate of pay, placement or any other employment related decision concerning ministers and other non-secular church employees."

The court dismissed the seminarian's claim that his religious employer had violated a state minimum wage law. It concluded:

> This claim concerns decisions regarding the rate of pay for non-secular church employees and must also be dismissed under the ministerial exception. The . . . ministerial exception applies to both state and federal claims, and prohibits a court from inquiring into the decisions of a religious organization concerning the hiring, firing, promotion, rate of pay, placement or any other employment related decision concerning ministers and other non-secular church employees. This most certainly includes questions concerning the amount of compensation owed a visiting seminarian student.[59]

Case 2. Shaliehsabou v. Hebrew Home of Greater Washington, 363 F.3d 299 (4th Cir. 2004)

For several years an Orthodox Jewish man (David) worked at a predominantly Jewish nursing home as a "kosher inspector." His primary duty was to guard against any violation of Jewish dietary laws. The nursing home is a nonprofit corporation whose mission, according to its bylaws, is to serve "aged of the Jewish faith in accordance with the precepts of Jewish law and customs, including the observance of dietary laws." While the nursing home accepts persons of all faiths, about 95% of its residents are Jewish. All members of its board of directors are Jewish. The facility maintains a synagogue on its premises and holds twice-daily religious services conducted by an ordained rabbi who serves as a full-time employee. Each resident's room contains a "mezuzah" (a parchment scroll inscribed with the biblical passages).

---

[59] Citing Bollard v. California Province of the Society of Jesus, 196 F.3d 940 (9th Cir. 1999).

Consistent with its mission to serve the spiritual needs of its residents, the nursing home provides its residents with kosher meals prepared in accordance with the Jewish dietary laws. To ensure that the food services department complied with these laws, the nursing home asked a council of local rabbis to recommend a person to serve as a kosher inspector at its facility. The council determined that a kosher inspector must have a knowledge of the basic Jewish dietary laws; must be a "Sabbath observer" and a "fully observant Jew"; and must have a knowledge of the dietary laws through experience and study at an Orthodox Jewish seminary. Compliance with the dietary laws, the council concluded, was "an integral and essential part of Jewish identity." The council recommended David as the nursing home's kosher inspector, and he was hired. David had been a devout Orthodox Jew his entire life and had obtained a Bachelor of Talmudic Law from a rabbinical college. He declared himself as "clergy" on his federal tax returns, and also claimed a parsonage exemption from his salary.

David's primary duties as kosher inspector included inspecting deliveries, opening and closing the refrigerators to insure the integrity of the kosher status of the kitchen, insuring that all meat and dairy products were stored and kept separate during food preparation, and lighting all ovens and heating equipment in accordance with the requirements of Jewish law. He also cleansed kitchen utensils and other items if they became non-kosher, and instructed kitchen staff on complying with the dietary laws and to report any violations.

David was paid for at least 80 hours of work each biweekly period. Although he occasionally received additional hourly compensation for hours worked over 80 per biweekly period, he claimed that he was not compensated for all of the overtime hours he worked. When he worked less than 80 hours during a biweekly period, hours were deducted from his "accrued leave" time to make sure that his total hours for the biweekly period equaled 80. If he exceeded his leave time, he would be docked pay for absences, including absences of less than one day.

David quit his job, and later sued the nursing home in a federal district court claiming that it had violated the federal Fair Labor Standards Act (FLSA), and a corresponding state law, by failing to pay him overtime wages. The district court ruled that David's claims were barred by a "ministerial exception" to the FLSA, and it dismissed the case. The court also ruled that even if David was not covered by the ministerial exception, he was exempt from the overtime pay requirements since he was a professional employee. David appealed. He claimed that the "ministerial exception" only applied to civil rights and employment laws, and not to the FLSA. He also asserted that he was not an exempt professional employee because he was paid an hourly wage rather than a salary.

the "ministerial exception"

Several state and federal laws prohibit various forms of discrimination in employment. For example, Title VII of the federal Civil Rights Act of 1964 prohibits discrimination in employment on the basis of race, color, national origin, sex, or religion. Employers engaged in interstate commerce and having at least 15 employees are subject to this law, including churches. However, for many years the courts have recognized a limited exception in the case of ministers. According to this exception (known as the "ministerial exception") the civil courts are barred by the First Amendment guaranty of religious freedom from resolving discrimination claims brought by ministers against a church. As one court has noted in a case involving a dismissed minister's claim of unlawful discrimination:

> This case involves the fundamental question of who will preach from the pulpit of a church, and who will occupy the church parsonage. The bare statement of the question should make obvious the lack of jurisdiction of a civil court. The answer to that question must come from the church.[60]

The ministerial exception has been applied by the courts to several other discrimination laws, including those banning discrimination in employment on the basis of age and disability. But what about the Fair Labor Standards Act? Does the ministerial exception prevent the civil courts from resolving cases involving the entitlement of ministers to overtime pay? The court noted that in a previous case it concluded that it did.[61] In the *Dole* case the court noted that the ministerial exception "is derived from the congressional debate [about the FLSA] and delineated in guidelines issued by the Labor Department's Wage and House Administrator." The relevant portion of those guidelines provides:

> Persons such as nuns, monks, priests, lay brothers, ministers, deacons, and other members of religious orders who serve pursuant to their religious obligations in schools, hospitals, and other institutions operated by their church or religious order shall not be considered to be "employees."[62]

The court noted that in the Title VII context it applied a "primary duties" test to determine whether an individual falls within the ministerial exception. This test focuses on the function of the position and whether the position is important to the spiritual and pastoral mission of the church, and not whether the individual holding that position is formally ordained. As a general rule, "if the employee's primary duties consist of teaching, spreading the faith, church governance, supervision of a religious order, or supervision or participation in religious ritual and worship, he or she should be considered clergy." The court concluded:

> Although the Title VII ministerial exception is based on constitutional principles and not on "congressional debate" and Labor Department guidelines as is the FLSA exception, we implicitly have held that the ministerial exceptions under the two Acts are coextensive in scope. For example, we have relied on Title VII ministerial exception cases in *Dole*, and we have cited both *Dole* and Title VII cases together in support of the proposition that "the ministerial exception operates to exempt from the coverage of various employment laws the employment relationships between religious institutions and their ministers." Accordingly, our precedent suggests that when determining who is a [minister] for purposes of the ministerial exception to the FLSA, we apply the same primary duties test that we apply for purposes of the Title VII minis-

---

[60] Simpson v. Wells Lamont Corporation, 494 F.2d 490 (5th Cir. 1974).

[61] Dole v. Shenandoah Baptist Church, 899 F.2d 1389 (4th Cir. 1990).

[62] Field Operations Handbook, Wage and Hour Division, U.S. Department of Labor § 10b03 (1967).

terial exception. This common sense approach creates continuity between the FLSA and Title VII, two employment laws of general applicability, and it allows us to avoid answering a difficult constitutional question—i.e., whether the First Amendment would otherwise compel an exception to the FLSA coextensive with that recognized as constitutionally mandated in the Title VII context.

The court noted that using a "primary duties" test to determine the scope of the FLSA's ministerial exception is "in accord with other statutory exceptions to the FLSA." It pointed out that the FLSA's minimum wage and overtime requirements do not apply to "any employee employed in a bona fide executive, administrative, or professional capacity." The regulations "look to the primary duties of a salaried position to determine whether an employee is a bona fide executive, administrator or professional. Courts are thus familiar and comfortable with examining the primary duties of an employee when determining the scope of exceptions under the FLSA. In sum, by determining whether a position is ministerial by referencing the primary duties of the position, the FLSA's ministerial exception is coextensive with that recognized under Title VII and parallels the inquiry made for other exceptions to the FLSA."

The court concluded that "the ministerial exception to the FLSA applies only where the employer is a religious institution and the employee's primary duties are ministerial in nature. The exception does not apply to the religious employees of secular employers or to the secular employees of religious employers."

The court then addressed David's contention that his primary duties were not ministerial, and that the nursing home was not a religious institution. In rejecting David's claim that his duties were not ministerial, the court noted that "in the Jewish faith, non-compliance with dietary laws is a sin. Jews view their dietary laws as divine commandments, and compliance therewith is as important to the spiritual well-being of its adherents as music and song are to the mission of the Catholic church. In short, failure to apply the ministerial exception in this case would denigrate the importance of keeping kosher to Orthodox Judaism."

The court then addressed David's contention that the ministerial exception should not apply to him because he was not employed by a religious institution. The court noted that the ministerial exception has been applied to religiously affiliated schools, hospitals, and corporations, and it concluded that "a religiously affiliated entity is a religious institution for purposes of the ministerial exception whenever that entity's mission is marked by clear or obvious religious characteristics." Applying that standard here, the court concluded that the nursing home was a religious institution. The court acknowledged that the home existed primarily to provide elder care and not religious services, but it concluded that "an entity can provide secular services and still have substantial religious character. The home is religiously affiliated, and its bylaws define it as a religious and charitable nonprofit corporation and declare that its mission is to provide elder care to aged of the Jewish faith in accordance with the precepts of Jewish law and customs." Pursuant to that mission, the home maintained a rabbi on its staff, employed a kosher inspector to ensure compliance with the Jewish dietary laws, and placed a mezuzah on every resident's doorpost."

The court noted that the FLSA exempted professional, administrative, and executive employees from its protections, and that these exceptions are limited to salaried employees. However, because it concluded that David's claims were barred by the ministerial exception, it did not address his status as an exempt professional employee.

This case was a ruling by the federal appeals court for the fourth federal circuit. The decisions of this court are binding only on courts within that circuit, which include the states of Maryland, North Carolina, South Carolina, Virginia, and West Virginia. While the ruling is not binding in any other state, the fact remains that this is one of the few cases to address the application of the ministerial exception to the Fair Labor Standards Act, and so it may be given special consideration by other courts addressing the same question.

Case Studies

The following examples illustrate the application of FLSA to ministers.

- *A youth pastor is employed full-time by a church, is paid an annual salary of $20,000, and in addition is permitted to live in the church parsonage without having to pay rent. The annual rental value of the parsonage is $12,000. Is the annual rental value of the parsonage considered in deciding if the youth pastor is paid on a salary basis of at least $455 per week ($23,660 per year)? The answer is yes. The final regulations specify that the value of "board" and "housing furnished for dwelling purposes" are not included in computing an employee's salary.*

- *Same facts as the previous case study. Since the youth pastor is paid an annual salary of less than $23,660, is he entitled to overtime pay? The final regulations specify that "there are some workers, such as . . . clergy, who are statutorily exempt or whose exempt status is not affected by the increased salary requirement in the final rule," and that "clergy and religious workers are not covered by the FLSA." This language indicates that the official position of the DOL is that clergy are not subject to the minimum wage and overtime pay requirements of the FLSA regardless of the amount of their compensation. Further, two federal courts have ruled that the so-called ministerial exception prohibits the DOL from applying the FLSA to ministers. These cases are binding only in states comprising the fourth federal circuit (Maryland, North Carolina, South Carolina, Virginia, and West Virginia), and a portion of Washington. They are persuasive, but not binding, precedent in other states. Therefore, this issue has not definitely been resolved by courts in other jurisdictions. However, even other jurisdictions the DOL regulations provide a basis for concluding that the FLSA minimum wage and overtime pay requirements do not apply to ministers.*

- *A youth pastor is employed full-time by a church in Virginia, and is paid an annual salary of $20,000, and in addition is paid an annual housing allowance of $12,000 that he uses to rent a home for his family. Is a housing allowance considered in deciding if the youth pastor is paid on a salary basis of at least $455 per week ($23,660 per year)? The final regulations do not address this issue directly, but they do state that the value of "board" and "housing furnished for dwelling purposes" are not included. These terms may be interpreted broadly to include compensation that is provided to a minister to provide housing in lieu of a parsonage, meaning that the youth pastor in this case study would not meet the $23,660 threshold for exempt status. This conclusion seems to be* *consistent with the purpose of the law to make the minimum wage and overtime pay protections of the Fair Labor Standards Act available to as many employees as possible. However, even if the salary requirement for exempt professional status is met, it is unlikely that the youth pastor would be entitled to overtime pay, for the same reasons mentioned in the previous case studies.*

• A church pays its pastor on an hourly basis of $15 per hour. Is the pastor entitled to overtime pay? In general, persons paid on an hourly basis cannot be exempt employees under the FLSA, and must receive overtime pay for hours worked in excess of 40 in any week. However, as noted above, the final DOL regulations state the ministers "are not covered by the FLSA." Further, two federal courts have ruled that the ministerial exception prohibits the DOL from applying the FLSA to ministers.

• A church pays its senior pastor an annual salary of $45,000. The pastor frequently works 60 hours or more per week, and asks the church treasurer if he is entitled to overtime pay. The answer is no. Even if the FLSA applies to ministers (which according to the DOL it does not), the pastor would satisfy the "professional employee" exemption under the FLSA since he performs professional duties and is compensated at a rate in excess of $23,660 per year.

State Laws § 8-08.7

Key Point 8-08.7 > *Several states have enacted minimum wage and overtime pay laws. The provisions of such laws will take priority over the minimum wage and overtime pay provisions of the federal Fair Labor Standards Act if they are a higher amount.*

The preamble to the DOL regulations cautions that "some state laws have stricter exemption standards than those described [in these regulations]. The FLSA does not preempt any such stricter state standards. If a state or local law establishes a higher standard than the provisions of the FLSA, the higher standard applies." This is an important point. Several states have enacted legislation mandating a higher minimum wage than the federal minimum wage. However, when Congress enacts increases in the federal minimum wage, the federal rate will transcend some state minimum wage rates. So, it is important for church leaders to be aware of both the federal and state rates. Whichever is higher applies.

"Several states have enacted legislation mandating a higher minimum wage than the federal minimum wage... whichever is higher applies."

Case Studies

Individual Coverage of Church Employees § 8-08.8

• A church has annual revenue of $300,000 and employs four persons (a pastor, a youth pastor, a church secretary, and a custodian). It engages in no "businesses" that compete

with for-profit companies, and does not operate a preschool or school. The church secretary asks the pastor if she is entitled to overtime pay for hours that she occasionally works in excess of 40 per week. The secretary is not entitled to the overtime provisions of the Fair Labor Standards Act on the basis of enterprise coverage for two reasons. First, the church is not engaged in commerce or in the production of goods for commerce; and second, the church does not have business income of $500,000 or more.

• Same facts as the previous case study except that the secretary purchases office supplies from a local office supply store two or three times each year. Do these purchases satisfy the individual coverage provisions of the Act, entitling the secretary to overtime pay for hours worked in excess of 40 each week? Probably not. The Department of Labor's Opinion Letter dated November 4, 1984, states that church employees are individually covered under FLSA, even if their employing church is not an "enterprise," if they "regularly and recurrently use the telephone, telegraph, or the mails for interstate communication or receive, prepare, or send written material across state lines." However, individual coverage will not be asserted "for office and clerical employees of a church who only occasionally or sporadically devote negligible amounts of time to writing interstate letters or otherwise handle interstate mail or make bookkeeping entries related to interstate transactions."

• Same facts as case study 1, except that the secretary purchased office supplies once or twice each year over the Internet from the same out-of-state office supply store. These purchases were always less than $100 per order. Do these purchases satisfy the individual coverage provisions of the FLSA, entitling the secretary to overtime pay for hours worked in excess of 40 each week? Probably not. See the analysis in case study 2.

• Same facts as case study 1, except that for the past 3 years the church secretary has purchased office supplies about 10 times each year over the Internet from various out-of-state office supply stores. These purchases included computers, computer software, office equipment, and office supplies, and averaged $4,000 per year. Do these purchases satisfy the individual coverage provisions of the FLSA, entitling the secretary to overtime pay for hours worked in excess of 40 each week? Probably. The court in the Boekemeier case (summarized in Section 8-08.3) concluded that a church employee satisfied the individual coverage provision and was entitled to overtime pay since he made "recurrent and frequent purchases" of goods from five out-of-state vendors, amounting to between 14 and 30 purchases over a five-year period (between three and six such purchases each year), for such items as custodial supplies and "important items to the church" such as a computer, electronic equipment, and a refrigerator. The secretary in this example made ten purchases from various out-of-state vendors each year, not only for office supplies but also for "important items to the church" such as computers and computer software.

• Same facts as case study 4, except that the church secretary makes all of these purchases from an office supply store a mile from the church (in the same state). Do these purchases satisfy the individual coverage provisions of the FLSA, entitling the secretary to overtime pay for hours worked in excess of 40 each week? No, they do not. In order for the secretary to qualify for individual coverage under the Act, she must be "engaged in commerce" or "engaged in the production of goods for commerce." The word "commerce" is defined by the FLSA as "trade, commerce, transportation, transmission, or communication among the several states or between any state and any place outside thereof." In other words, the "commerce" must be either interstate or foreign.

Exclusively local commercial transactions, such as the secretary's purchases of office supplies from a local office supply store, do not meet this definition.

• Same facts as case study 4, except that the office supply store is ten miles away in another state. The analysis would be the same as in case study 4.

• Same facts as case study 1, except that the church secretary purchases Sunday School literature from an out-of-state publisher twice each year. Each shipment costs an average of $5,000. Do these purchases satisfy the individual coverage provisions of the FLSA, entitling the secretary to overtime pay for hours worked in excess of 40 each week? Probably. The court in the Boekemeier case (summarized in Section 8-08.3) noted that "sporadic and occasional shipments of insubstantial amounts of goods" are not enough to invoke the overtime pay and minimum wage provisions of the Act. While the purchases of Sunday School literature were certainly "occasional," these purchases did not consist of "insubstantial amounts of goods." Literature for the church's education program would be substantial both in terms of amount of goods purchased from the out-of-state vendor and the importance of those goods to the church.

• Same facts as case study 1, except that the secretary places or receives between 5 and 10 long-distance calls each month involving persons in other states. Do these calls satisfy the individual coverage provisions of the FLSA, entitling the secretary to overtime pay for hours worked in excess of 40 each week? Probably so, according to the wording of the Fair Labor Standards Act and a Department of Labor publication. The Act defines "commerce" to include "transmission or communication among the several states or between any state and any place outside thereof." Further, a Department of Labor publication states that interstate commerce means "any work involving or related to the movement of persons or things (including intangibles, such as information) across state lines or from foreign countries." This publication gives the following example of an employee who is engaged in interstate commerce: "An employee such as an office or clerical worker who uses a telephone, facsimile machine, the U.S. mail, or a computer e-mail system to communicate with persons in another state." As a result, it is virtually certain that the Department of Labor would consider the secretary to be engaged in commerce, and therefore subject to the overtime pay and minimum wage provisions of the Act.

• Same facts as case study 1, except that the secretary sends and receives several e-mail messages each week from a computer in her church office. Many of these e-mails are sent to, and received from, persons in other states. The analysis in case study 8 would apply to this case study.

• Same facts as case study 1, except that the secretary occasionally travels to another state while performing her job. Do these trips satisfy the individual coverage provisions of the Act, entitling the secretary to overtime pay for hours worked in excess of 40 each week? Probably so, according to the wording of the Fair Labor Standards Act and publications issued by the United States Department of Labor. The word "commerce" is defined by the Act to include "transportation among the several states or between any state and any place outside thereof." A Department of Labor publication states that interstate commerce means "any work involving or related to the movement of persons or things (including intangibles, such as information) across state lines or from foreign countries." This publication gives the following example of an employee who is engaged in interstate commerce: "An employee who drives or flies to another state while performing his or her job duties." As a result, it is virtually certain that the Department of Labor *would consider the secretary to be engaged in commerce, and therefore subject to the overtime pay and minimum wage provisions of the Act.*

• Same facts as case study 10. What, if any, effect does the secretary's involvement in interstate commerce have upon the church custodian's entitlement to overtime pay and the minimum wage? The church does not meet the enterprise test since it is not engaged in commerce or in the production of goods for commerce, and does not have business income of $500,000 or more. Therefore, the only way for church employees to be covered by the Act's overtime pay and minimum wage provisions is by meeting the individual coverage requirements. Since individual coverage is on an individual basis, the fact that the secretary meets the individual coverage test has no effect on the church custodian. She will be entitled to overtime pay and the minimum wage only if she independently meets the individual coverage requirements summarized in this chapter.

Enterprise Coverage

• A church receives rental income of $550,000 each year from the rental of its facilities and several homes that it owns. In addition, it has at least two employees who are engaged in interstate commerce because of their frequent interstate purchases, telephone calls, and e-mail messages. The church meets the enterprise test since it "has employees engaged in commerce or in the production of goods for commerce" and has annual business income of at least $500,000. As a result, all of the church's nonexempt employees are covered by the Act's overtime pay and minimum wage provisions.

• A church does not operate any businesses, and has annual revenue of $300,000. It also operates a preschool that generates an additional $20,000 of income. Are employees of the preschool and church covered by the Act's overtime pay and minimum wage requirements? The Act defines an enterprise to include any organization that "is engaged in the operation of a . . . preschool, elementary or secondary school, or an institution of higher education (regardless of whether or not such . . . institution or school is public or private or operated for profit or not for profit)." Does this mean that both preschool and church employees are covered by the Act's protections? Probably. Note that the Act's definition of an enterprise includes an organization that "is engaged in the operation of" a school or preschool. This language would include a church that operates a school or preschool, and so it should be assumed that all of the nonexempt employees of a church that operates a school or preschool are covered by the Act's overtime pay and minimum wage requirements.

Occasional workers (including nursery attendants)

Lisa works for two hours on one Sunday each month in her church's nursery. She works as a volunteer, and receives no compensation. The FLSA has no application to her. The Department of Labor Opinion Letter of November 4, 1983 (summarized in Section 8-08.4) states: "Individuals who volunteer their services, usually on a part-time basis, to a church or synagogue not as employees or in contemplation of pay are not considered to be employees within the meaning of FLSA. For example, persons who volunteer their services as lectors, cantors, ushers or choir members would not be considered employees. Likewise, persons who volunteer to answer telephones, serve as doorkeepers, or perform general clerical or administrative functions would not be employees."

• *Same facts as the previous case study, except that the church pays Lisa $3 per hour for her services. Should the church pay Lisa the federal minimum wage? Assume that the state minimum wage is less than the federal minimum wage. Note the following factors that are relevant in answering this question. (1) The FLSA defines the term employee as "any individual employed by an employer," and adds that an employee includes a person who is "suffered or permitted" to work. This is a very broad definition, and is much broader than the definition used by the IRS for tax purposes. (2) The Department of Labor Opinion Letter of November 4, 1983 (quoted above) states: "In situations where the understanding is that the person will work for wages there will be an employment relationship." (3) If a church meets the definition of an enterprise, then compensated nursery workers (as well as other compensated staff positions) would be regarded by the Department of Labor as employees covered by the FLSA's protections. Note that the FLSA defines an enterprise to include any organization that is engaged "in the operation of a . . . preschool, elementary or secondary school, or an institution of higher education." So, churches that operate any of these entities will be regarded as enterprises by the Department of Labor. (4) If the church is not an enterprise, then nursery workers and other compensated workers will be covered by the FLSA's minimum wage and overtime pay provisions only if they meet the "individual coverage" requirement. In this regard, note that the Department of Labor Opinion Letter of November 4, 1983 (summarized in section 8-08.4) states: "Individual coverage will not be asserted, however, for office and clerical employees of a church or synagogue who only occasionally or sporadically devote negligible amounts of time to writing interstate letters or otherwise handle interstate mail or make bookkeeping entries related to interstate transactions." If there is any doubt concerning a compensated worker's entitlement to the minimum wage and overtime pay, church leaders should seek legal advice.*

Actual Time Worked in Commerce

• *A church has annual revenue of $300,000, and employs four persons (a pastor, a youth pastor, a church secretary, and a custodian). It engages in no "businesses" that compete with for-profit companies. The church secretary asks the pastor if she is entitled to overtime pay for hours that she occasionally works in excess of 40 per week. The secretary's "interstate" activities during year 2000 include (1) 7 purchases of church supplies over the Internet (each purchase was in a different week), and (2) 10 out-of-state telephone calls (each call was made during a different week, and no call was made during the same week as an Internet purchase). These purchases and telephone calls probably are enough to satisfy the individual coverage provisions of the Act, entitling the secretary to overtime pay for hours worked in excess of 40 each week. However, the church's records demonstrate that the secretary was engaged in interstate commerce only during 17 weeks of the year (the weeks in which Internet purchases and out-of-state telephone calls were made). Note that an employer's obligation to pay minimum wage or overtime compensation is determined on a weekly basis. As a result, the church could argue that the secretary was engaged in commerce only during these 17 weeks and was entitled to overtime pay only during these weeks and not for hours worked in excess of 40 during the remaining 35 weeks of the year when she was not engaged in commerce.*

• *Same facts as case study 16. The church keeps no records "clearly showing" the duties the secretary performed in interstate commerce and the wages she was paid during those weeks. The secretary is entitled to overtime pay for the entire year.*

• *A church operates a preschool five days each week. Can the church avoid the application of the Fair Labor Standards Act's overtime pay and minimum wage provisions by keeping records showing that its preschool employees are rarely if ever engaged in interstate commerce? Probably not. As noted above, the Act defines the term enterprise engaged in commerce or in the production of goods for commerce to include an enterprise that (1) "has employees engaged in commerce or in the production of goods for commerce" with annual business income of $500,000 or more, or (2) is engaged in the operation of a school. There is no requirement that preschool employees actually be engaged in commerce. They are covered by the Act because of the "enterprise" status of their employer.*

Church Board Minutes

• *A church custodian frequently works more than 40 hours per week, and is paid overtime compensation. The church board decides to place the custodian on a salary basis of $24,000 in order to avoid having to pay him overtime compensation. The board minutes state: "Custodian placed on salary of $24,000, to avoid overtime obligations." Church board members can be personally liable for violating the FLSA. This liability may be either criminal (in the case of willful violations) or civil. The Act specifies that "any person" who willfully violates the overtime pay or minimum wage provisions is subject to criminal prosecution. In addition, the Act specifies that any employer that violates the minimum wage or overtime pay provisions of the Act "shall be liable to the employee or employees affected in the amount of their unpaid minimum wages, or their unpaid overtime compensation, as the case may be, and in an additional equal amount as liquidated damages." In a recent federal court case, a church employee asserted that the church's board members were personally liable for their failure to pay him overtime compensation. He pointed to an excerpt in the minutes of the church board entitled "Concerns of the Board" which expressed concern over "overtime and compensatory time as it applies to hourly staff and to management." The court relied in part on this excerpt in concluding that the church and board may have "willfully" violated the overtime pay protections of the FLSA.*[63]

---

[63] Boekemeier v. Fourth Universalist Society, 86 F.Supp.2d 280 (S.D.N.Y. 2000).

PART THREE

Employment Discrimination

Legal Briefs

Congress has enacted a variety of employment and civil rights laws, including:

- Title VII of the Civil Rights Act of 1964
- Age Discrimination in Employment Act
- Fair Labor Standards Act
- Employee Polygraph Protection Act
- Americans with Disabilities Act
- Family and Medical Leave Act
- National Labor Relations Act
- Occupational Safety and Health Act

Congress enacted all of these laws under its constitutional authority to regulate interstate commerce. Is a church engaged in a business, industry, or activity affecting commerce? Maybe yes, maybe no. Churches can be exposed to substantial liability if they mistakenly assume that they are not subject to federal employment laws because they do not meet the commerce requirement.

Some federal civil rights and employment laws apply only to employers having a minimum number of employees. You'll want to be sure you understand the determining factors in whether or not your church is held to the federal requirements for these civil rights laws.

And don't be lulled into thinking the First Amendment guaranty of religious freedom means these civil rights laws don't apply to you and your church. Although the courts have applied a so-called ministerial exception in many cases, there have been several instances where the ministerial exception did not hold up in court. Here's a quick snapshot of how the civil rights laws may affect your church and ministers. If you have the required minimum number of employees.

Title VII & the Church
This law prevents against discrimination in hiring on the basis of race, color, national origin, gender, or religion. Religious organizations are exempt from the ban on religious discrimination, but not from the other prohibited forms of discrimination.

The Church & Sexual Harassment
Sexual harassment addresses unwelcome sexual contact, whether or not that contact is voluntary. Churches are held to the same standards of conduct regarding sexual harassment among employees.

The Age Discrimination in Employment Act
Churches can't discriminate in hiring on the basis of age.

The Americans with Disabilities Act
Religious organizations are not required to comply with the ADA requirements to hire and accommodate the mobility, transportation and communication needs of disabled employees.

Family and Medical Leave Act
Religious organizations are required to allow employees up to 12 weeks of unpaid leave each year on account of certain medical and family needs.

The Occupational Safety and Health Act
By law, churches are required to follow OSHA's regulations for safe and healthy work conditions.

Remember, many of these laws only apply to churches that employ the required number of staff. Read the rest of this chapter to learn the specifics.

Introduction to Federal Employment and Civil Rights Laws—The "Commerce" Requirement

§ 8-09

Key Point 8-09> *Congress has enacted a number of employment and civil rights laws regulating employers. These laws generally apply only to employers that are engaged in interstate commerce. This is because the legal basis for such laws is the constitutional power of Congress to regulate interstate commerce. As a result, religious organizations that are not engaged in commerce generally are not subject to these laws. In addition, several of these laws require that an employer have a minimum number of employees. The courts have defined "commerce" very broadly, and so many churches will be deemed to be engaged in commerce.*

Congress has enacted a variety of employment and civil rights laws that apply to some churches and religious organizations. These include Title VII of the Civil Rights Act of 1964, the Age Discrimination in Employment Act, the Americans with Disabilities Act, the Family and Medical Leave Act, the Fair Labor Standards Act, the National Labor Relations Act, the Employee Polygraph Protection Act, and the Occupational Safety and Health Act. See Table 8-6 for a summary of the more important laws.

Before turning to a direct examination of these laws, it is important to recognize that they all were enacted by Congress under its constitutional authority to regulate interstate commerce. As a result, these laws apply only to employers engaged in a business, industry, or activity "affecting commerce."[64] Is a church engaged in a business, industry, or activity affecting commerce? This is a complex question for which no simple answer can be given. In general, the answer in a particular case will depend upon how narrowly or expansively a court construes the term *affecting commerce,* and upon the size of the church and the nature of its operations. In general, the courts have interpreted the "affecting commerce" requirement broadly. As a result, church leaders should never assume that their church does not satisfy this requirement without legal advice. Churches can be exposed to substantial liability if the erroneously assume that they are not subject to federal employment laws because they do not meet the commerce requirement.

A federal appeals court concluded that a church-operated school was engaged in commerce.[65] A disabled woman who was turned down for a job at the school

---

[64] 29 U.S.C. § 142 (National Labor Relations Act); 29 U.S.C. § 203 (Fair Labor Standards Act); 29 U.S.C. § 630(b) (Age Discrimination in Employment Act); 29 U.S.C. § 652 (Occupational Safety and Health Act); 42 U.S.C. § 2000e(b) (Title VII of the Civil Rights Act of 1964). A more limited standard applies under the Fair Labor Standards Act (discussed earlier in this chapter).

[65] Equal Employment Opportunity Commission v. St. Francis Xavier Parochial School, 117 F.3d 621 (D.C. Cir. 1997).

filed a lawsuit claiming that the school discriminated against her in violation of the federal Americans with Disabilities Act. The ADA prohibits employers engaged in an activity "affecting commerce" *and* having at least 15 employees from discriminating in any employment decision on account of the disabled status of an employee or applicant for employment who is able to perform the essential functions of the job with or without reasonable accommodation by the employer. Was the school engaged in an industry affecting commerce? The court noted that the ADA defines this crucial term as "any activity, business, or industry in commerce or in which a labor dispute would hinder or obstruct commerce or the free flow of commerce." The church insisted that it was not an "industry affecting commerce" under this definition, but the court concluded that it was. It relied on an earlier case in which a federal appeals court found that an employer affected commerce since (1) it purchased products and supplies from out-of-state; (2) its employees traveled out-of-state on the employer's business; and (3) its employees made interstate telephone calls.[66] The court concluded:

> The school and its employees have engaged in activities that affect commerce. The school purchased supplies and books from companies outside of the District of Columbia. . . . Approximately five of its employees commuted to the school from outside of the District. Employees made interstate telephone calls and mailed letters to locations outside of the District of Columbia.

DID YOU KNOW?
IS A CHURCH ENGAGED IN COMMERCE?

There are a number of factors indicating that a church or other religious organization is engaged in commerce. These include any one or more of the following:

- operation of a private school
- sale of products (such as literature or tapes) to persons or churches in other states
- purchase of products (Sunday School literature, office equipment, etc.) from out-of-state vendors
- persons from other states attend your church
- operation of a church web page on the Internet

- operation of a commercial or "unrelated trade or business"
- employees travel out-of-state
- employees make out-of-state telephone calls
- the church sends mail out-of-state
- television or radio broadcasts

---

[66]   Martin v. United Way, 829 F.2d 445 (3d Cir.1987).

However, the court cautioned that the woman had not provided any evidence that the church had engaged in activities affecting interstate commerce, and so "this issue is inconclusive." The court added that "[we] presume that some of the same factors exist with respect to the church." There is little doubt that the court believed that the church was engaged in commerce.

Case Studies

• *A federal court in New Hampshire ruled that a church-operated school was engaged in an industry affecting commerce, and as a result was subject to the Age Discrimination in Employment Act.*[67]

• *A church is accused of engaging in sex discrimination in violation of Title VII of the Civil Rights Act of 1964. The church insists that it is not covered by Title VII since it is not engaged in commerce. The church operates a web page on the Internet. This single factor may persuade a court that the church is engaged in commerce.*

• *A church is accused of engaging in age discrimination in violation of federal law. The church insists that it is not covered by this law since it is not engaged in commerce. The church conducts a weekly 15-minute radio broadcast. This single factor indicates that the church is engaged in commerce.*

Key Point > *The United States Supreme Court issued a ruling in 1997 that defined commerce very broadly. The case is important because it involved a religious organization (a church-affiliated summer camp). This case makes it more likely that churches and other religious organizations will be deemed to be engaged in commerce. The Court observed: "Even though [the] camp does not make a profit, it is unquestionably engaged in commerce, not only as a purchaser . . . but also as a provider of goods and services. . . . The attendance of these campers necessarily generates the transportation of persons across state lines that has long been recognized as a form of commerce . . . . Our cases have frequently applied laws regulating commerce to not-for-profit institutions. . . . The nonprofit character of an enterprise does not place it beyond the purview of federal laws regulating commerce. We have already held that the commerce clause is applicable to activities undertaken without the intention of earning a profit. . . . We see no reason why the nonprofit character of an enterprise should exclude it from the coverage of [the commerce clause]."*[68]

The United States Supreme Court has ruled that an evangelistic association was engaged in activities affecting commerce since it was engaged in several commercial enterprises, including advertising, landscaping, service stations, restaurants, manufacture and sale of candy and clothing, record keeping, construction, plumbing, sand and gravel, electrical contracting, hog farms, feed and farm supplies, real estate development, and freight hauling.[69] Similarly, a federal appeals court concluded that

---

[67] Usery v. Manchester East Catholic Regional School Board, 430 F. Supp. 188 (D.N.H. 1977).

[68] Camps Newfound/Owatonna v. Town of Harrison, 117 S. Ct. 1590 (1997).

[69] Tony and Susan Alamo Foundation v. Secretary of Labor, 471 U.S. 290 (1985).

a religious organization that operated a hotel on a commercial basis was engaged in a business or activity affecting commerce.[70]

The United States Department of Labor has enacted a regulation specifying that

activities of eleemosynary, religious, or educational organizations may be performed for a business purpose. Thus, where such organizations engage in ordinary commercial activities, such as operating a printing and publishing plant, the business activities will be treated under the Act the same as when they are performed by the ordinary business enterprise.[71]

Table 8-6 **Application of Selected Federal Employment and Civil Rights Laws to Religious Organizations**

Statute	Main Provisions	Covered Employers
Title VII of 1964 Civil Rights Act	bars discrimination in employment decisions on the basis of race, color, national origin, sex, or religion	• 15 or more employees + interstate commerce • religious employers can discriminate on the basis of religion
Age Discrimination in Employment Act	bars discrimination in employment decisions on the basis of age (if 40 or over)	20 or more employees + interstate commerce
Americans with Disabilities Act	bars discrimination against a qualified individual with a disability who can perform essential job functions with or without reasonable employer accommodation (that does not impose undue hardship)	• 15 or more employees + interstate commerce • religious employers can discriminate on the basis of religion
Employee Polygraph Protection Act	employers cannot require, request, suggest, or cause any employee or applicant to take a polygraph exam	interstate commerce (no minimum number of employees)
Immigration Reform and Control Act	I-9 form must be completed by all new employees demonstrating identity and eligibility to work	all employers
Fair Labor Standards Act	requires minimum wage and overtime pay to be paid to employees	employers who employ employees who are engaged in commerce or in the production of goods for commerce, as well as any employee "employed in an enterprise engaged in commerce or in the production of goods for commerce"

---

[70] NLRB v. World Evangelism, Inc., 656 F.2d 1349 (9th Cir. 1981).

[71] 29 C.F.R. § 779.214.

Statute	Main Provisions	Covered Employers
Family and Medical Leave Act of 1993	eligible employees qualify for up to 12 weeks unpaid leave per year because of (1) birth or adoption of child, including care for such child, or (2) caring for spouse, child, or parent with a serious health condition, or (3) the employee's serious health condition	50 or more employees + interstate commerce
Occupational Safety and Health Act	mandates a safe and healthy workplace for covered employees	an organization "engaged in a business affecting commerce who has employees"
Older Workers Benefit Protection Act of 1991	bars employees at least 40 years old from "waiving" their rights under age discrimination law unless the waiver meets strict legal standards	20 or more employees + interstate commerce

The National Labor Relations Board has ruled that the publishing and distribution of Sunday Sschool literature by a religious denomination is an activity affecting commerce.[72] It is also possible that a church that operates a child care facility, an elementary school, a home for the aged, or an orphanage is engaged in an activity affecting commerce.

Counting Employees § 8-09.1

Key Point 8-09.1> *Many federal employment and civil rights laws apply only to those employers having a minimum number of employees. In determining whether or not an employer has the minimum number of employees, both full-time and part-time employees are counted. In addition, employees of unincorporated subsidiary ministries of a church are counted. The employees of incorporated subsidiary ministries may be counted if the church exercises sufficient control over the subsidiary.*

Some federal civil rights and employment laws apply only to employers having a minimum number of employees. To illustrate, employers must have 15 or more employees to be subject to the Americans with Disabilities Act and Title VII of the Civil Rights Act of 1964. An employer must have at least 20 employees to be subject to the federal age discrimination law. Such laws raise two important questions: (1) which employees are counted, and (2) are a parent organization and its affiliates or subsidiaries treated as a single employer? These questions will be addressed separately.

[72] Sunday School Board of the Southern Baptist Convention, 92 N.L.R.B. 801 (1950). *But cf.* Lutheran Church Missouri Synod, 109 N.L.R.B. 859 (1954).

A. Which Employees Are Counted?

Which employees should be counted in determining whether or not an employer has the minimum number of employees specified by a federal employment or civil rights law? Should part-time employees be counted? Hourly workers? Temporary workers? Persons on vacation or sick leave? These laws generally require that an employer have the minimum number of employees "for each working day in each of 20 or more calendar weeks in the current or preceding year." The United States Supreme Court has applied the "payroll method" for counting employees.[73] Under this approach, an "employee" is any person with whom the employer has an *employment relationship* during the week in question. The Court explained: "Under the interpretation we adopt . . . all one needs to know about a given employee for a given year is whether the employee started or ended employment during that year and, if so, when. He is counted as an employee for each working day after arrival and before departure." As a result, the Supreme Court's decision repudiates the argument made by the church, school, and preschool that they did not meet the 15 employee requirement since less than 15 employees were employed on Saturdays and Sundays.

Case Studies

• *A Louisiana court dismissed a Title VII sex discrimination claim brought against a church by a dismissed female choir director. The court noted that the church had fewer than 15 employees and therefore it was not subject to Title VII's ban on sex discrimination.*[74]

In summary, in determining whether an employer has 15 or more employees "for each working day in each of 20 or more calendar weeks in the current or preceding year," each week in which an employer has an employment relationship with 15 or more employees is counted.

The Supreme Court acknowledged that self-employed persons will appear on an employer's payroll, and that they should not be counted. It clarified that in counting employees under the "payroll method," only those persons who in fact are employees are counted.

Key Point > *One church insisted it was open on Saturdays and Sundays, and that a few of its employees (mostly its ministers) worked on those days. Therefore, if the workweek is defined to include Saturdays and Sundays, then it would not have the required number of employees "for each working day" since only a few persons worked on those days. Obviously, many churches have a few employees whose duties require them to work on Saturdays or Sundays. However, since the number of employees who work on these days usually is minimal, such churches could argue that they are not*

---

[73] Walters v. Metropolitan Educ. Enterprises, Inc., 117 S.Ct. 660 (1997).

[74] Steed v. St. Paul's United Methodist Church, 1999 WL 92626 (La. App. 1999).

covered by any civil rights law (federal or state) that applies to employers having a specified number of employees "for each working day in each of 20 or more calendar weeks in the current or preceding year." This argument was rejected by a federal appeals court on the basis of the Supreme Court's "payroll method" approach to counting employees.

B. Employees of Affiliated Organizations

Should the employees of an affiliated or subsidiary organization be combined with the employees of a parent organization when counting employees? That is, should the employees of a school, preschool, retirement facility, or other church-affiliated ministry be combined with the employees of the church when counting employees for purposes of applying federal civil rights and employment laws? This is an important question, given the large number of churches that operate affiliated ministries.

A federal appeals court addressed these questions in an important decision.[75] A woman (the "plaintiff") with multiple sclerosis claimed that she was not considered for a position as music director at a church-operated school because of her disability. She filed a complaint with the Equal Employment Opportunity Commission (EEOC), which determined that she had been a victim of discrimination. The EEOC sued the church and its school, claiming that they both had violated the Americans with Disabilities Act (ADA) as a result of their refusal to "accommodate" the plaintiff's disability, and their failure to hire her because of her disability. The church and school argued that they were not covered by the ADA since they each had less than 15 employees. The plaintiff asserted that under the so-called "single employer doctrine" the court should combine the employees of the church, the school, and a preschool to come up with the required 15 employees.

Under the single employer doctrine, separate entities that represent a "single, integrated enterprise" may be treated as a single employer for purposes of meeting the 15 employee test. The plaintiff asserted that the church operated the school and the preschool, and therefore these three entities should be considered as one.

In deciding whether or not the church, school, and preschool were a "single, integrated enterprise," a federal district court applied a four-part test announced by the Supreme Court in 1965.[76] This test focuses on the following four factors:

(1) interrelation of operations

(2) common management

(3) centralized control of labor relations, and

(4) common ownership or financial control

---

[75] Equal Employment Opportunity Commission v. St. Francis Xavier Parochial School, 117 F.3d 621 (D.C. Cir. 1997).

[76] Radio Union v. Broadcast Services, 380 U.S. 255 (1965).

The court clarified that "the absence or presence of any single factor is not conclusive," and that "control over the elements of labor relations is a central concern." The court cautioned that a plaintiff "must make a substantial showing to warrant a finding of single employer status," and that

> there must be sufficient indicia of an interrelationship between the immediate corporate employer and the affiliated corporation to justify the belief on the part of an aggrieved employee that the affiliated corporation is jointly responsible for the acts of the immediate employer.

INDICIA = Identifying marks; indications.

The court referred to an earlier federal appeals court case finding that the entities must be "highly integrated with respect to ownership and operations" in order for single employer status to be found.

The court's analysis of each of the four factors is summarized below.

(1) interrelation of operations

The court referred to combined accounting records, bank accounts, lines of credit, payroll preparation, telephone numbers, or offices as examples of "interrelated" operations. However, it concluded that there was insufficient interrelationship between the church, school, and preschool to consider them as a single employer. It did acknowledge that the pastor signed the school's budget, that a room in the church occasionally was used for school purposes, and that school children ate in a room that was also used by the preschool. However, the following factors demonstrated that there was insufficient interrelationship among the three entities (church, school, and preschool) to treat them as a single employer: (1) the school had a separate budget; (2) daily operations of the three entities (church, school, and preschool) were independent; (3) hours of operation of the three entities were significantly different (preschool was open earlier and later than the school, and the church alone was open on Saturdays and Sundays); (4) each of the three entities was operated by a different staff; (5) each of the three entities had its own principal or administrator; (6) each entity had different employment contacts and practices; (7) the school was located in a different building from the church and preschool; and (8) while the schoolchildren ate lunch in a room that was also used by the preschool, they did not use the room at the same time.

(2) common management

A second factor to consider in deciding whether or not to treat separate entities as a "single employer" is the presence or absence of common management. The court noted that the "focus of this factor . . . is on the existence of common directors and officers." In other words, are the directors and officers of the separate entities the same? The court concluded that this factor was not present in this case: "Here, there are separate management structures for the church, the day care center, and the school. These structures do not continuously monitor one another. The circumstances present here do not warrant a finding of common management."

The court cautioned that common management will exist when one organization runs another organization "in a direct, hands-on fashion, establishing the operating practices and management practices."

(3) centralized control of labor operations

A third factor to consider in deciding whether or not to treat separate entities as a "single employer" is the presence or absence of "centralized control of labor operations." The court observed that "the control required to meet the test of centralized control of labor relations is not potential control, but rather actual and active control of day-to-day labor practices." This test was not met, the court concluded:

> The enterprises here have separate employees, directors, and employment practices. The sole way in which the church is involved with the labor practices of the school is in the final phases of hiring. Plaintiff asserts that the pastor "interviews all applicants for the school," but plaintiff's own exhibits contradict this assertion. Rather, the principal and assistant principal screen resumes and conduct interviews; the pastor does not become involved until the end of the process, after the principal and assistant principal have selected two or three finalists, at which point he gives his input. When there is a disagreement, the pastor makes the final decision. The entities have different administrators and distinct labor pools. Plaintiff does not present adequate evidence of day-to-day active control by the church of the school's labor relations to justify a finding that the entities should be treated as a single employer.

(4) common ownership or financial control

A fourth factor to consider in deciding whether or not to treat separate entities as a "single employer" is the presence or absence of "common ownership or control." The court noted that "there is common ownership of the property and the buildings in which the day care center, the church, and the school are located, and that the pastor must sign the school's budget." On the other hand, the court noted that the church was part of the Archdiocese of Washington, "which is the corporate entity that owns the property and the buildings. Further . . . the Archdiocese has ultimate control over the school's budget." The court cautioned that "even if the Archdiocese were a party, common ownership alone is not enough to establish that separate employers are an integrated enterprise." The court continued:

> Even though the Archdiocese, rather than the church, is the owner and locus of financial control, the church does have some intermediary supervisory power over the school. However, given (1) the Archdiocese's ultimate control over the school's budget, (2) the Archdiocese's status as owner of the property and buildings, and (3) the fact that the school, the church, and the day care center have separate budgets, the court finds that this factor does not support a finding that the entities constitute a sin-

gle employer. Accordingly, the court declines to apply the integrated enterprise doctrine to consolidate defendants into constituting a single employer.

The EEOC appealed the district court's dismissal of the lawsuit. A federal appeals court for the District of Columbia reversed the district court's dismissal of the case on the ground that there was insufficient evidence to support the court's conclusion that the church, school, and preschool should not be treated as a single employer in applying the 15 employee requirement. Of most significance to the appeals court was the fact that the record did not reveal whether or not the church, school, and preschool were one corporate legal entity, or three separate entities. The court observed that "we cannot answer a question of utmost importance—whether the school (and the day care center) are distinct legal entities or whether they are merely parts of one legal entity—the church."

Why was this question so important? Because the Supreme Court's 4 factor test (discussed above) has only been applied in the context of *separate legal entities*. In other words, if the church, school, and preschool were a single corporate entity, with the school and preschool operating under the church's corporate umbrella, then they presumably would be treated as a single employer for purposes of applying the 15 employee requirement. There would be no need to apply the Supreme Court's 4 factor test. This test would be applied only if the three entities were legally distinct—that is, they were each separately incorporated. Only then would the 4 factor test be applied to determine whether or not the three entities were sufficiently related to be treated as a single employer for purposes of the 15 employee requirement.

The court conceded that "the door is at least open to apply the test to entities that have different names (a condition satisfied here)—even if they are not legally distinct (a condition that may or may not be satisfied here)," and that "leaving the door open allows the possibility that a single legal entity could . . . encompass divisions that are sufficiently independent of one another to warrant being treated as distinct employers within the meaning of the employment discrimination statutes." The court added that "such cases are perhaps rare, but we see no reason to think they are nonexistent."

The appeals court acknowledged that no other court has ever addressed the application of the Supreme Court's 4 factor test to religious organizations:

> The cases in which we have applied the [4 factor test] have all involved business corporations. We have found no cases in this circuit or elsewhere applying the test to a religious corporation. Because a religious corporation can possess unique attributes . . . it may be the case that even where there are multiple religious entities, aggregation (or non-aggregation) of employees in employment discrimination cases should not be resolved under [this test]. Although we express no opinion on the question, we note that the question to be answered by the [trial] court on remand may be [the first time any court has addressed this question].

In summary, the appeals court's analysis can be reduced to the following points:

1. Church with no affiliated entities. Consider only the church's employees in applying the 15 employee test under the Americans with Disabilities Act (or any other federal discrimination law—see Table 8-6).

2. Church with one or more affiliated entities that are not separately incorporated. Many churches operate a school, preschool, retirement facility, or other ministry. If these ministries are not separately incorporated, then the church along with its affiliates ordinarily will be treated as a single employer for purposes of applying the 15 employee test under the Americans with Disabilities Act (or any other federal discrimination law—see Table 8-6). In rare cases, this conclusion may not be automatic. For example, if the affiliates have different names, and are "sufficiently independent," then single employer status may not be automatic. Rather, the Supreme Court's 4 factor test (discussed above) may be applied to determine whether or not the church and its affiliates constitute a single employer for purposes of applying the 15 employee test. While such a result will be rare, it is not nonexistent.

3. Church with one or more affiliated entities that are separately incorporated. Many churches operate a school, preschool, retirement facility, or other ministry. If these ministries are separately incorporated, then the Supreme Court's 4 factor test (discussed above) is applied to determine whether the church along with its affiliates should be treated as a single employer for purposes of applying the 15 employee test under the Americans with Disabilities Act (or any other federal discrimination law—see Table 8-6).

The appeals court sent the case back to the district court for further proceedings to determine whether or not the church, school, and preschool were a single entity or three separate legal entities, and "whether to aggregate the employees of these entities in order to determine the number of employees defendants actually had." The district court began its opinion by observing:

> A determination that these entities are divisions of a corporation has two implications. First, it suggests that defendants are not proper parties to the lawsuit because case law reflects that unincorporated divisions of a corporation lack the capacity to sue or be sued. Second, assuming defendants can be sued, it leads to the conclusion that the employees of the church, the school, and the [preschool] should be aggregated for the purpose of the [15] employee requirement.[77]

While the church and school were unincorporated divisions of a corporation (the Archdiocese of Washington), the EEOC insisted that they were "sufficiently autonomous" from the Archdiocese to render them "suable entities." The court disagreed. The Archbishop of Washington is a "corporation sole," meaning that the office itself is a perpetual corporation. The Archdiocese is made up of all of the Catholic parishes and related facilities within its jurisdiction. Although the Canon Law of the Roman Catholic Church views each parish as a separate entity for religious purposes, the parishes are not separately incorporated under civil law. The church that operated the school in this case is a parish within the juris-

---

77 Equal Employment Opportunity Commission v. St. Francis Xavier Parochial School, 77 F.Supp.2d 71 (D.D.C. 1999).

diction of the Archdiocese, and it operates independently of other parishes within the jurisdiction. The Archdiocese owns all of the parish's property, and exerts varying degrees of control over different aspects of the parish's operations. As to financial matters, the Archdiocese maintains control over the parish's budget by requiring the parish to submit an annual financial report on all of its operations and to undergo periodic financial audits. Although the Archdiocese does not oversee the parish's daily expenditures, its approval is required for any expenditure exceeding $10,000. As to personnel matters, the Archdiocese appoints the pastor and, through the Archdiocese's personnel director, helps to determine the staffing of other priests assigned to work at the parish. The Archdiocese also influences other parish personnel decisions, such as the hiring of the school's teaching staff, by providing guidelines on appropriate hiring criteria.

The EEOC insisted that the church and school could be sued because the Federal Rules of Civil Procedure permit "unincorporated associations" to be sued. The court disagreed, noting that the church and school were not separately incorporated but rather were "unincorporated divisions of a corporation." The court continued:

> [As such] their presence in this case triggers a line of precedent holding that unincorporated divisions of a corporation lack legal capacity to be sued. . . . The rationale for this precedent is, above all, pragmatic, as an unincorporated division does not possess separate assets; all of its assets are owned by the corporation. Thus, "[u]nless the organization is liable there can be no levy of execution against the division's assets, and if the organization is not liable none of its assets can be used to satisfy the judgment."

The court disagreed with the contention of the EEOC that the church and school were "unincorporated associations," noting that it was "unaware of any reason to treat a division of a corporation in this manner." It explained:

> Although the term "unincorporated association" has not been defined uniformly under federal law, the definitions propounded by courts are substantially identical.... While all of these definitions describe an unincorporated association as a collection of persons working together for a common objective, they also describe it as an entity operating without a corporate charter. The court finds this latter characteristic determinative of whether an unincorporated division of a corporation meets the definition of an unincorporated association. Unlike unincorporated associations... a division of a corporation does operate with a charter—the charter of the larger corporation. Although the division is not separately incorporated, it is still governed by the terms of the corporate charter and still enjoys corporate status because it is a unit of the larger corporation. Thus, the court concludes that the federal law definition of an unincorporated association does not encompass an unincorporated division of a corporation.
>
> Finally, the religious character of the corporation involved in this case does not remove the normal prohibition on suing unincorporated divisions of a corporation. Although [the EEOC] cites to cases in which religious organizations were sued for violating employment discrimination laws, these cases do not suggest that the nature of an incorporated religious entity is such that its unincorporated divisions have the

legal capacity to be sued. Nor is there any reason to fragment the legal status of an incorporated religious entity in this manner.

The court referred to an earlier federal appeals court decision.[78] In the *F.E.L. Publications* case, the question before the court was whether a plaintiff could recover against a Bishop for interfering in the plaintiff's business relationship with one of the parishes in the Chicago Aarchdiocese. The Catholic Bishop of Chicago is organized as a "corporation sole" under Illinois law and, as such, owned all of the property in the Archdiocese. The court held that the plaintiff could not recover damages because "the parishes within the Archdiocese are not legal entities separate and independent from the Catholic Bishop, but are subsumed under the Catholic Bishop." This case "makes clear that an incorporated religious organization constitutes a single legal entity, and that unincorporated divisions of that organization lack any independently recognized legal status. Because the Archdiocese of Washington is incorporated as a corporation sole and holds title to all Archdiocese assets, its unincorporated divisions also lack any independently recognized legal status."

As a result, the court dismissed the EEOC's lawsuit against the church and school on the ground that they were divisions of a corporation and lacked the capacity to be sued.

This case suggests that an unincorporated division or department of a church or denomination cannot be sued individually. As a result, a lawsuit brought against such an entity should be dismissed. Of course, a plaintiff may be able to amend the lawsuit to include the church or denominational corporation as the defendant, but this will not always be possible because of the passage of time.

Case Studies

• *A church with 10 employees is accused of violating the federal age discrimination law by not hiring a job applicant who is 60 years old. Since the church does not have 20 employees, it is not subject to the federal age discrimination law (see Table 8-6).*

• *Same facts as the previous case study, except that the church operates a preschool that has 12 employees. The preschool is not separately incorporated. Since the preschool has no separate legal existence, the church and preschool probably will be treated as a "single employer" for purposes of applying the 20 employee test under the federal Age Discrimination in Employment Act (or any other federal discrimination law—see Table 8-6). This means that the 10 church employees and 12 preschool employees are combined, and therefore the 20 employee requirement is met. In rare cases, this conclusion may not be automatic. For example, if the affiliates have different names, and are "sufficiently independent," then single employer status may not be automatic. Rather, the Supreme Court's 4 factor test may be applied to determine whether or not the church and its affiliates constitute a single employer for purposes of applying the 20 employee test. While such a result will be rare, it is not nonexistent. This test focuses on the following four factors: (1) interrelation of operations; (2) common management; (3) centralized control of labor relations; and (4) common ownership or financial control. In applying this test, the absence or presence of any single factor is not conclusive,*

---

78 F.E.L. Publications, Ltd. v. Catholic Bishop of Chicago, 754 F.2d 216 (7th Cir. 1985).

116

and "control over the elements of labor relations is a central concern." A plaintiff "must make a substantial showing to warrant a finding of single employer status," and "there must be sufficient indicia of an interrelationship between the immediate corporate employer and the affiliated corporation to justify the belief on the part of an aggrieved employee that the affiliated corporation is jointly responsible for the acts of the imme- diate employer." This example assumes that the church is engaged in commerce. Finally, note that one court has cautioned that "the cases in which we have applied the [4 factor test] have all involved business corporations. We have found no cases . . . applying the test to a religious corporation. Because a religious corporation can possess unique attributes . . . it may be the case that even where there are multiple religious entities, aggregation (or non-aggregation) of employees in employment discrimination cases should not be resolved under [this test]." [79]

• Same facts as the previous case study, except that the preschool is separately incor- porated. The Supreme Court's 4 factor test is applied to determine whether the church along with its affiliates should be treated as a single employer for purposes of applying the 20 employee test under the federal Age Discrimination in Employment Act (or any other federal discrimination law—see Table 8-6). This test focuses on the following four factors: (1) interrelation of operations; (2) common management; (3) centralized control of labor relations; and (4) common ownership or financial control. In applying this test, the absence or presence of any single factor is not conclusive, and "control over the ele- ments of labor relations is a central concern." A plaintiff "must make a substantial showing to warrant a finding of single employer status," and "there must be sufficient indicia of an interrelationship between the immediate corporate employer and the affil- iated corporation to justify the belief on the part of an aggrieved employee that the affil- iated corporation is jointly responsible for the acts of the immediate employer." This case study assumes that the church is engaged in commerce. Finally, note that one court has cautioned that "the cases in which we have applied the [4 factor test] have all involved business corporations. We have found no cases . . . applying the test to a reli- gious corporation. Because a religious corporation can possess unique attributes . . . it may be the case that even where there are multiple religious entities, aggregation (or non-aggregation) of employees in employment discrimination cases should not be resolved under [this test]." [80]

• A federal court in New York ruled that a local church and denominational agency could be sued for the sexual harassment of a church employee by two pastors. The denomina- tional agency argued that it was not an employer under Title VII and as a result could not be liable for the pastors' acts of sexual harassment. The plaintiff argued that the denominational agency could be liable, even if it did not directly hire or employ her, under the so-called "joint employer" doctrine if it "controlled certain aspects of her employment with the church, including her compensation, privileges, terms, and condi- tions." The court concluded: "There is well-established authority under this theory that, in appropriate circumstances, an employee, who is technically employed on the books of one entity, which is deemed to be part of a larger single-employer entity, may impose liability for certain violations of employment law not only on the nominal employer but also on another entity comprising part of the single integrated employer. Under the sin- gle-employer doctrine, also known as the joint employer theory, an employee, formally employed by one entity, who has been assigned to work in circumstances that justify the

---

[79] Equal Employment Opportunity Commission v. St. Francis Xavier Parochial School, 117 F.3d 621 (D.C. Cir. 1997).

[80] Id.

conclusion that the employee is at the same time constructively employed by another entity, may impose liability for violations of employment law on the constructive employer, on the theory that this other entity is the employee's joint employer. In assessing whether a joint employer relationship exists, courts generally look for evidence of (1) interrelation of operations, (2) centralized control of labor relations, (3) common management, and (4) common ownership or financial control." The court noted that the denominational agency had offered no evidence disproving the elements of the single-employer theory. On the other hand, the plaintiff testified that she was directed to perform duties by the denominational agency; that she attended training offered by the denominational agency; that she participated in the denominational agency's group plan health insurance; and that the denominational agency controlled aspects of her compensation, hours, and job duties. These allegations were sufficient, with no contrary evidence from the denominational agency, to raise questions regarding common ownership and control between the employing church and denominational agency. As a result, the court declined the denominational agency's request to dismiss the claims against it.[81]

DID YOU KNOW?

15 Employee Requirement Not Jurisdictional

Title VII of the Civil Rights Act of 1964 prohibits employers engaged in interstate commerce and having at least 15 employees from discriminating in any employment decisions on the basis of race, color, national origin, gender, or religion. Some courts have ruled that the 15 employee requirement is jurisdictional, meaning that a court does not have the legal authority to resolve a Title VII case involving an employer with fewer than 15 employees. As a result, an employer can raise the "less than 15 employees" defense at any time, even after a court renders a judgment. Other courts have ruled that the 15 employee requirement is not jurisdictional, but rather is simply a requirement for a Title VII claim. Under this interpretation, the "less than 15 employees" defense must be asserted in an employer's response to a lawsuit or it will be waived.

In 2006 the United States Supreme Court ruled that the 15 employee requirement under Title VII is not jurisdictional, but rather is a requirement of a Title VII claim. As a result, it is waived if not raised in response to a lawsuit. It found no language in Title VII making this a jurisdictional requirement that can be raised at any time, and concluded that "when Congress does not rank a statutory limitation on coverage as jurisdictional, courts should treat the restriction as non-jurisdictional in character."

▶ *Some federal employment laws apply only to employers having a specified number of employees. According to the Supreme Court's recent decision, churches that are sued for violations of any of these laws must assert in their answer to the original lawsuit the "affirmative defense" that they have fewer than the required number of employees. A failure to do so will constitute a waiver of this defense.*[82]

---

[81]   Krasner v. Diocese, 431 F.Supp.2d 320 (E.D.N.Y. 2006).

[82]   Arbaugh v. Y & H Corporation, 126 S.Ct. 1235 (2006).

The "Ministerial Exception" under State and Federal Employment Laws

§ 8-10

Many courts have ruled that the First Amendment guaranty of religious freedom prevents state and federal employment discrimination laws from applying to the relationship between a church and its ministers. The courts have applied this so-called ministerial exception in many cases, as noted below. The exception has been applied in several cases to persons who are not ordained clergy but whose functions are central to the promotion and furtherance of a church's mission. A few courts have chosen not to apply the ministerial exception, usually because an employee's duties were not sufficiently ministerial in nature.

Cases Recognizing the Ministerial Exception

§ 8-10.1

Key Point 8-10.1> *The civil courts have consistently ruled that the First Amendment prevents them from applying employment laws to the relationship between a church and a minister.*

Summarized below are several illustrative cases applying the ministerial exception to discrimination claims brought by current or former church employees against their employer.

Case Studies

Federal Appeals Court Rulings

D.C. Circuit (District of Columbia)

• A federal appeals court made the following observation in a case involving a dismissed minister's claim of unlawful discrimination: "This case involves the fundamental question of who will preach from the pulpit of a church, and who will occupy the church parsonage. The bare statement of the question should make obvious the lack of jurisdiction of a civil court. The answer to that question must come from the church." The court acknowledged that the government's interest in preventing employment discrimination "is compelling," but it concluded that such an interest "does not override" the protection that the church claims under the constitutional guaranty of religious freedom." [83]

• A federal appeals court dismissed a lawsuit by a nun claiming that her employer, the Catholic University of America, discriminated against her on the basis of her sex in violation of Title VII of the Civil Rights Act of 1964. The nun was employed as a professor of canon law. She applied for academic tenure after 6 years of teaching, and

---

[83] Minker v. Baltimore Annual Conference of the United Methodist Church, 894 F.2d 1354 (D.C. Cir. 1990), quoting Simpson v. Wells Lamont Corporation, 494 F.2d 490 (5th Cir. 1974).

her application was denied. She sued the University, claiming that its decision to deny her tenure amounted to sex discrimination. The court upheld a federal district court's dismissal of the lawsuit, concluding that it was barred by the First Amendment guaranty of religious freedom: "The Supreme Court has shown a particular reluctance to interfere with a church's selection of its own clergy. . . . Relying on these and other cases [a number of federal courts] have long held that the free exercise [of religion] clause exempts the selection of clergy from Title VII and similar statutes and, as a consequence, precludes civil courts from adjudicating employment discrimination suits by ministers against the church or religious institution employing them." The court pointed out that the so-called "ministerial exemption" has not been limited to members of the clergy, but "has also been applied to lay employees of religious institutions whose primary duties consist of teaching, spreading the faith, church governance, supervision of a religious order, or supervision or participation in religious ritual and worship." Employees whose positions are "important to the spiritual and pastoral mission of the church should be considered clergy." The court concluded that "the ministerial exception encompasses all employees of a religious institution, whether ordained or not, whose primary functions serve its spiritual and pastoral mission," and this included a nun who taught in the canon law department of the Catholic University. The court noted that the canon law department performs "the vital function of instructing those who will in turn interpret, implement, and teach the law governing the Roman Catholic Church and the administration of its sacraments." [84]

3rd Circuit (Delaware, New Jersey, and Pennsylvania)

• *A federal appeals court ruled that a chaplain at a church-affiliated college was subject to the ministerial exception, and as a result it could not resolve her claims of sex discrimination. The court concluded that the ministerial exception "applies to any claim, the resolution of which would limit a religious institution's right to choose who will perform particular spiritual functions." The court rejected the plaintiff's claim that the college waived the ministerial exception by "repeatedly and publicly representing itself as an equal opportunity employer." However, the court concluded that the ministerial exception did not necessarily bar fraudulent misrepresentation and breach of contract claims, since these would not involve "government-imposed limits on the college's right to select its ministers."* [85]

4th Circuit (Maryland, North Carolina, South Carolina, Virginia, and West Virginia)

• *A female sued a religious denomination alleging sex discrimination in violation of Title VII when her application to serve as an "associate in pastoral care" was rejected. In rejecting this lawsuit, the court observed: "Courts must distinguish incidental burdens on free exercise in the service of a compelling state interest from burdens where the inroad on religious liberty is too substantial to be permissible. . . . This case is of the latter sort: introduction of government standards to the selection of spiritual leaders would significantly, and perniciously, rearrange the relationship between church and state. While an unfettered church may create minimal infidelity to the objective of Title VII, it provides maximum protection of the First Amendment right to the free exercise of religious beliefs. In other words, in a direct clash of highest order interests, the interest in protecting the free exercise of religion embodied in the First*

---

[84] E.E.O.C. v. Catholic University of America, 83 F.3rd 455 (D.C. Cir. 1996).

[85] Petruska v. Gannon University, 462 F.3d 294 (3rd Cir. 2006).

Amendment to the Constitution prevails over the interest in ending discrimination embodied in Title VII." [86]

• A woman was employed by a church as its music director. The job description for this position stated that the major duties were "to assist in the planning of all parish liturgies; to direct the parish choirs; to teach the congregation to actively and vocally participate in the music of the parish." The church conducted a parish survey that revealed considerable dissatisfaction with the music program, and this led to the director's termination. She later filed several charges of sex discrimination with the Equal Employment Opportunity Commission (EEOC), and the EEOC itself sued the church for discrimination on her behalf. A federal district court dismissed the lawsuit, and the former director appealed. A federal appeals court affirmed the district court's dismissal of the case. It began its opinion by noting that the ministerial exception "operates to exempt from the coverage of various employment laws the employment relationships between religious institutions and their ministers. This constitutionally compelled limitation on civil authority ensures that no branch of secular government trespasses on the most spiritually intimate grounds of a religious community's existence." The court concluded that the ministerial exception applied to the former music director in this case, even though she was not a credentialed minister, since her position was ministerial in nature and her primary duties "consisted of teaching, spreading the faith, church governance, supervision of a religious order, or supervision or participation in religious ritual and worship, he or she should be considered clergy." The court rejected the former director's claim that the ministerial exception did not apply to her since she was a mere "lay choir director and teacher, charged with the responsibility of training people to sing and perform music." It noted that "the music ministry at issue is ministerial because the position is important to the spiritual and pastoral mission of the church. The functions of the positions are bound up in the selection, presentation, and teaching of music, which is an integral part of [the church's] worship and belief. . . . At the heart of this case is the undeniable fact that music is a vital means of expressing and celebrating those beliefs which a religious community holds most sacred. . . . Thus, inasmuch as the music director's duties involved the expression of the church's musical tradition, it is a fallacy to denominate them as merely secular." [87]

5th Circuit (Louisiana, Mississippi, and Texas)

• A minister employee of the Salvation Army alleged that her employer had violated the Civil Rights Act of 1964 by paying female officers smaller salaries than similarly situated males. A federal appeals court concluded that the relationship of the Salvation Army to its officers was a church-minister relationship, and that the application of the provisions of Title VII to the employment relationship existing between a church and its minister would result in an impermissible encroachment by the government into an area of purely ecclesiastical concern. [88]

A woman began her employment as choirmaster of a church and thereafter became the director of music. While employed, she allegedly suffered from a variety of disabilities, including asthma, osteoarthritis of both knees, migraine headaches, and endometriosis. She claimed that the church refused to modify her work schedule to

---

[86] Rayburn v. General Conference of Seventh Day Adventists, 772 F.2d 1164 (4th Cir. 1985).

[87] Employment Opportunity Commission v. The Roman Catholic Diocese of Raleigh, 213 F. 3d 795 (4th Cir. 2000).

[88] McClure v. Salvation Army, 460 F.2d 553 (5th Cir. 1972), cert. denied, 409 U.S. 896 (1972).

allow full recovery from knee surgery and, after she suffered chemical exposures from cleaning materials, refused to accommodate her chemical sensitivities. Her employment was terminated, and she sued the church claiming that she was discharged in violation of the Americans with Disabilities Act. The church claimed that the woman's lawsuit was barred by the First Amendment's religion clauses. The court concluded that the woman's position at the church was "within the parameters" of the ministerial exception from civil rights laws. It pointed out that "the Director of Music was responsible for duties squarely within the conventional understanding of ecclesiastical or religious functions, and was not a position mainly performing tasks which are not traditionally ecclesiastical or religious." The court noted that "the ministerial exception has not been limited to members of the clergy," but rather "encompasses all employees of a religious institution, whether ordained or not, whose primary functions serve its spiritual and pastoral mission." This ruling was affirmed by a federal appeals court. The court noted the following three factors to consider in deciding if a church employee is a "minister" for purposes of the ministerial exception: (1) Are employment decisions regarding the position at issue made "largely on religious criteria"? (2) Is the employee authorized to perform the ceremonies of the church? (3) Does the employee engage in activities traditionally considered ecclesiastical or religious? The court concluded that the music director was a minister based on an analysis of these three factors. The court cautioned that the role of the civil courts in applying the "ministerial exception" was to focus on "the action taken, not possible motives," and that a church is "not required to advance a theological or religious explanation regarding its allegedly illegal employment actions." [89]

6th Circuit (Kentucky, Michigan, Ohio, and Tennessee)

• A federal appeals court ruled that the ministerial exception prevented a resident in a church-affiliated hospital's clinical pastoral education program from suing her employer for violating the Americans with Disabilities Act. The court concluded: "In order for the ministerial exception to bar an employment discrimination claim, the employer must be a religious institution and the employee must have been a ministerial employee. But, in order to invoke the exception, an employer need not be a traditional religious organization such as a church, diocese, or synagogue, or an entity operated by a traditional religious organization." The court concluded that a church-affiliated hospital was a religious institution, and that a resident in the hospital's clinical pastoral education program was a minister though she was not ordained. The court rejected the plaintiff's argument that the hospital waived the ministerial exception by its equal opportunity policy prohibiting discrimination on the basis of several grounds, including disability. The court noted a "presumption against waivers of constitutional rights and the heavy burden required to overcome that presumption, and concluded that the hospital "did not knowingly or voluntarily waive its constitutional right to be free from judicial interference with the selection of its ministers." [90]

7th Circuit (Illinois, Indiana, and Wisconsin)

• A black female sued her religious denomination, claiming both sex and race discrimination when her application for appointment as a member of the clergy was denied. A federal appeals court rejected her claim, noting that "religious bodies may make apparently arbitrary decisions affecting the employment status of their clergy members and be free from civil review having done so." The court added: "[The minister's] argu-

---

[89] Starkman v. Evans, 198 F.3d 173 (5th Cir. 1999).

[90] Hollins v. Methodist Healthcare, Inc., 474 F.3d 223 (6th Cir. 2006).

ment, that Title VII may be applied to decisions by churches affecting the employment of their clergy, is fruitless." The court concluded: "To accept [the minister's] position would require us to cast a blind eye to the overwhelming weight of precedent going back over a century in order to limit the scope of the protection granted to religious bodies by the free exercise clause." [91]

• A federal appeals court ruled that a "press secretary" was barred by the ministerial exception from suing her church for employment discrimination. A woman was hired by a Catholic Archdiocese to fill the post of Hispanic Communications Manager. Her duties included composing media releases for the Hispanic community; composing correspondence for the Cardinal; developing a working relationship with the Hispanic media and parishes in the Hispanic community to promote church activities; developing a working relationship with the Hispanic community to enhance community involvement; composing articles for church publications; and translating church materials into Spanish. After working for nearly a year, she resigned her employment. She later sued the Church, claiming that while she was employed she was discriminated against on the basis of her gender and national origin. The court concluded that the plaintiff was a "minister" subject to the ministerial exception. It observed: "In determining whether an employee is considered a minister for the purposes of applying this exception, we do not look to ordination but instead to the function of the position. . . . The role of the press secretary is critical in message dissemination, and a church's message, of course, is of singular importance. . . . Indeed, the rationale for the ministerial exception is founded upon the principle that "perpetuation of a church's existence may depend upon those whom it selects to preach its values, teach its message, and interpret its doctrines both to its own membership and to the world at large. . . ." As Hispanic Communications Manager, the plaintiff was integral in shaping the message that the Church presented to the Hispanic community. We therefore conclude that she served a ministerial function for the Church and her claims are therefore barred." [92]

• A federal appeals court ruled that the ministerial exception to employment discrimination laws prevented it from resolving an age discrimination lawsuit brought by a church music director against his employer. The director insisted that his job was not "religious" since "all I did was play music." The court disagreed, noting that "music is a vital means of expressing and celebrating those beliefs which a religious community holds most sacred." Since the director's duties "had a significant religious dimension," he "forfeited his rights under the Age Discrimination in Employment Act." The court also addressed the director's claim that the church represented itself to be an "equal opportunity" employer with respect to age and other factors, and by doing so voluntarily exposed itself to discrimination claims. The court disagreed, noting that "the ministerial exception . . . is not subject to waiver." [93]

8th Circuit (Arkansas, Iowa, Minnesota, Missouri, Nebraska, North Dakota, and South Dakota)

• A federal appeals court ruled that a hospital chaplain could not sue the hospital for alleged age and sex discrimination following her dismissal. The former chaplain was an ordained Episcopal priest who had served as chaplain of a church-affiliated hospital for

---

[91] Young v. Northern Illinois Conference of the United Methodist Church, 21 F.3d 184 (7th Cir. 1994).

[92] Alicea-Hernandez v. Catholic Bishop of Chicago, 320 F.3d 698 (7th Cir. 2003).

[93] Tomic v. Catholic Diocese, 442 F.3d 1036 (7th Cir. 2006).

10 years. Following her dismissal, the former chaplain sued the hospital on the grounds that her dismissal constituted sex discrimination in violation of Title VII of the Civil Rights Act of 1964, and violated the federal Age Discrimination in Employment Act. The court emphasized that the hospital was "without question a religious organization," and that the chaplain position "is primarily a ministerial position." The court conclud-ed: "We believe that the free exercise [of religion] clause of the First Amendment pro-hibits the courts from deciding cases such as this one. Personnel decisions by church-affiliated institutions affecting clergy are per se religious matters and cannot be reviewed by civil courts, for to review such decisions would require the courts to deter-mine the meaning of religious doctrine and canonical law and to impose a secular court's view of whether in the context of the particular case religious doctrine and canonical law support the decision the church authorities have made. This is precisely the kind of judicial second-guessing of decision-making by religious organizations that the free exercise [of religion] clause forbids." [94]

9th Circuit (Alaska, Arizona, California, Hawaii, Idaho, Montana, Nevada, Oregon, and Washington)

• *A federal appeals court ruled that it was barred by the ministerial exception from resolving a pastor's claim that he had been dismissed by his church because he suf-fered from Attention Deficit Disorder (ADD). A pastor sued his church, claiming that it violated the Americans with Disabilities Act (ADA) by dismissing him on account of his Attention Deficit Disorder, dyslexia, and heart problems, without attempting to accom-modate his needs. The pastor's lawsuit demanded that the church reinstate him, and pay him monetary damages. The church asked the court to dismiss the lawsuit on the ground that it was barred by the "ministerial exception" to employment discrimination laws. A federal district court agreed with the church and threw out the case. A federal appeals court agreed with this disposition. The appeals court noted that the ministeri-al exception "insulates a religious organization's employment decisions regarding its ministers from judicial scrutiny . . . . It derives from the [First Amendment religion clauses] and is intended to protect the relationship between a religious organization and its clergy from constitutionally impermissible interference by the government. Specifically, because clergy represent a religious institution to the people, a religious institution must retain unfettered freedom in its choice of clergy." The pastor insisted that the ministerial exception did not bar consideration of his claim that the church failed to "accommodate" his disability, as required by the ADA, since this claim was "not a personnel decision akin to hiring or firing." The court disagreed: "The ministeri-al exception does not apply solely to the hiring and firing of ministers, but also relates to the broader relationship between an organized religious institution and its clergy. . . . Matters touching this relationship must necessarily be recognized as of prime eccle-siastical concern." The court concluded that if the pastor were allowed to pursue his claims in civil court "the church would be required to provide a religious justification for its failure to accommodate and this is an area into which the First Amendment for-bids us to tread. We thus determine that the pastor's claims, grounded in the church's failure to accommodate his disabilities while he was still employed, are a part of the employment relationship between church and minister."* [95]

10th Circuit (Colorado, Kansas, New Mexico, Oklahoma, Utah, and Wyoming)

---

[94] Scharon v. St. Luke's Episcopal Presbyterian Hospitals, 929 F.2d 360 (8th Cir. 1991).

[95] Werft v. Desert Southwest Annual Conference of the United Methodist Church, 377 F.3d 1099 (9th Cir. 2004).

• *A federal appeals court ruled that it was barred by the ministerial exception from resolving a claim that a church had engaged in unlawful sex discrimination by dismissing a non-ordained female youth pastor because of her "marriage" to another woman. The court observed: "Courts have recognized a ministerial exception that prevents adjudication of Title VII employment discrimination cases brought by ministers against churches. The right to choose ministers is an important part of internal church governance and can be essential to the well-being of a church, for perpetuation of a church's existence may depend upon those whom it selects to preach its values, teach its message, and interpret its doctrines both to its own membership and to the world at large." The court concluded that "when a church makes a personnel decision based on religious doctrine, and holds meetings to discuss that decision and the ecclesiastical doctrine underlying it, the courts will not intervene." The court rejected the plaintiff's argument that the Supreme Court's 1990 ruling in the Smith case [96] effectively abolished the ministerial exception. In the Smith case the Court ruled that "neutral laws of general application" do not violate the First Amendment guaranty of religious freedom even if they impose substantial burdens on the exercise of religion. The plaintiff argued that this ruling meant that civil rights laws can be applied to churches and clergy without violating the First Amendment, since such laws are "neutral laws of general application." The court disagreed, noting that several federal appeals courts "have examined whether the ministerial exception survives in light of Smith and each has concluded that it does." Further, "the ministerial exception cases rely on a long line of Supreme Court cases affirming the church autonomy doctrine, which protects the fundamental right of churches to decide for themselves matters of church government, faith, and doctrine. These cases' rationale extends beyond the specific ministerial exception to the church autonomy doctrine generally, and we therefore find that the church autonomy doctrine remains viable after Smith." [97]*

11th Circuit (Alabama, Florida, and Georgia)

• *A federal appeals court ruled that the ministerial exception prevented it from resolving a claim by a minister that he had been "retaliated" against by his church for assisting a female employee in presenting a sexual harassment claim to church leaders. The court rejected the plaintiff's argument that the Supreme Court's 1990 ruling in the Smith case [98] effectively abolished the ministerial exception. In the Smith case the Court ruled that "neutral laws of general application" do not violate the First Amendment guaranty of religious freedom even if they impose substantial burdens on the exercise of religion. The plaintiff argued that this ruling meant that civil rights laws can be applied to churches and clergy without violating the First Amendment, since such laws are "neutral laws of general application." The court disagreed, noting that "the ministerial exception . . . has not been overruled by the Supreme Court's decision in Smith." The court concluded: "The relationship between an organized church and its ministers is its lifeblood. The minister is the chief instrument by which the church seeks to fulfill its purpose." Therefore, "an attempt by the government to regulate the relationship between a church and its clergy would infringe upon the church's right to be the sole governing body of its ecclesiastical rules and religious doctrine." [99]*

---

[96]   Employment Division v. Smith, 494 U.S. 872 (1990).

[97]   Bryce v. Episcopal Church in the Diocese of Colorado, 289 F.3d 648 (10th Cir. 2002).

[98]   Employment Division v. Smith, 494 U.S. 872 (1990).

[99]   Gellington v. Christian Methodist Episcopal Church, Inc., 203 F.3d 1299 (11th Cir. 2000), quoting McClure v. Salvation Army, 460 F.2d 553 (5th Cir. 1972).

"The relationship between an organized church and its ministers is its lifeblood. The minister is the chief instrument by which the church seeks to fulfill its purpose." Therefore, "an attempt by the government to regulate the relationship between a church and its clergy would infringe upon the church's right to be the sole governing body of its ecclesiastical rules and religious doctrine."

Federal District Court and State Court Rulings

• *A California court ruled that it was barred by the ministerial exception from resolving a sex discrimination claim brought by an ordained female chaplain against her employer, a church-affiliated university. The court concluded that "judicial review of [the university's] employment decision would absolutely result in excessive entanglement with religion. We would have to inquire into the good faith of the university's reasons for cutting back [the chaplain's] hours and adjudge the legitimacy of the church affiliated institution's own perception of its ministerial needs. Such a review is constitutionally forbidden." This was so despite the chaplain's argument that the decision to reduce her hours was an "economic" rather than a spiritual decision. The court noted simply that "the dispositive fact is the existence of an employment decision by a religious institution about a clergy employee. The courts do not cross that threshold."* [100]

• *A Washington, D.C. court ruled that a lawsuit brought against a church by the dismissed principal of a church-operated school had to be dismissed as a result of the ministerial exception. A woman sued a church under the District of Columbia Human Rights Act (the DCHRA) alleging discrimination and retaliation based on race. The court began its opinion by observing, "Although it would be difficult to exaggerate the magnitude of [the District's] interest in assuring equal employment opportunities for all, regardless of race, sex, or national origin, abundant decisional law from this court and others confirms the constitutional imperative of governmental non-interference with the ministerial employment decisions of churches." The court rejected the plaintiff's argument that most of her daily responsibilities were administrative and basically no different from those performed by her counterparts in public schools. It noted that "she was principal of a [church] school, and thus she, more than anyone else at the school except the pastor, was answerable to the religious authorities for providing, in myriad ways not reducible to a listing of tasks, spiritual leadership in and for the school community. These many responsibilities—some predominantly secular and some predominantly religious—are inextricably intertwined in the school's mission and in the principal's role in fulfilling it."* [101]

• *A federal district court in Florida ruled that the ministerial exception prevented it from applying the federal age discrimination law to a 68-year-old priest who was applying for a "nonministerial" position with a missions agency that involved the performance of ministerial functions. The court concluded that "because the primary functions of a brother involve teaching, ministering, and 'spreading the faith' in more than 27 countries around the world . . . a brother is the functional equivalent of a minister for the purposes of the ministerial exception," and therefore it was "barred by the First*

---

[100]   Schmoll v. Chapman University, 83 Cal.Rptr.2d 426 (Cal. App. 1999).

[101]   Pardue v. Center City Consortium Schools, 875 A.2d 669 (D.C. App. 2005).

Amendment from reviewing the [agency's] decision not to hire the [priest]." The court noted that "for more than a century the Supreme Court has followed a rule of deference to church authority in 'religious or ecclesiastical disputes,'" and that the Court has recognized the constitutional concerns raised by interference with administrative control of churches, stating that "legislation that regulates church administration, the operation of churches or the appointment of clergy . . . prohibits the free exercise of religion." [102]

• The Massachusetts Supreme Judicial Court ruled that it was barred by the ministerial exception from resolving a sex discrimination lawsuit brought by a former minister to the deaf. The court concluded: "It is true that the plaintiff's claims do not, on their face, question the verity of religious doctrines or beliefs. It is hard to conceive, however, how a court could inquire into the reasons for the defendants' decisions regarding the plaintiff's ministry without intruding into matters of the internal management of the [church]. The plaintiff's claims, by their very nature, implicate First Amendment rights. To argue otherwise diminishes the importance of the constitutional separation of church and state. . . . That the [church] may have acted in violation of antidiscrimination policies set forth in its own personnel handbook is irrelevant. We decline to venture into the realm of interpreting internal guidelines and procedures that have been adopted by the church. As discussed above, a church must be free to decide for itself what its obligations to its ministers are, without being subject to court interference." [103]

• A New Jersey court ruled that a lay teacher could sue a Catholic high school for age and sex discrimination. The teacher had been employed to teach English and history. After several years of teaching, she was informed that her position was being eliminated due to "budget problems." The teacher sued the school, claiming that the real reason she was being terminated was because of her gender and age. As proof, she alleged that the school later replaced her with a younger, male teacher. The school defended itself by insisting that all teaching positions at a Catholic high school are "religious" in nature, and that the First Amendment prohibits the civil courts from applying civil rights laws to such positions. In support of its position, the school noted that the contract signed by its teachers stated that all teachers are to "exemplify Christian principles and ideals" in the performance of their duties, and are to open each class with prayer. Further, the school asserted that "parochial school teachers, no matter what the subject matter being taught, are performing a ministerial function . . . inculcating faith, values, and moral precepts into the students" and that "secular subjects in a parochial school are important vehicles for the propagation of the faith." The court acknowledged that civil rights laws cannot be applied to ministers or lay employees performing ministerial functions for a church or religious school. However, the court concluded that the lay teacher in this case did not satisfy this test. It observed: "[T]he fact that faculty members serve as exemplars of practicing Christians does not automatically make their duties ministerial. . . . A teacher of secular subjects need not be considered a religious leader. Here . . . enforcing the prohibition against discrimination would have no impact on religious belief, doctrine, or practice. . . . Thus, since the underlying dispute does not turn on doctrine or polity, the court should not abdicate its duty to enforce secular rights." [104]

• A New Mexico court ruled that it was barred by the ministerial exception from resolving a rabbi's claim that a synagogue unlawfully dismissed him on the basis of his age

---

[102]   Sanchez v. Catholic Foreign Society of America, 82 F.Supp.2d 1338 (M.D. Fla. 1999).

[103]   Williams v. Episcopal Diocese, 766 N.E.2d 820 (2002).

[104]   Gallo v. Salesian Society, Inc., 676 A.2d 580 (N.J. Super. 1996).

and Parkinson's disease. The court quoted with approval from a federal appeals court decision: "The relationship between an organized church and its ministers is its lifeblood. The minister is the chief instrument by which the church seeks to fulfill its purpose. Matters touching this relationship must necessarily be recognized as of prime ecclesiastical concern. Just as the initial function of selecting a minister is a matter of church administration and government, so are the functions which accompany such a selection." [105]

• A federal court in North Carolina ruled that it was barred by the First Amendment guaranties of religious freedom and the nonestablishment of religion from resolving a sex discrimination lawsuit brought by a dismissed church music director. A church conducted a survey on all aspects of church life. The survey indicated a dissatisfaction among members with the music ministry. As a result of these concerns, the church dismissed its music director and hired a replacement. The dismissed music director sued her church, claiming that her dismissal amounted to sex discrimination in violation of Title VII of the Civil Rights Act of 1964. In particular, she alleged that she had been replaced by a male. The court dismissed the director's lawsuit on the ground that it was barred by the ministerial exception from resolving it. The court rejected the director's claim that the ministerial exception did not apply to her because her position was not ministerial in nature. It noted that she was a member of the church's worship committee and was responsible for planning music to complement the liturgy throughout the church season. The court concluded that "the function of planning and playing a part in the performance of the liturgy, the public worship of the church, is facially ministerial. [Her] duty as a member of the worship committee also [involved] teaching, spreading the faith . . . and supervision or participation in religious ritual and worship. . . . [Her] church considers the music leader a minister, someone who shares faith, serves the community, and expresses the love of God and neighbor through music. . . . Given the undisputed significance of the role of music in the church, and [the music director's] teaching and supervision of religious ritual and worship, her duties . . . fall within the ministerial exception." [106]

• A federal court in Tennessee ruled that it was barred by the ministerial exception from resolving a discrimination lawsuit brought by a hospital chaplain against her employer. A woman was employed by a church-affiliated hospital in its clinical pastoral education program. Her job description stated that she was required to initiate pastoral visits with patients and family members, be an on-call primary chaplain during non-work hours, and lead a Sunday worship service for patients, family and staff. The hospital later dismissed the employee after a psychological assessment, and other evidence, suggested that she was not a suitable candidate for the clinical pastoral education program. The former employee sued the hospital, claiming that its decision to dismiss her amounted to discrimination based on disability in violation of the Americans with Disabilities Act. Specifically, she asserted that the hospital violated the ADA by requiring her to submit to an unlawful medical examination performed by a staff psychologist, and by terminating her employment based on a perceived mental disability. The court noted that the ministerial exception prevents "any inquiry whatsoever into the reasons behind a church's ministerial employment decision." The court rejected the former employee's claim that the hospital waived the ministerial exception by obtaining [Association of

---

[105] Celnik v. Congregation B'Nai Israel, 131 P.3d 102 (N.M. 2006), quoting McClure v. Salvation Army, 460 F.2d 553 (5th Cir. 1972).

[106] Equal Employment Opportunity Commission v. The Roman Catholic Diocese of Raleigh, 48 F.Supp.2d 505 (E.D.N.C. 1999).

Clinical Pastoral Education] accreditation." The court noted that the former employee failed to demonstrate that the hospital "knew or intended to waive such rights by obtaining ACPE accreditation." Although the hospital's failure to adhere to the ACPE nondiscrimination clauses "might have some effect upon its accreditation by that agency, merely signing such an agreement does not, in and of itself, indicate a knowing, voluntary waiver of its constitutional right to be free from judicial interference with decisions relating to the employment of its ministers." [107]

• A Washington state court ruled that it was barred by the ministerial exception from resolving sexual harassment and retaliation claims made by a female associate pastor against her senior pastor. The court concluded: "[The plaintiff's] case centers on the claim that church authorities learned of the sexual harassment but failed to discipline [the senior pastor] and instead precluded her from seeking other work. But the church declined to discipline the senior pastor because its investigating committee and [national adjudicatory body] decided that insufficient evidence existed to file a charge. And the church's Book of Order prohibits allowing a minister to transfer while charges are pending. Thus . . . her retaliation claims would require a court to question and interpret the transfer rule in the church's Book of Order. We can do neither without effectively undermining the church's inherent autonomy. We thus affirm the trial court's order dismissing the claims against the church and the [regional church]." [108]

• A Wisconsin court ruled that a lawsuit brought by a former church employee claiming that her dismissal constituted unlawful sex discrimination had to be dismissed since the employee's position was "ministerial" and "ecclesiastical." [109] A female employee of a Catholic seminary, who served as "director of field education," claimed that the seminary's decision not to renew her contract of employment was based on her sex in violation of a state civil rights law. The law prohibits discrimination in employment decisions on the basis of an employee's "age, race, creed, color, handicap, marital status, sex, national origin, ancestry, arrest record, or conviction record." A state court rejected the seminary's claim that the civil courts lack jurisdiction to resolve employment discrimination suits brought against religious organizations. The court relied in part on a 1986 decision of the United States Supreme Court finding that the civil courts are not prohibited from "merely investigating" the circumstances of an employee's dismissal by a religious school. [110] The court observed that giving religious organizations immunity from employment discrimination laws "would dangerously encroach upon the [nonestablishment of religion] clause's prohibition against furthering religion by providing a benefit exclusively to a religious association." However, the court ruled that the First Amendment's protection of the free exercise of religion provides religious organizations with substantial protections that must be considered. These include the enforcement of state civil rights laws in cases involving employment decisions by religious organizations with respect to employees who perform a "ministerial" or "ecclesiastical" function. If an employee performs such a function, then "further enforcement of the [state civil rights law] against the religious association is constitutionally precluded, and the complaint should be dismissed." The court concluded that the employee in this case performed ministerial functions since her duties consisted of "teaching, spreading the faith, church governance, supervision of a religious order, or supervision or participation in religious ritual or worship."

---

[107] Hollins v. Methodist Healthcare, Inc., 379 F.Supp.2d 907 (W.D. Tenn. 2005).

[108] Elvig v. Ackles, 98 P.3d 524 (Wash. App. 2004).

[109] Jocz v. Labor and Industry Review Commission, 538 N.W.2d 588 (Wis. App. 1995).

[110] Ohio Civil Rights Commission v. Dayton Christian Schools, Inc., 477 U.S. 619 (1986).

• A federal district court in Wisconsin ruled that it was barred by the ministerial exception from resolving a former church music director's claim that she had been wrongfully terminated by her church on account of her race in violation of Title VII of the Civil Rights Act of 1964. The court dismissed the lawsuit on the ground that the director was a "minister," and that any resolution of her claims by a civil court would violate the First Amendment's guaranty of religious freedom. The court noted that an ecclesiastical or ministerial exception precludes the application of Title VII to the employment relationship between certain individuals and religious institutions, and that "the ministerial exception is aimed at preventing the introduction of government standards into a religious institution's selection of its own clergy." The court stressed that the ministerial exception has not been limited to cases involving clergy. Lay employees of religious institutions have been deemed "ministers" for the purposes of the exception where their "primary duties consist of teaching, spreading the faith, church governance, supervision of a religious order, or supervision or participation in religious ritual and worship." The court applied the three-part Starkman test in concluding that the director was a ministerial employee subject to the ministerial exception. [111]

Cases Not Recognizing the Ministerial Exception

§ 8-10.2

Key Point 8-10.2> *Some courts have not recognized the ministerial exception, usually because the complainant was not a minister in either status or function, or was employed by a secular organization.*

A few courts have not applied the ministerial exception, usually because the employee in question was not a "minister."

Case Studies

• A federal appeals court ruled that in some cases ministers can pursue sexual harassment claims against an employing church without violating the First Amendment. A woman served as associate pastor of a church for one year. Shortly after assuming this position, she claimed that the church's senior pastor began sexually harassing her and creating a "hostile work environment." Pastor Ruth made a formal complaint of sexual harassment to the church, which she claimed took no action to stop the harassment or alleviate the hostile working environment. She also claimed that the senior pastor retaliated against her by relieving her of certain duties, verbally abusing her and otherwise engaging in intimidating behavior. Again, the church, which knew or should have known of the senior pastor's behavior, failed to act. The court noted that to the extent the plaintiff's claims involved "an inquiry into the church's decision to terminate her ministry, those claims cannot proceed in civil court and were properly dismissed."

[111] Miller v. Bay View United Methodist Church, 141 F.Supp.2d 1174 (E.D. Wis. 2001). The *Starkman* case is a federal appeals court ruling summarized above under 5th Circuit cases.

However, the court concluded that she could, consistent with the First Amendment, "attempt to show that she was sexually harassed and that this harassment created a hostile work environment" since this would involve "a purely secular inquiry." The court concluded: "[There is] no First Amendment basis for shielding the church from its obligation to protect its employees from harassment when extending such protection would not contravene the church's doctrinal prerogatives or trench upon its protected ministerial decisions." [112]

• A California court ruled that the ministerial exception to employment discrimination laws did not necessarily apply to a married couple who taught marriage counseling at a church-affiliated university. The court could not "categorically" conclude that the plaintiffs were within the ministerial exception since "they are nonordained and they teach a subject (marriage and family counseling) that is not necessarily religious. . . . Psychology is not necessarily a religious subject. The world is full of psychologists who vehemently disagree about the role of religion in psychology." Of course, the relationship between marriage and family counseling and the institution's religious mission "was undeniable." Sex and marriage "are major topics in religion. Whole churches have sprung out of marital controversies . . . so we cannot say categorically that they could not come within the exception, either. All we can say is that, in this proceeding [the university] did not establish that they are required to come within the exception." The court sent the case back to the trial court for further consideration of the application of the ministerial exception. [113]

• A federal court in Connecticut ruled that a church-affiliated college could be sued by a homosexual ex-priest who was dismissed as a professor in the college's religion department. The court concluded that the professor's claims were not necessarily barred by the ministerial exception since the record was not clear as to the precise nature of his duties. While he was employed by a college sponsored by a Dominican Order of nuns, and he taught in the Department of Religious Studies and Philosophy, "questions remain as to his actual teaching and non-teaching functions. The evidence submitted does not establish that he taught Roman Catholic theology, canon law, or similar courses. It is also unclear whether the students at the College were required to take particular religion courses involving Catholic teachings and whether Michael taught those courses. Further, at this time the evidence does not establish that Michael led students in prayer or provided them with spiritual counseling." This case represents one of the most narrow interpretations of the ministerial exception. The court's conclusion that the ministerial exception "does not necessarily apply to a teacher of religion at a church-affiliated college is remarkable if not unbelievable. [114]

> "[There is] no First Amendment basis for shielding the church from its obligation to protect its employees from harassment when extending such protection would not contravene the church's doctrinal prerogatives or trench upon its protected ministerial decisions."

---

[112] Elvig v. Calvin Presbyterian Church, 375 F.3d 951 (9th Cir. 2004).

[113] Hope International University v. Superior Court, 14 Cal.Rptr.3d 643 (Cal. App. 2004).

[114] Hartwig v. Albertus Magnus College, 93 F.Supp.2d 200 (D. Conn. 2000).

• An Ohio court ruled that a church could be sued for disability discrimination as a result of its termination of a music director who suffered from severe depression. It noted that for the plaintiff to prove discrimination, he had to establish a prima facie case by proving (1) that he was disabled, (2) that he was terminated at least in part because of his disability, and (3) he could perform the essential functions of the job with or without a reasonable accommodation by the church. The court noted that the evidence supported all three of these factors. The court did not address the application of the ministerial exception. [115]

• A federal court in Pennsylvania ruled that the ministerial exception did not require the dismissal of a sex discrimination lawsuit brought by a lay church employee whose duties were not primarily religious in nature. The court noted that the employee's duties were clerical in nature. It concluded: "While she collected and maintained church documents and ensured that they contained all of the necessary information, she could not independently rule on the doctrinal legitimacy of documents submitted to her. . . . Filing and organizing documents, whether they are religious documents or tax forms, is a clerical function. . . . There is no evidence that her duties required any heightened religious knowledge or spiritual involvement." The court concluded that for purposes of the ministerial exception "whether an individual is important to the administrative functioning of the church is critically less significant than whether she is important to the spiritual functioning of the church. The lowest-ranking nun or monk in the abbey is still a minister, whereas a clerical or administrative employee, no matter how indispensable, is not. . . . [The plaintiff's] primary duties were not sufficiently important to the spiritual and pastoral mission of the church to render her a minister for purposes of the ministerial exception." [116]

Procedure for Establishing a Discrimination Claim

§ 8-11

Key Point 8-11> *Employees and applicants for employment who believe that an employer has violated a federal civil rights law must pursue their claim according to a specific procedure. Failure to do so will result in the dismissal of their claim.*

The procedures for filing claims under the federal discrimination laws discussed in this chapter are fairly consistent. Church leaders should be familiar with the following procedures in the event that a discrimination complaint is brought against their church:

1. Filing a charge with the EEOC. An "aggrieved" individual, a person acting on behalf of an aggrieved individual, or the Equal Employment Opportunity Commission (EEOC) itself may file a "charge" with the EEOC. The charge is a

---

[115] Mitnaul v. Fairmount Presbyterian Church, 778 N.E.2d 1093 (Ohio App. 2002).

[116] Patsakis v. Greek Orthodox Archdiocese of America, 339 F.Supp.2d 689 (W.D. Pa. 2004).

complaint filed on an EEOC form that alleges discrimination by an employer. In most cases, the charge is brought by the aggrieved individual claiming to have been a victim of discrimination in employment.

2. Notification of employer. Within ten days of the filing of the charge, the EEOC sends the employer a "notice" of the charge. The notice includes a summary of the alleged discrimination.

3. Investigations by state or local civil rights agencies. If the aggrieved person files a charge with a state or local civil rights agency, then no charge may be filed with the EEOC until at least 60 days have elapsed since the charge was filed with the state or local agency.

4. Time for filing charges. A charge must be filed with the EEOC within 180 days after the alleged discriminatory practice occurred. If a charge was initially filed with a state or local civil rights agency, then the charge must be filed with the EEOC by the earlier of the following two dates: (1) 300 days after the alleged discriminatory practice occurred, or (2) 30 days after notice from the state or local agency that it has terminated its proceedings regarding the charge.

5. EEOC investigation—no reasonable cause exists. The EEOC investigates the charge. If it determines that there is no reasonable cause to believe that the charge is true, it dismisses the charge and notifies the aggrieved person and employer of its decision. In deciding if reasonable cause exists, the EEOC must give "substantial weight" to the findings of any state or local civil rights agency that conducted its own investigation. If a charge is dismissed by the EEOC, or if the EEOC has not brought a civil lawsuit within 180 days of the filing of the charge, then the EEOC notifies the aggrieved person that he or she may file a civil lawsuit against the employer within 90 days of such notice. This is referred to as a "right-to-sue notice."

6. EEOC investigation—reasonable cause exists. If the EEOC determines that there is reasonable cause to believe that the charge is true, then it attempts to eliminate the alleged discriminatory practice by such informal methods as conferences, conciliation, and persuasion. If an employer accused of discrimination does not enter into a conciliation agreement with the EEOC within 30 days of the filing of the charge, then the EEOC may sue the employer in federal court on account of the alleged violation of the applicable federal civil rights law. Further, if the EEOC determines that reasonable cause exists, and the employer refuses to conciliate, then it sends the aggrieved party a "right to sue notice." A charging party may file a lawsuit within 90 days after receiving a right to sue notice from the EEOC. Under Title VII and the Americans with Disabilities Act, a charging party also can request a right to sue notice from EEOC 180 days after the charge was first filed, and may then bring suit within 90 days after receiving this notice. Under the Age Discrimination in Employment Act, a suit may be filed at any time 60 days after filing a charge with EEOC, but not later than 90 days after EEOC gives notice that it has completed action on the charge.

7. Federal court procedure. The plaintiff (the aggrieved person) bears the initial burden of proving that the employer engaged in the discriminatory practice. This can be done by direct evidence of discrimination, but more often it is done by showing "disparate treatment"—that is, the aggrieved party was treated less favorably than other employees who were not members of a protected group. The courts have ruled that a plaintiff can meet the initial burden of proof by establishing a "prima facie case" of discrimination by a preponderance of the evidence. This is done by showing that

> prima facie = plain or clear; self-evident; obvious

(1) the plaintiff is a member of a class protected by a federal, state, or local civil rights law; (2) the plaintiff suffered an adverse employment decision (such as not being hired if a job applicant, or being dismissed or disciplined if an employee); (3) a direct relationship exists between membership in the protected class and the adverse employment decision.

If the plaintiff is successful in making out a prima facie case of discrimination, then a presumption of discrimination exists, and the burden shifts to the employer to show a legitimate, nondiscriminatory reason for the adverse employment decision. If the employer demonstrates a nondiscriminatory reason for the adverse employment action, then the presumption is rebutted and the plaintiff must prove that the nondiscriminatory reason was a pretext for discrimination.[117]

8. Remedies. A variety of remedies are available to persons who establish that they were victims of employment discrimination. These include money damages and injunctive relief.

Case Study

• *An Ohio court ruled that a church school had not violated age discrimination law by dismissing an unmarried male teacher and female teacher who were living together in violation of church doctrine. Two teachers who had been dismissed by a church school sued the school claiming that their dismissals amounted to unlawful age discrimination. A court noted that employees who claim discrimination have the initial burden of establishing a "prima facie case" of discrimination. This requires proof that (1) they are a member of a class protected by a federal, state, or local civil rights law; (2) they suffered an adverse employment decision (such as being dismissed); (3) a direct relationship exists between membership in the protected class and the adverse employment decision. If an employee is successful in making out a prima facie case of discrimination, then a presumption of discrimination exists, and the burden shifts to the employer to show a legitimate, nondiscriminatory reason for the adverse employment decision. If the employer demonstrates a nondiscriminatory reason for the adverse employment action, then the presumption is rebutted and the employee must prove that the nondiscriminatory reason was a "pretext" for discrimination. The court conceded that the teachers had proven a prima facie case of discrimination since they were members of a protected class (40 years of age or older) and had been terminated*

---

[117] McDonnell Douglas Corporation v. Green, 411 U.S. 792 (1973).

and replaced with younger teachers. In response, the school alleged a nondiscriminatory reason for terminating the teachers. It asserted that the teachers had been dismissed because they failed to comply with church doctrine when they cohabited without being married. The teachers were unable to prove that the school's allegedly nondiscriminatory basis for terminating them was a "pretext." As a result, the court concluded that the teachers' age discrimination claim had to be dismissed.[118]

Title VII of the Civil Rights Act of 1964

§ 8-12

Key Point 8-12 > *Title VII of the Civil Rights Act of 1964 prohibits employers engaged in commerce and having at least 15 employees from discriminating in any employment decision on the basis of race, color, national origin, gender, or religion.*

The Civil Rights Act of 1964 was enacted by Congress "to achieve a peaceful and voluntary settlement of the persistent problem of racial and religious discrimination."[119] Title VII, Section 703(a), of the Civil Rights Act of 1964 specifies:

(a) It shall be an unlawful employment practice for an employer

(1) to fail or refuse to hire or to discharge any individual, or otherwise to discriminate against any individual with respect to his compensation, terms, conditions, or privileges of employment, because of such individual's race, color, religion, sex, or national origin; or

(2) to limit, segregate, or classify his employees or applicants for employment in any way which would deprive or tend to deprive any individual of employment opportunities or otherwise adversely affect his status as an employee, because of such individual's race, color, religion, sex, or national origin.

This general ban on discrimination applies to all employers, including religious organizations, that have 15 or more employees and that are engaged in an industry or activity "affecting commerce." The "commerce" and "15 employee" requirements are discussed earlier in this chapter.

---

[118]   Basinger v. Pilarczyk, 738 N.E.2d 814 (Ohio App. 2000).

[119]   SEN. REPORT NO. 872, 88TH CONG., 2ND SESS. (1964).

Note that Title VII only addresses discrimination committed by employers against employees or applicants for employment on the basis of any one or more of the following five grounds:

- race

- color

- religion

- sex

- national origin

Application to Religious Organizations

§ 8-12.1

Key Point 8-12.1> *Title VII of the Civil Rights Act of 1964 prohibits employers engaged in commerce and having at least 15 employees from discriminating in any employment decision on the basis of race, color, national origin, gender, or religion. Religious organizations are exempt from the ban on religious discrimination, but not from the other prohibited forms of discrimination.*

Title VII, section 702, of the Civil Rights Act of 1964 states:

This title shall not apply to . . . a religious corporation, association, educational institution, or society with respect to the employment of individuals of a particular religion to perform work connected with the carrying on by such corporation, association, educational institution, or society of its activities.

This provision permits religious corporations, associations, and educational institutions to discriminate on the basis of religion in the employment of any person for any position.

As originally enacted, section 702 permitted religious employers to discriminate on the basis of religion only in employment decisions pertaining to their "religious activities." Congress amended section 702 in 1972 to enable religious organizations to discriminate on the basis of religion in *all* employment decisions. In the years following the 1972 amendment, a number of federal courts suggested that the amendment violated the First Amendment's nonestablishment of religion clause. To illustrate, one court characterized the amendment as "a remarkably clumsy accommodation of religious freedom with the compelling interests of the state, providing . . . far too broad a shield for the secular activities of religiously affiliated entities with not the remotest claim to First Amendment protection...." [120]

---

[120] Equal Employment Opportunity Commission v. Southwestern Baptist Theological Seminary, 485 F. Supp. 255, 260 (N.D. Tex. 1980), *rev'd on other grounds*, 651 F.2d 277 (5th Cir. 1981), *cert. denied*, 102 S. Ct. 1749 (1982). *See also* Feldstein v. Christian Science Monitor, 555 F. Supp. 974 (D. Mass. 1983) (Christian Science Monitor held to be a religious activity of the First Church of Christ, Scientist, a religious organization, and thus it could discriminate in employment decisions on the basis of religion).

The court conceded that it would be unconstitutional to prohibit religious organizations from discriminating on the basis of religion in employment decisions pertaining to *religious activities*, but it concluded that allowing religious organizations to discriminate on the basis of religion in *any* employment decision went too far. Other courts reached the same result.[121]

In 1987, the United States Supreme Court resolved the controversy concerning the legal validity of section 702 by ruling unanimously that it did not violate the First Amendment's nonestablishment of religion clause.[122] The case involved a maintenance employee of a Mormon church-affiliated gymnasium in Salt Lake City, Utah, who was fired because he failed to comply with the church's standards regarding church attendance, tithing, and abstinence from coffee, tea, alcohol, and tobacco. The employee sued the church, alleging that his dismissal violated the ban on religious discrimination in employment decisions contained in Title VII of the Civil Rights Act of 1964. The church asserted that the exception contained in section 702 of the Act permitted it to discriminate in any employment decision on the basis of religion. The employee countered by claiming that the exception violated the First Amendment's ban on the establishment of a religion. A federal district court agreed with the employee, and ordered the employee reinstated with back pay. The church appealed directly to the Supreme Court.

The Supreme Court began its opinion by emphasizing that "there is ample room under the establishment clause for benevolent neutrality which will permit religious exercise to exist without sponsorship and without interference." It evaluated the constitutionality of the section 702 exemption on the basis of a three-part test it devised in 1971. Under this test, a law challenged on the basis of the nonestablishment of religion clause is permissible only if it satisfies three requirements—(1) it has a clearly secular purpose, (2) its primary effect is neither the advancement nor the inhibition of religion, and (3) it does not result in an excessive entanglement between church and state.[123] The Court concluded that "the exemption involved here is in no way questionable" under the three-part test. The section 702 exemption met the first part of the test since "under the *Lemon* analysis, it is a permissible legislative purpose to alleviate significant governmental interference with the ability of religious organizations to define and carry out their religious missions." In concluding that the section 702 exemption met the second part of the test, the Court observed that

> undoubtedly, religious organizations are better able now to advance their purposes than they were prior to the 1972 amendment to section 702. But religious groups have been better able to advance their purposes on account of many laws that have passed constitutional muster: for example, the property tax exemption . . . . A law is not unconstitutional simply because it allows churches to advance religion, which is

---

[121] *See, e.g.,* King's Garden, Inc. v. Federal Communications Commission, 498 F.2d 51 (D.C. Cir. 1974), *cert. denied,* 419 U.S. 996 (1974). *But cf.* Equal Employment Opportunity Commission v. Southwestern Baptist Theological Seminary, 651 F.2d 277 (5th Cir. 1981); Equal Employment Opportunity Commission v. Mississippi College, 626 F.2d 477 (5th Cir. 1980), *cert. denied,* 453 U.S. 912 (1981); Ritter v. Mount St. Mary's College, 495 F. Supp. 724 (D. Md. 1980).

[122] Corporation of the Presiding Bishop of the Church of Jesus Christ of Latter-Day Saints v. Amos, 483 U.S. 327 (1987).

[123] Lemon v. Kurtzman, 403 U.S. 602 (1971).

their very purpose. For a law to [have the primary effect of advancing religion] it must be fair to say that the government itself has advanced religion through its own activities and influence.

The Court also concluded that the section 702 exemption did not result in an excessive entanglement between church and state. On the contrary, "the statute effectuates a more complete separation of the two and avoids . . . intrusive inquiry into religious belief . . . ."

In responding to the dismissed employee's claim that section 702 provided adequate protection to religious employers prior to its amendment in 1972, the Court observed:

> [The dismissed employee argues] that . . . section 702 provided adequate protection for religious employers prior to the 1972 amendment, when it exempted only the religious activities of such employers from the statutory ban on religious discrimination. We may assume for the sake of argument that the pre-1972 exemption was adequate in the sense that the free exercise [of religion] clause required no more. Nonetheless, it is a significant burden on a religious organization to require it, on pain of substantial liability, to predict which of its activities a secular court will consider religious. The line is hardly a bright one, and an organization might understandably be concerned that a judge would not understand its religious tenets and sense of mission. Fear of potential liability might affect the way an organization carried out what it understood to be its religious mission.[124]

Religious organizations that are subject to Title VII are exempt only from the ban on religious discrimination in employment. They remain subject to Title VII's ban on employment discrimination based on race, color, national origin, or sex— except, as noted above, with respect to employment decisions involving clergy.

Case Study

• Religious organizations subject to Title VII are exempt from the ban on religious discrimination in employment, but they remain subject to the ban on employment discrimination based on race, color, national origin, or gender. However, not every allegation of discrimination has merit. To illustrate, a federal court in Pennsylvania ruled that a female employee of a Lutheran synod was not a victim of sex discrimination when her position was eliminated due to the merger of her synod with other synods. It observed: "[T]he 1984 decision of the three national Lutheran churches to merge had a significant impact on the future needs and direction of the Synod. Reflecting on these material changes, and their potential impact on the Synod's operational needs, the executive board of the Synod concluded that the coordinator of planning and communications position held by [the female employee] was expendable. While one may lament the fact that business principles and methods (e.g., budgets, income statements and time reports) have crept into our religious organizations, and regret the economic and personal pain that such bottom-line orientation caused the [dismissed

---

[124] *Id.* at 335-336. The Court noted that the present case illustrated the difficulties of distinguishing between "religious" and "secular" positions. The church maintained that the dismissed maintenance worker was engaged in a religious position, while the district court concluded that the position was entirely secular.

employee] in this case, this hand-wringing will not create a cause of action [for sex discrimination] where none exists."[125]

Application to Religious Educational Institutions

§ 8-12.2

Key Point 8-12.2> *Title VII of the Civil Rights Act of 1964 prohibits employers engaged in commerce and having at least 15 employees from discriminating in any employment decision on the basis of race, color, national origin, gender, or religion. Religious educational institutions are exempt from the ban on religious discrimination, but not from the other prohibited forms of discrimination.*

Title VII, Section 703(e)(2) of the Civil Rights Act of 1964 specifies:

[I]t shall not be an unlawful employment practice for a school, college, university, or other educational institution or institution of learning to hire and employ employees of a particular religion if such school, college, university, or other educational institution or institution of learning is, in whole or in substantial part, owned, supported, controlled, or managed by a particular religion or by a particular religious corporation, association, or society, or if the curriculum of such school, college, university, or other educational institution or institution of learning is directed toward the propagation of a particular religion.

This provision exempts religious educational institutions, whether at the primary, secondary, or college level, from the prohibition of religious discrimination contained in Title VII of the Civil Rights Act of 1964. Significantly, this provision speaks generally of the right of religious educational institutions to discriminate on the basis of religion in the hiring of employees who will directly promote religious belief, such as teachers, as well as those who will not, such as clerical, custodial, and administrative personnel. The United States Supreme Court has ruled that this exemption does not violate the First Amendment's "nonestablishment of religion" clause.[126]

Case Studies

• *A federal appeals court ruled that a teacher could not sue a church-operated school for discrimination after it refused to renew her contract because of her violation of the church's moral teachings. A divorced teacher at a Catholic school remarried, and was later informed by the school that she would not be rehired for the following school term. The school based its decision on the employment contract which noted that a*

---

[125] Yost v. Western Pennsylvania-West Virginia Synod of the Lutheran Church in America, Inc., 789 F. Supp. 191 (W.D. Pa. 1992).

[126] Corporation of Presiding Bishop v. Amos, 483 U.S. 327 (1987). This case is discussed below.

teacher could be dismissed "for serious public immorality, public scandal, or public rejection of the official teachings, doctrine or laws of the Roman Catholic Church." The school informed the teacher that she would not be rehired because she had remarried without pursuing "proper canonical process available from the Roman Church to obtain validation of her second marriage," and thereby had committed a serious offense against the "Church's teachings and laws on the indissolubility of Christian marriage and the sacramental nature of the marriage bond." The dismissed teacher sued the school, claiming that her dismissal violated Title VII of the Civil Rights Act of 1964. A federal appeals court rejected the teacher's claim. It concluded: "[I]t does not violate Title VII's prohibition of religious discrimination for a parochial school to discharge a Catholic or a non-Catholic teacher who has publicly engaged in conduct regarded by the school as inconsistent with its religious principles. We therefore hold that the exemptions to Title VII cover the parish's decision not to rehire [the teacher] because of her remarriage."[127]

• A federal appeals court ruled that a church-affiliated university did not commit unlawful discrimination when it dismissed a professor in its divinity school.[128] The professor had been employed to teach at a divinity school associated with Samford University—a Baptist university in Birmingham, Alabama. The professor claimed that he was dismissed by the divinity school's dean because he "did not adhere to and sometimes questioned the fundamentalist theology advanced by the leadership" of the divinity school. The professor sued the university, claiming that it had discriminated against him on account of his religious views in violation of Title VII of the Civil Rights Act of 1964. A federal district court dismissed the case, and the professor appealed. A federal appeals court upheld the district court's decision. It concluded that Title VII's exemption of "religious institutions" from the ban on religious discrimination in employment applied to the school. It based this conclusion on the following considerations: (1) the university was established as a "theological" institution. (2) The university's trustees are all Baptists. (3) Nearly 7 percent ($4 million) of the university's budget comes from the Alabama Baptist Convention (the "Convention")—representing the university's largest single course of funding. (4) The university submits financial reports to the Convention, and its audited financial statements are made available to all Baptist churches in Alabama. (5) All university professors who teach religious courses must subscribe to the Baptist "statement of faith," and this requirement is clearly set forth in the faculty handbook and in faculty contracts. (6) The university's charter states that its chief purpose is "the promotion of the Christian religion." (7) The university is exempt from federal income taxes as a "religious educational institution." The court also concluded that the school qualified for the exemption of "religious educational institutions" from Title VII's ban on religious discrimination in employment since it was "in substantial part" supported by the Convention: "Continuing support annually totaling over $4 million . . . accounting for seven percent of a university's budget, and constituting a university's largest single source of funding is of real worth and importance. This kind of support is neither illusory nor nominal. So, the Convention's support is substantial." The court concluded: "We . . . must give disputes about what particulars should or should not be taught in theological schools a wide berth. Congress, as we understand it, has told us to do so for purposes of Title VII. Also, such a construction allows us to avoid the First Amendment concerns which always tower over us when we face a case that is about religion."

---

[127] Little v. Wuerl, 929 F.2d 944 (3rd Cir. 1991).

[128] Killinger v. Samford University, 113 F.3d 196 (11th Cir. 1997).

Religion as a "Bona Fide Occupational Qualification" § 8-12.3

Key Point 8-12.3> *Title VII of the Civil Rights Act of 1964 prohibits employers engaged in commerce and having at least 15 employees from discriminating in any employment decision on the basis of race, color, national origin, gender, or religion. The Act permits religions organizations to discriminate in employment decisions on the basis of religion if religion is a bona fide occupational qualification.*

Title VII, Section 703(e)(1) of the Civil Rights Act of 1964 states:

Notwithstanding any other provision of this title . . . it shall not be an unlawful employment practice for an employer . . . to hire and employ employees . . . on the basis of his religion, sex, or national origin in those certain instances where religion, sex, or national origin is a bona fide occupational qualification reasonably necessary to the normal operation of that particular business or enterprise . . . .

If an employer otherwise subject to the Civil Rights Act of 1964 can demonstrate that religion is a bona fide occupational qualification for a particular position, then the employer may lawfully discriminate on the basis of religion in filling the position.

Discrimination Based on Religion or Morals § 8-12.4

Key Point 8-12.4> *Title VII of the Civil Rights Act of 1964 prohibits employers engaged in commerce and having at least 15 employees from discriminating in any employment decision on the basis of race, color, national origin, gender, or religion. The Act permits religions organizations to discriminate in employment decisions on the basis of religion. This exemption permits such organizations to discriminate on the basis of moral or scriptural standards so long as they do consistently and not in a way that adversely impacts employees who are members of a group that is protected under an applicable state or federal discrimination law.*

Can a church lawfully discriminate against an employee or applicant for employment on the basis of moral teachings? In some cases, religious organizations will be able to demonstrate that their moral teachings are integral to their religious beliefs, and therefore employment discrimination based on moral teachings is a form of religious discrimination that is permitted by Title VII. To avoid any confusion, religious organizations that take an adverse employment action against an employee or applicant for employment as a result of the organization's moral teachings should word their determination with references to relevant passages from Scripture. This will make it more likely that a court will view the decision as a protected form of religious discrimination.

Case Study

• *A federal district court in California refused to dismiss a lawsuit brought by a former church employee who was dismissed after church leaders learned that she was pregnant out of wedlock. A church operated a private school, and required all employees to be "born again believers living a consistent and practical Christian life." Employees were required to sign a statement of faith, and to commit themselves to the mission of the church and to a Christian lifestyle that emulates the life of Christ. The school's librarian, a female, signed an annual affirmation agreement in which she agreed that she would be bound by the moral values and religious beliefs of the church. As an employee, the librarian received an employee manual that repeatedly stressed the importance of employees living a life in conformity to the beliefs and values of the church. The librarian was fired when church leaders learned that she was pregnant out of wedlock. The librarian filed a lawsuit in federal court, asserting that the church and school discriminated against her on account of her pregnancy in violation of Title VII. The church and school filed a motion to dismiss, alleging that the librarian had been fired "for the sin of being pregnant without benefit of marriage" (a condition inconsistent with the religious values of the church and school). However, the church and school later asserted that the librarian's dismissal had nothing to do with her pregnancy, but rather was based on her adulterous relationship. Her pregnancy was evidence of the adultery but had nothing to do with the religious reason for her dismissal. A federal court acknowledged that the "new position" of the church and school—that the librarian was fired for adultery, and not on account of her pregnancy—would not give rise to a Title VII claim since Title VII specifically permits religious employers to discriminate on the basis of religion in employment decisions. However, the "old position" of the church and school—that the librarian was fired because she was pregnant and not married—raised the possibility of sex discrimination. This case illustrates the importance of accurately describing the basis for terminating an employee. There is a critical legal difference between dismissing an employee on account of pregnancy (even if out of wedlock) and dismissing an employee on account of adultery (of which pregnancy is merely evidence).* [129]

> There is a critical legal difference between dismissing an employee on account of pregnancy (even if out of wedlock) and dismissing an employee on account of adultery (of which pregnancy is merely evidence).

---

[129] Vigars v. Valley Christian Center, 805 F. Supp. 802 (N.D. Cal. 1992).

DID YOU KNOW?
DISMISSING AN EMPLOYEE FOR VIOLATION OF A CHURCH'S MORAL TEACHINGS

Before dismissing an employee for violating the church's moral teachings, church leaders should ask the following questions:

(1) Is there sufficient evidence to support our decision?

(2) Did we inform the employee, in an employee handbook or other document, that he or she would be subject to dismissal for engaging in behavior in violation of our moral teachings?

(3) How will we describe the basis for our decision? The best description will refer to the church's doctrinal tenets, and scriptural citations. Stay away from words such as "pregnancy" that can have a "secular" meaning, and that diminish the "religious exemption" available to churches under most federal and state civil rights and employment laws.

(4) How have we treated other employees in the past who were guilty of the same kind of misconduct? Have we treated all employees equally? Or, have we treated some employees less favorably than others? For example, have we dismissed female employees who were guilty of extramarital sexual relations, but only warned or reprimanded males employees guilty of the same behavior? Before dismissing an employee for misconduct, church leaders should review all other known cases involving similar misconduct by other employees. Be sure that an employee who is protected against discrimination by state or federal law is not being treated less favorably than other employees in previous cases.

(5) Have we consulted with an attorney before taking final action?

Case Studies

• *The Montana Supreme Court ruled that it was barred by the First Amendment guaranty of religious freedom from resolving a lawsuit brought by a woman who claimed that she had been unlawfully terminated from her employment at a church school on the basis of her cohabitation with a man to whom she was not married. The court concluded: "[No justification] has been offered to persuade us that [the plaintiff's] conduct involved a right of such high order that it would overcome the school's right to freely exercise its religion through its employment practices as guaranteed by the First Amendment to the United States Constitution . . . . We see no need to balance those religious rights . . . against [the plaintiff's] right to be free from discrimination based on marital status or her gender. This case is not about marital status or gender. It is about conduct which [she] agreed to avoid when she signed her employment agreement with [the school]. Even if she was terminated for the reason alleged, we conclude that her rights to be free from discrimination were not involved."[130]*

---

[130] Parker-Bigpack v. St. Labre School, 2000 WL 1101003 (Mont. 2000).

• *An Ohio court ruled that a church school had not violated age discrimination law by dismissing an unmarried male teacher and female teacher who were living together in violation of church doctrine. The school asserted that the teachers had been dismissed because they failed to comply with church doctrine when they cohabited without being married. The teachers were unable to prove that the school's allegedly nondiscriminatory basis for terminating them was a pretext. As a result, the court concluded that the teachers' age discrimination claim had to be dismissed.*[131]

A number of courts have ruled that Title VII's exemption of religious organizations from the ban on religious discrimination in employment does not apply if a religious organization uses religion as a "pretext" to discriminate against a member of a protected class. This is a very important qualification. Religious organizations can discriminate in their employment decisions on the basis of religion, but they must be consistent. To illustrate, a church that dismisses only female employees on the basis of adultery could not justify this practice on the basis of the Title VII exemption.

Case Studies

• *A minister employee of the Salvation Army alleged that her employer had violated the Civil Rights Act of 1964 by paying female officers smaller salaries than similarly situated males. A federal appeals court concluded that the relationship of the Salvation Army to its officers was a church minister relationship, and that the application of the provisions of Title VII to the employment relationship existing between a church and its minister would result in an impermissible encroachment by the government into an area of purely ecclesiastical concern.*[132]

• *A female teacher was hired to teach at a church-operated parochial school. The teacher later married, and shortly thereafter became so visibly pregnant that the church's pastor concluded that she had engaged in premarital sex. The teacher admitted that her pregnancy resulted from sex before her marriage. The pastor advised the teacher that the school would not renew her contract or hire her for the next school year. The teacher sued the church for discriminating against her on the basis of pregnancy in violation of Title VII of the Civil Rights Act of 1964. A federal appeals court refused to dismiss the teacher's complaint against the church. It noted that "courts have made clear that if the school's purported discrimination is based on a policy of preventing nonmarital sexual activity which emanates from the religious and moral precepts of the school, and if that policy is applied equally to its male and female employees, then the school has not discriminated based on pregnancy in violation of Title VII." But, the court noted that there were a number of ways for the teacher to prove that the school discriminated against her on the basis of pregnancy rather than on the basis of its moral and religious tenets. For example, she could show that the school "enforced its premarital sex policy in a discriminatory manner against only pregnant women, or against only women. This is because a school violates Title VII if, due purely to the fact that women can become pregnant and men cannot, it punishes only women for sexual relations because those relations are revealed through pregnancy. In other words, a school cannot use the mere observation or knowledge of pregnan-*

---

[131] Basinger v. Pilarczyk, 2000 WL 331630 (Ohio App. 2000).

[132] McClure v. Salvation Army, 460 F.2d 553 (5th Cir. 1972), *cert. denied*, 409 U.S. 896 (1972).

cy as its sole method of detecting violations of its premarital sex policy." The court also noted that the teacher "adduced evidence that the policy was not applied equally among men and women. School officials acknowledged in their depositions that the teacher's pregnancy alone had signaled them that she engaged in premarital sex, and that the school does not otherwise inquire as to whether male teachers engage in premarital sex. . . . These admissions raise an issue of material fact as to whether [the school] enforces its policy solely by observing the pregnancy of its female teachers, which would constitute a form of pregnancy discrimination."[133]

▶ It is common for church employment handbooks or employment contracts to state that employees will be expected to conform to the church's moral teachings. Some churches spell out with a high degree of specificity the moral teachings employees will be expected to follow. Other churches use vague references to moral or religious teachings. In the latter case, it is a good practice for the handbook or contract to specify that the church board, or some other officer or body, has the sole and final authority to determine the church's moral tenets. This will reduce any chance of confusion as to the meaning of these terms.

Case Studies

• A federal appeals court ruled that a church-operated preschool did not violate federal law when it dismissed an unmarried, pregnant preschool teacher. The school, which was affiliated with the Church of Christ, expects that its teachers will adhere to its religious tenets. All teachers are required to be Christians, and preference is given to those who are Church of Christ members. The school uses as its religious tenets the teachings of the New Testament, including the prohibition against sex outside of marriage. The dismissed worker knew that the school was a church-related school and indicated on her employment application that she had a Christian background and believed in God. The worker insisted that she was never told that she would be terminated if she engaged in sex outside of marriage. However, the school's faculty handbook (given to the worker after she was hired) reads: "Christian character, as well as professional ability, is the basis for hiring teachers at [the school]. Each teacher . . . is expected in all actions to be a Christian example for the students." When school administrators learned that the unmarried worker was pregnant, a decision was made to terminate her employment. However, the woman was informed that she would be eligible for re-employment if she married the father of the child. The school's president claimed that the woman was dismissed not because of pregnancy, but because the facts indicated that she engaged in sex outside of marriage. The woman sued the school, claiming that it committed unlawful sex discrimination when it fired her. The court ruled that the school lawfully dismissed the woman on the basis of her violation of its religious teachings against premarital sex and not because she was pregnant. The court rejected the woman's claim that the school applied its policy against premarital sex in a discriminatory way that was more strict when women were involved. The court observed that "although Title VII requires that [the school's] code of conduct be applied equally to both sexes, [the school] presented uncontroverted evidence . . . that [the administrator] had terminated at least four individuals, both male and female, who had engaged in extramarital sexual relationships

---

[133] Cline v. Catholic Diocese, 206 F.3d 651 (6th Cir. 2000).

that did not result in pregnancy." Further, the court acknowledged that the school's policy occasionally may have been violated because the administrator was unaware of every instance of premarital sex by his staff, but it insisted that "isolated inconsistent application" of the policy "was not sufficient to show that [the school's] articulated nondiscriminatory reason was not the real reason for [the woman's] termination."[134]

• A federal court ruled that a church-affiliated private school could be sued by a former employee who had been dismissed for extramarital sexual relations.[135] The school hired an unmarried woman as a math teacher. When she was hired, the woman signed a statement expressing her agreement with the school's "statement of belief" and agreed that her "lifestyle" would be "in accordance with the will of God and the Holy Scripture." A year later the school learned that the teacher (who was still unmarried) was pregnant. Because sexual activity outside of marriage violated the religious beliefs of the school, the teacher was dismissed. Shortly after being dismissed, the woman sued the school, claiming that the school had discriminated against her on the basis of pregnancy in violation of Title VII of the Civil Rights Act of 1964. She insisted that she was never informed, before her pregnancy, of any school policy against extramarital sexual relations, and she further claimed that she was told "I was terminated due to the fact that I was pregnant and unmarried and therefore a bad role model." The school denied that pregnancy rather than sexual activity was the basis for the teacher's dismissal. It conceded that this was the first case in which it had dismissed an employee for extramarital sex, but it insisted that it would treat male employees no differently if a case arose. The school asked the court to dismiss the lawsuit on the ground that Title VII permits religious employers to discriminate against employees on the basis of religion. The court declined to do so. It acknowledged that "Title VII explicitly provides exceptions for religious entities by allowing them to hire only employees of a given religion" and "permits employment of teachers based on religion if a school is controlled by a particular religion and qualification for employment is a religious requirement." This includes the right to "employ only teachers who adhere to the school's moral code". However, the court cautioned that "these exceptions to Title VII do not sanction gender discrimination" and that "religious codes of morality must be applied equally to male and female teachers." But if religious requirements "are applied equally to both males and females, the court will not evaluate the underlying dogma." The court then drew an important distinction between employment decisions based on pregnancy and those based on sexual activity. A rule that singles out pregnant employees for adverse treatment is not permitted because it is limited to females and therefore is discriminatory by definition. On the other hand, "restrictions on sexual activity, applied equally to males and females, are not discriminatory." The court was unwilling to dismiss the lawsuit because the evidence submitted by the school "does not indicate whether anyone else—male or female—has ever been fired as a teacher by the [school] for sexual intercourse outside of marriage."

Sexual Harassment

§ 8-12.5

Key Point 8-12.5> *Sexual harassment is a form of sex discrimination prohibited by Title VII of the Civil Rights Act of 1964. It consists of both "quid pro*

---

[134] Boyd v. Harding Academy of Memphis, Inc., 88 F.3d 410 (6th Cir. 1996).

[135] Ganzy v. Allen Christian School, 995 F. Supp. 340 (E.D.N.Y. 1998).

quo" harassment and "hostile environment" harassment. Religious organizations that are subject to Title VII are covered by this prohibition. An employer is automatically liable for supervisory employees' acts of harassment, but a defense is available to claims of hostile environment harassment if they have adopted a written harassment policy and an alleged victim fails to pursue remedies available under the policy. In some cases, an employer may be liable for acts of sexual harassment committed by nonsupervisory employees, and even nonemployees.

Sexual harassment is a form of "sex discrimination" prohibited by Title VII of the Civil Rights Act of 1964. Equal Employment Opportunity Commission (EEOC) regulations define sexual harassment as follows:

(a) Harassment on the basis of sex is a violation of Sec. 703 of Title VII. Unwelcome sexual advances, requests for sexual favors, and other verbal or physical conduct of a sexual nature constitute sexual harassment when (1) submission to such conduct is made either explicitly or implicitly a term or condition of an individual's employment, (2) submission to or rejection of such conduct by an individual is used as the basis for employment decisions affecting such individual, or (3) such conduct has the purpose or effect of unreasonably interfering with an individual's work performance or creating an intimidating, hostile, or offensive working environment.

> Sexual harassment addresses unwelcome sexual contact, whether or not that contact is voluntary.

This definition confirms the conclusion reached by numerous state and federal courts that sexual harassment includes *at least two separate types of conduct:*

(1) "quid pro quo" harassment, which refers to conditioning employment opportunities on submission to a sexual or social relationship, and

(2) "hostile environment" harassment, which refers to the creation of an intimidating, hostile, or offensive working environment through unwelcome verbal or physical conduct of a sexual nature.

Key Point > *A woman's "consent" is not a defense to an allegation of sexual harassment. The United States Supreme Court has observed: "The fact that sex-related conduct was voluntary in the sense that the complainant was not forced to participate against her will, is not a defense to a sexual harassment suit . . . . The gravamen of any sexual harassment claim is that the alleged sexual advances were unwelcome . . . . The correct inquiry is whether [the victim] by her conduct indicated that the alleged sexual advances were unwelcome, not whether her actual participation in sexual intercourse was voluntary." In other words, a female employee may engage in voluntary sexual contact with a supervisor because of her belief that her job (or advancement) depends on it. While such contact would be voluntary, it is not necessarily welcome. Sexual harassment addresses unwelcome sexual contact, whether or not that contact is voluntary.*

Key Point > *The United States Supreme Court has observed: "A sexually objectionable environment must be both objectively and subjectively offensive, one that a reasonable person would find hostile and abusive, and one that the victim in fact did perceive to be so. . . . Simple teasing, offhand comments and isolated incidents (unless extremely serious) will not amount to discriminatory changes in the terms and conditions of employment.*"[136]

When is an employer liable for sexual harassment? Consider the following rules:

rule #1 – quid pro quo harassment

If a supervisor conditions employment opportunities on an employee's submission to a sexual or social relationship, and the employee's "compensation, terms, conditions or privileges of employment" are adversely affected because of a refusal to submit, this constitutes quid pro quo sexual harassment for which the employer will be legally responsible. This is true whether or not the employer was aware of the harassment.

rule #2 – harassment committed by nonsupervisory employees

EEOC regulations address employer liability for the sexual harassment of nonsupervisory employees as follows:

> With respect to conduct between fellow employees, an employer is responsible for acts of sexual harassment in the workplace where the employer (or its agents or supervisory employees) knows or should have known of the conduct, unless it can show that it took immediate and appropriate corrective action.

rule #3 – harassment committed by non-employees

EEOC regulations address employer liability for the sexual harassment of non-employees as follows:

> An employer may also be responsible for the acts of non-employees, with respect to sexual harassment of employees in the workplace, where the employer (or its agents or supervisory employees) knows or should have known of the conduct and fails to take immediate and appropriate corrective action. In reviewing these cases the Commission will consider the extent of the employer's control and any other legal responsibility which the employer may have with respect to the conduct of such non-employees.

rule #4 – hostile environment harassment by a supervisor, with a tangible employment decision

If a supervisor creates an intimidating, hostile, or offensive working environment through unwelcome verbal or physical conduct of a sexual nature, this is "hostile environment" sexual harassment for which the employer will be legally responsible if the supervisor takes any "tangible employment action" against the employee. A tangible employment action includes "a significant change in employment status, such as hiring, firing, failing to promote, reassignment with significantly different responsibilities, or a decision causing a significant change

---

[136] Faragher v. City of Boca Raton, 524 U.S. 775 (1998).

in benefits." The employer is liable under such circumstances whether or not it was aware of the harassment.[137]

rule #5 – hostile environment harassment by a supervisor, with no tangible employment decision

If a supervisor creates an intimidating, hostile, or offensive working environment through unwelcome verbal or physical conduct of a sexual nature, this is "hostile environment" sexual harassment for which the employer will be legally responsible even if the supervisor takes no "tangible employment action" against the employee.[138]

rule #6 – the employer's "affirmative defense" to liability for a supervisor's hostile environment sexual harassment not accompanied by a tangible employment decision

If a supervisor engages in hostile environment sexual harassment but takes no "tangible employment decision" against a victim, the employer may assert an "affirmative defense" to liability. This defense consists of two elements:

(i) The employer "exercised reasonable care to prevent and correct promptly any sexually harassing behavior." This generally means that the employer adopted a written sexual harassment policy that was communicated to employees, and that contains a complaint procedure.

(ii) The victim "unreasonably failed to take advantage of any preventive or corrective opportunities provided by the employer or to avoid harm otherwise." This generally means that the victim failed to follow the complaint procedure described in the employer's sexual harassment policy.[139]

It is essential for any church having employees to adopt a sexual harassment policy, since this will serve as a defense to liability for a supervisor's acts of "hostile environment" sexual harassment to the extent that a victim of such harassment does not follow the policy.

Key Point> *A written sexual harassment policy does not insulate a church from all sexual harassment liability. It will not serve as a defense in any of these situations: (1) a "tangible employment decision" has been taken against an employee; (2) incidents of quid pro quo sexual harassment; or (3) a victim of a supervisor's hostile environment sexual harassment pursues his or her remedies under the employer's sexual harassment policy.*

What terms should be included in a sexual harassment policy? Unfortunately, the Supreme Court has not addressed this question directly. However, other courts have. Here is a list of some of the terms that should be incorporated into a written sexual harassment policy:

---

[137] Burlington Industries, Inc. v. Ellerth, 118 S. Ct. 2257 (1998); Faragher v. City of Boca Raton, 118 S. Ct. 2275 (1998).

[138] *Id.*

[139] *Id.*

- Define sexual harassment (both quid pro quo and hostile environment) and state unequivocally that it will not be tolerated and that it will be the basis for immediate discipline (up to and including dismissal).

- Contain a procedure for filing complaints of harassment with the employer.

- Encourage victims to report incidents of harassment.

- Assure employees that complaints will be investigated promptly.

- Assure employees that they will not suffer retaliation for filing a complaint.

- Discuss the discipline applicable to persons who violate the policy.

- Assure the confidentiality of all complaints.

In addition to implementing a written sexual harassment policy, a church should also take the following steps:

- Communicate the written policy to all workers.

- Investigate all complaints immediately. Some courts have commented on the reluctance expressed by some male supervisors in investigating claims of sexual harassment. To illustrate, a federal appeals court observed: "Because women are disproportionately the victims of rape and sexual assault, women have a stronger incentive to be concerned with sexual behavior. Women who are victims of mild forms of sexual harassment may understandably worry whether a harasser's conduct is merely a prelude to violent sexual assault. Men, who are rarely victims of sexual assault, may view sexual conduct in a vacuum without a full appreciation of the social setting or the underlying threat of violence that a woman may perceive."

- Discipline employees who are found guilty of harassment. However, be careful not to administer discipline without adequate proof of harassment. Discipline not involving dismissal should be accompanied by a warning that any future incidents of harassment will not be tolerated and may result in immediate dismissal.

- Follow up by periodically asking the victim if there have been any further incidents of harassment.

Key Point > *EEOC guidelines contain the following language: "Prevention is the best tool for the elimination of sexual harassment. An employer should take all steps necessary to prevent sexual harassment from occurring, such as affirmatively raising the subject, expressing strong disapproval, developing appropriate sanctions, informing employees of their right to raise and how to raise the issue of harassment under Title VII, and developing methods to sensitize all concerned."*

Key Point > *Most states have enacted their own civil rights laws that bar sexual harassment in employment, and it is far more likely that these laws will apply to churches since there is no "commerce" requirement and often fewer than 15 employees are needed to be covered by the law.*

The assistance of an attorney is vital in the drafting of a sexual harassment policy.

 Church insurance policies generally do not cover employment-related claims, including sexual harassment. If your church is sued for sexual harassment, you probably will need to retain and pay for your own attorney, and pay any judgment or settlement amount. This often comes as a shock to church leaders. You should immediately review your policy with your insurance agent to see if you have any coverage for such claims. If you do not, ask how it can be obtained. You may be able to obtain an endorsement for "employment practices." Also, a "directors and officers" policy may cover these claims.

The following case studies will illustrate the application of Title VII's ban on sexual harassment to religious organizations.

Case Studies

• *A church has four employees. A female employee believes that she has been subjected to sexual harassment, and threatens to contact the EEOC. Sexual harassment is a form of sex discrimination that is prohibited in employment by Title VII of the Civil Rights Act of 1964. This law applies only to those employers having at least 15 employees and that are engaged in commerce. Since the church in this example has fewer than 15 employees, it is not subject to Title VII, and therefore the EEOC (which has jurisdiction over Title VII claims) will not be able to process the employee's complaint.*

• *Assume that a church is covered by Title VII. A female bookkeeper claims that a male custodian has been sexually harassing her by creating a "hostile environment." She does not discuss the custodian's behavior with the senior pastor or church board. She later threatens to file a complaint with the EEOC, charging the church with responsibility for the custodian's behavior. Since the harassment was not committed by a supervisor having the authority to affect the bookkeeper's terms and conditions of employment, EEOC guidelines addressing employer liability for sexual harassment specify: "With respect to conduct between fellow employees, an employer is responsible for acts of sexual harassment in the workplace where the employer (or its agents or supervisory employees) knows or should have known of the conduct, unless it can show that it took immediate and appropriate corrective action." If the pastor and church board were not aware of the custodian's offensive behavior, then according to this regulation the church will not be legally responsible for it.*

• *Same facts as the previous case study, except that the bookkeeper complained on two occasions to the senior pastor about the custodian's behavior. The pastor delayed acting because he did not believe the matter was serious. According to the EEOC regulations quoted in the previous case study, it is likely that the church is liable for the custodian's behavior since the pastor was aware of the offensive behavior but failed to take "immediate and appropriate corrective action."*

• *Same facts as the previous case study, except that the pastor immediately informed the church board. The board conducted an investigation, determined the charges to be true on the basis of the testimony of other employees, and warned the custodian that one more* complaint of harassing behavior would result in his dismissal. This action was based on the bookkeeper's own recommendation. It is doubtful that the church will be liable for sexual harassment under these circumstances, since it took "immediate and appropriate corrective action."

• A church is subject to Title VII. A female secretary claims that she was harassed by a man who frequently was on church premises maintaining duplicating equipment. An EEOC regulation specifies that "[a]n employer may also be responsible for the acts of non-employees, with respect to sexual harassment of employees in the workplace, where the employer (or its agents or supervisory employees) knows or should have known of the conduct and fails to take immediate and appropriate corrective action. In reviewing these cases the Commission will consider the extent of the employer's control and any other legal responsibility which the employer may have with respect to the conduct of such non-employees."

• A church is subject to Title VII. A male supervisory employee informs a female employee that her continuing employment depends on engaging in sexual relations with him. This is an example of quid pro quo sexual harassment. The church is liable for such harassment by a supervisor whether or not it was aware of it. The fact that it had a written sexual harassment policy that prohibited such behavior will not relieve it from liability.

• A church is subject to Title VII. A male employee (with no supervisory authority) repeatedly asks another employee to go to dinner with him. This is not quid pro quo sexual harassment because the offending employee has no authority to affect the terms or conditions of the other employee's work if she refuses to accept his invitations. If the offending employee's behavior becomes sufficiently "severe and pervasive," it may become hostile environment sexual harassment. However, the church generally is not liable for hostile environment sexual harassment by a non-supervisory employee unless it was aware of it and failed to take "immediate and appropriate corrective action."

• A church is subject to Title VII. It adopts a written sexual harassment policy that defines harassment, encourages employees to report harassing behavior, and assures employees that they will not suffer retaliation for reporting harassment. A male supervisory employee engages in frequent offensive remarks and physical contact of a sexual nature with a female employee. The female employee is greatly disturbed by this behavior, and considers it inappropriate in a church. In fact, she had sought church employment because she considered it a safe environment and her job would be a ministry. The supervisor eventually dismisses the employee because of her refusal to "go along" with his offensive behavior. Throughout her employment, the employee never informed church leadership of the supervisor's behavior. Several months after her termination, the employee files a sexual harassment complaint with the EEOC. Will the church be liable for the supervisor's behavior under these circumstances? After all, it was not aware of the supervisor's behavior, and it adopted a written sexual harassment policy. The supervisor's behavior constituted "hostile environment" sexual harassment for which the church will be liable. The fact that the church leadership was unaware of his offensive behavior is not relevant. Further, the church's sexual harassment policy is no defense, since the employee suffered a "tangible employment decision" (dismissal) as a result of her refusal to go along with the supervisor's behavior.

• *Same facts as the previous case study, except that the employee was not dismissed and suffered no "tangible employment decision" (firing, failing to promote, reassignment with significantly different responsibilities, or a decision causing a significant change in benefits). The general rule is that an employer is liable for a supervisor's "hostile environment" sexual harassment that does not result in a tangible employment decision against the victim. However, the employer has an "affirmative defense" to liability if (1) it adopted a sexual harassment policy that was adequately communicated to employees, and (2) the victim failed to pursue her remedies under the policy. The church in this case qualifies for the affirmative defense. It adopted a sexual harassment policy, and the victim failed to follow the policy's complaint procedure. As a result, the church probably would not be liable for the supervisor's behavior.*

• *Same facts as the previous case study, except that the church is not subject to Title VII (it only has five employees). The church still may be liable under a state civil rights law, or under other legal theories (such as "intentional infliction of emotional distress," negligent selection or supervision, assault and battery, invasion of privacy, or false imprisonment).*

• *A church is subject to Title VII. It has not adopted a written sexual harassment policy. A female employee files a complaint with the EEOC, claiming that a supervisor has engaged in hostile environment sexual harassment. She never informed church leadership of the supervisor's behavior before filing her complaint with the EEOC. The church will be responsible for the supervisor's behavior under these circumstances. It does not qualify for the "affirmative defense" because it failed to implement a sexual harassment policy.*

• *Same facts as the previous case study, except that the church had adopted a written sexual harassment policy that was communicated to all employees. The church will have an "affirmative defense" to liability under these circumstances, because it adopted a sexual harassment policy and the victim failed to follow it by filing a complaint. These two examples demonstrate the importance of implementing a sexual harassment policy. Such a policy can insulate a church from liability for a supervisor's hostile environment sexual harassment—if no "tangible employment decision" was taken against the victim, and the victim failed to pursue his or her remedies under the policy.*

• *An associate pastor engaged in sexual relations with two female employees in the course of a counseling relationship. The women later informed the senior pastor. As a result, the two women were dismissed, and the associate pastor was forced to resign. The women later sued the church on the basis of several legal theories, including sexual harassment. A trial court threw out the sexual harassment claim, and the women appealed. A federal appeals court concluded that the church was not guilty of "hostile environment" sexual harassment. It noted that in order for the two women to establish "hostile environment" sexual harassment they needed to "produce evidence showing, among other things, that [the church] knew or should have known of the harassment in question and failed to take prompt remedial action." However, since it was established that the church "took prompt remedial action upon learning of [the minister's] misconduct," the two women had to prove that the church should have known of the minister's behavior before it was disclosed. The court concluded that the women failed to do so. The women claimed that the former minister had offended a few other women by complimenting them on their appearances and hugging them. This evidence, even if true, was not enough to demonstrate that the church "knew or should have known" of a "hos-*

tile environment." The court also rejected the women's claim that the church had engaged in "quid pro quo" sexual harassment. It noted that for the women to establish quid pro quo sexual harassment, they "were required to produce evidence showing, among other things, that the harassment complained of affected tangible aspects of their compensation, terms, conditions, or privileges of employment. In addition, they were required to develop evidence demonstrating that their acceptance or rejection of the harassment was an express or implied condition to the receipt of a job benefit or the cause of a tangible job detriment. [But the women's] own testimony that they were subjected to mild criticism of their work and told that they would not be promoted to positions they knew did not exist indicates that their jobs were not tangibly and detrimentally affected by their decisions to end their sexual relationships with [the minister] . . . . Further, there is no objective evidence in the record supporting the [women's] claims that they engaged in sex with [the minister] under an implied threat of discharge if they did not." [140]

• A federal appeals court ruled that a church-operated school was guilty of sexual harassment as a result of its failure to address its principal's offensive behavior with several female employees. A denominational agency operated a residential school for emotionally and physically impaired children. Over the course of several years, the principal of the school was accused on many occasions of sexual harassment by female employees. There was substantial evidence that school officials were aware of many of these complaints. School officials launched an investigation into the sexual harassment charges. They found that there was a significant basis to the harassment complaints. The school suspended the principal for five days without pay, ordered him to submit to a psychological assessment, and placed him on three months' probation. It also invited an outside consultant to conduct several days of seminars on sexual harassment. Even after this corrective action, there were several instances of inappropriate behavior involving the principal. During this same year, the principal was given a satisfactory performance evaluation and a raise. Several female employees who had been harassed by the principal sued the denominational agency on the ground that it was legally responsible for the principal's acts because of its failure to respond adequately to the accusations against him. A trial court ruled in favor of the women, and awarded them $300,000 in damages. A federal appeals court upheld this ruling. It referred to the "long-term, ostrich-like failure" by denominational and school officials to "deal forthrightly with [the principal's] treatment of female employees." The court observed that "the jury was entitled to conclude that [the agency] not only looked the other way for many years but that its corrective action was woefully inadequate, as demonstrated by [the principal's] later conduct." This case illustrates the importance of dealing promptly with complaints of sexual harassment. Letting years pass without addressing complaints of harassment will only increase significantly a church's risk of liability. After several years of complaints, the agency finally suspended the principal for five days, ordered a psychological assessment, imposed a three-month probationary period, and invited consultants to conduct sexual harassment training. These acts may seem thorough and adequate, but the court concluded that they were not sufficient to avoid liability for sexual harassment, because (1) the complaints against the principal had occurred over so many years; (2) the principal's acts of harassment were so pervasive; (3) the agency waited years before acting; (4) the

> "Letting years pass without addressing complaints of harassment will only increase significantly a church's risk of liability."

[140] Sanders v. Casa View Baptist Church, 134 F.3d 331 (5th Cir. 1998).

154

agency's response was insufficient, since the principal continued to engage in harassment even after he was disciplined; and (5) the principal received a satisfactory employee evaluation and a raise during the same year that he was disciplined for harassment.[141]

• *A federal appeals court ruled that in some cases ministers can pursue sexual harassment claims against an employing church without violating the First Amendment. A woman served as associate pastor of a church for one year. Shortly after assuming this position, she claimed that the church's senior pastor began sexually harassing her and creating a hostile work environment. She made a formal complaint of sexual harassment to the church, which she claimed took no action. She also claimed that the senior pastor retaliated against her by relieving her of certain duties, verbally abusing her and otherwise engaging in intimidating behavior. Again, the church, which knew or should have known of the senior pastor's behavior, failed to act. She sued her church in federal court, claiming that the church violated Title VII of the Civil Rights Act of 1964 which bars covered employers from engaging in sexual harassment or "retaliation" against employees. The court dismissed the lawsuit, concluding that any resolution of the plaintiff's claims would interfere with the church's constitutionally protected right to choose its ministers. The plaintiff appealed. A federal appeals court agreed that to the extent that the plaintiff's claims involved "an inquiry into the church's decision to terminate her ministry, those claims cannot proceed in civil court and were properly dismissed." However, the court concluded that she could, consistent with the First Amendment, "attempt to show that she was sexually harassed and that this harassment created a hostile work environment" since this would involve "a purely secular inquiry." The court noted that there are two ways for an employer to be liable for "hostile environment" sexual harassment: (1) An employer is liable for a hostile environment that "culminates in a tangible employment action." The court concluded that the ministerial exception prohibited it from assigning liability on this basis since it would directly implicate the church's practices regarding the employment of clergy. (2) When no tangible employment action has been taken, an employer is nevertheless liable for hostile environment sexual harassment unless it can establish an "affirmative defense" by showing that it exercised reasonable care to prevent and promptly correct any sexually harassing behavior, and the plaintiff unreasonably failed to take advantage of any preventive or corrective opportunities provided by the employer. An employer's adoption of a sexual harassment policy helps to demonstrate that an employer used reasonable care to prevent harassment, and, an employee's failure to use a complaint procedure provided by the employer will normally preclude the employee from pursing a sexual harassment claim. The court concluded that neither the First Amendment nor the ministerial exception barred the civil courts from resolving hostile environment sexual harassment lawsuits against churches based on this second form of liability. In other words, a church can be found liable for hostile environment sexual harassment unless it can establish an affirmative defense by having adopted a sexual harassment policy and complaint procedure which an employee chose not to follow.[142]*

• *A federal court in California ruled that a female minister failed to prove that her denomination engaged in sexual harassment. The woman, an ordained Buddhist minister, was employed as national director of a department of a denominational agency (the Buddhist Churches of America or BCA). While attending an annual meeting of Buddhist*

---

[141] Jonasson v. Lutheran Child and Family Services, 115 F.3d 436 (7th Cir. 1997).

[142] Elvig v. Calvin Presbyterian Church, 375 F.3d 951 (9th Cir. 2004).

ministers at a hotel in California, she received a sexually offensive anonymous telephone call. BCA officials conducted an investigation, and determined that a male Buddhist minister attending the same conference was the likely caller. The woman later sued the BCA, claiming that she had been a victim of sexual harassment. She claimed that BCA engaged in quid pro quo harassment by "the defunding of her department because of her refusal to quietly allow [the accused minister] to talk dirty to her." She claimed that her employment was conditional upon allowing this "sexual favor." The court rejected the woman's claim of sexual harassment, noting that she could not have suffered quid pro quo harassment because the accused minister did not hold any position giving him the power to affect the terms of her employment with BCA. Even if the accused minister held such a position, the contents of the harassing telephone call made at the hotel could not be construed as conditioning job benefits upon the woman's submission to the minister's sexual demands. The court also rejected the woman's claim that BCA was guilty of "hostile environment" sexual harassment. It noted that the telephone call she received while attending the conference "was not physically threatening or humiliating. It was not repeated at plaintiff's place of employment and was not accompanied by any other sexual conduct in the workplace. Moreover, the alleged co-employee who made the phone call was not a person who plaintiff was forced to work with on a daily basis . . . . This single isolated incident does not rise to the level of seriousness required to establish an abusive working environment." Further, the woman's claim that BCA did not quickly and thoroughly investigate her complaint did not by itself prove a hostile environment: "[A]n employer's lack of remedial action is not itself evidence of the hostile work environment. A hostile environment claim requires wrongful verbal or physical conduct of a sexual nature. Thus, although the action or inaction of an employer in response to an allegation of sexual harassment may be probative on the issue of the employer's liability, this evidence is relevant only if the plaintiff first establishes that that incident created a hostile work environment."[143]

• A Florida court ruled that it was barred by the First Amendment's ban on excessive entanglement between church and state from resolving a church secretary's claim of sexual harassment. A woman was employed as a church secretary and bookkeeper. She sued her church and a denominational agency alleging that a church volunteer who served as chairman of the pastor parish relations committee had sexually harassed her on the job. A state appeals court dismissed Anne's lawsuit on the ground that her claims, "which are based upon the actions of a volunteer rather than another employee, will require a secular court to review and interpret church law, policies, and practices to determine whether an agency relationship existed" between the alleged offender, the committee, the church, and denominational agency, and whether the church defendants could be held liable for the alleged offender's actions. The court concluded that "this examination would violate the First Amendment's excessive entanglement doctrine."[144]

• A federal court in Kansas ruled that a church could be liable for a staff member's repeated acts of sexual harassment. An ordained female pastor accepted a position with a church. Her duties required continuous contact with the church's director of music. She claimed that over the course of several years the director of music subjected her to sexually inappropriate behavior which was rude, offensive, oppressive, humiliating, degrading, embarrassing, annoying and emotionally upsetting. Such conduct included (1) embracing her in an extremely hard, suggestive and sexual manner; (2) making com-

---

[143] Himaka v. Buddhist Churches of America, 917 F.Supp. 698 (N.D. Cal. 1995).

[144] Carnesi v. Ferry Pass United Methodist Church, 770 So.2d 1286 (Fla. App. 2000).

ments about the drug Viagra; (3) telling her that he liked it when she wore short skirts; (4) making explicit gestures and comments; and (5) touching her breasts, buttocks and other personally sensitive areas. The church dismissed the pastor despite her satisfactory job performance. She sued the church in federal court for sexual harassment (a form of sex discrimination prohibited by Title VII of the Civil Rights Act of 1964), and an intentional failure to supervise. The court ruled that the church could be liable for the music director's acts on the basis of an intentional failure to supervise since it had the ability to control him and "knew or should have known of the necessity and opportunity for exercising such control." The court added that a church also can be liable for a negligent failure to supervise, where its failure is due to carelessness or inadvertence.[145]

• A woman was hired as an associate pastor of a church in Minnesota. A year later, she filed a discrimination charge with the state department of human rights against her supervising pastor. She claimed that her supervising pastor repeatedly made unwelcome sexual advances toward her. He allegedly referred to themselves as "lovers," physically contacted her in a sexual manner, and insisted on her companionship outside the work place despite her objections. The woman informed her local church leaders as well as her synod before filing the complaint with the state. Although the church and synod investigated the woman's allegations, no action was taken to stop the alleged harassment. Less than three months after the complaint was filed with the state, the church held a congregational meeting at which it voted to dismiss the woman as pastor. The reason stated for the discharge was the woman's "inability to conduct the pastoral office efficiently in this congregation in view of local conditions." A state appeals court ruled that the woman could sue her former supervising pastor for sexual harassment. The court also rejected the supervising pastor's claim that the woman was prevented from suing because she had "consented" to the supervising pastor's conduct.[146]

• A New York court ruled that a charity was liable for an executive officer's acts of sexual harassment.[147] A male executive director of the charity engaged in repeated acts of sexual harassment against female employees. The director was the charity's highest ranking employee. The harassment included inappropriate and demeaning communications, unwelcome sexual overtures, unwanted physical contact, and threats to fire the women (or make their jobs more unpleasant) if they did not submit to his advances. The director repeatedly begged each woman to be his "girlfriend" or "mistress," and to marry him or sleep with him. He frequently demanded that the women attend nonwork-related lunches with him. A personnel committee was apprised of these actions, and it conducted an investigation which came to the attention of the governing board. As a result of the investigation, the director was placed on a brief leave of absence. The women later sued the director for sexual harassment. They also sued the charity and each member of the governing board. The court concluded that the charity was liable for the director's acts of harassment. The court ruled that the director's acts constituted both quid pro quo and hostile environment sexual harassment, and it found the charity liable for those acts. The court noted that under federal law an employer is "strictly liable" for quid pro quo harassment, since the harasser has the authority to alter the terms or conditions of the victims' employment based on their response to his advances. Therefore, the charity was liable for the director's quid pro quo harassment. On the other hand, under federal law employers are strictly liable for a hostile work environment created by a victim's

---

[145] Dolquist v. Heartland Presbytery, 2004 WL 74318 (D. Kansas 2004).

[146] Black v. Snyder, 471 N.W.2d 715 (Minn. App. 1991).

[147] Father Belle v. State Division of Human Rights, 642 N.Y.S.2d 739 (A.D. 1996).

supervisor, but not by coworkers lacking supervisory authority. Since the director was the highest ranking supervisory employee, the charity was strictly liable for hostile environment harassment caused to his actions.

• *A federal court in North Carolina ruled that the First Amendment did not prevent it from resolving a sexual harassment claim brought by two nonminister church employees against their church. A church's receptionist and the pastor's secretary (both of whom were female) claimed that the pastor had sexually harassed them, and they sued the church and a denominational agency for damages. They claimed that the church defendants were responsible for the pastor's repeated acts of hostile environment sexual harassment since he was a supervisory employee. In particular, the women alleged that the defendants failed to take timely and appropriate action to correct the problem. The court noted that the women were "secular, lay employees who performed nonreligious, administrative tasks for a religious institution," and that a resolution of their sexual harassment claim would not violate the First Amendment. It further noted that "an employer's liability for its employee's sexual harassment of another individual may be premised on the employer's own negligence. An employer is negligent with respect to sexual harassment if it knew or should have known about the conduct but failed to stop it." The court concluded that it could decide whether or not the church and denomination "took some action that was reasonably calculated to put an end to the abusive environment" without any inquiry into religious doctrine.*[148]

• *A North Carolina appeals court ruled that the First Amendment did not prevent it from resolving a sexual harassment lawsuit brought by three female church employees against their church and denominational agencies. Three female church employees (the "plaintiffs") sued their Methodist church and various Methodist agencies as a result of the sexual misconduct of a pastor. The lawsuit alleged that the pastor "committed inappropriate, unwelcome, offensive and nonconsensual acts of a sexual nature against the plaintiffs, variously hugging, kissing and touching them, and made inappropriate, unwelcome, offensive and nonconsensual statements of a sexually suggestive nature to them." The plaintiffs further alleged that the pastor's actions amounted to sexual harassment and assault and battery, causing them emotional distress, embarrassment, humiliation, and damage to their reputations and career potential. The lawsuit alleged that the local church and Methodist agencies "knew or should have known" of the pastor's propensity for sexual harassment as well as assault and battery upon female employees and that they failed to take any actions to warn or protect the plaintiffs from his wrongful activity. A state appeals court concluded that if a resolution of the plaintiffs' legal claims did not require the interpretation of church doctrine, then "the First Amendment is not implicated and neutral principles of law are properly applied to adjudicate the claim."*[149]

• *An Ohio court ruled that an Episcopalian minister and his employing church could be sued for the minister's alleged acts of sexual harassment. A woman served some ten years as parish secretary of an Episcopal church prior to the arrival of a new minister. Soon after the arrival of the new minister, the secretary began alleging that the minister was engaging in acts of sexual harassment against her. Initially, the secretary contacted the bishop of the diocese with her complaint. He promised to make an investigation and apparently did, but concluded that, although he believed she was sincere in her allegations, there was nothing that he could do because the minister denied any wrongdoing. The bishop did order the work hours of the minister and secretary to be so staggered that they would*

---

[148] Smith v. Raleigh District of the North Carolina Conference of the United Methodist Church, 63 F.Supp.2d 694 (E.D.N.C. 1999).

[149] Smith v. Privette, 495 S.E.2d 395 (N.C. App. 1998).

not be working at the same time. After hearing that the bishop would take no further action, the woman wrote to the minister in question, the standing committee of the diocese, the vestry, the warden, and the bishop in an attempt to resolve what she called "this terrible problem." Upon receipt of this letter, the minister called the chancellor of the diocese, who advised him to fire the secretary. The minister thereafter was instructed by the vestry of the church to notify the congregation that the secretary had been fired and to give a reason. Accordingly, the minister published in the parish newsletter a statement that the secretary had been engaging in an open malicious endeavor to discredit him. Following her dismissal, the former secretary filed a lawsuit against the minister, her church, and the diocese. She based her lawsuit on a number of grounds, including sexual harassment. The appeals court ruled that the woman's claims were credible. It rejected the claim that the church could not be responsible for the minister's alleged actions since they were not performed within the "scope of his employment." It noted that "it is quite clear that the alleged sexual harassment did occur within the scope of [the minister's] employment with [the church]. He was the supervisor of [the secretary], and most of the alleged sexual harassment took place during working hours at the work place."[150]

• A federal court in Oklahoma ruled that a church was not liable on the basis of sexual harassment for the conduct of a minister. A woman was employed by a denominational office as an administrative assistant. Her supervisor was one of the regional church's officers. She sued the denomination for sexual harassment based on the following alleged acts of her supervisor: (1) The supervisor offered to boost her husband's compensation if she would "cooperate" with him, which she interpreted to mean a sexual relationship. Her husband was a pastor of a local church affiliated with the regional church. (2) She alleged that the supervisor blocked her path by standing in a doorway, and began rubbing her shoulders while saying that "I'm sorry it has to be this way." (3) The supervisor continued to sexually harass her for the next few months by brushing against her as he took things from her or handed them to her. The supervisor terminated her, and she sued the supervisor and denomination for sexual harassment. The court noted that for the denomination to be liable for the supervisor's hostile environment sexual harassment the plaintiff had to show that "the workplace was permeated with discriminatory intimidation, ridicule and insult, that was sufficiently severe or pervasive to alter the conditions of her employment and create an abusive working environment." The court concluded that the plaintiff failed to show that the conduct of her supervisor was "so extreme as to change the terms and conditions of her employment." It concluded, "While no woman should be made to feel uncomfortable in the workplace by virtue of a male supervisor leaning into her and brushing against her, because she can point to only two incidents, her work environment cannot be perceived as being pervaded by hostility toward women. Consequently, there is insufficient evidence to support a hostile work environment claim." The plaintiff also claimed that her supervisor's invitation to prevent financial harm to her family in exchange for sexual favors amounted to quid pro quo harassment. Once again, the court disagreed, noting that Title VII makes it unlawful for a covered employer to discriminate on the basis of sex against any individual with respect to his [or her] compensation, terms, conditions, or privileges of employment." The court concluded that "the plain text of Title VII requires that the person whose employment conditions are adversely affected also be the person who is discriminated against on the basis of sex."[151]

---

[150] Davis v. Black, N.E.2d, 70 Ohio App. 3d 359 (Ohio App. 1991).

[151] Bolin v. Oklahoma Conference, 397 F.Supp.2d 1293 (D. Okla. 2005).

• *A South Carolina court ruled that a denominational agency and one of its officials were not liable for a pastor's acts of sexual harassment. Three female church members claimed that their pastor sexually harassed and abused them over a period of several months. The pastor resigned from his denomination before it could review the charges of sexual harassment. The denomination accepted the resignation as a "withdrawal under complaint or charges," and discontinued its investigation into the women's charges. It later spent $4,000 for training pastors in handling sex abuse allegations and for sending the three women to a "survivors of clergy sexual abuse" retreat. The women later sued the denomination and one of its officers, claiming that they were responsible for the pastor's sexual harassment. The women asserted that the denomination "had a duty to prevent the sexual harassment of its parishioners by a member of the clergy and to help in healing afterward rather than being indifferent." They insisted that the denomination should be found guilty of negligence for violating this standard. The court disagreed, noting that the women "have cited no precedent and we are aware of none that stands for the proposition a church owes its parishioners a duty of care regarding its handling of their complaints." The court also rejected the women's claim that the denomination was liable for the pastor's harassment on the basis of a breach of a fiduciary duty. First, it concluded that no fiduciary relationship existed between the women and the denomination. It noted that the women had no contact with the denomination other than a single meeting with one official. Further, the women's personal expectation that the denomination would "take action" on their complaints did not create a fiduciary relationship: "The steps taken unilaterally by the [women] do not constitute an attempt on their part to establish the relationship alleged, and there is no evidence that [the denomination] accepted or induced any special, fiduciary bond with any of [the women] under these facts in any event." Even if a fiduciary relationship did exist, it was not violated since "there is no evidence of a breach of that duty. There is no evidence that [denomination] acted other than in good faith and with due regard to [the women's] interests."*[152]

• *A federal court in Washington ruled that the ministerial exception prevented it from resolving several claims brought by a seminary student against a religious organization, including sexual harassment. The student was assigned to a church in Washington to assist the officiating priest. The victim claimed that he was sexually harassed on numerous occasions by the priest. The student complained of this behavior to the archdiocese, which resulted in an investigation and transfer of the student to another parish. The victim claimed that the archdiocese took additional adverse actions against him on account of his accusations, and as a result he sued the archdiocese in federal court. The lawsuit asserted several grounds for relief, including sexual harassment. The court cautioned that the ministerial exception "does not foreclose all employment claims against a religious employer, but simply limits them." When a sexual harassment claim is made against a religious employer, a court may only consider the following three questions: (1) Was the victim subjected to a hostile work environment? (2) If so, did he exercise reasonable care to correct that environment? (3) Did he unreasonably fail to avail himself of those measures?*[153]

---

[152] Brown v. Pearson, 483 S.E.2d 477 (S.C. App. 1997).

[153] Alcazar v. Corporation of Catholic Archbishop of Seattle, 2006 WL 3791370 (W.D. Wash. 2006).

The Catholic Bishop Case   § 8-12.6

Key Point 8-12.6> *In the Catholic Bishop case the United States Supreme Court ruled that the National Labor Relations Act did not apply to church-affiliated schools. The court applied the following test, known as the Catholic Bishop test: First, determine if the application of the NLRA to a religious organization would give rise to serious constitutional questions under the First Amendment. Second, if a serious constitutional question would arise, then the NLRA cannot be applied without a showing of an "affirmative intention of the Congress clearly expressed" that it does apply. Third, if serious constitutional questions would not arise, then no inquiry is necessary as to whether Congress clearly expressed an intention for the law to apply. This test has been applied by some courts in assessing the applicability of other federal employment laws to churches.*

In a 1979 case the United States Supreme Court was faced with the issue of whether lay teachers in church-operated schools were under the jurisdiction of the National Labor Relations Board. The Court found that neither the language nor the legislative history of the National Labor Relations Act disclosed "an affirmative intention . . . clearly expressed" that the NLRB have such jurisdiction. Therefore, the Court declined to construe the Act in a manner that would require the resolution of "difficult and sensitive questions arising out of the guarantees of the First Amendment Religion Clauses."[154]

The Court's test for determining the validity of an exercise of jurisdiction by the NLRB over a religious organization may be summarized as follows:

Step #1. Determine if the exercise of jurisdiction by the NLRB over a religious organization would give rise to serious constitutional questions under the First Amendment (which guarantees the free exercise of religion).

Step #2. If a serious constitutional question would arise, then the NLRB may not exercise jurisdiction over the religious organization without a showing of an "affirmative intention of the Congress clearly expressed" to confer such jurisdiction.

Step #3. If serious constitutional questions would not arise from an exercise of jurisdiction by the NLRB over a religious organization, then no inquiry is necessary as to whether Congress clearly expressed an intention to confer jurisdiction.[155]

---

[154] NLRB v. Catholic Bishop of Chicago, 440 U.S. 490, 507 (1979). *See also* NLRB v. Bishop Ford Catholic High School, 623 F. 2d 818 (2nd Cir. 1980), *cert. denied*, 450 U.S. 996 (1980).

[155] In Dole v. Shenandoah Baptist Church, 899 F.2d 1389 (4th Cir. 1990), a federal appeals court suggested that the Supreme Court may have altered the *Catholic Bishop* test in a 1985 decision. In 1985, the Supreme Court ruled that "because we perceive no 'significant risk' of an infringement on First Amendment rights, we do not require any clearer expression of congressional intent to regulate these activities." Tony & Susan Alamo Foundation v. Secretary of Labor, 471 U.S. 290, 298 n.18 (1985). The federal appeals court observed that the Supreme Court may have intended to replace the *Catholic Bishop* test. If so, this objective is not clear, and has not been clarified in later decisions.

A few courts have applied the Catholic Bishop case in deciding if federal employment laws can be applied to religious organizations without violating the First Amendment.

Case Study

• A federal court in Delaware ruled that a church-operated school that fired a teacher for publicly advocating abortion rights could not be sued for violating a federal nondiscrimination law. The former teacher sued the school and supervising church, claiming that it was unlawful under Title VII of the Civil Rights Act of 1964 (which bans sex discrimination in employment) for the school to terminate an employee who advocated abortion rights. The court applied the Catholic Bishop test in evaluating the teacher's Title VII claim. The court concluded that the Title VII claim raised substantial constitutional questions, and that Congress had not "clearly expressed an intent that Title VII be applied" in a case like this.[156]

Failure to Accommodate Employees' Religious Practices

§ 8-12.7

Key Point 8-12.7> *Title VII of the Civil Rights Act of 1964 prohibits covered employers from discriminating against any employee on account of the employee's religion. Employers are required to "reasonably accommodate" employees' religious practices, so long as they can do so without undue hardship on the conduct of their business. Many state civil rights laws have a similar provision.*

Title VII of the Civil Rights Act of 1964 makes it unlawful for a covered employer to "discharge any individual, or otherwise to discriminate against any individual with respect to his compensation, terms, conditions, or privileges of employment, because of such individual's . . . religion." Religion is defined to include only those "aspects of religious observance and practice" that an employer is able to "reasonably accommodate . . . without undue hardship on the conduct of the employer's business." The intent and effect of this definition of "religion" is to make it a violation of Title VII for an employer *not* to make reasonable accommodations, short of undue hardship, for the religious practice of employees.

Courts have implemented a two-step procedure for evaluating claims and allocating burdens of proof under these provisions. First, plaintiff has the burden of establishing a "prima facie case." A plaintiff establishes a prima facie case of religious discrimination by proving that (1) he or she has a bona fide religious belief that conflicts with an employment requirement; (2) he or she informed the employer of this belief; and (3) he or she was disciplined for failure to comply with the conflicting employment requirement. Second, if a plaintiff has proven a

---

[156] Curay-Cramer v. Ursuline Academy, 344 F.Supp.2d 923 (D. Dela. 2004).

prima facie case, the burden shifts to the employer to show that it was unable reasonably to accommodate the plaintiff's religious needs without undue hardship.

Several courts have ordered employers to make "reasonable accommodations" of the religious needs of employees whose religious beliefs prevented them from working on certain days of the week. Most courts have required employers to attempt scheduling adjustments or reassignments prior to dismissing such employees.[157] If rescheduling, reassignments, or other accommodations would impose undue hardship on the employer, then accommodation of employees' religious practices is not required.[158]

Case Studies

• A county government employed a conservative Christian as director of its data processing department. The director was dismissed because of overtly religious practices, including: (1) his secretary typed Bible study notes for him; (2) he allowed employees to recite prayers in his office prior to the start of the workday and during departmental meetings; and (3) affirming his Christian faith during department meetings. The director sued the county claiming that his dismissal amounted to religious discrimination in violation of Title VII of the Civil Rights Act of 1964. A federal appeals court agreed in part with the director. It noted that Title VII prohibits covered employers from dismissing an employee on account of religion "unless an employer demonstrates that it is unable to reasonably accommodate an employee's religious observance or practice without undue hardship on the conduct of [its] business." The court noted that the county had made no attempt to accommodate the director's religious practices, and therefore it could defend against the charge of religious discrimination only by demonstrating that it would have suffered "undue hardship" had it not dismissed the director. The court cautioned that "undue hardship" must be real rather than speculative, and that it requires more than "some fellow worker's grumbling." An employer must demonstrate "actual imposition on coworkers or disruption of the work routine." The court agreed with the county that allowing the director to have his secretary type Bible study notes would impose an undue hardship on the county, and therefore a dismissal based on this conduct would not violate Title VII. The court reached the same conclusion with regard to the prayer meetings conducted in the director's office prior to the start of the workday. It noted that "nothing in Title VII requires that an employer open its premises for use before the start of the workday." However, the court disagreed that the county would have suffered "undue hardship" by allowing the director to utter occasional and spontaneous prayers during departmental meetings or to make occasional affirmations of religious faith. The court concluded that such expressions were "inconsequential . . . especially since they were apparently spontaneous and infrequent" and no employee complained about them. They did not result in "actual impo-

---

157 *See, e.g.,* Tincher v. WalMart Stores, Inc., 118 F.3d 1125 (7th Cir. 1997) (employer found liable); Heller v. EBB Auto Co., 8 F.3d 1433 (9th Cir. 1993) (employer found liable); Shpargel v. Stage & Co., 914 F.Supp. 1468 (E.D. Mich. 1996) (employer found liable); E.E.O.C. v. Arlington Transit Mix Inc., 734 F.Supp. 804 (E.D. Mich. 1990), *rev'd on other grounds,* 957 F.2d 219 (employer found liable); Riley v. Bendix Corp., 464 F.2d 1113 (5th Cir. 1972) (employer found liable); Jackson v. Veri Fresh Poultry, Inc., 304 F. Supp. 1276 (D. La. 1972) (employer found liable); Shaffield v. Northrop Worldwide Aircraft Services, Inc., 373 F. Supp. 937 (D. Ala. 1973) (employer found liable); Claybaugh v. Pacific Northwestern Bell Telephone Company, 355 F. Supp. 1 (D. Ore. 1973) (employer found liable).

158 *See, e.g.,* Hardison v. Trans World Airlines, 527 F.2d 22 (8th Cir. 1976) (employer proved undue hardship); Reid v. Memphis Publishing Company, 521 F.2d 512 (6th Cir. 1975) (employer proved undue hardship); Dixon v. Omaha Public Power District, 385 F. Supp. 1382 (D. Neb. 1976).

sition on coworkers or disruption of the work routine." As a result, the court concluded that the director could maintain his religious discrimination lawsuit against the county.[159]

• A federal court in Kansas ruled that an employer committed unlawful religious discrimination by dismissing two employees for engaging in religious speech with customers. The employees frequently greeted customers by saying "God bless you," "Praise the Lord," and other similar phrases. At certain times, because they felt that the Holy Spirit moved them to bless all GM employees, they extended such blessings to all of their food service customers. The employer deemed the employees' greetings to be inappropriate, and it eventually dismissed them. The employees sued the employer, claiming that its actions violated Title VII of the Civil Rights Act of 1964. The employees maintained that they were Christians who felt strongly that because of what God has done for them and the joy He has given them by changing their lives dramatically, they had to say things that were positive, uplifting, and inspirational to people with whom they spoke, and their religious greetings emanated from this belief. Honoring God through their speech, through such greetings, was a deep seated and sincerely held religious belief. The employer claimed that it did not have to tolerate these employees' religious practices if doing so would impose an undue hardship on it. It insisted that allowing them to continue their religious greetings would impose an undue hardship because it would jeopardize their business. The court concluded that the employees had met their "prima facie case" of religious discrimination by proving that (1) they had a bona fide religious belief that conflicted with an employment requirement; (2) they informed the employer of this belief; and (3) they were disciplined for failure to comply with the conflicting employment requirement. Having established a prima facie case, "the burden shifts to the employer to show that it was unable reasonably to accommodate the plaintiff's religious needs without undue hardship." Since the employer did not attempt to accommodate the employees' religious practice of blessing food service customers, the issue was whether its refusal to accommodate the employees' religious speech violated its obligation under Title VII to "reasonably accommodate" its employees' religious practice without undue hardship on the conduct of its business. The court concluded that allowing the employees to continue their religious greetings would not have imposed an undue hardship upon the employer. Allowing such a practice imposed only a "minimal burden" on the employer. It stressed that undue hardship cannot be proven by speculation, and yet this is what the employer was attempting to do.[160]

• A federal court in Nebraska ruled that an employer violated both state and federal law by dismissing an employee who refused to work on Easter Sunday. The employee, a devout Christian, was employed by a convenience store chain as a cashier. A previous manager accommodated the employee's desire not to work on Easter Sunday by allowing her to work on non-religious holidays (such as New Year's Day) instead. A new manager was not so accommodating. She scheduled the employee to work the evening shift on Easter Sunday even though she had been fully apprised in writing by the employee of her strong religious opposition to working on Easter Sunday. The employee attended church on Easter Sunday evening rather than go to work, and she was

---

[159] Brown v. Polk County, 61 F.3d 650 (8th Cir. 1995). The court also concluded that the county's actions may have violated the director's First Amendment right to freely exercise his religion. *See also* Shrum v. City of Coweta, 449 F.3d 1132 (10th Cir. 2006); Berry v. Department of Social Services, 447 F.3d 642 (9th Cir. 2006); Baker v. The Home Depot, 445 F.3d 541 (2nd Cir. 2006); Storey v. Burns International Security Services, 390 F.3d 760 (3rd Cir. 2004); Cloutier v. Costco Wholesale Corp., 390 F.3d 126 (1st Cir. 2004).

[160] Banks v. Service America Corporation, 72 EPD ¶45,018 (D. Kan. 1996).

promptly fired. She later sued her employer, claiming that she had been unlawfully discharged on account of her religion. The court concluded that the employee proved all three elements of her prima facie case, and therefore the employer violated Title VII by dismissing her. First, it pointed to the employee's long history of church atten-dance, including attending worship services on Sunday mornings and evenings, as evi-dence of her bona fide belief that working on Easter Sunday violated her religious beliefs. Second, it noted that the employee had informed her manager in writing of her desire not to work on Easter Sunday. Third, the employee clearly was dismissed because of her religious beliefs. The court rejected the employer's defense that it had offered the employee a "reasonable accommodation." It observed that the employer "knew that the entirety of Easter was of paramount religious significance to [the employee] and was unlike a normal Sunday." The court also rejected the employer's claim that accommodating the employee's religious beliefs would have imposed an undue burden on it. It noted that the previous manager was willing to allow the employee to work on secular holidays in lieu of working on Easter, and that other employees had indicated a willingness to work "at any time."[161]

The Religious Freedom Restoration Act

§ 8-12.8

Key Point 8-12.8> *Congress enacted the Religious Freedom Restoration Act to prevent the government from enacting any law or adopting any practice that substantially burdens the free exercise of religion unless the law or practice is support-ed by a compelling government interest. The compelling government interest require-ment applies to any law, including neutral laws of general applicability. The objective of the Act was to repudiate the Supreme Court's decision in the Smith case (1990) in which the Court ruled that neutral laws of general applicability that burden the free exercise of religion do not need to be supported by a compelling government interest in order to satisfy the First Amendment. In 1997, the Supreme Court ruled that the Act was unconstitutional. However, other courts have limited this ruling to state and local legislation, and have concluded that the Act continues to apply to federal laws.*

In 1963 the United States Supreme Court issued a major reinterpretation of the First Amendment's free exercise of religion clause in the case of *Sherbert v. Verner.*[162] In the *Sherbert* case, the Court announced that a government statute or regulation that imposes a "burden" on the free exercise of religion violates the free exercise clause unless the statute or regulation is justified by a "compelling state interest." This test was clarified a few years later in *Wisconsin v. Yoder.*[163] The Supreme Court articulated its understanding of the free exercise clause as follows:

1. Government may never interfere with an individual's right to believe whatever he or she wants.

---

[161] Pedersen v. Casey's General Stores, Inc., 978 F. Supp. 926 (D. Neb. 1997).

[162] 374 U.S. 398 (1963).

[163] 406 U.S. 205 (1971). The *Yoder* case is discussed in chapter 12, *supra*.

2. In determining whether the government may interfere with or restrict religiously motivated conduct, the courts must consider (a) whether the activity was motivated by and rooted in legitimate and sincerely held religious belief, (b) whether the activity was unduly and substantially burdened by the government's action, and (c) whether the government has a compelling interest in limiting the religious activity that cannot be accomplished by less restrictive means.

This general understanding of the free exercise clause was applied by the Supreme Court in several cases.[164]

In 1990 the United States Supreme Court ruled in the *Smith* case that a "neutral law of general applicability" that burdens the exercise of religion need not be supported by a compelling governmental interest to be permissible under the First Amendment's free exercise of religion clause.[165] In so ruling, the Court repudiated a quarter of a century of established precedent and severely diluted this basic constitutional protection. The results were predictable. Scores of lower federal courts and state courts sustained laws and governmental practices that directly restricted religious practices. In many of these cases, the courts based their actions directly on the *Smith* case, suggesting that the result would have been different had it not been for that decision.

Congress responded to the *Smith* case by enacting the Religious Freedom Restoration Act of 1993.[166] The Act restored the compelling interest test through the following provision:

> Government shall not burden a person's exercise of religion even if the burden results from a rule of general applicability [unless] it demonstrates that application of the burden to the person (1) is in furtherance of a compelling governmental interest; and (2) is the least restrictive means of furthering that compelling governmental interest.

In explaining this provision, the Senate Judiciary Committee commented that the Act "permits government to burden the exercise of religion only if it demonstrates a compelling state interest and that the burden in question is the least restrictive means of furthering the interest."

In the years following the enactment of RFRA a number of government attempts to regulate or interfere with religious practices were struck down by the courts on the basis of the Act.

A few courts have applied RFRA in evaluating claims of discrimination against religious employers under Title VII of the Civil Rights Act of 1964.

Case Study

• *A federal appeals court ruled that a minister's age discrimination lawsuit challenging a denominational policy requiring the retirement of ministers at 70 years of age was*

---

[164] *See, e.g.,* Hernandez v. Commissioner, 109 S. Ct. 2136 (1989); Hobbie v. Unemployment Appeals Commission, 480 U.S. 136 (1987); United States v. Lee, 455 U.S. 252 (1982).

[165] Employment Division v. Smith, 494 U.S. 872 (1990).

[166] 42 U.S.C. § 2000bb.

barred by the federal *Religious Freedom Restoration Act. The minister asserted that the mandatory retirement policy was a "secular" matter that was not influenced by any religious considerations. A federal appeals court ignored the ministerial exception to employment laws*[167] *and ruled that the lawsuit was barred by the federal Religious Freedom Restoration Act (RFRA). It noted that the ministerial exception "has no basis in statutory text, whereas RFRA, if applicable, is explicit legislation that could not be more on point. Given the absence of other relevant statutory language, the RFRA must be deemed the full expression of Congress's intent with regard to the religion-related issues before us and displace earlier judge-made doctrines that might have been used to ameliorate the age discrimination law's impact on religious organizations and activities." The court rejected the minister's claim that RFRA is unconstitutional. It concluded that RFRA represents a constitutional exercise of congressional power as it applies to the federal government. A dissenting judge argued that RFRA has no application to disputes between private parties, such as the present case, and that the case should have been dismissed on the basis of the ministerial exception.*[168]

The Civil Rights Act of 1991   § 8-12.9

Key Point 8-12.9> *The Civil Rights Act of 1991 permits victims of discrimination under various federal civil rights laws to sue their employer for money damages up to specified limits based on the size of the employer.*

The Civil Rights Act of 1991 allows, with limited exceptions, compensatory and punitive damages for intentional employment discrimination on the basis of race, color, religion, sex, national origin, age, or disability. However, the Act limits the amount of compensatory and punitive damages that are available to discrimination victims. The sum of punitive damages and compensatory damages cannot exceed the following amounts, per person: $50,000 for employers with 15-100 employees; $100,000 for employers with 101-200 employees; $200,000 for employers with 201-500 employees; $300,000 for employers with more than 500 employees. "Frontpay" (compensation for future services) is excluded from the definition of compensatory damages and is not included in the caps.

Case Studies

• *A denominational agency has 75 employees, and engages in the national distribution of religious literature to affiliated churches. A female sues the agency as a result of alleged intentional sex discrimination in employment. The agency clearly is subject to Title VII, and therefore is subject to "compensatory and punitive damages" not to exceed $50,000 if the woman can prove intentional sex discrimination.*

• *A church refuses to hire an applicant for employment because she is not a member of the same faith. The applicant cannot sue for monetary damages under Title VII since churches are not subject to the prohibition of religious discrimination in employment even if they are covered by Title VII.*

---

[167] *See* § 8-10, *supra.*

[168] Hankins v. Lyght, 441 F.3d 96 (2nd Cir. 2006).

The Civil Rights Act of 1991 provides that if an employer is charged with discrimination against a disabled person in violation of the Americans with Disabilities Act, no monetary damages will be available if the employer can demonstrate that it exercised good faith efforts (in consultation with the disabled person) to reasonably accommodate the disabled person.

The Civil Rights Act of 1991 also authorizes the award of attorneys fees to prevailing parties.

The Age Discrimination in Employment Act
§ 8-13

Key Point 8-13> *The federal Age Discrimination in Employment Act prohibits employers with 20 or more employees, and engaged in interstate commerce, from discriminating in any employment decision on the basis of the age of an employee or applicant for employment who is 40 years of age or older. The Act does not exempt religious organizations. Many states have similar laws that often apply to employers having fewer than 20 employees.*

In 1967, Congress enacted the Age Discrimination in Employment Act to prohibit employers engaged in an industry affecting commerce and employing at least 50 employees from making employment decisions that discriminate against individuals from 40 to 65 years old on account of age.[169] Congress later amended the Act to apply to employers employing 20 or more employees for each working day in each of 20 or more calendar weeks in the current or preceding year. Congress also expanded the class of protected employees to include all persons 40 years of age and older.

The Act specifies that "it shall not be unlawful for an employer . . . to observe the terms of . . . a bona fide employee benefit plan such as a retirement, pension, or insurance plan, which is not a subterfuge to evade the purposes of [the Act] . . . or to discharge or otherwise discipline an individual for good cause."[170] Ordinarily, an employee benefit plan will be considered to be "bona fide" if it is genuine and pays substantial benefits.

This ban on age discrimination applies to all employers, including religious organizations, that have 20 or more employees and that are engaged in an industry or activity "affecting commerce." The "commerce" and "employee" requirements are discussed earlier in this chapter. Note that the age discrimination law only addresses discrimination committed by employers against employees or applicants for employment.

---

[169] 29 U.S.C. §§ 621-634.

[170] 29 U.S.C. § 623(f).

Case Studies

• *The United States Supreme Court ruled that an employer cannot necessarily avoid an age discrimination claim by replacing one protected worker with another.*[171] *A long-term employee of a business corporation was dismissed at the age of 56, and replaced by a worker who was 40 years old. He sued his employer, claiming that it had committed unlawful age discrimination in violation of the federal Age Discrimination in Employment Act. The employer insisted that it could not be guilty of violating the Act if it replaced a worker at least 40 years of age with another worker who also was 40 years of age or older—since both employees are in the protected group of workers under the Act. The Supreme Court rejected this argument, noting that "the fact that one person in the protected class has lost out to another person in the protected class is . . . irrelevant, so long as he has lost out because of his age. Or to put the point more concretely, there can be no greater inference of age discrimination . . . when a 40-year-old is replaced by a 39-year-old than when a 56-year-old is replaced by a 40-year-old." The Court cautioned that "in the age-discrimination context . . . an inference [of discrimination] cannot be drawn from the replacement of one worker with another worker insignificantly younger." However, "the fact that a replacement is substantially younger than the plaintiff is a far more reliable indicator of age discrimination than is the fact that the plaintiff was replaced by someone outside the protected class."*

• *A federal appeals court ruled that the First Amendment guaranty of religious freedom prevented it from resolving a Methodist minister's claim that his dismissal violated federal age discrimination law.*[172] *The 63-year-old minister was employed by an annual conference of the United Methodist Church. After serving ten years as a counselor, he requested that he be returned to a pastoral appointment. He was assigned to a temporary post at a local church. The minister claimed that the new position paid him less than what a pastor with his qualifications and experience would normally receive. He complained to his district superintendent who, he alleged, assured him that he would be "moved to a congregation more suited to his training and skills, and more appropriate in level of income, at the earliest opportunity." The minister made repeated requests for reassignment, but four years passed without any change in his position. He then filed a lawsuit in federal court, alleging that he had been denied a rightful "promotion" solely on the basis of his age. The court rejected the minister's claim. It based its conclusion on a number of factors, including the following: (1) The Methodist Book of Discipline did mention age as one factor to consider in assigning clergy, and therefore a judicial finding that the church violated a minister's rights under federal age discrimination law could conceivably violate the church's right to freely exercise its religion. (2) The determination of "whose voice speaks for the church" is "per se a religious matter." The court noted that "we cannot imagine an area of inquiry less suited to a temporal court for decision; evaluation of the 'gifts and graces' of a minister must be left to ecclesiastical institutions. This is the view of every court that has been confronted by this [kind] of dispute." (3) The court acknowledged that churches have less protection when it comes to employment decisions involving non-clergy employees. However, cases reaching this conclusion were not relevant in this case, since a minister was involved.*

---

[171] O'Connor v. Consolidated Coin Caterers Corporation, 116 S. Ct. 1307 (1996).

[172] Minker v. United Methodist Church, 894 F.2d 1354 (D.C. Cir. 1990). *Accord* Gargano v. Diocese of Rockville Centre, 80 F.3d 87 (2nd Cir. 1996).

• *A federal appeals court ruled that federal age discrimination law applied to a church school.[173] A Catholic parochial school did not offer a teaching contract to a math teacher who had taught at the school for five years. The school noted that the teacher did not open classes with prayer and did not attend Mass with students. The former teacher sued the school for violating the federal Age Discrimination in Employment Act. The school argued that subjecting it to the provisions of the Act would create an "excessive entanglement" between church and state in violation of the First Amendment. The court disagreed, noting that "[t]he majority of courts considering the issue have determined that application of the [Age Discrimination in Employment Act] to religious institutions generally, and to lay teachers specifically, does not pose a serious risk of excessive entanglement. . . . [Age discrimination lawsuits] do not require extensive or continuous administrative or judicial intrusion into the functions of religious institutions. The sole question at issue . . . is whether the plaintiff was unjustifiably treated differently because of his age. . . . The Supreme Court has stated that 'routine regulatory interaction which involves no inquiries into religious doctrine, no delegation of state power to a religious body, and no detailed monitoring and close administrative contact between secular and religious bodies, does not of itself violate the [Establishment Clause's] nonentanglement command.' Application of the [Act] to the case at bar requires just such routine regulatory interaction between government and a religious institution." The court acknowledged that the Act is not applicable to claims brought by members of the clergy against their religious employers, since these cases involve "the pervasively religious relationship between a member of the clergy and his religious employer."*

• *A federal appeals court ruled that a hospital chaplain could not sue the hospital for alleged age and sex discrimination following her dismissal.[174] The former chaplain was an ordained Episcopal priest who had served as chaplain of a church-affiliated hospital for 10 years. Following her dismissal, the former chaplain sued the hospital on the grounds that her dismissal (1) violated the federal Civil Rights Act of 1964, which prohibits certain employers from dismissing employees on the basis of their sex, and (2) violated the federal Age Discrimination in Employment Act, which bans discrimination in employment against persons 40 years of age and older—on account of age. The court emphasized that the hospital was "without question a religious organization," and that the chaplain position "is primarily a ministerial position." The court concluded: "[W]e believe that the free exercise [of religion] clause of the First Amendment also prohibits the courts from deciding cases such as this one. Personnel decisions by church-affiliated institutions affecting clergy are per se religious matters and cannot be reviewed by civil courts, for to review such decisions would require the courts to determine the meaning of religious doctrine and canonical law and to impose a secular court's view of whether in the context of the particular case religious doctrine and canonical law support the decision the church authorities have made. This is precisely the kind of judicial second-guessing of decision-making by religious organizations that the free exercise [of religion] clause forbids."*

• *A Catholic college denied a priest's application for a one-year sabbatical, while at the same time approving the applications of two female professors. The priest sued the college, claiming that its denial of his application amounted to unlawful discrimination based on age, gender, and race (the priest was Asian). A federal appeals court dismissed the priest's claims.[175] It agreed that federal law banning discrimination based*

---

[173] DeMarco v. Holy Cross High School, 4 F.3d 166 (2nd Cir. 1993), quoting Hernandez v. Commissioner, 490 U.S. 680 (198

[174] Scharon v. St. Luke's Episcopal Presbyterian Hospitals, 929 F.2d 360 (8th Cir. 1991).

[175] Roxas v. Presentation College, 90 F.3d 310 (8th Cir. 1996).

on age, race, and gender can be applied to a college's policies regarding sabbatical leave. However, it concluded that the college had demonstrated a "legitimate, nondiscriminatory reason" for denying the priest's application for a sabbatical. In particular, it noted that the college was in the process of upgrading its two-year nursing program into an accredited four-year program, and that it granted the two female professors' requests for sabbaticals since they were involved with the nursing program and needed advanced degrees in order for the nursing program to be upgraded. Unfortunately, the college failed to claim that the priest's discrimination claims were barred by the First Amendment guaranty of religious freedom. The appeals court took the extraordinary step of asking the college to address this issue in a supplemental brief. The college eventually did so, but the court ruled that the First Amendment did not bar the priest's claims in this case since the college "failed to convince us that our consideration of [the priest's] claims would risk excessive entanglement" between church and state. The lesson is clear—churches and church schools should vigorously and at the earliest opportunity challenge any discrimination claims brought by a member of the clergy, emphasizing the religious role and functions of the minister. As this case illustrates, failure to do so may cause a civil court to reject such a defense.

• A federal court in Alabama ruled that a 59-year-old principal could sue his employing church-affiliated school for age discrimination when his one-year employment contract was not renewed. The court concluded that a lengthy employment relationship (in this case, seven years) without any negative employee evaluations casts serious doubt on an employer's allegedly nondiscriminatory basis for not renewing the principal's contract.[176]

> "The lesson is clear—churches and church schools should vigorously and at the earliest opportunity challenge any discrimination claims brought by a member of the clergy, emphasizing the religious role and functions of the minister."

• A federal court in Colorado ruled that a dismissed teacher at a Catholic high school could not bring an age discrimination claim against the school and archdiocese.[177] A teacher was employed to teach theology at a parochial high school. The school did not renew the teacher's contract of employment for two reasons: (1) a need for fewer teachers, and (2) the teacher's skills, abilities, and qualifications were deemed less desirable than other faculty members. The teacher alleged that the archdiocese failed to renew his employment contract on account of his age in violation of the Age Discrimination in Employment Act. In rejecting the teacher's claim, the court observed: "[T]he more pervasively religious the institution, the less religious the employee's role need be to risk First Amendment infringement. Conversely, the less religious an organization, the more religious an employee's role need be to risk First Amendment infringement. In this case [the teacher] does not challenge [the school's] religious affiliation. And, significantly he does not contest that his teaching role was primarily religious in nature. He taught Roman Catholic theology exclusively and even held some of his classes in [the school's] chapel so that his students could pray as part of his class. There is no

---

176 Shook v. St. Bede School, 74 F.Supp.2d 1172 (M.D. Ala. 1999). *Accord* Blackman v. Talmud Torah of Minnesota, 2001 WL 1558320 (D. Minn. 2002).

177 Powell v. Stafford, 859 F. Supp. 1343 (D. Colo. 1994).

genuine dispute that [his] duties were pervasively religious in nature. Courts have consistently held that the ADEA does not apply in cases involving employees performing primarily religious functions. . . . Simply put, there is no teaching position more closely tied to a Roman Catholic school's religious character than teaching Roman Catholic doctrine. I conclude that the archdiocese's free exercise [of religion] rights are substantially burdened by application of the ADEA under the circumstances here."

• *A federal court in Florida ruled that it was barred by the First Amendment guaranty of religious freedom from applying the federal age discrimination law to a 68-year-old priest who was applying for a "nonministerial" position with a missions agency that involved the performance of ministerial functions.*[178]

• *A federal court in Indiana rejected the claims of a 61-year-old employee of a church-operated hospital that she had been a victim of age discrimination.*[179] *A woman (the "plaintiff") worked for a church-operated hospital as a full-time cashier. Her position was reduced to part-time as a result of a reduction in force (RIF) caused by budget deficits. Eventually, the position was terminated. The plaintiff sued the hospital, claiming that the elimination of her position amounted to age discrimination in violation of federal law. The court observed: "[We] must determine whether a [jury] could find that the hospital's true reason for reducing her hours was the RIF going on at that time, and not whether that decision was a sound business decision. The evidence on which [the plaintiff] relies does not call into doubt the hospital's proffered reason for eliminating her cashier position. The hospital asserts that [the plaintiff's] position was eliminated because it was the department's only part-time position (and elimination of part time positions was a suggested method of cutting costs) and other full-time employees had the skills necessary to perform her duties, while she would have required additional training to perform their duties. [The plaintiff's] assertions that she was performing satisfactorily, that her duties still needed to be performed, and that a younger employee continued to perform her duties simply do not refute the specific reason given for her elimination, and therefore could not support a finding that the reason is a pretext for age discrimination."*

• *A Michigan court dismissed an age discrimination lawsuit brought against a Catholic church and archdiocese by a 62-year-old employee who was dismissed as a result of economic conditions.*[180] *The number of families in a Catholic parish declined from 1,500 to 1,250. This decline led to a deficit of $200,000. A CPA firm was called in to conduct a financial study and organizational analysis, and it recommended that the parish reorganize its staff and consolidate responsibilities. The pastor of the church responded by terminating five employees including the plaintiff (a 62-year-old custodian); a 40-year-old religious education secretary; a 31-year-old director of religious education; a 63-year-old school librarian; and a 68-year-old school secretary. The dismissed custodian sued the church and archdiocese, claiming that his dismissal violated a state civil rights law banning age discrimination in employment. He relied on the pastor's testimony that his decision to dismiss the custodian was based in part on the fact that the dismissed custodian would be able to retain his pension and medical benefits while two other custodians who were not dismissed would not. The court concluded that the pastor's consideration of the custodian's eligibility for retirement and med-*

---

[178] Sanchez v. Catholic Foreign Society of America, 82 F.Supp.2d 1338 (M.D. Fla. 1999).

[179] Humphrey v. Sisters of St. Francis Health Services, Inc., 979 F. Supp. 781 (N.D. Ind. 1997).

[180] Plieth v. St. Raymond Church, 534 N.W.2d 164 (Mich. App. 1995).

ical benefits did not automatically constitute unlawful age discrimination. It noted that in an age discrimination case the plaintiff has the burden of proving a "prima facie case" of discrimination by a preponderance of the evidence. It concluded that the custodian failed to meet this burden of proof, noting that "the mere fact that plaintiff was eligible for a pension is not enough for this court to infer age discrimination." The court pointed to a second basis for its decision: "When an employer lays off employees for economic reasons, the employee bears a greater burden of proof in establishing discrimination. In such a case, the employee must present evidence that age was a determining factor in the decision to discharge him. At best, plaintiff has offered evidence that his pension eligibility played some part in [the pastor's] decision to terminate him rather than the other two maintenance workers. Plaintiff has made no showing that his pension eligibility—and therefore, in plaintiff's argument, his age—was a determining factor in that decision."

• *A federal district court in Missouri ruled that it could not resolve a lawsuit brought against a synagogue by a former business administrator who claimed that he had been dismissed on the basis of age in violation of the Age Discrimination in Employment Act.*[181] *In deciding that the Act did not apply to the synagogue, the court relied on the Supreme Court's 1979 decision in N.L.R.B. Catholic Bishop of Chicago.*[182] *In the Catholic Bishop decision, the Supreme Court ruled that in deciding whether or not a federal law applies to religious organizations, a civil court first must ask if applying the law "would give rise to serious constitutional questions." If it would, then the law cannot be applied to religious organizations without a "clear expression of an affirmative intention" by Congress to apply the law to such organizations. The district court concluded that applying the Act to a church or synagogue would "give rise to serious constitutional questions." In reaching this conclusion, the court quoted from the business administrator's job description, and noted that his duties included "implementing Temple policies" and "having a positive attitude towards Jewish life and a Jewish background, enabling the administrator to understand the work of the Temple, its purposes and highest ideals and goals." The court then observed, again referring to the Catholic Bishop decision, that if a "serious constitutional question" exists, the court next must ascertain whether Congress has provided a "clear expression of an affirmative intention" that the Act apply to religious institutions. The court concluded that the Act did not specifically apply to churches of synagogues, and so this test was not met. As a result, the Act could not be applied in this case.*

• *A federal court in Missouri ruled that it lacked jurisdiction to resolve a seminary employee's claim that his dismissal violated federal age discrimination law.*[183] *The court, applying the analysis set forth by the United States Supreme Court in a previous ruling,*[184] *concluded that in deciding whether or not a federal law applies to religious organizations, a civil court first must ask if applying the law to religious organizations "would give rise to serious constitutional questions." If it would, then the law cannot be applied to religious organizations without an "affirmative expression of congressional intent" to apply the law to such organizations. Would application of the federal Age Discrimination in Employment Act to a seminary create "serious constitutional questions"? Yes, concluded the court. It emphasized that the seminary was "prima-*

---

181 Weissman v. Congregation Shaare Emeth, 839 F. Supp. 680 (E.D. Mo. 1993).

182 440 U.S. 490 (1979).

183 Cochran v. St. Louis Seminary, 717 F. Supp. 1413 (E.D. Mo. 1989).

184 NLRB v. Catholic Bishop, 440 U.S. 490 (1979).

rily a religious institution" whose objective was the preparation of students for the priesthood and the dissemination of religious values to its students. The court noted that "all faculty members, both lay and clerical, are expected to serve as religious role models, participate in spiritual activities and 'carry religious fervor and conviction' into the classroom." The court concluded that applying the federal age discrimination law to such an institution "would give rise to serious constitutional questions." In particular, discrimination claims would require the courts to determine whether a dismissal was based on religious considerations or age, and such inquiries "are fraught with the sort of entanglement [between church and state] that the Constitution forbids." Further, application of the Act to the seminary would cause the seminary to be more cautious in its religion-based employment decisions, thereby "imposing a chilling effect on the [seminary's] exercise of control over its religious mission." If "serious constitutional questions" would arise by applying a federal law to a religious organization, then the law cannot be applied without an affirmative and clear expression of congressional intent to apply the law to such organizations. The court found no clear indication that Congress intended the Act to apply to religious seminaries.

• A federal district court in Ohio rejected a religious school's claim that it was exempt from federal age discrimination law.[185] Xavier University is a Catholic institution of higher education operated by the Order of Jesuits. An employee brought an age discrimination lawsuit against the University. The University claimed that the court lacked jurisdiction over the case, since, as a religious institution, it was exempt from the antidiscrimination provisions of the federal Age Discrimination in Employment Act. The court agreed with the employee that the Act "gives no indication that religious institutions are exempt from its provisions." However, it also acknowledged that a religious institution could be exempted on the basis of the constitutional guaranty of religious freedom if application of the Act to the institution would "give rise to serious constitutional questions" under the religious freedom clause of the First Amendment. The court concluded that no "serious constitutional questions" were implicated by an application of the Act to the University and accordingly the claim of an exemption was rejected.

• A federal court in Pennsylvania ruled that a religious organization may have violated the Age Discrimination in Employment Act.[186] A Catholic monastery dismissed its chef after ten years of employment. The chef sued the monastery for violating the Act. The monastery asserted that the chef was not protected by the Act since he was not an employee (he owned a food service company that provided meals to the monastery). It also insisted that its decision was based on a deterioration in the quality and variety of food, and had nothing to do with the chef's age. The court refused to dismiss the case and ordered that it proceed to trial. It acknowledged that there was some evidence to support the conclusion that the chef was not an employee, including: (1) he insisted on being treated as an independent contractor for tax purposes, and received a 1099 rather than a W-2; (2) the monastery contracted with the chef's corporation for his services; (3) the monastery did not withhold taxes from the chef's pay; and (4) the monastery did not pay Social Security taxes for the chef, or extend to him any employee fringe benefit. However, the court concluded that there was evidence that the chef was an employee, and accordingly it could not dismiss the case. It cited the following

---

[185] Soriano v. Xavier University, 687 F. Supp. 1188 (S.D. Ohio 1988). *See also* Ritter v. Mount St. Mary's College, 738 F.2d 431 (4th Cir. 1984), *aff'd*, 814 F.2d 986 (4th Cir. 1987). Note, however, that while federal law prohibits sex discrimination under "any educational program or activity receiving federal financial assistance," the law does not apply "to an educational institution which is controlled by a religious organization if the application of this section would not be consistent with the religious tenets of such organization." 20 U.S.C. § 1681(a)(3).

[186] Stouch v. Brothers of the Order of Hermits of St. Augustine, 836 F. Supp. 1134 (E.D. Pa. 1993).

factors indicating employee status: (1) the monastery provided the chef's equipment; (2) the monastery hired and paid the chef's assistants; (3) the chef had worked for ten years at the monastery, and was required to work five or six days each week; (4) the chef had to comply with various reporting requirements imposed by the monastery; and (5) the chef's work was done at the monastery. The court concluded that from this evidence "there is a genuine issue whether [the chef] was an employee of the [monastery]." The court also rejected the monastery's claim that it dismissed the chef because of poor service. It quoted from a glowing reference letter a monastery representative had issued on behalf of the chef a short time before his dismissal. The letter stated, in part, that "[the chef] will not disappoint the client that entrusts with him their fondest culinary expectations." The court concluded that this letter, praising the chef's performance, and written just a few months before his dismissal, "creates a genuine issue of fact as to whether the proffered reason for his termination was the true reason." It left to the jury the task of deciding whether the monastery's dismissal was in fact based on unacceptable quality, or upon the chef's age.

• A California court ruled that a hospital affiliated with the Methodist church was a "religious corporation" for purposes of a state civil rights law banning discrimination in employment on the basis of age.[187] A 50-year-old nurse was dismissed by her employer (a hospital) for exceeding four months of medical leave in the same year. She sued the hospital, claiming that it was guilty of age discrimination in violation of a state civil rights law. The hospital claimed that the law exempted "religious corporations" and that it was therefore exempt because of its affiliation with the Methodist church. A state appeals court agreed, on the basis of the following factors: (1) the hospital was "created, organized, and is governed (at least partially) by members of the United Methodist Church"; (2) its articles of incorporation state that upon dissolution, its assets will revert to the United Methodist Church; (3) its bylaws require that a majority of its board members belong to the United Methodist Church, and that at least one other board member must be a Methodist minister; (4) its directors are elected annually by a Methodist agency; (5) it is accredited by the United Methodist Church; (6) a Methodist chaplain ministers to patients, and the hospital broadcasts daily sermons to patients' rooms. The court agreed with the hospital that it was a religious corporation and therefore was exempt from the state age discrimination law. It observed: "[I]t is far from clear that religiously affiliated hospitals serve a primarily secular purpose, as the [nurse] contends. To many religious adherents, the healing of the sick is closely associated with faith in a divine being. Many hospitals, even those without an official religious affiliation, offer on-site chapels and chaplains for the spiritual comfort of their patients and their families. This hospital, in particular, broadcasts daily religious sermons to its patients' rooms. We are not prepared to hold, as a matter of law, that a religiously affiliated hospital may not define and carry out its mission of healing the sick as a primarily religious mission."

Key Point > *Many laws refer specifically to "religious organizations." Examples include zoning ordinances, tax laws, civil rights laws, and copyright law. This case illustrates that an organization may be deemed "religious" for purposes of these laws even though it was created for charitable purposes—so long as it is affiliated with a church and furthers the church's religious mission.*

---

[187] Kelly v. Methodist Hospital of Southern California, 52 Cal. Rptr.2d 177 (Cal. App. 1996).

Case Studies

• *A Wisconsin appeals court ruled that a state agency's investigation into a dismissed teacher's complaint of age discrimination did not violate the constitutional rights of a church-operated school.*[188] *State law prohibits most employers, including church schools, from discriminating in employment decisions on the basis of age. A church school terminated a teacher whom it had employed for 16 years. The school cited "problems with the teacher's classroom management, her professionalism, and her maintenance of a prayerful environment." The teacher felt that she was fired on account of her age (she was 56), and she filed a complaint with the state equal rights agency. The agency concluded that there was reason to believe that the teacher had been a victim of age discrimination, largely on the ground that the school had given the teacher an excellent evaluation less than a year prior to her dismissal. The agency ordered a hearing to resolve the matter, but the school filed a lawsuit seeking to prevent a hearing on the ground that such a procedure would violate its constitutional right to religious freedom. A state appeals court concluded that the school's constitutional rights would not be violated by a hearing addressing the charge of age discrimination. The court relied solely on a 1986 decision of the United States Supreme Court in a similar case. The Supreme Court had ruled that an Ohio civil rights agency "violates no constitutional rights by merely investigating the circumstances of [the employee's] discharge in this case, if only to ascertain whether the ascribed religious-based reason was in fact the reason for the discharge." The court emphasized that the school "is still free to discharge employees for religious reasons," and that the school "will prevail in the [agency] investigation if [the dismissed teacher] cannot prove that the religious-based reason given for her discharge was only a pretext for age discrimination."*

• *A federal court in Wyoming ruled that a church did not commit unlawful age or disability discrimination when it did not renew the teaching contract of a teacher who had undergone four hip replacement surgeries. The court concluded that "there is no credible evidence at all in the record that suggests that the [church's] employment decisions had anything to do with age whatsoever. . . . [Her] argument that she was becoming more expensive to the school as a consequence of her longevity there as a teacher does not satisfy her burden of proof. [Her] self-serving conjecture and speculation do not serve to demonstrate that the employer's proffered reasons for the challenged actions are pretextual and unworthy of belief. There is no meaningful evidence, direct and indirect, of discrimination against plaintiff by defendant on the basis of age."*[189]

The Americans with Disabilities Act

§ 8-14

In enacting the Americans with Disabilities Act ("ADA") in 1990, Congress was responding to evidence that disabled persons occupy an inferior status in American life, and face persistent discrimination in employment, transportation, places of public accommodation, and communications. The ADA attempts to elim-

---

[188] Sacred Heart School Board v. Labor & Industry Review Commission, 460 N.W.2d 430 (Wis. App. 1990).

[189] Brown v. Holy Name Church, 80 F.Supp.2d 1261 (D. Wyo. 2000).

inate discrimination against individuals with disabilities, by (1) prohibiting covered employers from discriminating in any employment decision against a "qualified individual with a disability," and requiring employers to make "reasonable accommodations" for disabled persons unless doing so would impose an "undue hardship"; (2) prohibiting most places of public accommodation to discriminate against disabled individuals; (3) prohibiting discrimination in public transportation against disabled individuals; and (4) prohibiting discrimination in telecommunications against disabled individuals. The first two of these prohibitions are of the most relevance to religious organizations, and they are discussed separately below.

Discrimination in Employment

§ 8-14.1

Key Point 8-14.1> *The federal Americans with Disabilities Act prohibits employers with at least 15 employees, and that are engaged in interstate commerce, from discriminating in any employment decision against a qualified individual with a disability who is able, with or without reasonable accommodation from the employer, to perform the essential functions of the job. Accommodations that impose an undue hardship upon an employer are not required. Religious organizations may give preference to nondisabled members of their faith over disabled persons who are members of a different faith.*

Title I of the ADA prohibits discrimination in any employment decision against a qualified person with a disability. This section of the ADA applies to any employer that is engaged in a business or activity that "affects" interstate commerce and that has 15 or more employees. The prohibition of discrimination applies to all aspects of the employment relationship, including recruitment, advertising, processing of applications, hiring, promotion, awards, demotion, transfer, layoff, termination, right of return following layoff, rates of pay, job assignment, leaves of absence, sick leave, fringe benefits, financial support for training (e.g., apprenticeships, professional meetings and conferences), and employer-sponsored social or recreational programs. The word "discriminate" is defined broadly, and includes:

- segregating or classifying a job applicant or employee on the basis of a disability (if doing so adversely affects the person's job opportunities);

- utilizing standards or criteria that have the effect of discriminating on the basis of disability;

- not making reasonable accommodations to the known physical or mental limitations of an otherwise qualified individual with a disability who is an applicant or employee, unless the employer can demonstrate that the accommodation would impose an undue hardship on the operation of the business of the employer;

• using employment tests or other selection criteria that screen out or tend to screen out disabled individuals, unless the test or criteria is shown to be job-related for the position in question and is consistent with business necessity.

Prohibited discrimination must be against a *qualified individual with a disability*. This important term is defined as follows:

The term "qualified individual with a disability" means an individual with a disability who, with or without reasonable accommodation, can perform the essential functions of the employment position that such individual holds or desires. For purposes of this title, consideration shall be given to the employer's judgment as to what functions of a job are essential, and if an employer has prepared a written description before advertising or interviewing applicants for the job, this description shall be considered evidence of the essential functions of the job.

This definition contains several important terms. For example, a qualified individual with a disability is someone who, with or without reasonable accommodation by the employer, can perform the essential functions of the job. The regulations interpreting the ADA list the following factors to consider in deciding whether or not a particular function is essential: (1) the employer's judgment; (2) a written job description prepared by the employer before the employee is hired; (3) the amount of time spent on the job performing the function; (4) the consequences of not requiring an employee to perform the function; (5) the essentiality of the function in the work experience of current and former employees in similar positions. It is clear that qualified individuals with a disability cannot be discriminated against simply because they cannot perform marginal job functions. For example, job applicants with a disability that prevents them from using their hands would not be "qualified individuals with a disability" with respect to a clerk-typist position that involves mostly typing, since typing would be an essential function that such persons could not perform. However, these persons would be qualified individuals with a disability with respect to jobs requiring only occasional, light typing, since in such cases typing would be a marginal rather than an essential job function.

The ADA defines the term *disability* to mean "a physical or mental impairment that substantially limits one or more of the major life activities of such individual." The term also includes persons who are "regarded" as being disabled even though they are not. Examples of disabilities include orthopedic, visual, speech, and hearing impairments; cerebral palsy; epilepsy; HIV infection; muscular dystrophy; multiple sclerosis; cancer; heart disease; diabetes; mental retardation; and emotional illness.

The ADA also lists several behaviors and conditions that are *not* disabilities. These include homosexuality; bisexuality; illegal drug use; transvestism; pedophilia; exhibitionism; voyeurism; gender identity disorders and other sexual disorders; compulsive gambling; kleptomania; and pyromania.

Note that the term *qualified individual with a disability* includes persons who can perform the essential functions of a job with reasonable accommodation by the employer. Employers must recognize that they now have an affirmative duty to make reasonable accommodations to the known physical or mental limitations of an otherwise qualified individual with a disability who is an applicant or employee, unless they can demonstrate that the accommodation would impose an undue hardship on the operation of their business. The term *reasonable accommodation* is defined by the ADA as

> making existing facilities used by employees readily accessible to and usable by individuals with disabilities, and job restructuring, part-time or modified work schedules, reassignment to a vacant position, acquisition or modification of equipment or devices, appropriate adjustment or modifications of examinations, training materials or policies, the provision of qualified readers or interpreters, and other similar accommodations for individuals with disabilities.

The House Report to the ADA contains the following additional comments regarding reasonable accommodation:

> In [some] cases, the acquisition or modification of equipment, such as adaptive hardware or software for computers, telephone headset amplifiers, and telecommunication devices will enable persons with disabilities to do the job. For some people with disabilities, the assistance of another individual, such as a reader, interpreter or attendant, may be necessary for specified activities. . . .
>
> A reasonable accommodation should be tailored to the needs of the individual and the requirements of the job. Persons with disabilities have vast experience in all aspects of their lives with the types of accommodations which are effective for them. Employers should not assume that accommodations are required without consulting the applicant or employee with the disability. Stereotypes about disability can result in stereotypes about the need for accommodations, which may exceed what is actually required. Consultations between employers and persons with disabilities will result in an accurate assessment of what is required in order to perform the job duties.

Employers need not accommodate disabled individuals if the accommodation would impose an undue hardship on the operation of their business. The term *undue hardship* is defined by the ADA as

> an action requiring significant difficulty or expense, when considered in light of [the following factors]: (i) the nature and cost of the accommodation needed; (ii) the overall financial resources of the facility or facilities involved in the provision of the reasonable accommodation; the number of persons employed at such facility; the effect on expenses and resources; or the impact otherwise of such accommodation upon the operation of the facility; (iii) the overall financial resources of the covered entity; the overall size of the business of a covered entity with respect to the number of its employees; the number, type, and location of its facilities; and (iv) the type of operation or operations of the covered entity, including the composition, structure, and functions of the workforce of such entity; the geographic separateness, administrative, or fiscal relationship of the facility or facilities in question to the covered entity.

179

The ADA states that religious organizations (including religious educational institutions) are not prohibited "from giving preference in employment to individuals of a particular religion to perform work" connected with the carrying on by the organization of its activities. The ADA further provides that "a religious organization may require that all applicants and employees conform to the religious tenets of such organization."

The ADA also prohibits pre-employment medical tests, and requires covered employers to post notices to applicants and employees describing the applicable provisions of the Act.

What is the relevance to religious organizations of the ADA's prohibition of employment discrimination against qualified individuals with a disability? Consider the following three points:

- The ADA's employment discrimination provisions apply only to employers engaged in a business or activity that "affects" interstate commerce and that have 15 or more employees. Any religious organization with fewer than 15 employees is not covered by the ADA's employment discrimination provisions. Any religious organization having 15 or more employees will be covered only to the extent that it is engaged in a business or activity that "affects" interstate commerce. The application of the "commerce" and "employee" requirements to religious organizations are addressed fully earlier in this chapter.

- The ADA specifically permits religious organizations (including religious educational institutions) to "give preference in employment to individuals of a particular religion to perform work connected with the carrying on by organization of its activities."

- The ADA further provides that "a religious organization may require that all applicants and employees conform to the religious tenets of such organization."

Case Studies

- *A denominational agency employs D as a maintenance worker. D suffers a heart attack, and is no longer able to shovel snow. D's job description lists snow shoveling as an essential function of his position. Accordingly, the agency terminates D. Assuming that the agency is a covered employer under the ADA, it has violated the law. Consider the following analysis: the first question is whether or not D is a qualified individual with a disability. The term "qualified individual with a disability" is defined by the ADA as an individual with a disability who, with or without reasonable accommodation, can perform the essential functions of the employment position. D is clearly disabled. The ADA lists "heart disease" as a disability (assuming that it substantially limits one or more major life activities). The question then is whether or not D, with reasonable accommodation, can perform the essential functions of the job. Once again, it is clear that D's disability can be accommodated in such a way as to permit him to perform the essential function of snow shoveling. This could simply mean the purchase of a $500 snow blower. The final question is whether or not the reasonable accommodation (purchasing a snow blower) would impose an undue hardship on the employer. Several factors may be considered in answering this question. However, under these facts, it is unlikely that the purchase of a $500 snow blower would impose an undue hardship. Accordingly, the* *employer must accommodate D's disability. By firing D, the employer failed to reasonably accommodate D's disability, and thereby committed unlawful discrimination.*

• *Same facts as the previous case study, except that the employer is a local church with 3 employees. The ADA would not apply, since it applies only to employers having at least 15 employees.*

• *A denominational agency has an opening for a job requiring some use of a computer. K, a blind female, applies for the position. The agency informs K that she is not qualified for the position since she cannot type, and hires someone else. The House Report to the ADA states: "For example, in a job requiring the use of a computer, the essential function is the ability to access, input, and retrieve information from the computer. It is not essential that the person be able to use the keyboard or visually read the information from a computer screen. Adaptive equipment or software may enable a person with no arms or a person with impaired vision to control the computer and access information." Assuming that the agency is a covered employer under the ADA, it has violated the law. K clearly is a qualified individual with a disability. The term "qualified individual with a disability" is defined by the ADA as an individual with a disability who, with or without reasonable accommodation, can perform the essential functions of the employment position. Since the "essential function" of the job is the ability to access, input, and retrieve information from the computer (and not the ability to use the keyboard or visually read the information from a computer screen), K can perform this function with reasonable accommodation. This could simply mean the purchase of an "adaptive equipment or software." The final question is whether or not the reasonable accommodation (purchasing the adaptive equipment or software) would impose an undue hardship on the employer. Several factors may be considered in answering this question. However, under these facts, it is unlikely that the purchase of such equipment or software would impose an undue hardship, if its cost is insignificant in comparison to the agency's total budget. Accordingly, the employer must accommodate K's disability. By refusing to consider K, the employer failed to reasonably accommodate K's disability, and thereby committed unlawful discrimination.*

• *A denomination conducts a summer camping program for minors. It employs several "counselors" and attendants who help to conduct the program. The denomination requires that all counselors have a valid driver's license. This requirement is based on the fact that it is sometimes necessary for counselors to drive accident victims to a nearby hospital. G applied for a counselor position but was turned down when the denomination discovered that she had epilepsy and did not have a driver's license. The House Report to the ADA states, "While it was necessary that some of the group counselors be able to drive, it was not essential that all group counselors be able to drive. On any given shift, another group counselor could perform the driving duty. Hence, it is necessary to review the job duty not in isolation, but in the context of the actual work environment. . . . The 'essential functions' requirement assures that a person who cannot drive because of his or her disability is not disqualified for these reasons if he or she can do the actual duties of the job." Assuming that the denomination is a covered employer under the ADA, it has violated the law. G clearly is a qualified individual with a disability. The term "qualified individual with a disability" is defined by the ADA as an individual with a disability who, with or without reasonable accommodation, can perform the essential functions of the employment position. Since the "essential function" of the job is the ability to engage in counseling activities, and not the ability to drive a car, G can perform the essential job functions without any accommodation by the employer.*

Accordingly, the employer must accommodate G's disability. By refusing to consider G, the employer failed to reasonably accommodate G's disability, and thereby committed unlawful discrimination.

• *A denominational agency has a job opening for a warehouse worker. The job description states that the position requires a person capable of lifting 50-pound boxes. R, who suffers from multiple sclerosis, applies for the job although he is not able to lift 50-pound boxes. The House Report to the ADA states, "[Congress] does not intend to limit the ability of covered employers to choose and maintain a qualified workforce. Covered employers continue to have the ability to hire and employ employees who can perform the job. Employers can continue to use job-related criteria in choosing qualified employees. For example, in a job that requires lifting 50-pound boxes, an employer may test applicants and employees to determine whether or not they can lift 50-pound boxes." The ADA itself states that "it may be a defense to a charge of discrimination . . . that an alleged application of qualification standards, tests, or selection criteria that screen out or tend to screen out or otherwise deny a job or benefit to an individual with a disability has been shown to be job-related and consistent with business necessity, and such performance cannot be accomplished by reasonable accommodation." That is, the 50-pound box requirement is a legitimate requirement only if it in fact is job-related (i.e., workers in fact have to lift 50-pound boxes) and consistent with business necessity.*

• *A denomination plans to conduct an annual conference of affiliated clergy at Hotel Y. The denomination enters into a contract with Hotel Y for the conference. Assuming that the denomination is a covered employer under the ADA, it has an affirmative duty to investigate the accessibility of Hotel Y to disabled persons. The House Report to the ADA states, "Suggested approaches for determining accessibility would be for the employer to inspect the hotel first-hand, if possible, or to ask a local disability group to inspect the hotel. In any event, the employer can always protect itself in such situations by simply ensuring that the contract with the hotel specifies that all rooms to be used for the conference, including the exhibit and meeting rooms, be accessible in accordance with applicable standards. If the hotel breaches this accessibility provision, the hotel will be liable to the employer for the cost of any accommodation needed to provide access to the disabled individual during the conference, as well as for any other costs accrued by the employer."*

• *A religious organization subject to the ADA has a job opening for a typist. One of the essential functions of the job is the ability to type at least 75 words per minute. Two persons apply for the job. One is a disabled person who can type 50 words per minute. The other is a nondisabled person who can type 75 words per minute. The employer is free to hire the nondisabled person. This will not violate the ADA. The House Report to the ADA states: "An employer can continue to give typists typing tests to determine their abilities. [Congress] does not intend that covered employers have an obligation to prefer applicants with disabilities over other applicants on the basis of disability."*

• *A religious organization subject to the ADA has an opening for an accountant. The job description requires that the individual be a college graduate with a degree in accounting. A blind applicant satisfies these requirements. She can perform all the essential functions of the job if she is provided with a part-time reader. If providing a part-time reader is a reasonable accommodation, then the applicant is a qualified individual with a disability, and she cannot be denied the job on the basis of her impairment unless providing the reader would constitute an undue hardship to the employer. Whether or not an undue hardship would exist depends upon an analysis of several factors, including the* size, financial resources, and number of employees of the employer. Obviously, the concept of undue hardship will be much narrower for larger employers having substantial financial resources. The House Report to the ADA states, "For some people with disabilities, the assistance of another individual, such as a reader, interpreter or attendant, may be necessary for specified activities."

• A denominational agency subject to the ADA restricts its hiring to persons who are members of affiliated churches. J, a disabled person, applies for a position with the agency. J is not a member of an affiliated church. The agency hires T for the position, since T is a member of an affiliated church (even though T had lower test scores than J). This discrimination is permitted under ADA.

• Same facts as the previous case study, except that both J and T are members of an affiliated church. The denomination may not discriminate against J on the basis of disability.

• A federal appeals court ruled that a church-operated school violated the Americans with Disabilities Act by failing to accommodate a disabled job applicant.[190] A church school placed an ad in a local newspaper for a part-time music teacher. A woman with multiple sclerosis and confined to a wheelchair called the school in response to the ad. She claimed that school employees refused to grant her an interview after she asked if the building was "wheelchair accessible." The woman filed a complaint with the Equal Employment Opportunity Commission (EEOC), which determined that the she had been a victim of discrimination on account of her disability. The EEOC sued the church and its school, claiming that they both had violated the Americans with Disabilities Act (ADA) as a result of their refusal to "accommodate" the woman's disability, and their failure to hire her because of her disability. The church and school argued that they were not covered by the ADA since they were not engaged in "commerce" and had less than 15 employees. A federal appeals court rejected this argument, and ruled that the woman could sue for a violation of the ADA. This case is addressed fully in section 8-14.

• A federal court in Louisiana ruled that a church school did not violate the Americans with Disabilities Act by not rehiring a teacher (the "plaintiff") who had to temporarily quit her job because of pregnancy-related varicose veins.[191] The school accommodated her by providing her with a first-floor classroom because of her discomfort in climbing stairs. While pregnant with her fifth child, the plaintiff did not teach and received disability payments from the school. She returned to the school for the next school year but left during the middle of the year when she became pregnant with her sixth child. She received disability payments during this time period. When her doctor released her to return to teaching, the school had no available positions since the release occurred during the middle of the school year. The school's principal informed the plaintiff that she would probably not be hired for the next school year because the school would be retaining her replacement. When the replacement teacher indicated that she would not be returning the next year, the principal hired another teacher from a list of 75 applicants. She chose not to rehire the plaintiff because of her evaluation of the plaintiff's professional capabilities and past attendance record. The principal felt that the new teacher, who had 11 years of teaching experience, was better qualified than the plaintiff. The plaintiff sued the school, claiming that its decision not to rehire her violated the Americans with Disabilities Act (ADA). The court noted that the school offered nondis-

---

[190] Equal Employment Opportunity Commission v. St. Francis Xavier Parochial School, 117 F.3d 621 (D.C. Cir. 1997).

[191] Kent v. Roman Catholic Church, 7 A.D. Cases 884 (E.D. La. 1997).

183

criminatory reasons for the principal's decision not to rehire the plaintiff. It was then up to the plaintiff to prove that the employer's reason was a "pretext" for discrimination. The court concluded that the plaintiff failed to meet this burden.

• A Washington state court ruled that a Catholic archdiocese was liable for handicap discrimination.[192] The archdiocese maintains a conference facility that hired a female housekeeper. The housekeeper injured her hand while working, and had to have surgery. Following the surgery, she returned to work for a brief time before she underwent a second surgery. When she left for this second surgery, she alleged that her supervisor assured her that there "would always be a place for her" at the conference facility and that another employee would fill her position only on a temporary basis. Eight months later, the housekeeper was released by her doctor to return to work. When she returned to work, she was informed by her supervisor that her position had been filled after she had been absent for 60 days. She was not notified of any other job openings nor offered any other jobs with the archdiocese, even though there were three job openings at the conference facility following her discharge. The housekeeper sued the archdiocese, alleging handicap discrimination. A jury awarded her $150,000 in damages, and a state appeals court affirmed this verdict. The court noted that once the employee demonstrated that she was handicapped, and that she was qualified to fill vacant positions, then the burden "shifted" to the employer "to demonstrate a nondiscriminatory reason for refusing to accommodate" the employee. The court noted that the housekeeper had established that she was handicapped (because of her hand injury), and that three job openings later occurred that she was qualified to fill. Accordingly, the archdiocese then had the duty to demonstrate that it had a valid nondiscriminatory reason for not "accommodating" the housekeeper by taking affirmative measures to notify her of the job openings. The court insisted that when an employee becomes handicapped on the job, the employer has a continuing duty to inform the employee of job openings beyond the termination of the employer-employee relationship—until such time as "such attempts to accommodate become an undue burden rather than a reasonable requirement." Since the archdiocese failed to notify the former employee of these job openings, and failed to demonstrate a nondiscriminatory reason for not doing so, the former employee had proven her claim of handicap discrimination.

Discrimination in Public Accommodations
§ 8-14.2

Key Point 8-14.2> *The federal Americans with Disabilities Act prohibits discrimination against disabled persons by privately owned places of public accommodation. The Act exempts religious organizations from this provision. Some states and cities have enacted laws prohibiting discrimination against disabled persons in some places of public accommodation, and these laws may apply to religious organizations.*

---

[192] Wheeler v. Catholic Archdiocese of Seattle, 829 P.2d 196 (Wash. App. 1992).

DID YOU KNOW?

STEPS EMPLOYERS SHOULD TAKE TO COMPLY WITH THE ADA

1. Prepare job descriptions for all employees. Be sure to itemize essential job functions. These are functions that are job-related and required by business necessity. Do not list functions that will not in fact be required in performing the job in question.

2. Review job application forms and eliminate any question that segregates or classifies applicants on the basis of disability.

3. Review all employee selection criteria and procedures to ensure that they (1) provide an accurate measure of an applicant's actual ability to perform the essential functions of the job, and (2) offer disabled applicants a reasonable accommodation to meet the criteria that relate to the essential job functions.

4. Review all pre-employment tests to ensure that they do not discriminate against disabled individuals.

5. Eliminate any pre-employment medical examination requirement.

6. Post required notices informing applicants and employees of their rights under the ADA.

7. Interview procedures and questions should be reviewed carefully. It is not permissible to ask applicants about disabilities. For example, if driving is an essential job function, an employer may ask a job applicant whether or not he or she has a driver's license, but it would be improper to ask whether or not the applicant has a visual impairment.

8. Designate an employee who will be responsible for ensuring ADA compliance, and be sure that this individual receives sufficient training.

9. Educate supervisory personnel regarding ADA requirements and prohibitions.

Another major provision (Title III) of the ADA prohibits discrimination against disabled persons by privately owned places of public accommodation. The ADA states that "no individual shall be discriminated against on the basis of disability in the full and equal enjoyment of the goods, services, facilities, privileges, advantages, or accommodations of any place of public accommodation by any person who owns, leases (or leases to), or operates a place of public accommodation." The ADA defines the term *public accommodation* to include 12 types of facilities, including auditoriums or other places of public gathering, private schools (including nursery, elementary, secondary, undergraduate, and postgraduate), and day care centers.

The ADA defines discrimination in public accommodations broadly to include the following:

- Denying an individual (or class of individuals) the opportunity to use the accommodations on the basis of a disability.

- Providing disabled individuals with use or enjoyment of the accommodations that is not equal to that afforded nondisabled persons.

- Providing disabled individuals with use or enjoyment of the accommodations separate from those afforded nondisabled persons.

- Establishing eligibility criteria that screen out disabled individuals.

- Failure to make reasonable modifications in policies, practices, or procedures, if necessary to make the accommodations available to disabled individuals.

- Failure to take steps to ensure that disabled persons are not denied use of the accommodations because of the absence of "auxiliary aids and services."

- Failure to remove architectural barriers in existing facilities if such removal is "readily achievable." The term readily achievable is defined by the ADA to mean "easily accomplishable and able to be carried out without much difficulty or expense." Factors to be considered in making this determination include (1) the nature and cost of the action needed, and (2) the overall financial resources of the facility, the number of employees, and the impact of the removal on the operation of the facility.

- Failure to employ readily achievable alternatives if the removal of architectural barriers is not readily achievable.

Disabled persons are permitted to sue an organization that owns or operates a place of public accommodation that engages in one or more of these discriminatory practices. They can either obtain a court injunction ordering the place of public accommodation to comply with the law, or they can obtain monetary damages (up to $50,000 for a first violation, and up to $100,000 for subsequent violations).

The ADA specifies that its public accommodation provisions "shall not apply to . . . religious organizations or entities controlled by religious organizations, including places of worship." Accordingly, most types of religious organizations are excluded from the prohibition of discrimination in places of public accommodation. The House Report to the ADA specifies that "places of worship and schools controlled by religious organizations are among those organizations and entities which fall within this exemption." The House Report further specifies that "activities conducted by a religious organization or an entity controlled by a religious organization on its own property, which are open to nonmembers of that organization or entity are included in this exemption."

It is important to note that while religious organizations are not subject to the ADA's public accommodation provisions, they may be subject to similar provisions under state or local law.

Case Study

> • Local churches, denominational agencies, and church-controlled schools do not have to comply with the public accommodation provisions of the ADA. For example, they would not need to remove architectural barriers to make their facilities more accessible to disabled persons. This exemption applies both to existing and future construction. But be sure to check state and local laws for possible application.

Family and Medical Leave Act § 8-15

Key Point 8-15> *The federal Family and Medical Leave Act requires employers with 50 or more employees and engaged in interstate commerce to allow employees up to 12 weeks of unpaid leave each year on account of certain medical and family needs. There is no exemption for religious organizations.*

A. In General—the "Leave" Requirement

The Family and Medical Leave Act[193] requires every employer that is "engaged in commerce or in any industry or activity affecting commerce that employs 50 or more employees" to grant eligible employees up to 12 workweeks of unpaid leave during any 12-month period in any one or more of the following situations:

- Because of the birth of a son or daughter of the employee and in order to care for such son or daughter.

- Because of the placement of a son or daughter with the employee for adoption or foster care.

- In order to care for the spouse, or a son, daughter, or parent, of the employee, if such spouse, son, daughter, or parent has a serious health condition.

- Because of a serious health condition that makes the employee unable to perform the functions of the position of such employee.

An eligible employee (entitled to up to 12 workweeks of leave) is an employee who has been employed for at least 12 months by the employer and who has at least 1,250 hours of service with that employer during the previous 12-month period (an average of 25 hours per week).

Note that only those employers "engaged in commerce or in any industry or activity affecting commerce" and that employ 50 or more employees are covered by the Act. One senator estimated that this restrictive definition has the effect of exempting 95 percent of the employers in this country from the new law, and "leaving over 60 percent of the work force unprotected."

Another important term under the Act is "serious medical condition," since leave is required (1) in order to enable an employee to care for a spouse, son, daughter, or parent if such person has *a serious medical condition*, or (2) if an

---

[193] 29 U.S.C. § 2601 *et seq.*

employee has *a serious health condition* that makes the employee unable to perform the functions of his or her job. What is a "serious medical condition"? The Act defines the term as "an illness, injury, impairment, or physical or mental condition that involves inpatient care in a hospital, hospice, or residential medical care facility; or continuing treatment by a health care provider." Note that the terms "son" and "daughter" include a biological, adopted, or foster child, a stepchild, or a legal ward, who is under 18 years of age or who is 18 years of age or older and incapable of self-care because of a mental or physical disability.

There are a few other provisions of the Act that deserve comment:

intermittent leave

The Act specifies that employees cannot necessarily take their leave "intermittently" or on a "reduced leave" basis. For example, employees entitled to leave because of the birth or adoption (or foster care placement) of a child may not take their leave intermittently or on a reduced leave schedule unless the employee and the employer agree.

unpaid leave

Note that all the Act requires is unpaid leave. Employers are not required to pay employees during their medical or family leave.

effect on existing leave policy

If an employer already makes less than 12 weeks of paid leave available to an employee for the conditions specified in the Act, then "the additional weeks of leave necessary to attain the 12 workweeks of leave required under this Act may be provided without compensation."

employees' duties

Employees have certain duties under the Act. One such duty is the "notice" requirement. The Act specifies that in cases involving the birth or adoption of a child, "the employee shall provide the employer with not less than 30 days' notice, before the date the leave is to begin, of the employee's intention to take leave . . . except that if the date of the birth or placement requires leave to begin in less than 30 days, the employee shall provide such notice as is practicable." Further, if medical care or treatment (for the employee or the employee's spouse, child, or parent) is foreseeable, then the employee is required to "make a reasonable effort to schedule the treatment so as not to disrupt unduly the operations of the employer, subject to the approval of the health care provider of the employee or the health care provider of the son, daughter, spouse, or parent of the employee, as appropriate; and shall provide the employer with not less than 30 days' notice, before the date the leave is to begin, of the employee's intention to take leave . . . except that if the date of the treatment requires leave to begin in less than 30 days, the employee shall provide such notice as is practicable." The Act also clarifies that an employer may require an employee on leave to report periodically to the employer on the status and intention of the employee to return to work.

certification

As an accommodation to employers, the Act contains a provision that permits employers to certify that an employee (or an employee's spouse, child, or parent) has a "serious health condition" warranting leave. The Act specifies that an employer may require that a request for leave under such circumstances "be supported by a certification issued by the health care provider of the eligible employee or of the son, daughter, spouse, or parent of the employee, as appropriate. The employee shall provide, in a timely manner, a copy of such certification to the employer." The certification is sufficient if it states

> (1) the date on which the serious health condition commenced; (2) the probable duration of the condition; (3) the appropriate medical facts within the knowledge of the health care provider regarding the condition; (4) a statement that the eligible employee is needed to care for the son, daughter, spouse, or parent and an estimate of the amount of time that such employee is needed to care for the son, daughter, spouse, or parent, or a statement that the employee is unable to perform the functions of the position of the employee; and (5) in the case of certification for intermittent leave for planned medical treatment, the dates on which such treatment is expected to be given and the duration of such treatment.

The Act permits employers to obtain a "second opinion" concerning the medical condition of an employee or of an employee's spouse, child, or parent. It provides: "In any case in which the employer has reason to doubt the validity of the certification provided [by an employee] the employer may require, at the expense of the employer, that the eligible employee obtain the opinion of a second health care provider designated or approved by the employer concerning any information [in the original certification]." However, an employer may not obtain a second opinion from a health care provider that is "employed on a regular basis by the employer." If a second opinion differs from the original certification, then "the employer may require, at the expense of the employer, that the employee obtain the opinion of a third health care provider designated or approved jointly by the employer and the employee concerning the information certified [in the original certification]. The opinion of the third health care provider . . . shall be considered to be final and shall be binding on the employer and the employee."

The Act further specifies that an employer "may require that the eligible employee obtain subsequent recertifications on a reasonable basis."

returning to work

What happens when an employee who has been on medical or family leave returns to work? Must the employee be returned to his or her former job? This is what the Act says: "Any eligible employee who takes leave . . . shall be entitled, on return from such leave, to be restored by the employer to the position of employment held by the employee when the leave commenced, or to be restored to an equivalent position with equivalent employment benefits, pay, and other terms and conditions of employment." With regard to the accrual of seniority and fringe benefits during periods of unpaid medical or family leave, the Act provides that "the taking of leave shall not result in the loss of any employment benefit accrued prior to the date on which the leave commenced." However, nothing in the Act "shall be construed to entitle any restored employee to the accrual of any seniority or employment benefits during any period of leave, or any right, benefit, or position of employment other than any right, benefit, or position to which the employee would have been entitled had the employee not taken the leave." While an employee is on leave required by the Act, the employer "shall maintain coverage under any group health plan for the duration of such leave at the level and under the conditions coverage would have been provided if the employee had continued in employment continuously for the duration of such leave." If the employee does not return from leave, the employer in some cases is entitled to recover the premium that the employer paid for maintaining coverage for the employee under a group health plan.

If an employee has been on leave because of his or her own medical condition, the Act specifies that "as a condition of restoration . . . the employer may have a uniformly applied practice or policy that requires each such employee to receive certification from the health care provider of the employee that the employee is able to resume work, except that nothing in this paragraph shall supersede a valid state or local law or a collective bargaining agreement that governs the return to work of such employees."

notice

The Act requires employers to "post and keep posted, in conspicuous places on the premises of the employer where notices to employees and applicants for employment are customarily posted, a notice . . . setting forth excerpts from, or summaries of, the pertinent provisions of this Act." The penalty for noncompliance with the notice requirement is $100 for each separate offense.

B. Application to Churches and other Religious Organizations

There is no exemption in the Act for religious organizations. However, the Act will have minimal impact on most churches, since it applies only to employers that are "engaged in commerce or in any industry or activity affecting commerce that employ 50 or more employees." Most churches employ fewer than 50 persons, and these churches will not be affected at all by the new law. A church employing 50 or more persons can establish that it is exempt by demonstrating that it is not engaged in a business or activity "affecting commerce." Whether or not a church or other religious organization is engaged in "commerce" is a question addressed fully in section 8-09 of this chapter.

There is no doubt that some religious organizations will be covered by the Act, including many denominational headquarters, publishers, religious educational institutions, and larger churches. Administrators of such institutions should review this section carefully, and consult with their own legal counsel to discuss coverage and implementation issues.

Some churches will voluntarily comply with the Act, even though they have fewer than 50 employees or are not engaged in commerce. After all, Congress has determined that a 12-week medical and family leave policy is essential to preserve the family. As one senator remarked, "to lose your job and to lose health care coverage when your child is sick or your spouse is ill or a parent you are caring for is in trouble, to lose a job and lose the health care coverage, what more cruel set of facts could strike a family? So this legislation will do an awful lot just to save and protect good people who are trying to hold body and soul and family together at a time when they need it most. . . . The Family and Medical Leave Act establishes a basic standard of human decency."

Churches considering voluntary compliance with the Act should keep in mind the following points:

- The medical and family leave mandated under the Act is unpaid leave. This is a noncash fringe benefit.

- The cost to an employer in granting unpaid leave can be significantly less than the cost of training a permanent replacement for an employee who needs time off due to the birth of a child or an illness in the family. Much congressional testimony was devoted to proving this point.

- Employers who voluntarily comply with the Act will realize a benefit in the form of improved employee morale. Many church employees will expect their church to provide medical and family leave, even though the church may not be subject to the Act. Church employees will expect their church to comply with a law designed to protect the family rather than hide behind the "legal technicality" that they are exempt.

- Recall that employers can require verification that an employee is eligible for the leave. This will reduce the risk that employees will abuse the medical and family leave policy.

Case Studies

- *A federal court in Michigan ruled that a church school did not violate the Family and Medical Leave Act, or a state employment discrimination law, when it refused to return a female employee to her former job following a 33-week leave of absence caused by pregnancy-related complications. A female employee was unable to work three months into a pregnancy. She did not return to work until 33 weeks after she began pregnancy leave. When she reported for work, the school principal informed her that she was assigned to a new position with the same salary and benefits, according to a plan he had devised to reorganize the office. The employee perceived this reassignment as a demotion, tendered a letter of resignation a few days later, and then filed a lawsuit claiming that the church violated her rights under the Family and Medical Leave Act (FMLA). Federal regulations state that "it is the employer's responsibility to designate leave, paid or unpaid, as FMLA-qualifying, and to give notice of the designation to the employee as provided in this section." According to the regulations, an employer's failure to give an appropriate notice designating leave as FMLA-qualifying leave precludes the employer from counting any of the absences against the FMLA's 12 weeks. An employer may not designate leave as FMLA leave retroactively. In this case the church failed to notify the employee that any of her disability leave commencing on the day she left her job due to pregnancy was considered FMLA leave. She claimed that her absence from work before the church designated her leave as FMLA leave could not be counted against FMLA's 12 weeks, and since she returned to work within 12 weeks of the church's designation she enjoys the protection of the FMLA despite an actual absence that exceeded 12 weeks. The court relied on a decision by the United States Supreme Court in which the Court concluded that an employer's violation of the notice regulations does not automatically entitle an employee to additional leave beyond 12 weeks or establish a right to recovery.[194] Rather, the employee must prove that she suffered prejudice by the employer's failure to properly notify her of her rights under the FMLA or that certain leave would be counted against her FMLA allotment. The court concluded that there was no evidence that the employee could have returned to work within 12 weeks of the time she began her pregnancy leave regardless of the notice the church might have given her regarding her rights and responsibilities under the FMLA. An employee "who does not return to work within the 12-week period specified by the FMLA may not claim the protection provided by the Act."[195]*

• A federal district court in New York ruled that a church agency did not violate the Family and Medical Leave Act by dismissing an employee whose investment decisions resulted in a loss of $8 million in church funds.[196] Before dismissing the employee, the agency attempted to work out a severance agreement with the employee. While these negotiations were proceeding, the employee took medical leave. He was later dismissed when efforts to negotiate a severance agreement failed. The employee sued the agency, claiming that his dismissal violated the Family and Medical Leave Act (FMLA), which makes it unlawful for covered employers to "discharge or in any other manner discriminate" against any individual for exercising rights provided by the Act. A federal district court dismissed the lawsuit. It noted that "the FMLA provides that an employee on protected leave is not entitled to any greater rights or benefits than he would be entitled to had he not taken the leave." It further observed that it was undisputed that the church had announced its determination to terminate the director before he went on medical leave, but deferred doing so only to provide an opportunity for the parties to try to negotiate a resignation agreement. Further, the church reserved the right to terminate the director if no such agreement were negotiated. As a result, the director "was not denied any right, for none was preserved." The FMLA "does not require employers to give returning employees any assurances of job security to which they would not have been entitled, prior to taking sick leave." The court also observed that "FMLA is not a shield to protect employees from legitimate disciplinary action by their employers if their performance is lacking in some manner unrelated to their FMLA leave."

Employer "Retaliation" Against Victims of Discrimination § 8-16

Key Point 8-16> *State and federal civil rights laws generally prohibit employers from retaliating against an employee for filing a discrimination claim or otherwise exercising rights provided by the law.*

---

[194] Ragsdale v. Wolverine World Wide, Inc., 535 U.S. 81 (2002).

[195] Thompson v. Diocese of Saginaw, 2004 WL 45519 (E.D. Mich. 2004).

[196] Carrillo v. The National Council of the Churches of Christ in the U.S.A., 976 F. Supp. 254 (S.D.N.Y. 1997).

Many federal and state civil rights laws that ban discrimination in employment prohibit employers from "retaliating" against employees who oppose discriminatory practices or pursue claims of discrimination. To illustrate, Title VII of the Civil Rights Act of 1964,[197] the federal Age Discrimination in Employment Act,[198] and the Americans with Disabilities Act[199] all prohibit employer retaliation.

Case Studies

• *The Colorado Supreme Court threw out a lawsuit brought by a woman alleging that her church acted improperly and unlawfully when it dismissed her after she made complaints of sexual harassment against another minister. The woman alleged that her stepfather committed various acts of sexual assault against her when she was a minor. Her stepfather was a minister at the time, and later became president of his denomination. The woman pursued ministerial studies and was licensed as a minister. She later learned that her stepfather was harassing female church employees and parishioners in another church, and she reported this to denominational officers. In response, the stepfather filed charges with the denomination against the woman, claiming that her allegations were false and demanding a full investigation. After an investigation, denominational officers revoked the woman's license and denied her the opportunity to open a new church. The woman responded by filing a lawsuit against her stepfather, and her denomination, alleging several theories of liability including illegal retaliation by denominational officials in response to her charges of sexual harassment, in violation of Title VII of the Civil Rights Act of 1964. The court rejected this claim on the ground that it arose from the denomination's decision to revoke her minister's license. The court concluded that it was barred from resolving the woman's lawsuit on the basis of the First Amendment's free exercise and nonestablishment of religion clauses.[200]*

• *A male associate pastor engaged in sexual relations with two female church employees. The two women eventually disclosed the affairs to the church's senior pastor. This led to their termination, and the forced resignation of the associate pastor. The women later sued the church, claiming that it committed unlawful "retaliation" against them in violation of Title VII by dismissing them for disclosing the associate pastor's behavior. A federal district court disagreed, noting that the church could not be responsible for retaliation since its decision to dismiss the women was not sex discrimination. This conclusion was affirmed on appeal by a federal appeals court.[201] The court observed: "The [women] did not . . . produce any evidence suggesting that they were fired because of their gender. In fact, the record shows that [the former minister], who also committed adultery, was forced to resign, and that [the church's] position against adultery was neutral with respect to sex, longstanding, and understood by both [women] at the time they engaged in sexual conduct with [the minister]."*

---

[197] 42 U.S.C. § 2000e-3(a).

[198] 29 U.S.C. § 623(d).

[199] 42 U.S.C. § 12203.

[200] Van Osdol v. Vogt, 908 P.2d 402 (Colo. 1996).

[201] Sanders v. Casa View Baptist Church, 134 F.3d 331 (5th Cir. 1998).

• *A federal court in California ruled that a female minister failed to prove that her denominational agency had engaged in sexual harassment.[202] A woman (the victim) was employed as national director of a department of a denominational agency (the Buddhist Churches of America, or BCA). She was ordained as a Buddhist minister. She alleged that another minister made a sexually harassing telephone call to her during a BCA conference. She filed a complaint with the Equal Employment Opportunity Commission (EEOC) regarding the harassing call. She later sued the BCA in federal court, claiming that it had engaged in unlawful "retaliation" against her by cutting off all funding of her department following the filing of her EEOC claim. The court noted that to prove a "prima facie case" of unlawful retaliation, a plaintiff must establish that she acted to protect her Title VII rights, that an adverse employment action was thereafter taken against her, and that a connection existed between these two events. At that point, the burden of production then shifts to the employer to advance legitimate, non-retaliatory reasons for any adverse actions taken against the plaintiff. The court concluded that it could not resolve the victim's retaliation claim, since "[i]f plaintiff makes out a prima facie case of retaliation, the court would be placed in the position of evaluating whether BCA had any legitimate, non-retaliatory reasons for the defunding of [her] department. . . . Although the financial decisions of a church are not, strictly speaking, part of the church's "spiritual function," these decisions remain vital to a religious organization's ministerial and religious planning. Determining whether the decision to eliminate funding from [the victim's] department—a religious education department—was legitimate seems likely to draw this court into judgments on matters of faith and doctrine, as well as matters of general church governance. Because it appears that plaintiff's retaliation claim would result in an intolerably close relationship between church and state both on a substantive and procedural level, plaintiff's retaliation claim is dismissed . . . on First Amendment grounds.*

Discrimination Based on Military Status

§ 8-17

Key Point 8-17> *Federal law prohibits all employers, including churches, from discriminating against any person on account of military service. This includes discriminating against an applicant for employment, or an employee, who has an obligation to perform services on active duty or in the National Guard.*

The Uniformed Services Employment and Reemployment Rights Act (USERRA) applies to persons who perform work in the "uniformed services," which include the Army, Navy, Marine Corps, Air Force, Coast Guard, and Public Health Service commissioned corps, as well as the reserve components of each of these services. Federal training or service in the Army National Guard and Air National Guard also gives rise to rights under USERRA. In addition, under the Public Health Security and Bioterrorism Response Act, certain disaster response work is considered "service in the uniformed services."

Uniformed service includes active duty, active duty for training, inactive duty training (such as drills), initial active duty training, and funeral honors duty per-

---

[202] Himaka v. Buddhist Churches of America, 917 F.Supp. 698 (N.D. Cal. 1995).

formed by National Guard and reserve members, as well as the period for which a person is absent from a position of employment for the purpose of an examination to determine fitness to perform any such duty.

USERRA covers nearly all employees, including part-time and probationary employees. USERRA applies to virtually all U.S. employers, regardless of size. *Religious employers are not exempt.*

In general, an employer must reemploy service members returning from a period of service in the uniformed services if those service members meet five criteria: (1) the person must have held a civilian job; (2) the person must have given notice to the employer that he or she was leaving the job for service in the uniformed services, unless giving notice was precluded by military necessity or otherwise impossible or unreasonable; (3) the cumulative period of service must not have exceeded five years; (4) the person must not have been released from service under dishonorable conditions; and (5) the person must have reported back to the civilian job in a timely manner or have submitted a timely application for reemployment.

USERRA establishes a five-year "cumulative total" on military service with a single employer, with certain exceptions allowed for situations such as call-ups during emergencies, reserve drills, and annually scheduled active duty for training.

Key Point > *USERRA also allows an employee to complete an initial period of active duty that exceeds five years (e.g., enlistees in the Navy's nuclear power program are required to serve six years).*

Key Point > *Laws in some states provide additional protections to military personnel.*

Employee Polygraph Protection Act

§ 8-18

Key Point 8-18 > *Federal law prohibits employers that are engaged in interstate commerce (regardless of the number of employees) to require or even suggest that an employee or prospective employee submit to a polygraph examination. There is no exemption for religious organizations. A very limited exception exists for "ongoing investigations" into employee theft.*

A. Background

The Employee Polygraph Protection Act (EPPA),[203] which was enacted by Congress in 1988, prohibits any "employer" (defined as an employer "engaged in or affecting commerce") from doing any one of the following three acts:

(1) directly or indirectly, to require, request, suggest, or cause any employee or prospective employee to take or submit to any lie detector test;

---

[203] 29 U.S.C. § 2001 *et seq.*

(2) to use, accept, refer to, or inquire concerning the results of any lie detector test of any employee or prospective employee;

(3) to discharge, discipline, discriminate against in any manner, or deny employment or promotion to, or threaten to take any such action against—(A) any employee or prospective employee who refuses, declines, or fails to take or submit to any lie detector test, or (B) any employee or prospective employee on the basis of the results of any lie detector test . . . .

A church is subject to the Act if it is "engaged in or affecting commerce." There is no requirement that an employer have a minimum number of employees. Whether or not churches and other religious organizations are engaged in "commerce" is a question that is addressed in section 8-09 of this chapter.

▶ *The Act not only prohibits covered employers from requiring that employees take polygraph exams, but it also prohibits an employer from requesting or suggesting that an employee or prospective employee take such an exam.*

B. An Important Exception for "Ongoing Investigations" into Employee Theft

The Act contains a few narrow exceptions. One permits employers to ask employees to submit to a polygraph exam if they are suspected of theft and there is an ongoing investigation. Here are the details of this exception:

[This Act] shall not prohibit an employer from requesting an employee to submit to a polygraph test if—

(1) the test is administered in connection with an ongoing investigation involving economic loss or injury to the employer's business, such as theft, embezzlement, misappropriation, or an act of unlawful industrial espionage or sabotage;

(2) the employee had access to the property that is the subject of the investigation;

(3) the employer had a reasonable suspicion that the employee was involved in the incident or activity under investigation; and

(4) the employer executes a statement, provided to the examinee before the test, that—(A) sets forth with particularity the specific incident or activity being investigated and the basis for testing particular employees, (B) is signed by a person (other than a polygraph examiner) authorized to legally bind the employer, (C) is retained by the employer for at least 3 years, and (D) contains at a minimum—(i) an identification of the specific economic loss or injury to the business of the employer, (ii) a statement indicating that the employee had access to the property that is the subject of the investigation, and (iii) a statement describing the basis of the employer's reasonable suspicion that the employee was involved in the incident or activity under investigation.[204]

---

[204] 29 U.S.C. § 2006(d).

If your church is subject to the Employee Polygraph Protection Act, then the following prohibitions apply:

• You cannot "require, request, suggest, or cause" any employee or prospective employee to take a polygraph exam.

• You cannot "actively participate" with the police in administering a polygraph exam to an employee. You can engage in "passive cooperation." This includes allowing the police to conduct an exam on your premises, or releasing an employee during working hours to take a test at a police station.

• You cannot "use, accept, refer to, or inquire concerning the results" of a polygraph exam.

• You cannot discharge, discipline, discriminate against, or deny employment or promotion to an employee or applicant for employment on the basis of (1) a refusal to take a polygraph exam, or (2) the results of a polygraph exam. Nor can you threaten to do so.

Know the details of the "ongoing investigation" exception. Under very limited circumstances, you can request that an employee take a polygraph exam if you suspect the employee of theft and you are conducting an ongoing investigation. Do not rely on this exception without fully complying with all of the requirements quoted above. Also, consult with legal counsel to be sure the exception is available to you.

Case Studies

• A church board suspects the church's volunteer treasurer of embezzling several thousands of dollars of church funds. The treasurer is called into a board meeting, and is told "you can clear your name if you submit to a polygraph exam." Does this conduct violate the Employee Polygraph Protection Act? Possibly not. The Act only protects "employees," and so a volunteer treasurer presumably would not be covered. However, if the treasurer receives any compensation whatever for her services, or is a "prospective employee," then the Act would apply. Because of the possibility that volunteer workers may in some cases be deemed "employees," you should not suggest or request that they take a polygraph exam without the advice of legal counsel.

• Same facts as the previous case study, except that the church suspects a full-time secretary of embezzlement. Can it suggest that the secretary take a polygraph exam? Only if all the requirements of the "ongoing investigation" exception apply. These include: (1) the test is administered in connection with an ongoing investigation

*involving economic loss or injury to the employer's business, such as theft or embez-
zlement; (2) the employee had access to the property that is the subject of the investigation; (3) the employer had a reasonable suspicion that the employee was involved in
the incident or activity under investigation; and (4) the employer executes a statement, provided to the examinee before the test, that—(A) sets forth with particularity
the specific incident or activity being investigated and the basis for testing particular
employees, (B) is signed by a person (other than a polygraph examiner) authorized to
legally bind the employer, (C) is retained by the employer for at least 3 years, and (D)
contains at a minimum—(i) an identification of the specific economic loss or injury to
the business of the employer, (ii) a statement indicating that the employee had access
to the property that is the subject of the investigation, and (iii) a statement describing
the basis of the employer's reasonable suspicion that the employee was involved in the
incident or activity under investigation.*

The EPPA provides that an employer that violates the Act is liable to the
employee or prospective employee for "such relief as may be appropriate, including, but not limited to, employment, reinstatement, promotion, and the payment
of lost wages and benefits." A court may also award damages based on "emotional distress," and punitive damages.

Key Point > *Damages awarded for violating the Employee Polygraph Protection
Act may not be covered under a church's liability insurance policy. This is another reason for church leaders to assume that the Act applies to their church, and to interpret
its provisions prudently.*

Occupational Safety and Health Act

§ 8-19

Key Point 8-19> *The Occupational Safety and Health Act imposes various
requirements upon employers in order to achieve safe and healthful working conditions. The Act applies to any employer engaged in commerce, regardless of the number of employees. There is no exemption for religious organizations, but the
Occupational Safety and Health Administration has not applied the Act, as a matter of
discretion, to employees engaged in religious services.*

In 1970, Congress enacted the Occupational Safety and Health Act (OSHA)
"to assure so far as is possible every working man and woman in the nation safe
and healthful working conditions."[205] The Act achieves its aim primarily through
imposing various duties upon employers. The Act defines covered employers to
include any organization "engaged in a business affecting commerce that has
employees." If an employer is engaged in a business that affects commerce it will
be subject to OSHA even it if has only one employee. In enacting the Act,
Congress "intended to exercise the full extent of the authority granted" to it by
the Constitution's "commerce clause."[206]

---

[205] 29 U.S.C. § 651(b).

[206] Chao v. Occupational Safety and Health Review Commission, 401 F.3d 355 (5th Cir. 2005).

OSHA regulations clearly specify that nonprofit organizations are subject to OSHA regulations:

> The basic purpose of the Act is to improve working environments in the sense that they impair, or could impair, the lives and health of employees. Therefore, certain economic tests such as whether the employer's business is operated for the purpose of making a profit or has other economic ends, may not properly be used as tests for coverage of an employer's activity under the Act. To permit such economic tests to serve as criteria for excluding certain employers, such as nonprofit and charitable organizations which employ one or more employees, would result in thousands of employees being left outside the protections of the Act in disregard of the clear mandate of Congress to assure "every working man and woman in the nation safe and healthful working conditions." Therefore, any charitable or nonprofit organization which employs one or more employees is covered under the Act and is required to comply with its provisions and the regulations issued thereunder.

However, OSHA regulations treat churches as a special case. Here is what the regulations say:

> Churches or religious organizations, like charitable and nonprofit organizations, are considered employers under the Act where they employ one or more persons in secular activities. As a matter of enforcement policy, the performance of, or participation in, religious services (as distinguished from secular or proprietary activities whether for charitable or religion-related purposes) will be regarded as not constituting employment under the Act. Any person, while performing religious services or participating in them in any degree is not regarded as an employer or employee under the Act, notwithstanding the fact that such person may be regarded as an employer or employee for other purposes—for example, giving or receiving remuneration in connection with the performance of religious services.

This language is very important. It demonstrates that OSHA considers churches to be subject to the provisions of the Act and regulations, but for policy reasons no "enforcement" action will be taken against a church that violates OSHA regulations in the course of "the performance of, or participation in religious services" since "any person, while performing religious services or participating in them in any degree is not regarded as an employer or employee under the Act, notwithstanding the fact that such person may be regarded as an employer or employee for other purposes."

The regulations[207] list the following examples of religious organizations that *would be covered* employers under the law:

- a private hospital owned or operated by a religious organization
- a private school or orphanage owned or operated by a religious organization
- commercial establishments of religious organizations engaged in producing or selling products such as alcoholic beverages, bakery goods, religious goods, etc.

---

[207] 29 C.F.R. 1975.4(c).

• administrative, executive, and other office personnel employed by religious organizations

On the other hand, the regulations[208] list the following examples of religious organizations that *would not be covered* employers under the law:

• churches with respect to clergymen while performing or participating in religious services

• churches with respect to other participants in religious services such as choir masters, organists, other musicians, choir members, ushers, and the like

The special treatment of churches and church employees under the OSHA regulations helps to explain why no court has addressed the application of the Act to churches. The fact is that most churches would be considered "employers" under the Act because they are engaged in interstate commerce, but, OSHA has chosen not to assert jurisdiction over churches except in special circumstances.

The partial exemption of churches from OSHA coverage is illustrated by the following case studies:

Case Studies

• *A church uses a small band during worship services. A church member brings an audiometer to a worship service and measures peaks of 105 decibels on the front row with a sustained reading of 95 decibels. The church's music minister (a full-time employee) is exposed for several minutes during each worship service to decibel levels exceeding those specified by OSHA. Must the church implement "administrative or engineering controls" to reduce the noise to levels to acceptable levels or provide "personal protective equipment" to its music minister? The OSHA regulations specify that "as a matter of enforcement policy, the performance of, or participation in, religious services will be regarded as not constituting employment under the Act. Any person, while performing religious services or participating in them in any degree is not regarded as an employer or employee under the Act."*

• *A church uses a small orchestra during worship services twice each week. The orchestra practices for two hours each week in addition to performing in worship services. Members of the orchestra are exposed to decibel levels exceeding the permissible levels specified by OSHA. Is the church liable for exceeding these limits? The OSHA regulations specify that "as a matter of enforcement policy, the performance of, or participation in, religious services will be regarded as not constituting employment under the Act. Any person, while performing religious services or participating in them in any degree is not regarded as an employer or employee under the Act." In addition, OSHA regulations list "participants in religious services such as choir masters, organists, other musicians, choir members, ushers, and the like" as an example of persons who are outside of the scope of OSHA coverage.*

• *Helen is a church organist. She plays the organ several times each week at worship services, choir rehearsals, funerals, weddings, and other special functions. She is frequently exposed to decibel levels exceeding the permissible levels specified by OSHA.*

[208] *Id.*

Is the church liable for exceeding these limits? The OSHA regulations specify that "as a matter of enforcement policy, the performance of, or participation in, religious services will be regarded as not constituting employment under the Act. Any person, while performing religious services or participating in them in any degree is not regarded as an employer or employee under the Act." In addition, OSHA regulations list "participants in religious services such as choir masters, organists, other musicians, choir members, ushers, and the like" as an example of persons who are outside of the scope of OSHA coverage.

• Jon is a sound technician employed by a church. His job is to make sure that sound levels are adequate during all church services and functions. He is required to be present at all rehearsals as well as services and special functions. He is often exposed to music that exceeds the permissible levels specified by OSHA. Is the church liable for exceeding these limits? The OSHA regulations specify that "as a matter of enforcement policy, the performance of, or participation in, religious services will be regarded as not constituting employment under the Act. Any person, while performing religious services or participating in them in any degree is not regarded as an employer or employee under the Act." In addition, OSHA regulations list "participants in religious services such as choir masters, organists, other musicians, choir members, ushers, and the like" as an example of persons who are outside of the scope of OSHA coverage. Does this exception apply to a sound technician? Does his work constitute participation in a religious service "in any degree"? Neither OSHA, nor any court, has addressed this issue. It remains a possibility.

• Pastor Ted has heard that churches are exempt from OSHA. Is this correct? The answer is no. The Occupational Safety and Health Act specifies that "each employer shall furnish to each of his employees a place of employment free from recognized hazards that are causing or are likely to cause . . . serious physical harm." It defines covered employers to include any organization "engaged in a business affecting commerce that has employees." If an employer is engaged in a business that affects commerce it will be subject to OSHA even it if has only one employee. In enacting the Act, Congress "intended to exercise the full extent of the authority granted" to it by the Constitution's "commerce clause." This language is so broad that there is no doubt that most churches are subject to OSHA. However, as a matter of discretion, OSHA regulations specify that "as a matter of enforcement policy" the "performance of, or participation in, religious services will be regarded as not constituting employment under the Act." As a result, "any person, while performing religious services or participating in them in any degree is not regarded as an employer or employee under the Act" even though that person is regarded as an employee for other purposes (such as tax reporting). However, OSHA regulations list the following examples of religious organizations that would be covered employers under the law: (1) a private hospital owned or operated by a religious organization; (2) a private school or orphanage owned or operated by a religious organization; (3) commercial establishments of religious organizations engaged in producing or selling products such as alcoholic beverages, bakery goods, or religious goods; (4) administrative, executive, and other office personnel employed by religious organizations. In summary, churches are subject to OSHA with regard to any of these situations.

Key Point > OSHA violations can result in substantial penalties. These penalties depend on a number of factors. To illustrate, willful or repeated violations of OSHA requirements may result in a penalty of up to $70,000 for each violation (with a minimum penalty of $5,000 in the case of willful violations). Employers who fail to *correct a citation issued by OSHA may be assessed a penalty of up to $7,000 for each day that the violation continues. The Occupational Safety and Health Act specifies that OSHA has authority "to assess all civil penalties provided in this section, giving due consideration to the appropriateness of the penalty with respect to the size of the business of the employer being charged, the gravity of the violation, the good faith of the employer, and the history of previous violations."*

The courts consistently apply a "ministerial exception" to state and federal employment laws based on the assumption that resolution of employment disputes between churches and ministers would entangle the courts in internal church matters in violation of the First Amendment.[209] As one court aptly noted in a case involving a dismissed minister's claim of wrongful termination, "This case involves the fundamental question of who will preach from the pulpit of a church. . . . The bare statement of the question should make obvious the lack of jurisdiction of a civil court. The answer to that question must come from the church." A federal appeals court has applied the ministerial exception to a minister's claim for overtime pay under the federal Fair Labor Standards Act.[210]

Such rulings suggest that ministers may not be able to pursue monetary damages against their employing church for OSHA violations. This issue has never been addressed by a court. It is possible that the ministerial exception would not be applied in an OSHA case, since it pertains to compliance with federal safety regulations that likely would involve no interpretation of church doctrine. Even if the ministerial exception did apply to OSHA claims, it would not bar claims by lay employees.

A covered employer's legal obligation under the Act is to provide employees with a safe place to work. OSHA regulations prescribe several rules to assist employers in complying with this basic requirement. In effect, the regulations could be viewed as reasonable "standards of care." As a result, they might be used by church employees and members to establish a standard of care applicable to churches even with respect to "exempt" positions.

Display of Posters

§ 8-20

Key Point 8-20> *Several federal and state laws require certain employers to display workplace posters in order to inform employees of their rights. Some poster requirements apply to religious organizations, while others do not. Even those that do often require modification to avoid confusion.*

Churches often receive ominous and unsolicited advertisements warning them to begin displaying workplace posters or face substantial fines and penalties. These advertisements have created considerable confusion and apprehension among church leaders. Are churches required to display posters? If so, which ones?

---

[209] See § 8-10, *supra.*

[210] Shaliehsabou v. Hebrew Home of Greater Washington, 363 F.3d 299 (4th Cir. 2004)

A. Poster Requirements Under Federal Law

There are several poster requirements that are imposed by federal law. Those most relevant to churches are summarized below.

1. Minimum Wage and Overtime Pay

The Fair Labor Standards Act is the federal law that contains the minimum wage and overtime pay requirements. More than eighty million American workers are protected (or "covered") by the FLSA, which is enforced by the Wage and Hour Division of the U.S. Department of Labor.

The minimum wage and overtime pay protections of the FLSA will apply to church employees if their work regularly involves them in interstate commerce. The definition of commerce is very broad, and includes such tasks as typing letters that are sent out-of-state in the mail, making telephone calls to persons located in other states, and traveling to other states in their work. Most church employees will meet this broad definition, and are therefore subject to the protections of the FLSA.

There are certain exceptions that are recognized by the FLSA. For example, administrative, executive, and professional workers are not covered. Generally, these are persons who perform duties specified by the Act, and who are paid on a salary basis of at least $455 per week. In addition, Department of Labor regulations specify that "clergy and religious workers are not covered by the FLSA." This language indicates that the official position of the DOL is that clergy are not subject to the minimum wage and overtime pay requirements of the FLSA regardless of the amount of their compensation.

Every employer that employs workers subject to the federal minimum wage and overtime pay requirements is required by law to post "a notice explaining the Act . . . in conspicuous places in every establishment where such employees are employed so as to permit them to observe readily a copy." You can obtain a free copy of a poster from any local office of the United States Department of Labor (Wage and Hours Division), or by visiting the DOL website (www.dol.gov/esa).

The official poster is very generic, and simply notes the current minimum wage, and informs employees that they have a right to "overtime pay at least one and a half times your regular rate of pay for all hours worked over 40 in a workweek." The official poster does not address the unique status of ministers under the law. Therefore, use of the official FLSA poster by churches may lead to confusion and a misinterpretation of the law unless properly modified.

Case Study

• A youth pastor is employed full-time by a church and is paid an annual salary of $20,000. Since he is paid less than $455 per week is he entitled to overtime pay? Department of Labor regulations specify that "clergy and religious workers are not covered by the FLSA." This language indicates that the official position of the DOL is that clergy are not subject to the minimum wage and overtime pay requirements of the FLSA regardless of the amount of their compensation. The DOL regulations provide a basis for concluding that the FLSA minimum wage and overtime pay requirements do not apply to ministers. This clarification is not mentioned in the official FLSA poster.

To the contrary, if the youth pastor read the official FLSA poster, he would assume that the church was legally required to provide him with overtime pay at a rate of one-and-a-half times his regular compensation for hours worked in excess of 40 during the same week.

2. Equal Employment Opportunity

Every employer covered by federal nondiscrimination laws prohibiting employment discrimination based on race, color, sex, national origin, religion, age, equal pay, and disability is required to display on its premises the poster "Equal Employment Opportunity Is the Law." The poster must be displayed prominently, where it can be readily seen by employees and job applicants. You can obtain a free copy of the poster "Equal Employment Opportunity Is the Law" by contacting any local EEOC office, or by visiting the EEOC website (www.eeoc.gov).

Key Point > *To obtain free copies of other federal required posters please contact the U.S. Department of Labor by calling 888-972-7332.*

Churches are subject to these laws only if they are engaged in commerce (most are), and have at least 15 employees (20 in the case of the age discrimination law).

Case Study

• *A church has six employees. It is not subject to federal laws banning employment discrimination based on race, color, sex, national origin, religion, age, equal pay, and disability. It is not required to display on its premises the poster "Equal Employment Opportunity Is the Law."*

The official EEOC poster specifies:

Applicants to and employees of most private employers, state and local governments, educational institutions, employment agencies and labor organizations are protected under the following Federal laws:

RACE, COLOR, RELIGION, SEX, NATIONAL ORIGIN

Title VII of the Civil Rights Act of 1964, as amended, prohibits discrimination in hiring, promotion, discharge, pay, fringe benefits, job training, classification, referral, and other aspects of employment, on the basis of race, color, religion, sex or national origin.

DISABILITY

The Americans with Disabilities Act of 1990, as amended, protects qualified applicants and employees with disabilities from discrimination in hiring, promotion, discharge, pay, job training, fringe benefits, classification, referral, and other aspects of employment on the basis of disability. The law also requires that covered entities provide qualified applicants and employees with disabilities with reasonable accommodations that do not impose undue hardship.

AGE

The Age Discrimination in Employment Act of 1967, as amended, protects applicants and employees 40 years of age or older from discrimination on the basis of age in hiring, promotion, discharge, compensation, terms, conditions or privileges of employment.

SEX (WAGES)

In addition to sex discrimination prohibited by Title VII of the Civil Rights Act of 1964, as amended (see above), the Equal Pay Act of 1963, as amended, prohibits sex discrimination in payment of wages to women and men performing substantially equal work in the same establishment. Retaliation against a person who files a charge of discrimination, participates in an investigation, or opposes an unlawful employment practice is prohibited by all of these Federal laws. If you believe that you have been discriminated against under any of the above laws, you should contact immediately: The U.S. Equal Employment Opportunity Commission (EEOC), 1801 L Street, N.W., Washington, D.C. 20507 or an EEOC field office by calling toll free (800) 669-4000.

Note that the "official" EEOC poster does not address the unique status of ministers and churches under these laws. In particular, note the following two points:

First, the courts have refused to apply these discrimination laws to the relationship between a church and its pastor. This so-called "ministerial exception" is rooted in the First Amendment guaranty of religious freedom. As one court has noted, in a case involving a dismissed minister's claim of unlawful discrimination: "This case involves the fundamental question of who will preach from the pulpit of a church, and who will occupy the church parsonage. The bare statement of the question should make obvious the lack of jurisdiction of a civil court. The answer to that question must come from the church." *Minker v. Baltimore Annual Conference of the United Methodist Church, 894 F.2d 1354 (D.C. Cir. 1990).*

Second, Title VII and the Americans with Disabilities Act contain specific exemptions for religious employers. Both allow churches to discriminate in many employment decisions on the basis of religion.

Neither of these two unique rules is reflected in the Equal Employment Opportunity Is the Law poster, and so the poster will create confusion if posted in a church without appropriate modifications. Consider the following case studies.

Case Studies

• A church has more than 15 employees, and displays the Equal Opportunity Is the Law poster on its premises. An applicant for a bookkeeping position is rejected because she is a member of a different religious faith. The applicant sees the poster, and notes that covered employers cannot discriminate on the basis of religion. She files a formal complaint of discrimination with a civil rights agency. The complaint is quickly dismissed since the ban on religious discrimination in employment does not apply to a church. This unfounded complaint was filed because the official poster does not address the unique rules that pertain to churches.

• A church has more than 20 employees, and displays the Equal Opportunity Is the Law poster on its premises. The church dismisses a 60-year-old associate pastor, and replaces him with a pastor who is 30 years old. The dismissed pastor on many occasions had reviewed the poster, and is now convinced that his dismissal constitutes age discrimination in violation of federal law. As a result, he files a formal claim of discrimination with a civil rights agency. The complaint is quickly dismissed because of the "ministerial exception" to employment discrimination laws. This unfounded complaint was filed because the official poster does not address the unique rules that pertain to churches and ministers.

3. Employee Polygraph Protection Act

The federal Employee Polygraph Protection Act makes it unlawful for an employer engaged in interstate commerce (regardless of the number of employees) to require or even suggest that an employee or job applicant take a polygraph examination. Federal regulations specify that "every employer subject to the [Act] shall post and keep posted on its premises a notice explaining the Act . . . . Such notice must be posted in a prominent and conspicuous place in every establishment of the employer where it can readily be observed by employees and applicants for employment." A free copy of the required notice can be obtained from the nearest office of the U.S. Department of Labor, Wage and Hour Division, or by visiting the DOL website (www.dol.gov/esa). The official poster states, in part:

> The Employee Polygraph Protection Act prohibits most private employers from using lie detector tests either for pre-employment screening or during the course of employment.

PROHIBITIONS

Employers are generally prohibited from requiring or requesting any employee or job applicant to take a lie detector test, and from discharging, disciplining, or discriminating against an employee or prospective employee for refusing to take a test or for exercising other rights under the Act.

EXEMPTIONS

The Act permits polygraph testing, subject to restrictions, of certain employees of private firms who are reasonably suspected of involvement in a workplace incident (theft, embezzlement, etc.) that resulted in economic loss to the employer.

EXAMINEE RIGHTS

Where polygraph tests are permitted, they are subject to numerous strict standards concerning the conduct and length of the test. Examinees have a number of specific rights, including the right to a written notice before testing, the right to refuse or discontinue a test, and the right not to have test results disclosed to unauthorized persons.

The Employee Polygraph Protection Act contains no special rules or exceptions for religious organizations, and so the official poster can be used without modification.

4. Occupational Safety and Health Act (OSHA)

Employers covered by the Occupational Safety and Health Act are required to display a poster prepared by the U.S. Department of Labor summarizing the major provisions of the Act and telling employees how to file a complaint. The newly revised OSHA poster contains the following text:

- You have the right to notify your employer or OSHA about workplace hazards. You may ask OSHA to keep your name confidential.

- You have the right to request an OSHA inspection if you believe that there are unsafe and unhealthful conditions in your workplace. You or your representative may participate in the inspection.

- You can file a complaint with OSHA within 30 days of discrimination by your employer for making safety and health complaints or for exercising your rights under the OSHA Act.

- You have a right to see OSHA citations issued to your employer. Your employer must post the citations at or near the place of the alleged violation.

- Your employer must correct workplace hazards by the date indicated on the citation and must certify that these hazards have been reduced or eliminated.

- You have the right to copies of your medical records or records of your exposure to toxic and harmful substances or conditions.

- Your employer must post this notice in your workplace.

Churches are required to post the OSHA poster if they are covered by the federal Occupational Safety and Health Act. As noted in section 8-19 of this text, religious organizations are only partially subject to OSHA regulations. The official OSHA poster does not take the unique status of churches into account, and may cause confusion unless properly modified.

The OSHA poster can be ordered without charge on the OSHA website (www.osha.gov).

5. Family and Medical Leave Act

The Family and Medical Leave Act provides certain employees with up to 12 weeks of unpaid, "job-protected" leave each year to give birth or to care for a family member, and requires group health benefits to be maintained during the leave as if the employee continued to work instead of taking leave. This law only applies to employers having *50 or more employees.*

All covered employers are required to display and keep displayed a poster prepared by the Department of Labor summarizing the major provisions of the Act and telling employees how to file a complaint. The poster must be displayed in a conspicuous place where employees and applicants for employment can see it.

The official FMLA poster prepared by the Department of Labor is one page long. Here are some of the key provisions:

• FMLA requires covered employers to provide up to 12 weeks of unpaid, job-protected leave to "eligible" employees for certain family and medical reasons. Employees are eligible if they have worked for their employer for at least one year, and for 1,250 hours over the previous 12 months, and if there are at least 50 employees within 75 miles.

• Unpaid leave must be granted for any of the following reasons: (1) to care for the employee's child after birth, or placement for adoption or foster care; (2) to care for the employee's spouse, son or daughter, or parent who has a serious health condition; or (3) for a serious health condition that makes the employee unable to perform the employee's job.

• At the employee's or employer's option, certain kinds of paid leave may be substituted for unpaid leave.

• The employee may be required to provide advance leave notice and medical certification. Taking of leave may be denied if requirements are not met. The employee ordinarily must provide 30 days' advance notice when the leave is "foreseeable." An employer may require medical certification to support a request for leave because of a serious health condition, and may require second or third opinions (at the employer's expense) and a fitness for duty report to return to work.

• For the duration of FMLA leave, the employer must maintain the employee's health coverage under any "group health plan."

• Upon return from FMLA leave, most employees must be restored to their original or equivalent positions with equivalent pay, benefits, and other employment terms.

• The use of FMLA leave cannot result in the loss of any employment benefit that accrued prior to the start of an employee's leave.

• FMLA makes it unlawful for any employer to: (1) interfere with, restrain, or deny the exercise of any right provided under FMLA; or (2) discharge or discriminate against any person for opposing any practice made unlawful by FMLA or for involvement in any proceeding under or relating to FMLA.

The Family and Medical Leave Act contains no special rules or exceptions for religious organizations, and so the official poster can be used without modification.

You can obtain a free copy of a poster from any local office of the United States Department of Labor, Wage and Hours Division, or by visiting the DOL website (www.dol.gov/esa).

Case Study

• *A church has 20 employees. It is not subject to the Family and Medical Leave Act (which only applies to employers having 50 or more employees). It is not required to display on its premises the Family Medical Leave Act poster.*

6. Uniformed Services Employment and Reemployment Rights Act

The Uniformed Services Employment and Reemployment Rights Act (USER-RA) applies to persons who perform work in the "uniformed services," which include the Army, Navy, Marine Corps, Air Force, Coast Guard, and Public Health Service commissioned corps, as well as the reserve components of each of these services. Federal training or service in the Army National Guard and Air National Guard also gives rise to rights under USERRA. In addition, under the Public Health Security and Bioterrorism Response Act of 2002, certain disaster response work is considered "service in the uniformed services."

Uniformed service includes active duty, active duty for training, inactive duty training (such as drills), initial active duty training, and funeral honors duty performed by National Guard and reserve members, as well as the period for which a person is absent from a position of employment for the purpose of an examination to determine fitness to perform any such duty.

USERRA covers nearly all employees, including part-time and probationary employees. USERRA applies to virtually all U.S. employers, regardless of size. *Religious employers are not exempt.*

In general, an employer must reemploy service members returning from a period of service in the uniformed services if those service members meet five criteria: (1) the person must have held a civilian job; (2) the person must have given notice to the employer that he or she was leaving the job for service in the uniformed services, unless giving notice was precluded by military necessity or otherwise impossible or unreasonable; (3) the cumulative period of service must not have exceeded five years; (4) the person must not have been released from service under dishonorable conditions; and (5) the person must have reported back to the civilian job in a timely manner or have submitted a timely application for reemployment.

USERRA establishes a five-year "cumulative total" on military service with a single employer, with certain exceptions allowed for situations such as call-ups during emergencies, reserve drills, and annually scheduled active duty for training.

Key Point > *USERRA also allows an employee to complete an initial period of active duty that exceeds five years (e.g., enlistees in the Navy's nuclear power program are required to serve six years).*

Employers are required to display a poster explaining the rights, benefits, and obligations of employees and employers under the law. The official USERRA poster published by the Department of Labor contains the following text:

USERRA protects the job rights of individuals who voluntarily or involuntarily leave employment positions to undertake military service or certain types of service in the

National Disaster Medical System. USERRA also prohibits employers from discriminating against past and present members of the uniformed services, and applicants to the uniformed services.

REEMPLOYMENT RIGHTS

You have the right to be reemployed in your civilian job if you leave that job to perform service in the uniformed service and:

• you ensure that your employer receives advance written or verbal notice of your service;

• you have five years or less of cumulative service in the uniformed services while with that particular employer;

• you return to work or apply for reemployment in a timely manner after conclusion of service; and

• you have not been separated from service with a disqualifying discharge or under other than honorable conditions.

If you are eligible to be reemployed, you must be restored to the job and benefits you would have attained if you had not been absent due to military service or, in some cases, a comparable job.

RIGHT TO BE FREE FROM DISCRIMINATION AND RETALIATION

If you:

• are a past or present member of the uniformed service;

• have applied for membership in the uniformed service; or

• are obligated to serve in the uniformed service;

then an employer may not deny you:

• initial employment;

• reemployment;

• retention in employment;

• promotion; or

• any benefit of employment

because of this status. In addition, an employer may not retaliate against anyone assisting in the enforcement of USERRA rights, including testifying or making a statement in connection with a proceeding under USERRA, even if that person has no service connection.

HEALTH INSURANCE PROTECTION

- If you leave your job to perform military service, you have the right to elect to continue your existing employer-based health plan coverage for you and your dependents for up to 24 months while in the military.

- Even if you don't elect to continue coverage during your military service, you have the right to be reinstated in your employer's health plan when you are reemployed, generally without any waiting periods or exclusions (e.g., pre-existing condition exclusions) except for service-connected illnesses or injuries.

The official USERRA poster can be downloaded or ordered on the Department of Labor website, without charge. There are no special exceptions for religious employers under USERRA, but the so-called "ministerial exception" may prevent the application of this law to ministers. No court has addressed this issue directly.

The official poster contains the following disclaimer that would cover the potential application of the ministerial exception: "The rights listed here may vary depending on the circumstances."

B. Penalties for Failing to Display a Required Federal Poster

Can pastors and church board members be sent to jail for failing to display a required poster? Can a church that fails to display a required federal poster be assessed a substantial fine or other penalty? Despite what you may have read in the fear-mongering advertisements you have received from private companies offering to sell you a poster that will enable your church to be "in compliance'" with the law, there are few penalties that can be assessed for failing to display a poster. And, the penalties that do exist are insignificant and rarely imposed.

The U.S. Department of Labor website contains the following information regarding penalties for failure to display workplace posters:

Poster	Penalty for Failure to Display
Occupational Safety and Health Act (OSHA)	Any employer covered by the Act is subject to a "citation and penalty" for failing to display the required poster.
FLSA (overtime and minimum wage)	No citations or penalties for failure to post.
Family and Medical Leave Act	Willful refusal to post may result in a civil money penalty by the Wage and Hour Division not to exceed $100 for each separate offense.
Uniformed Services Employment and Reemployment Rights Act (USERRA)	No citations or penalties for failure to notify. An individual could ask the Department of Labor to investigate and seek compliance, or file a private enforcement action to require the employer to provide the notice to employees.
Employee Polygraph Protection Act	The Secretary of Labor can bring court actions and assess civil penalties for failing to post.

Failure to display a required poster may have consequences besides a fine or penalty. To illustrate, in order for an employee to sue an employer for violating federal discrimination laws, the employee generally must file a "charge" or complaint with the Equal Employment Opportunity Commission (EEOC) within 180 days from the date of the alleged violation (this deadline may be extended to 300 days if the complaint is covered by a state or local nondiscrimination laws). However, several courts have ruled that an employer's failure to display required workplace posters may *extend the time that employees have to file discrimination claims*, thereby exposing an employer to potential liability for a protracted period of time. This is a good reason to comply with applicable poster requirements, even if the monetary penalty that can be imposed for noncompliance is minimal.

Case Study

- *A church has 20 employees. It fails to display any workplace posters. An employee files a charge of age discrimination with the EEOC two years after the alleged act of discrimination occurred. The church claims that the claim is barred because it was filed more than 180 days after the alleged act of discrimination. The employee points out that the church failed to display the Department of Labor's "Equal Employment Opportunity Is the Law" workplace poster. This omission may have the effect of extending the employee's deadline for filing her discrimination complaint, since she could argue that she was not aware of her rights under the law and could not take advantage of them in a timely manner.*

Key Point > *No reported court ruling addresses the imposition of fines or other penalties on a church for failure to display a required workplace poster. This does not suggest that churches should disregard poster requirements. Instead, it demonstrates that innocent failures to comply with poster requirements will not necessarily result in fines, penalties, or prison sentences, especially if a church begins to comply with those requirements.*

C. Commercially Available Posters

Posters that claim to comply with federal employment laws are available from a number of vendors. Before purchasing one of them, note the following considerations:

- Many of these posters are expensive. Some cost as much as $150 or more for doing nothing more than reproducing the free Department of Labor posters on one large, laminated chart.

- Do not purchase a poster from any vendor that engages in fear tactics or intimidation.

- No commercially available poster that we have seen mentions the special exceptions and rules that apply to churches and clergy as noted in this section. In addition, they often contain information about laws that do not apply to churches. As a result, such posters will often create confusion among church staff members.

Case Study

A church has five employees. The church treasurer receives an unsolicited ad warning of substantial fines and penalties for failure to display a workplace poster. The church pays $100 for the poster. The poster presents the same material that is available for free in Department of Labor posters. It includes the Equal Employment Opportunity Is the Law and Family Medical and Leave Act posters, neither of which applies to a church with only five employees.

D. State Law

Many states have their own poster requirements in addition to those mandated by federal law. For example, many states require that employers subject to the following laws post notices described by state law: (1) a state civil rights law; (2) a state minimum wage law; (3) unemployment compensation; and (4) workers compensation. Many states make these posters available free of charge. Also, note that the official posters often do not address the special rules or exemptions that may apply to churches and clergy. We recommend that church leaders contact a local attorney for an explanation of the poster requirements that apply under state or local law.

E. Conclusions

In summary, some or perhaps all of the poster requirements described in this section may apply to a church, depending on the circumstances. Some churches display a "unified" poster containing the required language under each federal and state law, while others simply display applicable posters copied from federal and state agency websites. In either case, your posters should be accompanied by a notice (prepared by the church) to the effect that the posters do not take into account the special rules and exceptions that apply to churches and clergy.

▶ *Federal posters can be obtained here,*
http://www.dol.gov/osbp/sbrefa/poster/matrix.htm.

▶ *Some churches display the applicable federal and state posters (obtained for free from government websites), and also post a conspicuous notice above or below the posters that cautions employees that the posters do not necessarily reflect the unique legal rules and exceptions that apply to churches and clergy.*

Discrimination Under State Laws

§ 8-21

General Employment Discrimination Laws

§ 8-21.1

Key Point 8-21.1> *Many state civil rights laws prohibit employers with a specified number of employees from discriminating in any employment decision on the basis of a variety of characteristics that may include race, color, national origin, religion, gender, age, disability, marital status, and sexual orientation. In some cases, these laws exempt religious organizations or clergy.*

Most states have enacted laws banning a variety of forms of discrimination by employers. Many of these laws are patterned after federal laws summarized in this chapter, but some add additional kinds of prohibited discrimination, including marital status and sexual orientation. Many of these laws permit religious organizations to discriminate in employment decisions on the basis of religion.[211]

Discrimination Based on Sexual Orientation

§ 8-21.2

Key Point 8-21.2> *Many state civil rights laws prohibit employers with a specified number of employees from discriminating in any employment decision on the basis of the sexual orientation of an employee or applicant for employment. Such laws generally exempt religious organizations.*

Several states have enacted laws prohibiting employers from discriminating against employees and applicants for employment on the basis of their sexual orientation. The application of these laws is summarized in Table 8-7. All of them contain an exemption for religious organizations. Even without such an exemption, it is unlikely that the civil courts would apply such a law to the relationship between a church and its ministers.

A few courts have addressed the liability of religious organizations for discriminating against employees on the basis of their sexual orientation. The leading cases are summarized below.

Case Studies

• *A federal appeals court ruled that it was barred by the First Amendment guaranty of religious freedom from resolving a claim that a church had engaged in unlawful sex discrim-*

---

[211] *See, e.g.*, Gabriel v. Immanuel Evangelical Lutheran Church, 640 N.E.2d 681 (Ill. App. 4 Dist. 1994); Montrose Christian School v. Walsh, 770 A.2d 111 (Md. 2001); Porth v. Roman Catholic Diocese, 532 N.W.2d 195 (Mich. App. 1995); Assemany v. Archdiocese of Detroit, 434 N.W.2d 233 (Mich. App. 1988); Geraci v. ECKANAR, 526 N.W.2d 3 (Minn. App. 1995); Sabatino v. Saint Aloysius Parish, 672 A.2d 217 (N.J. Super. 1996); Scheiber v. St. John's University, 600 N.Y.S.2d 734 (A.D. 2 Dept. 1993); Speer v. Presbyterian Children's Home and Service Agency, 847 S.W.2d 227 (Tex. 1993); Jocz v. Labor and Industry Review Commission, 538 N.W.2d 588 (Wis. App. 1995).

ination by dismissing a non-ordained female youth pastor because of her "marriage" to another woman. It noted that "the courts have recognized a ministerial exception that prevents adjudication of Title VII employment discrimination cases brought by ministers against churches. The right to choose ministers is an important part of internal church governance and can be essential to the well-being of a church, for perpetuation of a church's existence may depend upon those whom it selects to preach its values, teach its message, and interpret its doctrines both to its own membership and to the world at large." The court concluded that "when a church makes a personnel decision based on religious doctrine, and holds meetings to discuss that decision and the ecclesiastical doctrine underlying it, the courts will not intervene."[212]

• A federal court in Connecticut ruled that the a church-affiliated college could be sued by a homosexual ex-priest who was dismissed as a professor in the college's religion department. The professor introduced his male life partner to faculty and members of the college administration. No negative comments were made, no criticism of his sexual preference was voiced, and he experienced a general acceptance by the faculty and staff. However, a few years later college administrators began reading articles in Catholic newspapers identifying the professor as a homosexual ex-priest who was "married" to another man. These articles did not affect his employment with the college. However, the college president later dismissed him when she learned that he had identified himself as a "priest (on leave)" in a letter to the editor of a newspaper. The former professor sued the college on several grounds. The court concluded that his claims were not necessarily barred by the ministerial exception since the record was not clear as to the precise nature of his duties.[213]

• Georgetown University was sued by various homosexual student groups for its refusal to officially recognize them. The students cited the District of Columbia "Civil Rights Act," which bans discrimination based on sexual orientation by any educational institution within the District. The University (a private Catholic educational institution) argued that recognition of the groups would violate its constitutional right to religious freedom since recognition would imply endorsement of conduct contrary to Catholic doctrine. The court concluded that the District's Civil Rights Act did not require that a private religious university recognize a student group whose beliefs and practices were contrary to church teachings. However, it held that the Act did require equal access to University facilities and services, and, since the University denied the homosexual groups certain services (a mailbox, computer labeling, mailing services, and the right to apply for funding), it was in violation of the Act. The court found that any burden on the University's religious freedom that might result from providing these incidental services was so minimal that it was overridden by the compelling governmental interest of eradicating discrimination.[214]

• A Massachusetts court ruled that the civil courts are barred by the First Amendment from resolving clergy employment disputes regardless of whether the church is congregational or hierarchical in polity. A church dismissed its pastor. The former pastor sued the church on several grounds, including unlawful employment discrimination based on his "perceived sexual orientation." A state appeals court concluded that the First Amendment barred the civil courts from resolving all clergy employment disputes regardless of church polity. It concluded, "Congregational as well as hierarchical churches are entitled to autonomy over church disputes touching on matters of doctrine, canon law, polity, discipline, and minis-

---

[212] Bryce v. Episcopal Church in the Diocese of Colorado, 289 F.3d 648 (10th Cir. 2002).

[213] Hartwig v. Albertus Magnus College, 93 F.Supp.2d 200 (D. Conn. 2000).

[214] Rights Coalition v. Georgetown University, 536 A.2d 1 (D.C. App. 1987)

terial relationships. To conclude otherwise would violate fundamental precepts of the First Amendment . . . guaranteeing free exercise of religion."[215]

• A Massachusetts court ruled that a church could not be sued for dismissing a homosexual employee. The court noted that because the employee had been terminated "for being gay . . . and [was based on the] religious belief [of the church] that homosexuality is a sin for which one must repent," the imposition of liability in such a case "would burden the church's right to free exercise of religion."[216]

• A church hired a bisexual music director (the plaintiff). The plaintiff was fired when he refused to apologize to a church member for calling him homophobic. He filed a charge of discrimination with the Minnesota Department of Human Rights (MDHR), alleging discrimination and retaliation by the church on the basis of sexual orientation under the Minnesota Human Rights Act (MHRA). The MDHR dismissed the claim, finding no probable cause to charge the church. The plaintiff then sued the church in court. A trial court ruled that churches were exempt from the MHRA, and it dismissed the case. A state appeals court concluded: (1) Churches can discriminate in hiring decisions on the basis of sexual orientation, but only for (a) "ministerial" positions, or (b) non-ministerial positions for which heterosexuality is a "bona fide occupational qualification." (2) Churches can discriminate in all other employment decisions (other than hiring) on the basis of sexual orientation. This is true for ministerial and non-ministerial positions.[217]

• A Minnesota court ruled that a religious school and a parent denomination did not unlawfully discriminate against a homosexual teacher who was forced to resign after disclosing his sexual orientation. It concluded that any analysis of the teacher's claims would require delving into church doctrine: "[The plaintiff], an ordained minister, was initially called to his position, a process which, according to church doctrine, is guided by the Holy Spirit and God's will. The high school is a sacred community administered according to the Christian understanding of the Gospel. The education provided to students is based on the scriptures of the Old and New Testament, to which teachers are asked to ascribe when teaching. The national church's position is that homosexuality is intrinsically sinful. The plaintiff's assertion that he should not have been discharged based on his sexual orientation would require the court to analyze and apply church doctrine to assess his argument. We must conclude that this type of searching inquiry intrudes into church doctrine and church administrative matters and engenders a prohibited relationship between the church and the judiciary. Consequently, resolution of his claims would violate the establishment doctrine of the First Amendment." The teacher claimed that because the school and national church never incorporated the religious belief that homosexuality is a sin into their employment policies and because they have no stated policy, either written or unwritten, that forbids homosexuality among its employees, the employment decision did not implicate religious beliefs, procedures, or law. The court stressed that the teacher was not merely a lay employee but instead was a campus pastor as well as a teacher of religious subjects. The school and national church decided that he should be discharged because of their ecclesiastical concerns based on their firmly held religious beliefs. As a result, any analysis of his qualification for employment would require analysis of those beliefs.[218]

[215] Callahan v. First Congregational Church, 808 N.E.2d 301 (Mass. Sup. 2004).

[216] Madsen v. Ervin, 481 N.E.2d 1160 (Mass. App. 1985).

[217] Egan v. Hamline United Methodist Church, 2004 WL 771461 (Minn. App. 2004).

[218] Doe v. Lutheran High School, 702 N.W.2d 322 (Minn. App. 2005).

- A Minnesota appeals court ruled a local civil rights ordinance banning discrimination against homosexuals could not be applied to a religious organization. A Catholic religious center in Minneapolis rented space to a number of community groups, including Alcoholics Anonymous, Weight Watchers, and Dignity (an organization composed largely of homosexual Catholics). In 1986, the local archbishop was instructed by the Vatican to determine whether or not pastoral practices in the diocese were consistent with the Vatican's "Letter to Bishops on the Pastoral Care of Homosexual Persons." This letter prohibits church facilities from being used by organizations that oppose the Vatican's position on homosexuality. Since Dignity's beliefs were in conflict with the Vatican's position, its lease of space in the religious center was terminated. Dignity filed a complaint with the Minneapolis "department of civil rights," claiming that a municipal civil rights ordinance banning discrimination against homosexuals had been violated by the termination of its lease. It named the center along with the diocese and archbishop as defendants. The complaint was dismissed, and Dignity appealed to an appeals board which concluded that Dignity's civil rights had been violated by the defendants. It assessed fines, and ordered the defendants to refrain from any further discrimination against homosexuals. The defendants appealed this order to a state appeals court. The court ruled that application of the civil rights ordinance to the center, diocese, and archbishop constituted prohibited "entanglement" of the government in religious affairs in violation of the First Amendment. It concluded: "In determining whether state action constitutes excessive entanglement, a court must undertake an examination of the character and purposes of the groups involved, the nature of the state's involvement, and the relationship that results between the state and religious authority. In this case, we conclude the nature of the state's activity clearly evinces excessive entanglement. . . . A city or municipality is without jurisdiction to enforce civil rights protections against a religious organization enforcing conformity of its members to certain standards of conduct and morals. We therefore conclude the order of the [appeals board] must be reversed as excessive entanglement in religious affairs contrary to the First Amendment of the United States Constitution." This case is one of a few decisions recognizing that the First Amendment permits a church to "enforce conformity of its members to certain standards of conduct or morals," notwithstanding a civil rights law to the contrary.[219]

- A New York court ruled that a church could be sued by a former employee for discriminating against him on the basis of his religion and sexual orientation. A homosexual, Jewish man was employed by a church in an administrative capacity. The employee claimed that his supervisor acted in a hostile manner toward him because of his sexual orientation and religious background, and that she undermined him in his job performance and treated him differently than she did heterosexual employees. The former employee sued the church, claiming that it was responsible for its supervisor's acts of religious and sexual orientation discrimination. He asked the court to award him back pay, front pay or reinstatement, compensatory and punitive damages, interest, attorney's fees, and costs. The church argued that it was exempt from the anti-discrimination provisions of the civil rights laws of the State of New York and New York City. The court conceded that both laws permit religious organizations to limit employment or give preference to persons of the same religion or denomination, or to promote the religious principles of the organization. However, the court noted, "those limited exemptions for religious organizations are a far cry from letting them harass their employees and treat the employees in an odiously discriminatory manner during their employment, and to use derogatory expressions toward the employees. . . . Thus, the claims cannot be dismissed due to defendant's status as a religious organization."[220]

---

[219] Dignity Twin Cities v. Newman Center and Chapel, 472 N.W.2d 355 (Minn. App. 1991).

[220] Logan v. Salvation Army, 809 N.Y.S.2d 846 (Sup. Ct. 2005).

Table 8-7 **State Laws Barring Private Employers from Discriminating on the Basis of Sexual Orientation** Note: Since laws may change, this table should not be relied upon without first consulting with an attorney.

state	applies to employers with at least this many employees	effective date	exemption for religious organizations
CA	5	1992	Does not apply to "a religious association or corporation not organized for private profit."
CT	3	1991	Does not apply to "a religious corporation, entity, association, educational institution or society with respect to the employment of individuals to perform work connected with the carrying on by such corporation, entity, association, educational institution or society of its activities, or with respect to matters of discipline, faith, internal organization or ecclesiastical rule, custom or law which are established by such corporation, entity, association, educational institution or society."
D.C.	1	1977	"Nothing in this chapter shall be construed to bar any religious organization, or any organization operated for charitable or educational purposes, which is operated, supervised or controlled by or in connection with a religious organization, from limiting employment, or admission to or giving preference to persons of the same religious persuasion as is calculated by the organization to promote the religious principles for which it is established or maintained."
HI	1	1991	Does not "prohibit or prevent any religious or denominational institution or organization, or any organization operated for charitable or educational purposes, that is operated, supervised, or controlled by or in connection with a religious organization, from giving preference to individuals of the same religion or denomination or from making a selection calculated to promote the religious principles for which the organization is established or maintained."
IL	15	2006	Does not apply to "a religious corporation" with respect to members of their faith.
ME	1	2006	"'Employer' does not include a religious or fraternal corporation or association, not organized for private profit and in fact not conducted for private profit, with respect to employment of its members of the same religion, sect or fraternity, except for purposes of disability-related discrimination, in which case the corporation or association is considered to be an employer." "This subchapter does not prohibit a religious corporation, association, educational institution or society from giving preference in employment to individuals of its same religion to perform work connected with the carrying on by the corporation, association, educational institution or society of its activities. Under this subchapter, a religious organization may require that all applicants and employees conform to the religious tenets of that organization."
MD	15	2001	Does not apply to a "religious corporation, association, educational institution or society with respect to the employment of individuals of a particular religion or sexual orientation to perform work connected with the carrying on by such corporation, association, educational institution or society of its activities."
MA	6	1995	"Nothing herein shall be construed to bar any religious or denominational institution or organization, or any organization operated for charitable or educational purposes, which is operated, supervised or controlled by or in connection with a religious organization, and which limits membership, enrollment, admission, or participation to members of that religion, from giving preference in hiring or employment to members of the same religion or from taking any action with respect to matters of employment, discipline, faith, internal organization, or ecclesiastical rule, custom, or law which are calculated by such organization to promote the religious principles for which it is established or maintained."
MN	1	1993	Does not apply to "a religious corporation, association, or society, with respect to qualifications based on religion or sexual orientation, when religion or sexual orientation shall be a bona fide occupational qualification for employment." In addition, "Nothing in this chapter prohibits any religious association, religious corporation, or religious society that is not organized for private profit, or any institution organized for educational purposes that is operated, supervised, or controlled by a religious association, religious corporation, or religious society that is not organized for private profit, from: (1) limiting admission to or

state	applies to employers with at least this many employees	effective date	exemption for religious organizations
			giving preference to persons of the same religion or denomination; or (2) in matters relating to sexual orientation, taking any action with respect to education, employment, housing and real property, or use of facilities. This clause shall not apply to secular business activities engaged in by the religious association, religious corporation, or religious society, the conduct of which is unrelated to the religious and educational purposes for which it is organized."
NV	15	1995	Does not apply to "any religious corporation, association or society with respect to the employment of individuals of a particular religion to perform work connected with the carrying on of its religious activities."
NH	6	1997	"Nothing contained in this chapter shall be construed to bar any religious or denominational institution or organization, or any organization operated for charitable or educational purposes, which is operated, supervised or controlled by or in connection with a religious organization, from limiting admission to or giving preference to persons of the same religion or denomination or from making such selection as is calculated by such organization to promote the religious principles for which it is established or maintained."
NJ	1	1992	"It shall not be an unlawful employment practice for a religious association or organization to utilize religious affiliation as a uniform qualification in the employment of clergy, religious teachers or other employees engaged in the religious activities of the association or organization, or in following the tenets of its religion in establishing and utilizing criteria for employment of an employee."
NM	15		"Nothing contained in the Human Rights Act shall... bar any religious or denominational institution or organization that is operated, supervised or controlled by or that is operated in connection with a religious or denominational organization from imposing discriminatory employment or renting practices that are based upon sexual orientation or gender identity; provided, that the provisions of the Human Rights Act with respect to sexual orientation and gender identity shall apply to any other (1) for-profit activities of a religious or denominational institution or religious organization . . . or (2) nonprofit activities of a religious or denominational institution or religious organization...."
NY	1	2003	"Nothing contained in this section shall be construed to bar any religious or denominational institution or organization, or any organization operated for charitable or educational purposes, which is operated, supervised or controlled by or in connection with a religious organization, from limiting employment... or giving preference to persons of the same religion or denomination or from taking such action as is calculated by such organization to promote the religious principles for which it is established or maintained."
RI	4	1995	"Nothing in this subdivision shall be construed to apply to a religious corporation, association, educational institution, or society with respect to the employment of individuals of its religion to perform work connected with the carrying on of its activities."
VT	1	1992	"The provisions of this section prohibiting discrimination on the basis of sexual orientation shall not be construed to prohibit or prevent any religious or denominational institution or organization, or any organization operated for charitable or educational purposes, which is operated, supervised, or controlled by or in connection with a religious organization, from giving preference to persons of the same religion or denomination or from taking any action with respect to matters of employment which is calculated by the organization to promote the religious principles for which it is established or maintained."
WA	8	2006	"'Employer' includes any person acting in the interest of an employer, directly or indirectly, who employs eight or more persons, and does not include any religious or sectarian organization not organized for private profit."
WI	1	1981	No specific exemption, but a state law allows religious organizations, under some circumstances, to give preference to an applicant or employee who "adheres to the religious association's creed."

Nearly 100 cities have enacted their own civil rights laws that in some cases bar employers from discriminating against employees and applicants for employment based on their sexual orientation. For example, 33 cities in California have enacted such laws.

Many courts have ruled that the First Amendment guaranty of religious freedom prevents civil rights laws from applying to the relationship between a church and its pastor. This so-called "ministerial exception" is explained fully in section 8-10 of this chapter.

Q Can a church waive its exemption from state laws prohibiting employers from discriminating in employment decisions on the basis of sexual orientation?

A One court ruled that churches may waive an exemption through "nondiscrimination" provisions in personnel handbooks or policy manuals, but only if the waiver is "specific and unequivocal, and the scope of that waiver is evident."[221] However, "a pronouncement by the religious organization that it will conform to the principle of nondiscrimination only indicates an intent to voluntarily embrace that principle. Without greater clarity, we would be compelled to conduct an examination and interpret statements of the church on doctrinal policy as it relates to the alleged reasons for an employee's discharge. This invites an unconstitutional entanglement of the church with the judicial and administrative branches of government. We conclude that there is not an effective waiver in this case."

Q Should churches that choose to discriminate in employment decisions on the basis of sexual orientation amend their bylaws to say so?

A This is not required in any state. Table 8-7 summarizes the exemption of religious organizations from state laws prohibiting discrimination in employment on the basis of sexual orientation. This table demonstrates that religious organizations are exempt regardless of whether they have a special clause in their bylaws that states their theological opposition to hiring homosexual employees. The only current exception to this rule may be Minnesota. The Minnesota Human Rights Act, as interpreted by a state appeals court, exempts churches from the ban on discrimination based on sexual orientation in hiring decisions only with respect to (1) lay employees for whom heterosexuality is a bona fide occupational qualification, and (2) ministers. Minnesota churches can help demonstrate that heterosexuality is a bona fide occupational qualification for lay employees by adopting a policy to this effect that clearly articulates a theological basis. Such a policy can be in the church's policy manual, or in a resolution adopted by the board or membership. No amendment to the church bylaws is necessary.[222]

---

[221] Egan v. Hamline United Methodist Church, 2004 WL 771461 (Minn. App. 2004).

[222] Id.

Q Does the Civil Rights Restoration Act prevent churches from discriminating against persons on the basis of sexual orientation?

A The Rehabilitation Act of 1973,[223] as amended by the Civil Rights Restoration Act, forbids discrimination on the basis of handicap by any institution that receives federal financial assistance. In 1987, the Supreme Court ruled that a public school teacher suffering from tuberculosis was a "handicapped individual" entitled to protection under the Act.[224] The Court emphasized that the teacher was handicapped because her tuberculosis caused physical impairment, not because the disease was contagious. "This case does not present, and we therefore do not reach," concluded the Court, "the questions whether a carrier of a contagious disease such as AIDS could be considered to have a physical impairment, or whether such a person could be considered, solely on the basis of contagiousness, a handicapped person." To clarify that a contagious disease (such as AIDS) does not render a person "handicapped" in the absence of physical impairment, the Act was amended to read that the term handicapped does not include "an individual who has a currently contagious disease or infection and who, by reason of such disease or infection, would constitute a direct threat to the health or safety of other individuals or who, by reason of the currently contagious disease or infection, is unable to perform the duties of the job."[225] According to this language, an AIDS victim could be classified as handicapped if he or she was physically impaired by the disease and did not constitute a threat to the health or safety of others. A few courts have ruled that under these circumstances AIDS is a handicap.[226]

While it is possible that the federal courts will interpret the term handicapped to include homosexuals, such a result is unlikely as a result of the overwhelming expression by Congress that homosexuality is not a handicap. Consider the following sampling of comments (contained in the Congressional Record) of some of the sponsors and co-sponsors of the bill (many other examples could be cited). "[The Act] does not prohibit discrimination against homosexuals and does not give sweeping protection to alcoholics and drug addicts" (Senator Kennedy). "The bill does not change the definition of who is handicapped. There are no Supreme Court rulings which require anyone to consider alcoholics, drug addicts, active homosexuals or transvestites to be handicapped. [Some have suggested that] churches and religious leaders could be forced to hire a practicing homosexual drug addict with AIDS to be a teacher or youth pastor. This is the most blatant untruth of all. No American government has ever had or could ever get the power, under our Constitution, to dictate any choice of

---

[223] 29 U.S.C. § 794.

[224] Arline v. School Board of Nassau County, 107 S. Ct. 1123 (1987).

[225] 29 U.S.C. § 706(8)(C).

[226] See, e.g., Thomas v. Atascadero Unified School District, 662 F. Supp. 376 (C.D. Cal. 1987); District 27 Community School Board v. Board of Education, 502 N.Y.S.2d 325 (1986).

pastor in a church—whether it be a youth pastor or any other" (Senator Mitchell). "There is no truth to the charges that the Act would require schools, churches, or any employer to hire homosexuals, alcoholics, drug abusers, or victims of AIDS" (Senator Conrad). "The Civil Rights Restoration Act absolutely does not expand coverage of the civil rights laws to homosexuals" (Senator Ford). "This law will not require churches to hire homosexuals" (Senator Bentsen). "If, for instance, the religious tenets of an organization require it to take disciplinary action against a homosexual because of that person's sexual preference . . . the Act would not protect the individual" (Senator DeConcini). "Is it true that churches and religious schools will have to hire homosexuals as a result of this bill? No, it is not true" (Senator Levin).

One federal court has concluded that transvestites are protected by federal anti-discrimination law. The court concluded that "while homosexuals are not handicapped it is clear that transvestites are, because many experience strong social rejection in the work place as a result of their mental ailment made blatantly apparent by their cross-dressing life-style."[227] This decision ignored testimony in the Congressional Record by the sponsors and co-sponsors of the Civil Rights Restoration Act demonstrating that it was not the intent of Congress to treat transvestites as handicapped. Such testimony will be relevant in future judicial decisions interpreting the term handicapped. But again, it cannot be said with certainty that the courts will not treat transvestites as handicapped, and therefore that churches covered by the Act will not be required to hire transvestites.

Discrimination Based on Use of Legal Substances § 8-21.3

Key Point 8-21.3> *Many states have enacted laws prohibiting employers from disciplining employees for using lawful products (such as tobacco) during non-working hours. Some of these laws exempt religious organizations.*

Many states have enacted laws prohibiting employers from disciplining employees for using lawful products (such as tobacco) during non-working hours. Some of these laws exempt religious organizations. Even without such an exemption, it is unlikely that most courts would apply such a law to the relationship between a church and its ministers.

Case Studies

• *The North Dakota Supreme Court ruled that an employer may have violated a minister's legal rights by dismissing him for engaging in private sexual behavior (masturbation) in a*

---

[227] Blackwell v. United States Department of Treasury, 656 F. Supp. 713 (D.D.C. 1986)

private stall in a public restroom.[228] *A state law prohibits an employer from discharging an employee "for participation in lawful activity off the employer's premises during non-working hours which is not in direct conflict with the essential business related interests of the employer." Further, employers can dismiss employees who engage in lawful behavior during non-working hours if "contrary to a bona fide occupational qualification that reasonably and rationally relates to employment activities and the responsibilities of a particular employee . . . ." This law was enacted to prevent employers from "inquiring into an employee's non-work conduct, including an employee's weight and smoking, marital, or sexual habits." The minister acknowledged that state law prohibits masturbation in a public place, but he insisted that a private stall in a public restroom is not a "public place" and therefore his behavior was legal. And, since it was legal, he could not be dismissed for engaging in such behavior. The court noted that several other courts have concluded that "activities conducted in an enclosed stall in a public restroom do not occur in a public place." On the other hand, it acknowledged that state law allows employers to dismiss an employee for engaging in lawful behavior during non-working hours if (1) the behavior is in direct conflict with the essential business-related interests of the employer, or (2) is contrary to a bona fide occupational qualification that reasonably and rationally relates to employment activities and the responsibilities of a particular employee. The court conceded that the retirement home might be able to establish either or both of these exceptions, and it sent the case back to the trial court for further consideration.*

DID YOU KNOW?
DISMISSING AN EMPLOYEE FOR ENGAGING IN LAWFUL ACTIVITIES DURING NON-WORKING HOURS

Many states have enacted laws preventing employers from dismissing employees on account of lawful behavior during non-working hours. These laws vary from state to state. Church leaders should review their own state law and be able to answer the following questions:

(1) Does our state have such a law?

(2) Does it apply to churches? In many states, such laws exempt churches.

(3) If our church is covered, which employees are protected? All employees? Only lay employees? What about clergy?

(4) If our church is covered, what activities are prohibited? This is critical. You need to know how your church can violate the law.

(5) What exemptions exist? It is common for such laws to exempt behavior that is contrary to a "bona fide occupational qualification" that reasonably relates to employment activities and responsibilities. Church leaders need to be familiar with any available exemptions.

---

[228] Hougum v. Valley Memorial Homes, 574 N.W.2d 812 (N.D. 1998).

Termination

Legal Briefs

In most states, employees who are hired for an indefinite period are considered "at will" employees. This means that the employment relationship may be terminated at will by either the employer or employee, with or without cause, and with or without notice. The courts and state legislatures have created a number of exceptions to the at will employment rule. These exceptions limit the right of an employer to terminate an at will employee. Employees who are hired for a specific term are not at will employees, and they may be terminated only if the employer has "good cause."

The dismissal of an employee can be a traumatic experience. When an employee is dismissed who has been employed by the church for many years, there often is a desire by other employees and the congregation itself for information about the dismissal. After all, what could this trusted and faithful employee have done to warrant such harsh treatment? Often, church leaders resist sharing any of the details, fearing they will be sued if they do. This concern is understandable. However, problems can occur when nothing is disclosed to the staff or membership. Church leaders under these circumstances often are accused of acting arbitrarily, and there is a demand for an explanation. Refusal to respond to such demands may place the church leadership in an even worse light.

There is a possible answer to this dilemma. Many states recognize the concept of "qualified privilege." This means that statements made to others concerning a matter of common interest cannot be defamatory unless made with malice. Statements are made with malice if they are made with a knowledge that they are false, or with a reckless disregard as to their truth or falsity. In the church context, this privilege protects statements made by members to other members concerning matters of common interest. Such communications cannot be defamatory unless malice is proven. Church leaders who decide to disclose why an employee was dismissed can reduce the legal risk to the church and themselves by following a few basic precautions:

- **Only share information with active voting members of the church—at a membership meeting or by letter. The qualified privilege does not apply if the communication is made to non-members.**

- **Adopt procedures that will confirm that no non-member received the information.**

- **Limit your remarks to factual information and do not express opinions.**

- **Prepare a written statement that will be shared with members, and have it reviewed in advance by an attorney.**

Termination of Employees

§ 8-22

Key Point 8-22> *In most states, employees who are hired for an indefinite period are considered "at will" employees. This means that the employment relationship may be terminated at will by either the employer or employee, with or without cause, and with or without notice. The courts and state legislatures have created a number of exceptions to the at will employment rule. These exceptions limit the right of an employer to terminate an at will employee. Employees who are hired for a specific term are not at will employees, and they may be terminated only if the employer has "good cause."*

A. The "At Will" Employment Rule, and Its Exceptions

In most states an employee hired for an *indefinite term* may be discharged by the employer at any time with or without cause.[229] This principle is referred to as the "at will" employment rule. The idea is that either the employer or the employee has the right to terminate the employment relationship "at will." This rule only applies to employees hired for indefinite terms of employment. The "at will" employment rule is subject to a number of exceptions in each state, including some or all of the following:

1. *Discrimination based on race, color, national origin, sex, or religion.* Title VII of the Civil Rights Act of 1964 is a federal law that makes it unlawful for an employer that is engaged in "commerce" and that has at least 15 employees to discharge any individual on the basis of race, color, national origin, religion, or sex (including both pregnancy and sexual harassment). The Act does permit religious organizations to discharge or otherwise discriminate against employees on the basis of religion. Many states have their own civil rights laws that ban this type of employment discrimination, and they are more likely to apply to churches since there is no "commerce" requirement and the minimum number of employees often is fewer than 15.

2. *Discrimination based on age.* The federal Age Discrimination in Employment Act makes it unlawful for an employer that is engaged in "commerce" and that has at least 20 employees to discharge any individual on the basis of age (if the person is at least 40 years of age). Many states have their own civil rights laws that ban this type of employment discrimination, and they are more likely to apply to churches since there is no "commerce" requirement and the minimum number of employees often is fewer than 20.

3. *Discrimination based on disability.* The federal Americans with Disabilities Act is a federal law that makes it unlawful for an employer that is engaged in "commerce" and that has at least 15 employees to discharge any indi-

---

[229] *See generally* L. Larson, Unjust Dismissal (2007 supplement); Larson's Employment Discrimination (2007 supplement); W. Holloway and M. Leech, Employment Termination (2nd ed. 1993).

vidual on the basis of disability—if the employee is able to perform the essential functions of the job with or without reasonable accommodation by the employer (so long as the accommodation would not impose an undue hardship on the employer). The Act does permit religious organizations to discriminate against employees on the basis of religion. Many states have their own civil rights laws that ban this type of employment discrimination, and they are more likely to apply to churches since there is no "commerce" requirement and the minimum number of employees often is fewer than 15.

4. *Discrimination based on military status.* The Uniformed Services Employment and Reemployment Rights Act specifies that a person "who is a member of, applies to be a member of, performs, has performed, applies to perform, or has an obligation to perform service in a uniformed service shall not be denied initial employment, reemployment, retention in employment, promotion, or any benefit of employment by an employer" on the basis of his or her military service or application for service. The law applies to all employers, including churches, whether or not they are engaged in interstate commerce and regardless of the number of their employees. The law defines "service in the uniformed services" to include "active duty, active duty for training, initial active duty for training, inactive duty training, full-time National Guard duty, and a period for which a person is absent from a position of employment for the purpose of an examination to determine the fitness of the person to perform any such duty." The law only protects employees whose military absences from an employer have not exceeded five years, with certain exceptions. An employee's reinstatement rights depend upon the time he or she is away on military leave.

5. *Discrimination based on sexual orientation.* A number of states have enacted laws prohibiting employers from discriminating against employees and applicants for employment on the basis of their sexual orientation. Most of these laws exempt religious organizations. Even without such an exemption, it is unlikely that most courts would apply such a law to the relationship between a church and its ministers.

▶ *A church should avoid dismissing an employee who is a member of a protected class under a federal or state civil rights law unless there is a legitimate, nondiscriminatory basis for the dismissal. For example, a church should avoid dismissing a 60-year-old employee unless there is clear and convincing evidence of incompetency, incapacity, insubordination, or some other nondiscriminatory basis for dismissal.*

▶ *Dismissed employees often point to "performance reviews" as proof that their termination was discriminatory. To illustrate, assume that a church conducts annual "performance reviews" for all employees, and that a disabled employee consistently received excellent or above average scores. Within a few months of such a review, the employee is dismissed because of the "poor quality" of his work. The employee sues*

227

the church, claiming that it discriminated against him on the basis of his disability. The church insists that the disability had nothing to do with its decision, but the employee points to the annual performance reviews as proof that the church's alleged basis for termination was a "pretext."

6. *Dismissal based on polygraph testing.* The federal Employee Polygraph Protection Act prohibits any employer engaged in commerce, regardless of the number of employees, from requiring, requesting, suggesting, or causing any employee or applicant for employment to take a polygraph exam. This law applies to all employers, including religious organizations, engaged in an activity affecting interstate commerce. The law contains a few exceptions that ordinarily will not apply to churches. For example, employers can ask an employee to take a polygraph exam if an incident of theft or embezzlement has occurred and there is evidence pointing to the employee as the perpetrator. Employers relying on this exception must comply with several requirements. The assistance of legal counsel is essential.

7. *State laws regulating off-hours conduct of employees.* Many states have enacted laws prohibiting employers from disciplining employees for using lawful products (such as tobacco or alcohol) off of the employer's premises during non-working hours. Some of these laws exempt religious organizations.

8. *Violation of public policy.* A number of courts have protected "at will" employees by permitting them to sue their former employer if their dismissal violated "public policy."[230] To illustrate, employees terminated for refusing to commit perjury or some other crime, for performing jury service, or for filing a workers compensation claim against their employer have been allowed to sue their employer for wrongful discharge. The "public policy" exception to the employer's right to discharge employees hired for indefinite terms has been narrowly construed, and is rejected by some courts. One court rejected the argument that the "national policy" against religious discrimination is sufficiently compelling to create an exception to the "at will" doctrine in the context of religious employers.[231]

9. *Employment handbook exception.* Some courts have restricted an employer's right to fire "at will" employees as a result of binding assurances and commitments contained in an employee manual or handbook.[232] This

---

[230] *See generally* Note, *Protecting At Will Employees Against Wrongful Discharge: The Duty to Terminate Only in Good Faith,* 93 HARV. L. REV. 1816 (1980).

[231] Amos v. Corporation of Presiding Bishop, 594 F. Supp. 791 (D. Utah 1984), *rev'd on other grounds,* 483 U.S. 327 (1987).

[232] *See, e.g.,* Guz v. Bechtel National, 8 P.3d 1089 (Cal. 2000); Gaudio v. Griffin Health Services Corporation, 733 A.2d 197 (Conn. 1999); Orr v. Westminster Village North, 689 N.E.2d 712 (Ind. 1997); Lytle v. Malady, 579 N.W.2d 906 (Mich. 1998); Tenet Healthcare Limited v. Cooper, 960 S.W.2d 386 (Tex. App. 1998).

view has been rejected by other courts.[233] Many courts have upheld the validity of "disclaimers" appearing in employment contracts and handbooks, which purport to disclaim any contractual meaning or intent.

10. *Invasion of privacy.* Some courts have allowed dismissed employees to sue their former employer if their dismissal was based on an "invasion of privacy" by the employer. Examples include dismissals based on evidence obtained through illegal telephone wiretapping, or through unauthorized access to the employee's personal property.[234]

11. *"True cause" letters.* Although not directly limiting an employer's right to discharge an employee engaged for an indefinite term, some states have enacted laws requiring employers to provide discharged employees with a letter setting forth the "true cause" of the discharge.[235] Ordinarily, however, the employer is not obligated to provide such a letter unless it receives a written request from a discharged employee.

12. *Fraud.* A few courts have permitted dismissed employees to sue their former employers on the basis of fraudulent representations. For example, an employee who was assured by his employer that his position would be "permanent" was fired. While the court concluded that an employee hired on a "permanent" basis is in fact an "at will" employee who ordinarily can be terminated at any time with or without cause, the employee could sue his former employer on the basis of the fraudulent representation.[236]

13. *Statutory elimination of the "at will" rule.* At least one state (Montana) has enacted a statute prohibiting employers from dismissing employees except for "good cause."[237] Such a statute in effect repeals the "at will" rule.

14. *Covenant of fair dealing.* A few courts have ruled that a "covenant of fair dealing" is implied in every contract of employment. A dismissed employee can sue a former employer for violating this covenant.

15. *Union activities.* The National Labor Relations Act makes it unlawful for an employer engaged in a business or activity "affecting commerce" to discharge an employee on the basis of union activities.[238]

---

[233] *See, e.g.,* Chin v. American Telephone and Telegraph Co., 410 N.Y.S.2d 737 (1978); Rosby v. General Baptist State Convention of North Carolina, Inc., 370 S.E.2d 605 (N.C. App. 1988); Reynolds Manufacturing Co. v. Mendoza, 644 S.W.2d 536 (Tex. App. 1982).

[234] *See, e.g.,* Fischer v. Mt. Olive Lutheran Church, Inc., 207 F.Supp.2d 914 (W.D. Wis. 2002).

[235] *See, e.g.,* MO. REV. STAT. § 290.140.

[236] Hamlen v. Fairchilds Industries, Inc., 413 So.2d 800 (Fla. App. 1982); Silver v. Mohasco Corp., 462 N.Y.S.2d 917 (1983).

[237] The Montana Wrongful Discharge From Employment Act (1987).

[238] *See* § 8-09, § E, *supra,* for a discussion of the meaning of the term *affecting commerce.*

In 1991 the Model Employment Terminations Act was adopted by the Uniform Law Commissioners and offered to the state legislatures for their consideration. So far, no state has adopted the Act, although it is possible that some will do so. As a result, church leaders should be familiar with the Act's major provisions, which are summarized below:

1. The Act prohibits employers from dismissing an employee without good cause. However, this limitation only applies to employees who have been employed by the same employer for at least one year.

2. The Act defines good cause as (1) a "reasonable basis" for termination based on such considerations as the employee's job performance or employment record; or (2) an employer's "business judgment" (for example, the reorganization, consolidation, or discontinuation of positions or departments, or "changing standards of performance for positions").

3. Only those employers with five or more employees are covered by the Act.

4. The Act does not apply to self-employed persons.

5. The Act permits employees to waive the Act's requirement that terminations be based on good cause by entering into a severance agreement with their employer. The Act defines the terms that must appear in such an agreement.

B. The Dismissal of Employees Hired for a Definite Term

The courts generally hold that employees hired for a definite term may not be discharged before the end of their term of employment unless *good cause* exists. An employer need not demonstrate good cause to justify a failure to rehire an employee upon the expiration of a definite term of employment.

Good cause may include serious illness; abandonment of employment; breach of contract; refusal to perform assigned duties; incompetency; neglect of duties; misconduct; insubordination; intoxication; intemperance; doctrinal deviation; or conduct contrary to the church's moral teachings.

> *Many churches reserve the right to dismiss an employee for conduct in violation of the church's moral teachings. Unfortunately, this can lead to confusion since dismissed employees often insist that their behavior did not violate such teachings. One way to reduce the likelihood of such disputes is to state (in the church's employee handbook, or in some other appropriate document) that the church board is the sole arbiter of what behavior violates the church's moral teachings.*

An employee who is discharged without good cause before the end of a specified term of employment generally is entitled to recover as damages the salary and other benefits agreed upon for the remainder of the employment term less the amount the employee earned, or with reasonable diligence might have earned, from other employment of the same or a similar nature during the period.

Key Point > *The civil courts generally will not interfere with a church's decision to terminate a minister's services. This subject is covered fully in chapter 2.*

C. Communicating with Other Employees and the Congregation

The dismissal of an employee can be a traumatic experience. When an employee is dismissed who has been employed by the church for many years, there often is a desire by other employees and the congregation itself for information about the dismissal. After all, what could this trusted and faithful employee have done to warrant such harsh treatment? Often, church leaders resist sharing any of the details, fearing they will be sued if they do. This concern is understandable. However, problems can occur when nothing is disclosed to the staff or membership. Church leaders under these circumstances often are accused of acting arbitrarily, and there is a demand for an explanation. Refusal to respond to such demands may place the church leadership in an even worse light.

There is a possible answer to this dilemma. Many states recognize the concept of "qualified privilege." This means that statements made to others concerning a matter of common interest cannot be defamatory unless made with malice. Statements are made with malice if they are made with a knowledge that they are false, or with a reckless disregard as to their truth or falsity. In the church context, this privilege protects statements made by members to other members concerning matters of common interest. Such communications cannot be defamatory unless malice is proven. Church leaders who decide to disclose why an employee was dismissed can reduce the legal risk to the church and themselves by following a few basic precautions:

• Only share information with active voting members of the church—at a membership meeting or by letter. The qualified privilege does not apply if the communication is made to non-members.

• Adopt procedures that will confirm that no non-member received the information.

• Limit your remarks to factual information and do not express opinions.

• Prepare a written statement that will be shared with members, and have it reviewed in advance by an attorney.

In some cases, it is helpful to obtain a signed confession from an employee who is being terminated because of misconduct. The confession should state that it can be read to the staff and congregation.

Case Studies

• An Indiana court concluded that it was barred by the First Amendment from resolving a claim by a dismissed pastoral associate that she had been defamed by church officials.[239] The dismissed employee sued her church for defamation, claiming that the senior pastor had "unlawfully, untruthfully, and intentionally made misleading and slanderous remarks" about her and had "implied that there was something of a bad and sinister nature" about her, "thereby causing her irreparable harm, injury, and damages and rendering her sick, stressed, and physically debilitated." Specifically, Linda alleged that after she was fired the pastor stated that she "cannot be trusted with seven-year-old children"; that the reasons for her termination were "personal and confidential"; and that she was "incapable of Christian ministry" and had a "vindictive heart." The court dismissed the defamation claim. It concluded: "When officials of a religious organization state their reasons for terminating a pastoral employee in ostensibly ecclesiastical terms, the First Amendment effectively prohibits civil tribunals from reviewing these reasons to determine whether the statements are either defamatory or capable of a religious interpretation related to the employee's performance of her duties."

• A Massachusetts court ruled that a pastor could sue his denomination for publishing a statement informing other pastors and the media that he had been suspended from all pastoral duties because of "formal charges of sexual misconduct."[240] However, the court acknowledged that the denomination's public statements concerning the pastor's sexual misconduct may well have been protected by a conditional privilege. It stated the general rule as follows: "An occasion makes a publication conditionally privileged if the circumstances lead any one of several persons having a common interest in a particular subject matter correctly or reasonably to believe that there is information that another sharing the common interest is entitled to know. . . . The common interest of members of religious associations is recognized as sufficient to support a privilege for communications among themselves concerning the qualifications of the officers and members and their participation in the activities of the society." In summary, the First Amendment did not prevent the pastor from suing his denomination for libel or slander as a result of public statements concerning his alleged sexual misconduct, but the denomination might be exempted from liability on the basis of the common interest privilege.

• A church business administrator, upon returning from a two-month leave of absence, suspected that another church employee had been signing unauthorized church checks. She shared her concerns with the church's finance council. The employee later sued the church, claiming that she had been defamed. A Minnesota appeals court dismissed the lawsuit. It noted that a person who makes a defamatory statement may be protected from legal liability by a "qualified privilege." Statements are protected by a qualified privilege if they address a matter of common concern among church members. This means that they cannot be defamatory. The court cautioned that a qualified privilege may be lost if it is "abused," meaning that the person making defamatory statements did so with "malice." Malice exists if the statements were made out of "ill will and improper motives or . . . wantonly for the purpose of injuring the [victim]." Was the church guilty of malice in this case? The court rejected the employee's claim that malice was established by the church's failure to publish a retraction, and by its failure to investigate fully the facts of the case before making the allegedly defamatory state-

---

239 Brazauskas v. Fort Wayne-South Bend Diocese, Inc., 714 N.E.2d 253 (Ind. App. 1999).

240 Hiles v. Episcopal Diocese, 744 N.E.2d 1116 (Mass. App. 2001).

ments. The court cautioned that the following factors may tend to establish malice: (1) exaggerated language; (2) the character of the language; (3) an extensive distribution of the defamatory statements; and (4) "other matters in excess of the privilege." The court concluded: "Employers have legitimate interests in protecting themselves against dishonest employees. Employers are entitled to a qualified privilege if they have reasonable grounds for believing in the validity of a statement, even though hindsight might show the statement to be false. [The business administrator] was understandably bothered by the situation and took steps to address the apparent breach of authority. She spoke to the person who chairs the committee responsible for monitoring church funds and, on his request, to the entire finance council. [Her] actions were reasonable to protect her employer."[241]

• A New Jersey court ruled that a church acted properly in dismissing its music director for criminal acts.[242] The music director entered into a one-year employment contract with a church. The contract contained the following provision for termination: "The parties involved shall give notice of termination of employment at least 30 days in advance of the termination. The termination time must be completed by the employee or if the employer does not wish the termination to be completed the employer shall fulfill all contractual financial agreements." After working for the church for a few months, the music director was arrested for possession of illegal anabolic steroids. It was later disclosed that the music director had been taking steroids to assist him with bodybuilding, and that he had previously ordered several shipments of steroids shipped directly to the church to avoid detection. One package recovered by the police contained 290 tablets of methandrostenolone, 240 tablets of oxandrolone, and 9 vials of decadurabolin. A few days later the pastor of the church learned of his music director's arrest from a newspaper article. A few days later, the music director's employment was terminated. The music director sued the church for wrongful termination. A state appeals court, in rejecting the music director's claim, noted that "in every contract there is an implied covenant of good faith and fair dealing." The music director violated this covenant by his behavior: "Even where, as here, the employee performs the duties contracted for satisfactorily, criminal activity by the employee can justify his discharge for breach of an employment contract. . . . It is clear that [the music director] intentionally ordered the anabolic steroids for his personal use and had them shipped to [the church] address. This constituted a breach of the implied conditions of [his] contract of employment. The receipt of anabolic steroids at work indirectly involved [the church] in the commission of a criminal offense and constituted gross misconduct." Second, the court concluded that employees have a "duty of good conduct." It based this duty on the following language from a respected legal treatise: "[An employee] is subject to a duty not to conduct himself with such impropriety that he brings disrepute upon the [employer] or upon the business in which he is engaged . . . . The nature of the business and the position of the agent determine what reputation the agent has agreed to maintain and what conduct can be expected from him. . . . [A]lthough the employer has no control over the conduct of such persons when they are not engaged in his work, he has such interest in the general integrity of his business household that it may be a breach of duty for one of them to acquire a deserved reputation for loose living, or to commit a serious crime." The court concluded that "when the duty of good conduct is violated by an employee, the employer has good cause to terminate a contract and the termination will not support a cause of action for breach of contract."

---

[241] Kozar v. Church of St. John the Baptist, 1997 WL 89144 (unpublished decision, Minn. App. 1997).

[242] McGarry v. Saint Anthony of Padua Roman Catholic Church, 704 A.2d 1353 (N.J. Super. 1998) (quoting Restatement (Second) of Agency, § 380 and comment).

• An Ohio court ruled that a preschool teacher who was dismissed for striking a child could not sue the preschool for defamation. A preschool director entered a classroom of 2-year-old children upon hearing hysterical crying. A worker informed the director that the teacher had struck the child. The director noticed a hand-mark on the child's face. Upon being questioned, the boy stated (and demonstrated) that the teacher had put her hand over his mouth and shook him. The teacher was confronted with this information, but denied it. However, she offered no other explanation as to the boy's condition. The director was not satisfied that the teacher was being truthful, and dismissed her. The director later reported the incident to the boy's mother, and to the state department of human services. The fired teacher sued the center, alleging that she had been defamed by the director's communications to the boy's mother, to other workers at the center, to the president of the center's board of directors, and to the state. A state appeals court rejected the teacher's claims. It noted that the director was required by state law to report suspected cases of abuse to the department of human services, and so this communication did not constitute defamation. Further, there was no evidence that the director ever informed other workers at the center as to the reason that the teacher had been terminated. With respect to the communications made to the boy's mother, and to the president of the center's board of directors, the court concluded that such communications "enjoyed at least a qualified privilege" since they were matters of "common interest." As such, the communications would not be defamatory unless they were made with "malice." The court observed that "the record is devoid of evidence of actual malice on the part of [the director in communicating] the statements. On the contrary, the record reveals that [she] acted properly and reasonably under the circumstances."[243]

• An Ohio court ruled that a former teacher at a church-operated school could not sue school officials for defamation since the allegedly defamatory statements made by the school officials concerned a matter of "common interest" and accordingly were privileged. The teacher was convicted of contributing to the delinquency of a minor for providing alcohol to one of his students. He advised school officials of his conviction, and was permitted to remain on the faculty both as a teacher and yearbook adviser. A few years later, his teaching contract was not renewed. A priest was hired to replace him as teacher and yearbook adviser. When the former teacher continued to associate with student members of the yearbook staff, two priests (who served as administrators at the school) contacted the parents of two of these students and informed them that the former teacher had been convicted of "corrupting a minor," implied that he was a homosexual, and recommended that they not permit their sons to associate with such a person. The former teacher learned of these statements, and sued the priests for defamation. A state appeals court ruled that the statements made by the priests were not defamatory since they were protected by a qualified privilege. It observed: "As a matter of public policy, educators and parents share a common interest in the training, morality and well-being of the children in their care. . . . [S]tatements made by a teacher and a principal which relate to a former teacher's . . . commission of acts which are potentially harmful to the well-being of a student, when made to the parents of the student involved, can be motivated by a common interest in the education or safety of that student."[244]

• A Texas court ruled that a church was not liable for defaming a former secretary as a result of statements made to church members claiming that she had misappropriated church funds. A church operated a private school. Its minister of education, who also served as principal of the school, resigned after admitting that he misappropriated

---

[243] Lail v. Madisonville Child Care Project, 561 N.E.2d 1063 (Ohio App. 1990).

[244] McCartney v. Oblates of St. Francis de Sales, 609 N.E.2d 216 (Ohio App. 1992).

church funds, destroyed church records, forged signatures, and committed other criminal acts. He later pleaded guilty to criminal charges for his admitted conduct in misappropriating school funds. He informed the church that a woman who served as a secretary at the school participated in the misappropriations. After an audit confirmed the principal's accusations the church asked the secretary to resign. The church published (1) a letter to its members claiming that the secretary misappropriated school funds; (2) a letter to the school children's parents claiming that the secretary deposited tuition funds into the wrong accounts and later used the funds for her personal benefit; destroyed checks, financial records, and bank records; forged signatures; covered up these indiscretions; received seventy dollars extra per pay period for nearly two years as well as other undocumented "reimbursements"; and (3) a report to the church members reporting the secretary's resignation and claiming that she deposited tuition funds into the wrong account and then used the funds to support programs and individuals outside of and over the budget adopted by the congregation. At a meeting of church members, church officials orally accused the secretary of depositing tuition funds into the wrong account and then using the funds for her personal benefit or for other people or projects as she and the principal saw fit; destroying checks, bank records, and financial records; forging signatures; and covering up many of these indiscretions. The secretary later sued the church and the individual members of the church audit committee, claiming that the church's actions defamed her. A state appeals court rejected all of the secretary's claims. It concluded that words that otherwise might be defamatory may be "legally excused" by a qualified privilege. It observed: "All of the members of [the church] have a common interest in the church's use of their financial contributions to the church; thus, the members have a common interest in information about those funds. The members who made the statements in question reasonably believed that the misappropriation took place and that the board, the members, and the parents shared a common interest in the use of the funds and information about those funds. [The church] reasonably believed that these people were entitled to know of the misappropriation. [It] had a duty to perform for the board, the members, and the parents. [It] made the communications without actual malice. [The principal] confessed his and [the secretary's] involvement, and [he] later pleaded guilty to criminal charges. [The church's] audit confirmed all of [his] statements. [The secretary] never swore under oath in an affidavit in opposition to summary judgment that the statements were lies. [She] kept the misappropriated funds in a shoe box in her closet and returned the funds when accused. [The principal] testified that the statements were true. [The secretary] admits receiving personal benefit from the misappropriation of funds. [She] admits she destroyed records. [The church] neither entertained serious doubts as to the truth of the statements nor made these statements with a high degree of awareness of their probable falsity. The communications appeared accurate, [the church] reasonably believed [the principal], and church members and parents who received information had an interest in the funds and information about the funds."[245]

A few courts have ruled that employers, including churches, are more exposed to liability for statements made about employees following their termination than for statements made prior to termination.

> • *A Missouri appeals court ruled that it was barred by the First Amendment from resolving a former church school principal's claim that she had been defamed by statements made by her former employer prior to her termination, but it did allow her to sue on the*

---

[245] Hanssen v. Our Redeemer Lutheran Church, 938 S.W.2d 85 (Tex. App. 1997).

basis of a defamatory statement allegedly made when she was no longer an employee. While most of the allegedly defamatory statements were made prior to the non-renewal of her contract, one was made afterwards. She alleged that a church official, knowing that she no longer was an employee[246], sent a memo to another person in which he accused her of "ineffective leadership" and being involved in a "situation" that was "a violation of professional boundaries that is giving public scandal." The court concluded that this communication "was not connected to the non-renewal issue, but instead came a substantial period of time after the personnel issues were resolved." As a result, the court allowed the former principal to sue the church on the basis of this communication, and sent the case back to the trial court for further deliberations. However, it cautioned that the trial court "must consider First Amendment protections related generally to the governance of the [church] and also the defense of common law conditional privilege, as well as any other defenses."

Severance Agreements   § 8-22.1

Key Point 8-22.1> *Churches should consider using a severance agreement when a decision is made to dismiss an employee. Such agreements set forth the terms and conditions of an employee's separation. In most cases, the employer agrees to pay the employee a specified sum of money (often expressed in terms of so many weeks of pay) in exchange for the employee's consent to the termination of the employment relationship and a release of any legal claims against the employer. Such agreements should be drafted by an attorney to ensure enforceability.*

The termination of an employee is often a traumatic event that can expose a church to litigation. This risk should be taken seriously, since such disputes are a common form of church litigation, and many church insurance policies contain no coverage for employment practices. If your church does not have employment practices coverage, you may have to retain and compensate your own attorney if sued by a current or former employee, and pay any settlement amount or court judgment.

> *Ask your church insurance agent if your church has employment practices coverage. If not, find out how you can obtain this coverage.*

> *Some churches have purchased officers and directors insurance. In some cases, this insurance may cover some employment claims, often with a large retention (deductible).*

Many employers resolve employment disputes by using severance agreements. A severance agreement is an enforceable contract, signed by both the church and employee, in which the employee agrees to voluntarily terminate his or her employment and release the church from any liability in exchange for the church's agreement to pay specified benefits. These agreements avoid the expense

---

[246] State ex rel. Gaydos v. Blaeuer, 81 S.W.3d 186 (Mo. App. 2002).

and inconvenience of litigation, and often result in an amicable resolution of an employment dispute.

There are several points that church leaders should consider when proposing a severance agreement, including the following:

1. *Voluntary termination of employment.* The employee voluntarily terminates his or her employment, as of a specified date.

2. *Release of rights.* The employee releases specified claims against the employer. It is important for these released claims to be described fully. For example, the agreement should identify by name all state and federal statutes that confer rights that are being released. When severance agreements contain only vague references to released rights, employees may later argue that they did not understand what rights were being released and so the agreement is void.

3. *Consideration.* The employer must provide the employee with something of value in order for the employee's duties under a severance agreement to be legally enforceable. The legal term for the "value" that must be provided by the employer is consideration. Often, it is in the form of a lump sum amount of money, or a continuation of salary and benefits for a specified number of weeks. The value provided by the employer should exceed what is provided to employees who voluntarily terminate their employment without being asked to sign a severance agreement.

4. *Legal review by employee.* The agreement should encourage the employee to retain an attorney to review the agreement's provisions.

5. *Legal review by employer.* The employer should have the agreement drafted by an attorney to ensure compliance with all applicable laws. Some states impose specific requirements upon severance agreements.

6. *No duress.* Several courts have found severance agreements to be null and void on the ground that the employee was "coerced" into signing it. This a good reason to allow the employee several days to evaluate the agreement, and to seek legal counsel.

7. *Older workers.* The Older Workers Benefit Protection Act, which applies to any employer with 20 or more employees that is engaged in interstate commerce, prohibits employees at least 40 years of age from "waiving" their rights under federal age discrimination law unless the waiver meets several specific requirements, including the following: (1) the waiver is in simple language; (2) the waiver specifically refers to rights arising under the federal Age Discrimination in Employment Act; (3) the employee does not waive rights or claims that may arise after the date the waiver is executed; (4) the employee must receive some benefit for signing the waiver in addition to salary; (5) the individual is

advised in writing to consult with an attorney prior to executing the agreement; (6) the individual is given a period of at least 21 days within which to consider the agreement; and (7) the agreement provides that for a period of at least 7 days following the execution of such agreement, the individual may revoke the agreement. This law will not apply to most local churches, since they have fewer than 20 employees. Even churches with 20 or more employees are not subject to these requirements unless they are engaged in interstate commerce.

8. *Confidentiality.* It is common for severance agreements to contain a confidentiality clause that prohibits the employer and the employee from disclosing the terms of the agreement, except as specifically permitted (such as discussions with a tax advisor).

9. *Fringe benefits.* A severance agreement should clarify the status of fringe benefits. For example, what happens to accrued vacation or sick time? Retirement plan benefits (such as those payable under a rabbi trust)? Unreimbursed business expenses? Also, the agreement should address the continuation of medical insurance.

10. *Employer property.* The agreement should address the return of all employer property (keys, computers, cell phones, credit cards, etc.).

11. *Board approval.* Have the final agreement reviewed by the church board prior to legal review and signature.

12. *Tax withholding.* Payments made to a former employee pursuant to a severance agreement ordinarily constitute taxable income and therefore payroll taxes need to be withheld (unless the person is a minister who was employed to perform ministerial services, and did not elect voluntary withholding). The tax regulations state: "Any payments made by an employer to an employee on account of dismissal, that is, involuntary separation from the service of the employer, constitute wages regardless of whether the employer is legally bound by contract, statute, or otherwise to make such payments." There is one exclusion that may apply in some cases. Section 104(a)(2) of the tax code specifies that gross income does not include the amount of any damages received (whether by suit or agreement and whether as lump sums or as periodic payments) "on account of personal physical injuries or physical sickness." However, section 104(a) specifies that "emotional distress shall not be treated as physical injury or physical sickness" except for "damages not in excess of the amount paid for medical care . . . attributable to emotional distress." As a result, jury awards and settlements for employment discrimination and wrongful dismissal claims are fully taxable to the extent that they are based on emotional distress. Church leaders must determine whether severance pay is taxable so that it can be prop-

erly reported (on a W-2 and 941 forms), and taxes withheld. Failure to properly report severance pay can result in penalties for both a church and the recipient.

13. *Housing allowances.* Can a church designate any portion of a minister's severance pay as a housing allowance? This question has never been addressed by either the IRS or any court. However, an argument can be made that a church can designate a portion of severance pay as a housing allowance if the severance pay is treated as taxable compensation rather than as damages in settlement of a personal injury claim. If the severance pay represents taxable income, as the IRS will almost certainly insist in most cases, it is because the amount paid represents compensation based on services rendered. Since a housing allowance must be designated out of compensation paid to a minister for services rendered in the exercise of ministry, a reasonable case can be made that a housing allowance can be designated with respect to taxable severance pay. Of course, a housing allowance can only be designated for ministers. And, designating severance pay as a housing allowance will be of little value if a minister transfers immediately to another church that designates a timely housing allowance. But a designation of a housing allowance will be useful in the case of a minister who is not immediately employed by another church or religious organization.

14. *Arbitration.* Some employers include a clause in severance agreements that requires any dispute associated with the agreement to be resolved through mediation or binding arbitration.

Case Study

• *An Indiana court ruled that a lawsuit brought by a dismissed pastor against his former church was barred by the First Amendment guaranty of religious freedom, and by the fact that the pastor's acceptance of a 90-day severance check amounted to an "accord and satisfaction" of all claims against the church. An accord and satisfaction is a binding settlement of a disputed claim that occurs when one party offers less than the disputed amount to the other with the understanding that its acceptance will constitute a settlement of the entire claim, and the other party accepts the lower amount. Under these circumstances, the party who accepted the lower amount cannot later claim any additional amount.*[247]

---

[247] Stewart v. Kingsley Terrace Church of Christ, 767 N.E.2d 542 (Ind. App. 2002).

PART FIVE

Miscellaneous Issues

Legal Briefs

HERE ARE A VARIETY OF MISCELLANEOUS ISSUES THAT MAY AFFECT YOU AND YOUR CHURCH:

National Labor Relations Act
The National Labor Relations Act gives employees the legal right to form labor unions. Some religious organizations are exempt from the provisions of this law.

Reference letters
A reference letter evaluates the qualifications and suitability of a person for a particular position. Churches, like other employers, often use reference letters to screen new employees and volunteers. Churches often are asked to provide reference letters on current or former workers. The law generally provides employers with important protections when responding to a reference letter request. However, liability may still arise in some cases, such as if the employer acts with malice in drafting a reference letter.

Church leaders often are reluctant to provide a reference letter containing negative information because of a fear of legal liability. Some churches and secular employers have been sued by former employees or volunteers because of negative information shared in a reference letter. Liability generally is based on defamation, the infliction of emotional distress, or "interference with contract." While it is possible for churches to be sued, and found liable, for information contained in reference letters that they provide to other churches or employers, there are precautions that church leaders can take to reduce this risk.

Evaluations
Many churches perform periodic evaluations of their employees. In many cases, supervisors give inflated evaluations in order to avoid conflict. This common practice can expose a church to an increased risk of liability for employees who are protected by a state or federal employment discrimination law. How can a church avoid such a scenario? By insisting that all employee evaluations be objective assessments of clearly defined goals or standards.

Interviews
Employers must be familiar with what questions they can and can't ask at different stages of the interview process. Many pre-offer interview questions can be deemed as discriminatory, especially as they relate to disabilities. Be sure you know how to conduct interviews correctly.

Arbitration
By adopting an arbitration policy, a church can compel members to arbitrate specified disputes with their church rather than pursue their claim in the civil courts.

Handbooks
Employee handbooks can provide employees with valuable information on the terms and conditions of their employment. However, they may also expose a church to an increased risk of liability. Have an attorney prepare or review your employee handbook before it is adopted.

Privacy
Do employees have a "right of privacy" in their workspace? Are the contents of their desk off limits to prying staff? Can church leaders dismiss an employee if they find pornographic files on his office computer? Or, would this amount to an invasion of the employee's privacy or a violation of wiretap laws?

Courts have ruled on these questions and determined that employees may have a limited right of privacy in their workspace that may extend to the contents of their desk and cabinet drawers, and employer-provided computers. This right of privacy can be superseded by a policy that clearly authorizes the employer to inspect these items.

Insurance
Employment disputes are one of the most common sources of litigation involving churches. However, many churches are not insured against this risk, because most church general liability insurance policies exclude employment practices. This means that many churches face a potentially significant uninsured risk.

How can church leaders respond to this potentially uninsured risk? Two ways:

1. Implement an effective risk management program that addresses the most common types of employer liability.

2. Purchase employment practices liability insurance (EPLI). Often, EPLI insurance can be purchased as a special endorsement to a comprehensive general liability (CGL) policy.

National Labor Relations Act   § 8-23

Key Point 8-23> *The National Labor Relations Act gives employees the legal right to form labor unions. Some religious organizations are exempt from the provisions of this law.*

In 1935 Congress decided that disturbances in the area of labor relations led to undesirable burdens on and obstructions of interstate commerce, and it passed the National Labor Relations Act.[248] The Act, building on the National Industrial Recovery Act (1933), gave employees a federally protected right to join labor organizations and bargain collectively through their chosen representatives on issues affecting their employment. Congress also created the National Labor Relations Board (NLRB) to supervise the collective bargaining process. The Board was empowered to investigate disputes about which union, if any, represented employees, and to certify the appropriate representatives as the designated collective bargaining agent. The employer was then required to bargain with these representatives, and the Board was authorized to make sure that such bargaining did in fact occur. In general, the Act stipulated that an employer's refusal to bargain was an unfair labor practice. Thus a general process was established that would ensure that employees as a group could express their opinions and exert their influence over the terms and conditions of their employment. The Board would act to see that the process worked. Congress enacted the Labor Management Relations Act in 1947 to adjust and minimize any differences in the rights granted to unions, employees, and employers.

Does the National Labor Relations Act apply to religious organizations? This question has caused considerable controversy. Initially, it should be noted that the stated purpose of the Act was to

> eliminate the causes of certain substantial obstructions to the free flow of commerce and to mitigate and eliminate these obstructions when they have occurred by encouraging the practice and procedure of collective bargaining and by protecting the exercise by workers of full freedom of association, self-organization, and designation of representatives of their own choosing, for the purpose of negotiating the terms and conditions of their employment or other mutual aid or protection.[249]

Clearly, then, the Act was designed to apply only to those employment relationships that affect commerce. The Act defines the term *affecting commerce* to mean "in commerce, or burdening or obstructing commerce or the free flow of commerce, or having led or tending to lead to a labor dispute burdening or obstructing commerce or the free flow of commerce."[250] Further, the Act defines *employer* as

---

[248] 29 U.S.C. §§ 151-168.

[249] 29 U.S.C. § 151.

[250] 29 U.S.C. § 152(7).

any person acting as an agent of an employer, directly or indirectly, but shall not include the United States or any wholly owned Government corporation, or any Federal Reserve Bank, or any state or political subdivision thereof, or any person subject to the Railway Labor Act, as amended from time to time, or any labor organization (other than when acting as an employer), or anyone acting in the capacity of officer or agent of such labor organization.[251]

In summary, the Act covers any employer that is not covered by one of the eight exceptions mentioned in the preceding paragraph. Since religious organizations do not fit within any of the eight exempt categories, the National Labor Relations Board has held that such organizations are covered by the Act at least to the extent that they are engaged in some proprietary activity affecting commerce.[252] To illustrate, the NLRB has asserted jurisdiction over the Sunday School Board of the Southern Baptist Convention since it was engaged in the sale of literature on a nationwide basis and thus could be viewed as being involved in a proprietary activity affecting commerce. The NLRB observed:

> The employer asserts that as it is a nonprofit organization which is engaged in purely religious activities, it is not engaged in commerce within the meaning of the Act. We find no merit in this contention. . . . As this Board and the courts have held, it is immaterial that the employer may be a nonprofit organization, or that its activities may be motivated by considerations other than those applicable to enterprises which are, in the generally accepted sense, commercial.[253]

Similarly, the Board asserted jurisdiction over an evangelistic organization that was engaged in substantial commercial activities that were unrelated, except as a revenue source, to the organization's religious activities.[254]

The "Catholic Bishop" Test

A number of religious organizations have challenged the constitutionality of NLRB determinations that they are covered by the Act. In a leading case, the United States Supreme Court was faced with the issue of whether lay teachers in church-operated schools were under the jurisdiction of the NLRB. The Court found that neither the language nor the legislative history of the National Labor Relations Act disclosed "an affirmative intention . . . clearly expressed" that the

---

[251] 29 U.S.C. § 152(2).

[252] First Church of Christ, Scientist, 194 N.L.R.B. 1006 (1972). Although the NLRB has traditionally assumed jurisdiction over all religious organizations, it has, as a matter of discretion, refused to assert jurisdiction over religious organizations not engaged in commercial activities or religious organizations engaged in commercial activities that earn less than prescribed levels of income. This principle is referred to as the worthy cause doctrine. *See generally* Sherman & Black, *The Labor Board and the Private Nonprofit Employer: A Critical Examination of the Board's Worthy Cause Exemption,* 83 HARV. L. REV. 1323 (1970). *See also* Laycock, *Towards a General Theory of the Religions Clauses: The Case of Church Labor Relations and the Right to Church Autonomy,* 81 COLUM. L. REV. 1373 (1981) (arguing that NLRB assertions of jurisdiction over religious organizations may result in a violation of the First Amendment's guaranty of religious freedom).

[253] Sunday School Board of the Southern Baptist Convention, 92 N.L.R.B. 801, 802 (1950).

[254] NLRB v. World Evangelism, Inc., 656 F.2d 1349 (9th Cir. 1981). *See also* Tressler Lutheran Home for Children v. NLRB, 677 F.2d 302 (3rd Cir. 1982) (NLRB jurisdiction over church-operated children's home upheld); Jacobo Marti & Sons, Inc. v. NLRB, 676 F.2d 975 (3rd Cir. 1982) (NLRB jurisdiction over cheese processing plant having a close connection with the Amish faith upheld).

NLRB have such jurisdiction. Therefore, the Court declined to construe the Act in a manner that would require the resolution of "difficult and sensitive questions arising out of the guarantees of the First Amendment Religion Clauses."[255]

The Court's test for determining the validity of an exercise of jurisdiction by the NLRB over a religious organization may be summarized as follows:

Step #1. Determine if the exercise of jurisdiction by the NLRB over a religious organization would give rise to serious constitutional questions under the First Amendment (which guarantees the free exercise of religion).

Step #2. If a serious constitutional question would arise, then the NLRB may not exercise jurisdiction over the religious organization without a showing of an "affirmative intention of the Congress clearly expressed" to confer such jurisdiction.

Step #3. If serious constitutional questions are not an exercise of jurisdiction by the NLRB over a religious organization, then no inquiry is necessary as to whether Congress clearly expressed an intention to confer jurisdiction.[256]

In applying this test, one court has upheld an exercise of jurisdiction by the NLRB over a Christian evangelistic organization engaged in substantial commercial activities. The court noted that no serious First Amendment questions were raised since NLRB jurisdiction resulted in only a "minimal infringement" on the organization's constitutional rights.[257] Serious constitutional questions are raised by an NLRB assertion of jurisdiction over church school teachers, concluded the court, but this is not true of an exercise of jurisdiction over lay employees engaged in the commercial activities of a religious organization.

NLRB assertions of jurisdiction similarly have been upheld over church affiliated hospitals[258] and nursing homes[259] that (1) receive a substantial percentage of their income from governmental sources; (2) hire employees without regard to religious beliefs; and (3) engage in no specific religious indoctrination of patients or employees. A number of courts have concluded that Congress has "clearly

---

[255] NLRB v. Catholic Bishop of Chicago, 440 U.S. 490, 507 (1979). *See also* NLRB v. Bishop Ford Catholic High School, 623 F. 2d 818 (2nd Cir. 1980), *cert. denied*, 450 U.S. 996 (1980).

[256] In Dole v. Shenandoah Baptist Church, 899 F.2d 1389 (4th Cir. 1990), a federal appeals court suggested that the Supreme Court may have altered the *Catholic Bishop* test in a 1985 decision. In 1985, the Supreme Court ruled that "because we perceive no 'significant risk' of an infringement on First Amendment rights, we do not require any clearer expression of congressional intent to regulate these activities." Tony & Susan Alamo Foundation v. Secretary of Labor, 471 U.S. 290, 298 n.18 (1985). The federal appeals court observed that the Supreme Court may have intended to replace the *Catholic Bishop* test. If so, this objective is not clear, and has not been clarified in later decisions.

[257] NLRB v. World Evangelism, Inc., 656 F.2d 1349 (9th Cir. 1981).

[258] St. Elizabeth Community Hospital v. NLRB, 708 F.2d 1436 (9th Cir. 1983); Bon Secours Hospital, Inc., 248 N.L.R.B. 743 (1980) (Catholic social service agency whose purpose was the provision of social services on a nondenominational basis and that hired employees without regard to religious beliefs held to be subject to NLRB jurisdiction).

[259] Mid American Health Services, Inc., 247 N.L.R.B. 752 (1980).

expressed an intention to confer [NLRB] jurisdiction" over church-affiliated hospitals, since in 1974 it removed the pre-existing exemption of all nonprofit hospitals under section 2 of the National Labor Relations Act, and rejected an amendment that would have retained the exemption for church-affiliated hospitals.

Another court reached the same conclusion with respect to employees of a church-operated home for neglected children.[260] The court agreed with the Supreme Court that an exercise of jurisdiction by the NLRB over church-operated schools raised serious constitutional questions since such schools actively propagate religious faith. However, the court did not believe that serious constitutional questions were raised by an assertion of jurisdiction by the NLRB over church-operated homes for neglected children since such institutions are not devoted to the propagation of religion. Since no serious constitutional question was raised, the court concluded that an "affirmative intention of Congress clearly expressed" to confer jurisdiction over church-operated homes for neglected children was not necessary.

Significantly, the court emphasized that (1) governmental funding comprised over half of the home's income; (2) the home hired employees without regard to their religious affiliation; (3) the home accepted only abused children and kept them an average of six weeks during which time they remained wards of the state; (4) all children were referrals from a state agency; and (5) children could not attend religious services contrary to the beliefs of their parents without parental consent. The court concluded that under these facts the home was indistinguishable from a nonreligious institution, and, accordingly, no serious First Amendment questions were implicated.

A federal appeals court ruled that a child care center operated by the Salvation Army was subject to NLRB jurisdiction.[261] The court emphasized that serious constitutional questions were not created by NLRB jurisdiction over the facility, since

> [t]he program's function is primarily to provide care for the children, not education. It involves no religious instruction, indoctrination, or extracurricular activities. Neither the teachers, children, nor parents are chosen for their religious affiliation. Nor do they receive any religious training. The director, who oversees the workplace, need not be, and is not presently, a clergyman. . . . [T]here is not evidence that the [facility] serves anything other than a secular function with respect to the children, parents, and teachers.[262]

The court emphasized that

> if the [facility] provided not just day care for children but also religious instruction and religiously oriented extracurricular activities, a different result might be required. Instead, we have an institution whose primary business is the provision of care and

---

[260] NLRB v. St. Louis Christian Home, 663 F.2d 60 (8th Cir. 1981); *See also* *Tressler Lutheran Home for Children v. NLRB, 677 F.2d 302 (3rd Cir. 1982).

[261] NLRB v. Salvation Army, 763 F.2d 1 (1st Cir. 1985).

[262] *Id.* at 6.

whose operation is indistinguishable from that of secular day care centers. The risk of serious constitutional questions being raised in these circumstances is simply too insignificant and speculative . . . . [W]ere we not to find jurisdiction, we might inadvertently be offering all private day care centers and other private providers of care a formalistic means of circumventing federal labor laws. By articulating some religious affiliation and mission, no matter how little effect it might have on the social programs' functions or operations, providers of care could easily avoid the Board's jurisdiction . . . .[263]

Many children's homes affiliated with churches are not subject to NLRB jurisdiction because their activities are inherently religious. The New Testament itself states: "Pure religion and undefiled before God and the Father is this, To visit the fatherless and widows in their affliction . . . ."[264] Children's homes that are affiliated with and controlled by bona fide churches, that receive all or most of their income from nongovernmental sources, that actively propagate the church's religious tenets to their children, and that require employees to be members of the church, undoubtedly are exempt from NLRB jurisdiction under the Supreme Court's three part test. However, church-affiliated children's homes that lack most of these characteristics may be subject to NLRB jurisdiction.

Conclusion

It is likely that the NLRB will continue to exercise jurisdiction over religious organizations engaged in substantial commercial activities, and that the courts will uphold such exercises of jurisdiction. As one court has observed, when a religious or nonprofit organization operates in the same way as a secular institution, the NLRB may treat such an organization like a secular institution.[265] But NLRB assertions of jurisdiction over religious organizations probably will not be upheld in any of the following situations:

a. The organization is not involved in substantial commercial activities.[266]

b. The organization is not engaged in a business or activity affecting commerce. Commerce is defined by the National Labor Relations Act as trade, traffic, commerce, transportation, or communication among the several states.[267] A religious organization that purchases all of its supplies from local vendors and sells no product or service to persons residing in other states may not be engaged in any activity affecting commerce. Note, however, that the Act defines commerce to include "communication" among the several states. This would include radio or television broadcasts, and may include the operation of a "web page" on the Internet. The purchase

---

[263] *Id.* at 6-7.

[264] James 1:27 (KJV).

[265] NLRB v. St. Louis Christian Home, 663 F.2d 60 (8th Cir. 1981).

[266] The NLRB claims to possess jurisdiction over all religious organizations, but it declines to assert jurisdiction over religious organizations not engaged in substantial commercial activities. An assertion of jurisdiction over a religious organization not engaged in substantial commercial activities might violate the First Amendment. NLRB v. Catholic Bishop of Chicago, 440 U.S. 490 (1979).

[267] 29 U.S.C. § 152(6).

of electricity and natural gas from a utility company engaged in interstate commerce also may constitute commerce.[268] In general, the discussion in section 8-05 regarding the meaning of "commerce" in the context of federal civil rights laws is relevant here as well.

c. An assertion of NLRB jurisdiction inhibits a religious organization's ability to propagate its beliefs.[269]

d. An assertion of NLRB jurisdiction raises serious constitutional questions under the First Amendment and no "affirmative intention of Congress clearly expressed" confers jurisdiction.[270]

Reference Letters

Key Point 8-24> *A reference letter is a letter that evaluates the qualifications and suitability of a person for a particular position. Churches, like other employers, often use reference letters to screen new employees and volunteers. Churches often are asked to provide reference letters on current or former workers. The law generally provides employers with important protections when responding to a reference letter request. However, liability may still arise in some cases, such as if the employer acts with malice in drafting a reference letter.*

A "reference letter" is a letter that evaluates the qualifications and suitability of a person for a particular position. There are a number of important legal issues associated with the use of reference letters, and some of them are addressed in this section.

A. Requesting Reference Letters as a Screening Device

The use of reference letters when hiring employees and selecting volunteer workers is becoming an increasingly common church practice, since it is a way for churches to reduce the risk of liability for "negligent selection" of employees and volunteers. The use of reference letters in screening workers is addressed in chapter 12 of this text.

> *The use of reference letters, and several sample forms, is available in several resources available from the publisher of this text.[271]*

---

[268] *See generally* NLRB v. St. Louis Christian Home, 663 F.2d 60 (8th Cir. 1981). The expansive interpretation of the term *commerce* has not gone without objection. One judge has commented that "it is virtually unthinkable that the Founding Fathers could have foreseen the extent to which an increasingly expansive interpretation of the Commerce Clause could so infringe local authority." Godwin v. Occupational Safety and Health Review Commission, 540 F.2d 1013, 1017 (9th Cir. 1976) (Ely, J., concurring).

[269] NLRB v. Catholic Bishop of Chicago, 440 U.S. 490 (1979).

[270] *Id.*

[271] *See, e.g.,* J. COBBLE, R. HAMMAR, and S. KLIPOWICZ, REDUCING THE RISK OF CHILD SEXUAL ABUSE IN YOUR CHURCH; J. COBBLE and R. HAMMAR, SELECTING AND SCREENING CHURCH WORKERS; J. COBBLE and R. HAMMAR, SELECTION AND SCREENING KIT FOR CHURCH EMPLOYEES; J. COBBLE and R. HAMMAR, SELECTION AND SCREENING KIT FOR CHURCH VOLUNTEERS; J. COBBLE and R. HAMMAR, SELECTION AND SCREENING KIT FOR MINISTERS. All of these resources are available from the publisher of this text.

B. Responding to Reference Letter Requests

Many churches have been asked to provide reference letters on a current or former employee or volunteer. Unfortunately, such letters can expose a church to legal liability if not handled properly. While liability ordinarily is associated with negative information disclosed in a reference letter, it also may arise because of positive references. Both kinds of liability are addressed in this section.

Some churches, like many secular employers, refuse to respond to any reference request, other than to confirm the fact that a person worked for the church and the dates of employment or volunteer service. While such an approach certainly reduces if not eliminates a church's liability for providing an inappropriate reference, it does so in some cases at the risk of exposing innocent people to potential harm. To illustrate, assume that First Church dismisses Bill as a volunteer children's worker because of inappropriate sexual contact with children. Bill applies for a similar position at Second Church. Second Church asks First Church for a reference letter describing Bill's suitability for working with children. The pastor and board at First Church refuse to respond because of a fear of legal liability. Within a few months, Bill molests four children while acting as a volunteer worker at Second Church. Are the pastor and board members of First Church morally responsible, at least in part, for the molestation of the four children? Many church leaders would answer yes to this question. As a result, many church leaders have a desire to share information about former employees or volunteers with other churches when asked to do so, even if that information involves inappropriate behavior.

While it is possible for churches to be sued, and found liable, for information contained in reference letters that they provide to other churches or employers, there are precautions that church leaders can take to reduce this risk. Several of these precautions are addressed in the following paragraphs.

liability for providing negative references

Church leaders often are reluctant to provide a reference letter containing negative information because of a fear of legal liability. Some churches and secular employers have been sued by former employees or volunteers because of negative information shared in a reference letter. Liability generally is based on defamation, the infliction of emotional distress, or "interference with contract."

Case Study

• *An employee of a church-affiliated college was terminated for not returning a paycheck that had been inadvertently issued to him for a time period in which he had performed no services. The employee applied for work at a local business as a security guard. A company supervisor called the college's personnel department for a reference. A supervisor in the personnel department responded to the reference request with laughter, and then advised the caller that the former employee "has a problem of dishonesty concerning money." Because of this negative reference, the company decided not to hire the individual. He later sued the college for slander and "interference with business relations." A Massachusetts appeals court concluded that the col-*

lege was liable under these circumstances. This case illustrates the legal risks that one assumes in providing negative references to other employers. This is particularly so when "opinions," as opposed to statements of fact, are expressed.[272]

Many courts and legislatures have recognized a number of legal defenses that are available to employers when responding to a request for a reference letter. These defenses include the following:

(1) truth

Employers cannot be liable for defamation when the information shared in a reference letter is true. Of course, to qualify for this defense, an employer must limit its reference letter to assertions of fact that are verifiable through documents or the testimony of witnesses. Truth is not an absolute defense to claims of emotional distress and interference with contract, but it certainly makes such claims less likely to succeed.

(2) qualified privilege

In many states, employers are protected by a "qualified privilege" when giving references on former employees. This qualified privilege generally prohibits an employer from being guilty of defamation unless the former employee can prove that statements of fact given by the employer in a reference letter were false, and made with malice. Malice in this context generally means that the employer either knew the statements were false, or made them with a reckless disregard as to their truth or falsity. Note that not all states recognize the qualified privilege. As a result, employers should not make potentially defamatory statements about former employees without the advice of a local attorney.

The concept of qualified privilege was described by one court as follows:

> One who in the regular course of business is asked by a prospective employer . . . for information concerning a person, is entitled to the defense of qualified privilege if his reply would otherwise be regarded as defamatory. . . . The qualified privilege serves an important public function in the employment context. Without the privilege, references would be even more hesitant than they are to provide candid evaluations of former employees. In order to overcome the qualified privilege, the plaintiff must show that the statements were made with malice. Once a communication is deemed privileged, the burden of proof to demonstrate malice rests with the plaintiff. To show malice, the plaintiff must show either that the statements were made with knowing falsity, in bad faith, or with reckless disregard of the truth.[273]

Several states have enacted legislation incorporating the concept of qualified privilege as a matter of law. Such statutes typically protect information shared by employers in reference letters, unless the information is shared with malice.

---

[272] St. Clair v. Trustees of Boston University, 521 N.E.2d 1044 (Mass. App. 1988).

[273] Hargrow v. Long, 760 F. Supp. 1 (D.D.C. 1991).

Case Studies

• *A New York court ruled that disparaging statements made by a minister about a member of his congregation when asked by a prospective employer for a reference were not defamatory because they were protected by a qualified privilege and had not been made with malice.*[274] *A woman sued her minister for defamation as a result of a reference he provided on her behalf to a prospective employer (a college affiliated with her church). The minister informed an employee of the college's personnel department that the woman was an "unstable person" and that "her children are disturbed." The court ruled that these statements were not defamatory since they were protected by a qualified privilege. Many courts have concluded that the law should encourage members of churches and other organizations to share with each other about matters of common interest without undue concern about being sued for defamation. As a result, many courts have ruled that church members are protected by a qualified privilege when sharing with other church members about matters of mutual concern or common interest. This means that such communications cannot be defamatory unless made with "malice." Malice in this context means that the person who made the allegedly defamatory remark knew that it was false, or made it with a reckless disregard as to its truth or falsity. The court concluded that statements made by the minister to the college personnel department were protected by the qualified privilege based on a common interest, and that the minister had not been guilty of malice and therefore his comments were not defamatory. It concluded: "Such statements were protected by a qualified privilege, the issue being whether plaintiff's allegations of malice are sufficient to overcome the privilege, i.e., sufficient to permit an inference that defendant acted out of spite or ill will, with reckless disregard for the statements' truth or falsity, or with a high degree of belief that [his] statements were probably false. They do not.... While the statements were frank, the expressions used were not beyond what was necessary for the purposes of the communication, both speaker and listener having a common interest in plaintiff's character and fitness as a prospective teacher and promoter of their faith, or otherwise so vituperative as to warrant an inference of malice.... Suspicion, surmise and accusation are not enough to infer malice."*

• *A federal court in the District of Columbia threw out a lawsuit brought by a worker against his former employer for allegedly defamatory references given to prospective employers.*[275] *The worker was employed as a bookkeeper for a secular company. His employment was marked by difficulties with fellow employees. Without explanation or advance notice, the worker quit his job. He later applied for another job, and the prospective employer sought references from the former employer. One supervisor stated that the worker was "wholly incompetent" and "not eligible for rehire." Another supervisor stated that the worker was "undesirable as a candidate for rehire," and that he had "personality conflicts" with coworkers. The worker sued his former employer, and these supervisors, for defamation on the basis of these statements. The defendants asked the court to dismiss the case, and the court did so. It emphasized that all of the allegedly defamatory statements were protected by a "qualified privilege" which it defined as follows: "One who in the regular course of business is asked by a prospective employer . . . for information concerning a person, is entitled to the defense of qualified privilege if his reply would otherwise be regarded as defamatory.... The qualified privilege serves an important public function in the employment context. Without the privilege, references would be even more hesitant than they are to provide candid*

---

[274] Sborgi v. Green, 722 N.Y.S.2d 14 (Sup. Ct. 2001).

[275] *Id.*

evaluations of former employees. In order to overcome the qualified privilege, the plaintiff must show that the statements were made with malice. Once a communication is deemed privileged, the burden of proof to demonstrate malice rests with the plaintiff. To show malice, the plaintiff must show either that the statements were made with knowing falsity, in bad faith, or with reckless disregard of the truth."
Applying this standard, the court concluded that the former employer and supervisors were protected by the qualified privilege with regard to information they shared in their references, and that the former worker had the burden of proving that the reference statements were made with malice. The court concluded that the former worker had produced no evidence to demonstrate that any of the statements had been made with malice.

(3) release

Current or former employees and volunteers who are adults can release a church from liability associated with information disclosed in a reference letter. As noted above, it is advisable to obtain such a release before issuing a reference letter that will contain negative information. Ideally, a release form should require the person's signature to be made before a notary public. At a minimum, a release form should require the signer's signature to be witnessed by one or two other persons whose signatures appear on the form.

Case Study

• *A Texas appeals court ruled that a "release form" signed by an employee prevented her from suing a former employer for statements it made about the employee to a prospective employer. An employee who had been terminated by her employer applied to another employer for a job. The new employer had the employee sign a form entitled "authorization for release of information." This form provided, in part: "I hereby authorize any investigator . . . bearing this release to obtain any information from schools, residential management agents, employers, criminal justice agencies, or individuals, relating to my activities. This information may include, but is not limited to, academic, residential, achievement, performance, attendance, personal history, disciplinary, arrest, and conviction records. I hereby direct you to release such information upon request to the bearer. . . . I hereby release any individual, including record custodians, from any and all liability for damages of whatever kind or nature which may at any time result to me on account of compliance or any attempts to comply, with this authorization." The prospective employer contacted the former employer as part of its background check of the employee, and was informed about her negative job performance. On the basis of this information, the prospective employer declined to hire the individual. She promptly sued the former employer for defamation, and a jury awarded her $1 million in damages. The former employer appealed this verdict. A state appeals court reversed the jury's verdict, and ruled that the former employer should pay the employee nothing. The court noted that statements made by a former employer to a prospective employer about a former employee are protected by a "qualified privilege." This ordinarily means that such statements cannot be the basis for defamation unless they are made with "malice." The court concluded, however, that the statements made by the former employer in this case were protected by an absolute privilege because of the release form signed by the former employee, and accordingly it was impossible for the employee to sue her former employer for defamation.*[276]

---

[276] Smith v. Holley, 827 S.W.2d 433 (Tex. App. 1992).

Churches wanting to respond to a request for a reference letter on a former employee or volunteer who did not perform satisfactorily, or who was guilty of some form of misconduct, can reduce the risk of liability in a number of ways, including one or more of the following:

1. Do not respond.

2. Respond with a reference letter (or telephone call) that limits the response to statements of fact that can be verified with documents or testimony. So long as there is a factual basis for a reference, a church will be eligible for the "qualified privilege" in most states that makes employers immune from liability for negative references unless they act with malice. In this context, malice means that the employer knew that a statement was false, or acted with reckless disregard or indifference regarding the statement's truth or falsity. In no case should opinions be expressed, since these are difficult to establish in a court of law.

3. Respond only if you receive, in advance, a "release form" signed by the former employee or volunteer releasing your church and its agents, officers, and employees, from liability based on information shared in the reference letter. Of course, persons with a history of unsatisfactory work or inappropriate behavior often will refuse to sign such a form, which should serve as a warning to the church or other organization that asked you for the reference letter.

Because the availability of these defenses varies from state to state, it is advisable for a church to check with an attorney before making a negative reference.

interference with contract

In many states, one who interferes with an existing contract between two other parties can be sued for "interference with contract." To illustrate, assume that a church dismisses a pastor for adultery. The pastor is later hired by another church. After a few months, a denominational official learns of the pastor's new job, and contacts the board members of the new church to inform them of the pastor's previous misconduct. As a result of this unsolicited disclosure, the church board decides to terminate the pastor's employment. The pastor may be able to sue the denominational official for interference with contract. Note that this basis of liability requires the existence of a contract. If the church had asked the denominational official for a letter of reference *prior* to the date the pastor was hired, there can be no interference with contract. The timing of a letter of reference is critical. If it comes before the prospective employee is hired, there can be no interference with contract. If it comes after the employee is hired, there may be liability.

Case Studies

• *The Alaska Supreme Court ruled that a denominational official in the Presbyterian Church (USA) could be sued on the basis of interference with contract for making disparaging comments about another minister who recently had been hired by a local church.*[277] *A Presbyterian minister left a pastoral position in Alaska and accepted a call as minister of a Presbyterian church in Tennessee. When he presented himself to the church to begin his duties, he was informed by church officials that because of derogatory information the church had received from a denominational official (an executive presbyter in Alaska), the church would not hire him. The presbyter had informed church leaders that the minister was divorced, dishonest, unable to perform pastoral duties because of throat surgery, and that he had made an improper sexual advance to a church member in Alaska. The minister sued the presbyter for intentional interference with his employment contract with the Tennessee church. Generally, one who intentionally interferes with a known contract can be sued for damages. The state supreme court concluded that the civil courts can make this determination without any inquiries into internal church discipline. The court drew an important distinction between clergy who are seeking a pastoral position and those who have been hired. If a church official makes derogatory remarks about a minister who already has been hired by a local church, and if those remarks induce local church leaders to terminate the employment agreement, then the church official can be sued for "interference with contract." The court insisted that such claims ordinarily will not involve inquiries into core ecclesiastical issues. This suggests that church officials should be more cautious in making remarks about clergy who already have been hired by a local church or other religious organization.*

• *A Louisiana court suggested that it could not resolve a priest's claim that a church official was guilty of interference with contract as a result of the contents of a letter of reference.*[278] *A Catholic priest who had been accused of molesting a child was investigated by church officials. He later filed a lawsuit claiming that a church official interfered with his employment prospects as a Navy chaplain as a result of a letter of reference that referred to "some accusations of questionable behavior and some complaints about [the priest's] ministry." The church official insisted that the letter of reference pertained to the fitness of the priest for assignment to a chaplaincy position—a matter beyond the reach of the civil courts. The court did not address this issue directly, but seemed to acknowledge that internal communications among clergy or church leaders regarding the fitness of a minister cannot give rise to civil liability.*

• *A New Jersey court ruled that a church acted properly in dismissing its music director for criminal acts.*[279] *After working for the church for a few months, the music director was arrested for possession of illegal anabolic steroids. It was later disclosed that the music director had been taking steroids to assist him with bodybuilding, and that he had ordered several shipments of steroids shipped directly to the church to avoid detection. The music director was dismissed, and later applied to another church for similar employment. His application was rejected when the church contacted the previous church and was informed by the pastor of what had happened. The music director sued*

---

[277] Marshall v. Munro, 845 P.2d 424 (Alaska 1993).

[278] Hayden v. Schulte, 701 So.2d 1354 (La. App. 1997).

[279] McGarry v. Saint Anthony of Padua Roman Catholic Church, 704 A.2d 1353 (N.J. Super. 1998).

his former church, alleging breach of contract. He also claimed that the pastor, by informing the other church of the music director's criminal activities, had wrongfully "interfered with his prospective economic advantage." The trial court dismissed the music director's assertion that the church had wrongfully interfered with a "prospective economic advantage." It noted that the music director could not show that "there was an intentional, without justification, interference" with his economic advantage. Further, the court pointed out that the pastor had disclosed the information only after it was requested, and the information was of criminal conduct admitted by the music director and covered in the newspaper. Additionally, the pastor was protected by a "qualified privilege" for employment references, meaning that he could not be liable unless his reference contained information that the pastor knew to be false.

liability for refusing to respond to a request for a reference letter

It is a fundamental principle of law that there can be no liability for a failure to protect another from harm or peril. As one court observed: "One human being, seeing a fellow man in dire peril, is under no legal obligation to aid him, but may sit on the dock, smoke his cigar, and watch the other fellow drown."[280] This principle means that a church cannot be liable for failing to warn another church of the dangerous propensities of a former employee or volunteer. To illustrate, if Jack molests children at First Church while serving as a volunteer worker, and later begins working as a volunteer children's worker at Second Church, First Church is under no legal obligation to warn Second Church of Jack's dangerous behavior. There are practical reasons for this rule. After all, the leadership of First Church cannot be expected to hire an investigator to track Jack down and find out every church that he attends.

Some courts have created a limited exception to the general rule of no liability for a failure to warn others of a former worker's dangerous propensities. If a "special relationship" exists between church leaders and a potential victim, then the church has a legal duty to warn the potential victim of the dangerous propensities of an employee or volunteer. This exception was recognized in the following case study.

Case Study

- *A Washington state court ruled that a church and a member of the church board could be sued by three women who had been molested by a volunteer youth worker when they were minors.[281] The board member had received information indicating that the worker was a child molester, but failed to disclose this information for 23 years. Because of the board member's failure to disclose this information, the molester was able to molest the sisters over a period of several years. The court found that the church had a "special relationship" with minors that imposed upon it a duty to protect them from the criminal and intentional acts of others. The court acknowledged that "as a general rule, there is no legal duty to protect another from the criminal acts of a third person." However, there is an exception if a "special relationship" exists between a church and a potential victim which imposes upon the church a duty to "protect" the victim from harm. The court concluded that a special relationship exists between*

---

[280] Evans v. Ohio State University, 680 N.E.2d 161 (Ohio App. 1996).

[281] Funkhouser v. Wilson, 950 P.2d 501 (Wash. App. 1998).

churches and children who participate in church programs and activities: "[W]e believe that churches and the adult church workers who assume responsibility for the spiritual well being of children of the congregation, whether as paid clergy or as volunteers, have a special relationship with those children that gives rise to a duty to protect them from reasonably foreseeable risk of harm from those members of the congregation whom the church places in positions of responsibility and authority over them."

The conclusion reached by the court in the previous case study is extraordinary. It exposes church leaders to liability for failing to protect children against "reasonably foreseeable risks of harm" by volunteer or paid youth workers. Note that the victims in the case study were members of the same church as the molester. But what if the molester began attending a different church? Would church leaders at the former church have a legal duty to warn the second church of the molester's dangerous propensities? Probably not. It is doubtful that the court would have concluded that a "special relationship" existed between the former church and children in the second church that would give rise to a duty to protect them from the molester by notifying the church of his dangerous behavior.

liability for providing positive references

In two historic cases that will be of direct relevance to churches, the supreme courts of Texas and California have ruled that individuals and their employers face potential legal liability for providing positive and unqualified references on former workers *who they know pose a risk of harm to others*. In both cases, positive references were provided on individuals with a known background of sexual misconduct involving minors. The molesters were hired on the basis of these references, and they later molested other minors in the course of their new duties. Both courts ruled that persons who provide positive references under these circumstances, without any disclosure of the negative information, are legally responsible for the harm the worker inflicts on others. It is essential for church leaders to be familiar with both of these rulings. While they apply only in the states of Texas and California, it is likely they will be followed in other states. The cases are summarized in the following two examples.

Case Studies

- *The Texas Supreme Court ruled that a local Boy Scout council could be liable for a scoutmaster's acts of child molestation because it was aware of rumors suggesting that the scoutmaster had engaged in inappropriate behavior with boys but still recommended him to a leadership position in a local troop.*[282] *The court concluded that if the council knew or should have known that the molester was "peculiarly likely to molest boys," it had a duty not to recommend him as a scoutmaster. Further, the council's "affirmative act of recommending [the molester] as a potential scoutmaster . . . created a duty on the part of [the council] to use reasonable care in light of the information it had received." It continued: "[W]e hold that if [the local council] knew or should have known that [the molester] was peculiarly likely to molest boys, it had a duty not to recommend him as a scoutmaster." The court concluded: "[W]e recognize that there is no way to ensure that this type of conduct will never happen, despite an organization's best efforts.*

[282] Golden Spread Council, Inc. v. Akins, 926 S.W.2d 287 (Tex. 1996).

However, [the local council] and similar organizations deal with children. The public has a strong interest in protecting children from abuse, and parents put their trust in such organizations. Having undertaken to recommend a potential scoutmaster for the church, [the council] had a duty to use reasonable care in doing so to prevent an unreasonable risk of harm to [the victim] and others who would be affected. [The council] breached that duty if it knew or should have known that [the molester] was peculiarly likely to molest boys. On this record, this is the issue determinative of [the council's] liability."

• *The California Supreme Court ruled that the former employers of a teacher who molested an adolescent girl were liable for his actions because they provided his current employer with positive references despite their knowledge of his previous misconduct.*[283] *A teacher was employed by a public school based in part on the glowing letters of recommendation from the principals of three schools in which he had previously been employed. One of the letters of recommendation stated that "due in large part to [his] efforts, our campus is a safe, orderly and clean environment for students and staff. . . . I recommend [him] without reservation." In fact, each of the principals was aware of prior incidents or reports of sexual misconduct by the teacher. They all failed to disclose the teacher's misconduct in their letters of recommendation. Unfortunately, the teacher sexually molested a 13-year-old girl (the victim) shortly after beginning his new assignment. The victim later sued the three prior schools and their principals, claiming that they were responsible for her injuries because they were aware of prior incidents of sexual misconduct involving the teacher but failed to disclose this information in their letters of recommendation. The three principals (and their schools) insisted that "a rule imposing liability on writers of recommendation letters could have one very predictable consequence—employers would seldom write such letters, even in praise of exceptionally qualified employees." The principals pointed out few persons will provide "full disclosure" of all negative information in reference letters since doing so would expose them to liability for defamation or invasion of privacy. This threat of liability will "inhibit employers from freely providing reference information," and this in turn will restrict the flow of information prospective employers need and impede job applicants in finding new employment. On the other hand, the victim insisted that employers providing references on former employees are protected under California law by a "qualified privilege." The qualified privilege renders employers immune from liability for their communications pertaining to a former employee's "job performance or qualifications" so long as they do not act maliciously and provide the information "to, and upon request of, the prospective employer." The court concluded that this qualified privilege greatly reduces the concerns expressed by the principals (and their schools). The court went so far as to observe that the qualified privilege ordinarily would prevent liability in a case such as this involving negligent misrepresentations made by employers about a former employee. However, the court noted that the qualified privilege did not help the principals in this case since it applies only to communications made "upon request of" a prospective employer. The principals "do not claim that they wrote [their letters of recommendation] in response to [the school's] request, and, accordingly, the privilege is inapplicable." Having concluded that the principals (and their schools) owed the victim a duty of care, the court addressed the question of whether or not they breached this duty by making misrepresentations or giving false information in their letters of recommendation concerning the teacher. The court conceded that there is no liability for "nondisclosure," meaning that an employer cannot be legally responsible for a victim's injuries on the basis of its refusal to disclose information about a former worker. However, the court concluded that this case presented an exception to the general rule: "[T]hese letters,*

283 Randi W. v. Muroc Joint Unified School District, 60 Cal. Rptr.2d 263 (Cal. 1997).

256

essentially recommending [the teacher] for any position without reservation or qualification, constituted affirmative representations that strongly implied [the teacher] was fit to interact appropriately and safely with female students. These representations were false and misleading in light of [the principals'] alleged knowledge of charges of [the teacher's] repeated sexual improprieties." The court summarized its ruling as follows: "[W]e conclude that [the principals'] letters of recommendation, containing unreserved and unconditional praise for [a former teacher] despite [their] alleged knowledge of complaints or charges of his sexual misconduct with students, constituted misleading statements that could form the basis for . . . liability for fraud or negligent misrepresentation. Although policy considerations dictate that ordinarily a recommending employer should not be held accountable for failing to disclose negative information regarding a former employee, nonetheless liability may be imposed if, as alleged here, the recommendation letter amounts to an affirmative misrepresentation presenting a foreseeable and substantial risk of physical harm to a prospective employer or third person."

• G worked as a volunteer children's worker at First Church. After parents complained to the senior pastor about G's inappropriate touching of a number of children, G is removed from his position. A few months later G leaves First Church and begins attending Second Church. When he applies as a children's worker, Second Church contacts First Church for a reference. First Church sends a letter containing a strong and unqualified recommendation of G. Nothing is disclosed regarding G's inappropriate touching of several children. G later molests a child at Second Church. When the child's parents learn of First Church's recommendation, they sue the church. In Texas and California, or in any state that follows the decisions of the Texas and California supreme courts (summarized above), First Church may be legally responsible for G's acts of molestation occurring at Second Church. It knew that G was "peculiarly likely" to molest minors and therefore had a duty not to recommend him.

• Same facts as the previous case study, except that First Church refused to respond to Second Church's request for a reference regarding G. The Texas Supreme Court ruled that there can be no liability under these circumstances, since First Church has not "recommended" G.

• B, a former member of First Church, has attended Second Church for a few years and recently applied to work in the church nursery. Second Church asks First Church for a letter of recommendation. The staff at First Church is aware of no information regarding B that would indicate she would be unsuitable for working with minors, and so it sends a letter of recommendation. It does no investigation. B later is accused of abusing a child in the nursery at Second Church. The Texas Supreme Court's ruling would not make First Church legally responsible for B's actions under these circumstances. While it recommended her, it had no knowledge indicating that she posed a risk of harm to others. According to the court's decision, First Church had no independent duty to investigate B on its own.
• Same facts as the previous case study, except that the staff at First Church was aware that B had been accused of child molestation on two different occasions, but it did not believe that the accusations were credible and so ignored them when preparing its letter of recommendation. Under these circumstances, it is possible that a court would conclude that First Church should have known, on the basis of information available to it without an independent investigation, that B posed a risk of harm to children. As a result, it had a duty not to recommend her. In Texas and California, or in any state that follows the decisions of the Texas and California supreme courts (summarized above), First Church may be liable for acts of abuse committed by B at Second Church.

C. Confidentiality

Churches should be careful to treat as confidential any reference letter they receive on a current or former employee or volunteer worker. In some states, employees have a legal right to inspect their personnel records, but this right does not extend to reference letters that may be in their personnel file.[284]

Case Study

- *The Pennsylvania Supreme Court ruled that a state nonprofit corporation law giving members the right to inspect corporate records was "limited by considerations of privacy, privilege and confidentiality." As an example, the court referred to reference letters, noting that releasing "confidential references . . . would infringe upon the legitimate expectations of confidentiality of those who submitted the references. Further, releasing such references would ensure that very few persons in the future would ever respond to requests for references."[285]*

Employee Evaluations §8-25

Key Point 8-25> *Employers often evaluate some or all of their employees on a periodic basis. Such evaluations can help employees be more productive, but they also can be used as evidence of discrimination if an employee who is a member of a protected class under a state or federal employment law is terminated despite average or above-average evaluations.*

Many churches perform periodic evaluations of their employees. In many cases, supervisors give inflated evaluations in order to avoid conflict. This common practice can expose a church to an increased risk of liability for employees who are protected by a state or federal employment discrimination law. To illustrate, let's say that a church decides to fire a 62-year-old custodian. The custodian has worked for the church for 15 years, and throughout this entire time her work has been inefficient and of poor quality. However, her supervisor has always given her above average scores on her annual employee evaluations. Eventually, the church board decides that the custodian must be terminated. Following her termination, the employee sues the church for discriminating against her on account of age in violation of a state age discrimination law. The church attempts to prove that it terminated the custodian due to her poor quality work, but a

---

[284] *See, e.g.,* MINN. STAT. § 181.961 (employees can inspect their personnel records, but the term "personnel record" does not include "written references respecting the employee, including letters of reference supplied to an employer by another person").

[285] Lewis v. Pennsylvania Bar Association, 701 A.2d 551 (Pa. 1997).

court rejects this defense on the basis of the annual performance reviews that consistently and without exception portrayed the custodian as an "above average" worker. These evaluations convinced the court that the real reason for the custodian's termination was her age.

How can a church avoid such a scenario? By insisting that all employee evaluations be objective assessments of clearly defined goals or standards. Unfortunately, this is easier said than done.

> ▶ *If your church performs employee evaluations, and all employees score above average, this is a good sign that supervisors are not providing objective and accurate assessments. This may expose the church to an increased risk of liability if it is sued for violating a state or federal employment discrimination law.*

> ▶ *Does your church evaluate employees? If so, be sure the evaluations are objective. In addition, be aware that positive evaluations may be used against you if you dismiss an employee for violating the church's moral teachings, and one or more positive evaluations were issued after church leaders became aware of the employee's violation of the church's moral teachings.*

Case Studies

• *A federal appeals court ruled that a church school may have violated a federal ban on pregnancy discrimination by terminating a female teacher who was pregnant on the day she was married. While the school insisted that its decision was based solely on its moral teachings, the court was not persuaded. It relied in part on a "glowing" teacher performance evaluation the teacher had received two months after the school concluded that she had engaged in premarital sex. In addition to noting her "successful" performance in almost all of 15 objective criteria, the school's principal praised her for "adjusting very well" to the "busy and changing year in regard to her classroom reassignment and personal life." The court concluded that the very positive employee evaluation the teacher received prior to her termination was evidence that the school had not terminated her on the basis of her violation of its moral teachings. After all, if the school had such standards, and they were as important as church officials insisted, then how could someone who so blatantly violated them receive an exemplary performance evaluation?*[286]*

• *A federal court ruled that a 59-year-old principal could sue his employing church-affiliated school for age discrimination when his one-year employment contract was not renewed. The court concluded that a lengthy employment relationship (in this case, seven years) without any negative employee evaluations casts serious doubt on an employer's allegedly nondiscriminatory basis for an adverse employment action regarding that employee. The importance of this point cannot be overstated. Churches that perform employee evaluations should recognize that a series of positive evaluations could place the church in a weak position in the event it dismisses or disciplines the employee and is hit with a discrimination claim.*[287]

---

[286] Kline v. Catholic Diocese, 206 F.3d 651 (6th Cir. 2000).

[287] Shook v. St. Bede School, 74 F.Supp.2d 1172 (M.D. Ala. 1999).

A federal court in Puerto Rico ruled that a church agency did not commit age discrimination by terminating a 48-year-old employee whose performance evaluations consistently rated his work as "poor" and whose position was eliminated when his department was relocated.[288]

Employment Interviews

§ 8-26

Key Point 8-26> *Many employers interview applicants for employment. There are several state and federal laws that regulate the kinds of questions that may be asked.*

A. In General

It is common for employers to interview applicants for employment in addition to having them complete a written application. This practice provides the employer with an opportunity to assess applicants' suitability for a particular position. Church leaders should understand that several state and federal laws may restrict the kinds of questions that may be asked during an employment interview.

Employers are legally entitled to ask questions that will help them determine if an applicant meets the requirements for a job. But, certain questions are not relevant to an applicant's qualifications and should not be asked. For example, questions about an applicant's race, national origin, disabilities, or age generally are not relevant to an applicant's ability to perform the requirements of a job, and should not be asked. In rare cases, such questions may be permissible if they are intended if based on a "bona fide occupational qualification." Also, state and federal laws banning discrimination in employment on the basis of religion generally contain broad exemptions for religious organizations. As a result, it generally is permissible for religious organizations to exclude or prefer persons for employment on the basis of religion.

> *Church leaders should periodically review questions that are asked during interviews, or on employment applications. Look at each question and ask, "Why are we asking this question? Is this information relevant to the qualifications for this position?"*

Table 8-8 summarizes the legal status of several kinds of questions. The table is not exhaustive and there may be exceptions. It assumes that an employer is covered under applicable state or federal nondiscrimination laws. The coverage of churches and other religious employers under state and federal employment discrimination laws is addressed previously in this chapter.

Also, note that the "ministerial exception" generally bars the civil courts from reviewing decisions by churches and other religious organizations regarding the selection of ministers. This exception permits religious organizations to ask applicants for ministerial positions any questions they wish. See section 8-10 in this chapter.

---

[288] Soto v. Corporation of the Presiding Bishop of the Church of Jesus Christ of Latter-Day Saints, 73 F.Supp.2d 116 (D. Puerto Rico 1999).

B. The Americans with Disabilities Act

The Americans with Disabilities Act (ADA) makes it unlawful for a covered employer to discriminate against a qualified applicant or employee with a disability. The ADA applies to private employers having 15 or more employees and engaged in commerce. The U.S. Equal Employment Opportunity Commission (EEOC) enforces the employment provisions of the ADA.

Table 8-8 **Interview Questions**

Question	Acceptable	Inadvisable
Race or color	No.	Applicant's race or color of skin.
Arrest record	No, unless job related.	Number and kinds of arrests.
Conviction record	Questions about actual criminal convictions if substantially related to a person's ability or suitability for performing a specific job.	Questions about convictions unrelated to job requirements.
Military service	Military experience or training if job related.	Type or condition of discharge; questions about military service for another country.
Credit records	None, unless job related.	Questions about charge accounts, credit rating, bankruptcies, and garnishments.
Religion	Religious organizations can ask applicants their religious affiliation, and give preference to applicants who share the organization's religious beliefs.	—
References	Names of professional and character references, including the applicant's pastor or other religious leader.	—
Birthplace and residence	Applicant's place of residence, length of residence at that location and prior locations, and location of current employer.	Birthplace of applicant, or the applicant's parents or other relatives; birth certificate, naturalization or baptismal certificate prior to hiring.
Language	Languages the applicant speaks or writes fluently, if job related.	Applicant's mother tongue; language used at home; how the applicant acquired the ability to read, write, or speak a foreign language.

Question	Acceptable	Inadvisable
Name	Whether applicant has worked under a different name if necessary to allow a check of work or education records.	The original name of an applicant whose name has been legally changed or the national origin of the applicant's name.
Marital status	Whether the applicant is married, single, divorced, separated, or engaged, if relevant in assessing the applicant's suitability for employment with a religious employer based on doctrinal considerations.	Whether the applicant is married, single, divorced, separated, engaged, or widowed, unless these questions are relevant in assessing an applicant's suitability for employment with a religious employer based on doctrinal considerations.
Citizenship	Documentation to establish the applicant's identity and employment eligibility.	Birthplace of the applicant or any information not relevant to making employment decisions.
Age	None, unless age is a bona fide occupational qualification.	Requesting age on employment application, using phrases such as "young, boy, girl, recent college graduate" on help wanted notices or advertisements.
Sex	None, unless sex is a bona fide occupational qualification (such as an applicant for a pastoral position with a church that is doctrinally opposed to the ordination of women).	An applicant's sex, unless sex is a bona fide occupational qualification (such as an applicant for a pastoral position with a church that is doctrinally opposed to the ordination of women).
Family status	If applicant has responsibilities or commitments that prevent him or her from meeting work schedules if asked of all applicants regardless of sex.	Marital status, number and age of children, spouse's job.
Pregnancy	Applicant's anticipated duration of employment, if asked of all applicants.	Any questions about pregnancy, medical history, or family plans.
Child care	None, unless job related and asked of all applicants.	Questions about child care arrangements that are only addressed to female applicants.
Height and weight	None, unless job related.	Any question unrelated to job requirements.
Disability	Whether the applicant can perform the essential functions of the job in question.	Questions about an applicant's disabilities.
Organizations	Applicant's membership in professional organizations if job related.	All clubs, social organizations, societies, and other non-job-related organizations to which the applicant belongs.
Relatives and friends	Names of applicant's relatives already employed by the employer.	Names of friends working for the employer or relatives other than those working for the employer.

Question	Acceptable	Inadvisable
Photographs	None, except after hiring.	Photographs with an application or after an interview but prior to hiring.
Sexual orientation	Many states have enacted laws prohibiting private employers from discriminating in employment decisions on the basis of sexual orientation. All of these laws exempt religious employers. As a result, religious employers may ask applicants questions about their sexual orientation if required by the employer's doctrine.	Many states have enacted laws prohibiting private employers from discriminating in employment decisions on the basis of sexual orientation. All of these laws exempt religious employers. As a result, religious employers may ask applicants questions about their sexual orientation if required by the employer's doctrine.

The ADA defines an individual with a disability as a person who: (1) has a physical or mental impairment that substantially limits a major life activity, (2) has a record or history of a substantially limiting impairment, or (3) is regarded or perceived by an employer as having a substantially limiting impairment.

An applicant with a disability, like all other applicants, must be able to meet the employer's requirements for the job, such as education, training, employment experience, skills, or licenses. In addition, an applicant with a disability must be able to perform the "essential functions" of the job (the fundamental duties) either on her own or with the help of "reasonable accommodation." However, an employer does not have to provide a reasonable accommodation that will cause "undue hardship," with significant difficulty or expense.

The ADA prohibits employers from asking questions that are likely to reveal the existence of a disability *before* making a job offer (i.e., the pre-offer period). This prohibition covers written questionnaires and inquiries made during interviews, as well as medical examinations. However, such questions and medical examinations are permitted *after* extending a job offer but before the individual begins work (i.e., the post-offer period).

Although employers may not ask disability-related questions or require medical examinations at the pre-offer stage, they may do a wide variety of things to evaluate whether an applicant is qualified for the job, including the following:

- Employers may ask about an applicant's ability to perform specific job functions. For example, an employer may state the physical requirements of a job (such as the ability to lift a certain amount of weight, or the ability to climb ladders), and ask if an applicant can satisfy these requirements.

- Employers may ask about an applicant's non-medical qualifications and skills, such as the applicant's education, work history, and required certifications and licenses.

- Employers may ask applicants to describe or demonstrate how they would perform job tasks.

Once a conditional job offer is made, the employer may ask disability-related questions and require medical examinations as long as this is done for all entering employees in that job category. If the employer rejects the applicant after a disability-related question or medical examination, investigators will closely scrutinize whether the rejection was based on the results of that question or examination. If the question or examination screens out an individual because of a disability, the employer must demonstrate that the reason for the rejection is "job-related and consistent with business necessity."

In 1995, the EEOC issued a document entitled "ADA Enforcement Guidance: Preemployment Disability-Related Questions and Medical Examinations." This document addresses the kinds of questions that can, and cannot, be asked by employers. Its conclusions are summarized in Table 8-9.

Key Point > At the pre-offer stage, an employer cannot ask questions that are likely to elicit information about a disability. This includes directly asking whether an applicant has a particular disability. It also means that an employer cannot ask questions that are closely related to disability. On the other hand, if there are many possible answers to a question and only some of those answers would contain disability-related information, that question is not "disability-related."

Key Point > An employer may not ask a third party (such as a service that provides information about workers compensation claims, a state agency, or an applicant's friends, family, or former employers) any questions that it could not directly ask the applicant.

Table 8-9 **Permitted and Prohibited Interview Questions under the ADA**

Pre-Offer Stage	
Question	**Acceptable**
Can you perform the job?	Yes. An employer may ask whether applicants can perform any or all job functions, including whether applicants can perform job functions "with or without reasonable accommodation."
Describe or demonstrate how you would perform the job, with or without reasonable accommodations.	Yes. An employer may ask applicants to describe how they would perform any or all job functions, as long as all applicants in the job category are asked to do this. Employers should remember that if an applicant says that he or she will need a reasonable accommodation to do a job demonstration, the employer must either provide a reasonable accommodation that does not create an undue hardship upon it, or allow the applicant to simply describe how he or she would perform the job function.
Describe or demonstrate how you would perform the job, with or without reasonable accommodations [if other applicants are not asked to do so].	Yes. When an employer reasonably believes that an applicant will not be able to perform a job function because of a known disability, the employer may ask that particular applicant to describe or demonstrate how he or she would perform the function. An applicant's disability would be a "known disability" either because it is obvious (for example, the applicant uses a wheelchair), or because the applicant has voluntarily disclosed that s/he has a hidden disability.

Pre-Offer Stage	
Question	**Acceptable**
An employer asks applicants if they will need reasonable accommodations for the hiring process.	Yes. An employer may tell applicants what the hiring process involves (for example, an interview, timed written test, or job demonstration), and may ask applicants whether they will need a reasonable accommodation for this process.
An employer asks applicants if they will need reasonable accommodations to perform the functions of the job.	No. In general, an employer may not ask questions on an application or in an interview about whether an applicant will need reasonable accommodation for a job. This is because these questions are likely to elicit whether the applicant has a disability (generally, only people who have disabilities will need reasonable accommodations).
An applicant with no known disability is being interviewed for a job. He has not asked for any reasonable accommodation, either for the application process or for the job. The employer asks him, "Will you need reasonable accommodation to perform this job?"	No. In general, an employer may not ask questions on an application or in an interview about whether an applicant will need reasonable accommodation for a job. This is because these questions are likely to elicit whether the applicant has a disability (generally, only people who have disabilities will need reasonable accommodations).
An employer reasonably believes that an applicant will need reasonable accommodation to perform the functions of the job. The employer asks the applicant if he or she needs reasonable accommodations and what type of reasonable accommodations would be needed to perform the functions of the job.	The employer could ask these questions if: (1) the employer reasonably believes the applicant will need reasonable accommodation because of an obvious disability; (2) the employer reasonably believes the applicant will need reasonable accommodation because of a hidden disability that the applicant has voluntarily disclosed to the employer; or (3) an applicant has voluntarily disclosed to the employer that he or she needs reasonable accommodation to perform the job.
An employer asks if an applicant can meet the employer's attendance requirements.	Yes. An employer may state its attendance requirements and ask whether an applicant can meet them. An employer also may ask about an applicant's prior attendance record (for example, how many days the applicant was absent from his/her last job). These questions are not likely to elicit information about a disability because there may be many reasons unrelated to disability why someone cannot meet attendance requirements or was frequently absent from a previous job (for example, an applicant may have had daycare problems).
An employer asks an applicant, "How many Mondays or Fridays were you absent last year on leave other than approved vacation leave?"	Yes. This question is not likely to elicit information about a disability.
An employer asks an applicant, "How many days were you sick last year?"	No. This question relates directly to the severity of an individual's impairments, and so it is likely to elicit information about a disability.

Pre-Offer Stage	
Question	**Acceptable**
An employer asks an applicant about licenses or certifications required for a job.	Yes. An employer may ask an applicant at the pre-offer stage whether he or she has certifications or licenses required for job duties. An employer also may ask an applicant whether he or she intends to get a particular job-related certification or license, or why he or she does not have the certification or license. These questions are not likely to elicit information about an applicant's disability because there may be a number of reasons unrelated to disability why someone does not have — or does not intend to get — a certification or license.
An employer asks an applicant about prior arrests or convictions.	Yes. Questions about an applicant's arrest or conviction records are not likely to elicit information about disability because there are many reasons unrelated to disability why someone may have an arrest or conviction record. However, questions about arrests or convictions in some cases may violate Title VII of the Civil Rights Act of 1964.
An employer asks an applicant if he or she has any impairments.	Yes, if the particular question is not likely to elicit information about whether the applicant has a disability. Not all impairments are disabilities; an impairment is a disability only if it substantially limits a major life activity.
An employer asks an applicant with a broken leg how she broke her leg.	Yes. Since a broken leg normally is a temporary condition which does not rise to the level of a disability, this question is not likely to disclose whether the applicant has a disability.
An employer asks an applicant with a broken leg: "Do you expect the leg to heal normally?" or "Do you break bones easily?"	No. This question may disclose whether the applicant has a disability.
An employer asks an applicant if he can perform major life activities, such as standing, lifting, walking, etc.	No. Questions about whether an applicant can perform major life activities are almost always disability-related because they are likely to elicit information about a disability. For example, if an applicant cannot stand or walk, it is likely to be a result of a disability. So, these questions are prohibited at the pre-offer stage unless they are specifically about the ability to perform job functions.
An employer asks an applicant about her workers compensation history.	No. An employer may not ask applicants about job-related injuries or workers compensation history. These questions relate directly to the severity of an applicant's impairments. Therefore, these questions are likely to elicit information about disability.
An employer asks applicants if they are taking illegal drugs.	Yes. An individual who currently uses illegal drugs is not protected under the ADA (when the employer acts on the basis of the drug use).
An employer asks applicants about legal drug use.	No. If the question is likely to elicit information about disability. Employers should know that many questions about current or prior lawful drug use are likely to elicit information about a disability, and are therefore impermissible at the pre-offer stage. For example, questions like, "What medications are you currently taking?" or "Have you ever taken AZT?" certainly elicit information about whether an applicant has a disability. However, some innocuous questions about lawful drug use are not likely to elicit information about disability.

Pre-Offer Stage	
Question	Acceptable
An employer ask applicants about their prior illegal drug use.	Yes, provided that the particular question is not likely to elicit information about a disability. It is important to remember that past addiction to illegal drugs or controlled substances is a covered disability under the ADA (as long as the person is not a current illegal drug user), but past casual use is not a covered disability. Therefore, the question is fine as long as it does not go to past drug addiction. An employer may ask, "Have you ever used illegal drugs?" "When is the last time you used illegal drugs?" or "Have you used illegal drugs in the last six months?" These questions are not likely to tell the employer anything about whether the applicant was addicted to drugs. However, questions that ask how much the applicant used drugs in the past are likely to elicit information about whether the applicant was a past drug addict. These questions are therefore impermissible at the pre-offer stage. At the pre-offer stage, an employer may not ask an applicant questions such as, "How often did you use illegal drugs in the past?" "Have you ever been addicted to drugs?" "Have you ever been treated for drug addiction?" or "Have you ever been treated for drug abuse?"
An employer asks applicants about their consumption of alcoholic beverages.	Yes, unless the particular question is likely to elicit information about alcoholism, which is a disability. An employer may ask an applicant whether he or she drinks alcohol, or whether he or she has been arrested for driving under the influence because these questions do not reveal whether someone has alcoholism. However, questions asking how much alcohol an applicant drinks or whether he or she has participated in an alcohol rehabilitation program are likely to elicit information about whether the applicant has alcoholism.

After giving a job offer to an applicant, an employer may ask disability-related questions and perform medical examinations. The job offer may be conditioned on the results of post-offer disability-related questions or medical examinations. At the "post-offer" stage, an employer may ask about an individual's workers compensation history, prior sick leave usage, illnesses, impairments, and general physical and mental health. Disability-related questions and medical examinations at the post-offer stage do not have to be related to the job. If an employer asks post-offer disability-related questions, or requires post-offer medical examinations, it must make sure that it follows certain procedures: (1) all entering employees in the same job category must be subjected to the examination or inquiry, regardless of disability; and (2) medical information obtained must be kept confidential.

Arbitration

Key Point 8-27> *Churches have various defenses available to them if they are sued as a result of a personal injury. One such defense is an arbitration policy. By adopting an arbitration policy, a church can compel members to arbitrate specified disputes with their church rather than pursue their claim in the civil courts.*

The arbitration of disputes has many potential advantages over litigation in the civil courts. Consider the following:

- faster resolution of disputes

- lower attorneys' fees

- arbitration awards are often less than civil court judgments

- little if any risk of punitive damages, or astronomical verdicts out of proportion to the alleged wrong

- disputes are resolved privately, with little or no media attention

- the spectacle of plaintiffs' attorneys appealing to the emotions of juries through courtroom theatrics is eliminated

- arbitration can reconcile the parties to a dispute unlike civil litigation in which the parties almost always enter and leave court as enemies

- no threatening letters from attorneys demanding exorbitant payoffs in order to avoid litigation

- parties to a dispute can select one or more arbitrators having specialized knowledge concerning the issues involved (unlike civil court judges who often have limited familiarity with applicable law)

- arbitration awards are final (no time-consuming appeals)

With these numerous advantages, arbitration is becoming an increasingly common way of resolving disputes. The United States Supreme Court has stressed the advantages of arbitration agreements in the context of employment disputes:

There are real benefits to the enforcement of arbitration provisions. We have been clear in rejecting the supposition that the advantages of the arbitration process somehow disappear when transferred to the employment context. Arbitration agreements allow parties to avoid the costs of litigation, a benefit that may be of particular importance in employment litigation, which often involves smaller sums of money than disputes concerning commercial contracts. These litigation costs to parties (and the accompanying burden to the courts) would be compounded by the difficult choice-of-law questions that are often presented in disputes arising from the employment relationship and the necessity of bifurcation of proceedings in those cases where state law precludes arbitration of certain types of employment claims but not others.[289]

---

[289] Circuit City Stores, Inc. v. Adams, 532 U.S. 105 (2001).

Key Point > *Employment-related claims are significant not only because of their number, but also because they represent an uninsured risk for most churches. Most church general liability insurance policies contain no coverage for such claims. This means that a church that is sued for such a claim will be compelled to hire and pay its own attorney, and pay any settlement or court judgment. The costs associated with even a single claim can be substantial, and this can force a church to divert funds budgeted for ministry to the payment of attorneys and possibly a settlement or judgment. Further, if a discrimination complaint is filed by a current or former employee with the Equal Employment Opportunity Commission (EEOC) or its state or local counterparts, this can lead time-consuming and often unpleasant interaction with government investigators that many church leaders have found to be condescending if not hostile toward religion. Clearly, it is in the best interests of every church to consider alternatives to civil litigation, such as mediation and arbitration.*

A. Arbitration of Employment Disputes under State Law

In the past, some courts and state legislatures attempted to impose limits on the enforceability of arbitration provisions in employment contracts under state law. The United States Supreme Court addressed the enforceability of arbitration provisions in the context of *state* employment or civil rights claims in a 2001 decision.[290] The Court concluded that (1) arbitration provisions are enforceable, and are not barred by the Federal Arbitration Act (for employees not directly engaged in transportation); and (2) the FAA preempts states laws that seek to impose limits on the enforceability of arbitration provisions in employment contracts. It is now clear that employers can compel employees to arbitrate wrongful dismissal and discrimination claims under state law by inserting valid arbitration provisions in employment contracts and applications.

B. Arbitration of Employment Disputes under Federal Law

Can a clause in an employment application or contract calling for binding arbitration of employment disputes preempt the jurisdiction of the federal Equal Employment Opportunity Commission (EEOC) under federal employment and civil rights laws? Consider the following case study:

Case Study

• *A church employs Barb as an office secretary. After working for the church for two years, Barb is dismissed because of extramarital sexual relations in violation of the church's religious and moral teachings. Barb files a complaint with the EEOC claiming that her dismissal constituted unlawful sex discrimination in violation of Title VII of the federal Civil Rights Act of 1964 since the church had not dismissed a male youth pastor who was guilty of the same kind of misconduct a year earlier. The church insists that the EEOC must drop its investigation since Barb signed an employment application prior to being hired in which she agreed to resolve all legal disputes with the church, including discrimination claims under Title VII, through binding arbitration.*

Is the EEOC deprived of jurisdiction over this claim by virtue of the arbitration clause in the church's employment application? This issue was not addressed

---

[290] *Id.*

directly by the Supreme Court in the *Circuit City* case. The Supreme Court addressed this issue in the "Waffle House" case in 2002.[291] An applicant for employment (Eric) signed an employment application with a local Waffle House restaurant that required him to submit to binding arbitration "any dispute or claim concerning [his] employment with Waffle House, Inc., or any subsidiary or Franchisee of Waffle House, Inc., or the terms, conditions or benefits of such employment." Eric was hired, and a few weeks later he suffered a seizure while at work. Waffle House dismissed him, stating in the separation notice that "we decided that for [his] benefit and safety, and Waffle House, it would be best he not work here any more."

Eric filed a charge of discrimination with the EEOC, complaining that his discharge violated the federal Americans With Disabilities Act of 1990 (ADA). The EEOC later sued Waffle House and sought (1) a court order prohibiting Waffle House from discriminating on the basis of disability in any employment decision; (2) a court order requiring Waffle House to institute an anti-discrimination policy; (3) backpay for Eric and reinstatement in his job; and (4) compensatory and punitive damages for Eric. Waffle House insisted that the arbitration provision in the employment contract required the court to dismiss the ADA suit and refer the matter to arbitration.

The Supreme Court ruled that an arbitration agreement between an employer and employee does not bar the EEOC from pursuing victim-specific relief, such as backpay, reinstatement, and damages in an enforcement action brought by the EEOC. In other words, the EEOC is not bound by an arbitration agreement to which it was not a party, and is free to sue an employer for violations of federal employment laws.

Key Point > *Arbitration clauses in employment applications and contracts do not deprive the EEOC of jurisdiction to process discrimination complaints under federal law (including both injunctive relief and money damages for individual victims of discrimination). However, note that there is still a significant advantage to using arbitration clauses in employment applications and contracts. The Supreme Court concluded in the Circuit City case that arbitration clauses prevent employees from pursuing discrimination or wrongful dismissal claims under state law. And, it is these state law claims that expose employers to the greatest amount of money damages since there are limits on employer liability under Title VII of the federal Civil Rights Act of 1964. The Civil Rights Act of 1991 limits the amount of compensatory and punitive damages that are available to most discrimination victims. For example, employers with fewer than 101 employees (the vast majority of churches) cannot be liable for more than $50,000 to any one person. Because of these limits, plaintiffs' attorneys who represent current and former employees routinely file claims under state law. It is these state law claims that expose employers to substantial jury verdicts, and it is these that the Supreme Court has said may be preempted by arbitration provisions. Further, note that the EEOC only sues several hundred employers each year, and so the Supreme Court's decision (in the Waffle House case) that the EEOC is not deprived of jurisdiction to sue employers in its own name as a result of arbitration agreements is of limited significance.*

---

[291] EEOC v. Waffle House, Inc., 534 U.S. 279 (2002).

C. Should Our Church Compel Employees to Arbitrate Employment Disputes?

This is a question that every church should consider. In answering this question, there are a number of points that should be considered:

(1) The advantages to arbitration, listed at the beginning of this article, should be reviewed.

(2) Remember that employment claims currently represent the most likely basis for lawsuits involving churches.

(3) Is your church subject to state or federal civil rights laws protecting employees against various forms of discrimination? What about other kinds of employment claims, such as wrongful dismissal?

(4) Employment lawsuits generally are not covered under church general liability insurance policies. This means that if your church is sued for such a claim, you may be required to hire and pay your own attorney, and pay any settlement or court judgment. The costs associated with a single claim can be substantial.

(5) Check with your insurance agent to see if your church has insurance to cover employment claims. Remember that such coverage may be available under a directors and officers insurance policy, if you have one, even if it is not provided under your general liability policy.

▶ *If you don't have coverage for employment claims, then arbitration may help your church limit the costs associated with such claims. But remember, the costs associated with a single claim may be substantial. As a result, church leaders should discuss with their insurance agent or broker the availability of employment practices insurance coverage. And, they should take steps to minimize or manage the risk of employment-related legal claims.*

(6) If you have insurance to cover employment claims, then check with your insurance company to be sure that an arbitration award would be honored under your insurance policy up to your coverage limits.

(7) Be sure to consult with an attorney concerning the advantages and disadvantages of an arbitration policy. You may want to have an attorney meet with your board or congregation concerning this issue. If possible, use an attorney who specializes in employment law.

(8) Many cite 1 Corinthians 6:1-8 as scriptural support for the arbitration of internal church disputes. This passage is quoted below:

If any of you has a dispute with another, dare he take it before the ungodly for judgment instead of before the saints? Do you not know that the saints will judge the world? And if you are to judge the world, are you not competent to judge trivial cases? Do you not know that we will judge angels? How much more the things of this life! Therefore, if you have disputes about such matters, appoint as judges even men of little account in the church! I say this to shame you. Is it possible that there is nobody among you wise enough to judge a dispute between believers? But instead, one brother goes to law against another-and this in front of unbelievers! The very fact that you have lawsuits among you means you have been completely defeated already. Why not rather be wronged? Why not rather be cheated? Instead, you yourselves cheat and do wrong, and you do this to your brothers.

D. How Do We Implement an Arbitration Policy?

If your church decides to implement an arbitration policy for the resolution of disputes with employees, how do you do so? Given the importance of having a policy that complies with local law, it is imperative that any church wanting to adopt an arbitration policy retain the services of a local attorney who specializes in employment law. The last thing you want is a false sense of security based on a home-made and unenforceable arbitration policy. Here are some recommendations you may want to share with your attorney:

(1) Check with other churches in your state and find some that have adopted arbitration policies. Ask if you can see their policies.

(2) Ask your insurance company if it has sample arbitration policies for churches.

(3) Be sure that the arbitration policy covers claims under federal, state, and local civil rights and employment laws. Ideally, you will want to refer to applicable laws by name. If you don't, then employees may be able to avoid arbitration by saying that they did not understand what they were agreeing to arbitrate because the arbitration clause was not specific enough.

(4) Be sure the arbitration policy contains a "severability" clause. Such a clause states that if any provision of the policy is determined to be invalid by a court of law, the remaining provisions will remain valid.

Your attorney will assist you in deciding whether to place the arbitration policy in your employment application, in an employee handbook, or both.

E. What about Employment Disputes Involving Ministers?

There is no reason to exclude ministers from a church's arbitration policy. However, note the following unique rules:

(1) Most courts have ruled that ministers are not protected by federal and state civil rights laws since the first amendment religious clauses prevent the civil courts from deciding "who will preach from the pulpit."[292] Therefore, you may want to exclude ministers, or those serving in positions that would be deemed "ministerial," from your arbitration policy. In other words, why submit claims to arbitration that the civil courts would not accept? On the other hand, some churches may prefer to arbitrate all employee claims, including those brought by ministers.

---

[292] *See* § 8-10, *supra.*

(2) Many churches have governing documents (such as bylaws) that prescribe how ministers are selected and removed. If a congregation acts to remove a minister in accordance with its governing document and the minister threatens to challenge the church's decision, you need to decide if this is the kind of claim you want to submit to arbitration. That is, if the church acts consistently with its bylaws in removing the pastor, should the pastor be able to use the church's arbitration policy to challenge the church's decision? Once again, the courts generally have not been willing to resolve such claims.

(3) In some churches, ministers are selected and removed only through action of a parent denominational agency. Employment claims involving ministers may be resolved within the denomination using existing procedures. Arbitrating such claims may conflict with denominational rules. This issue must be clarified with denominational officers before adopting an arbitration policy.

F. What about the Arbitration of Other Claims?

This section is addressing only the arbitration of employment disputes. Church leaders may want to consider adopting a separate policy to resolve disputes involving members and the church, or disputes between members.

G. Civil Court Review of Arbitration Awards

Note that the Federal Arbitration Act cautions that "an agreement in writing to submit to arbitration an existing controversy . . . shall be valid, irrevocable, and enforceable, save upon such grounds as exist at law or in equity for the revocation of any contract." In other words, an agreement to arbitrate is a contract, and like any contract, is subject to challenge on the basis of a number of legal theories. This is why it is so important for churches to have arbitration policies drafted by an attorney who specializes in employment law.

H. What about Current Employees Who Have Not Signed an Arbitration Agreement?

Let's say that your church has seven employees, and that you decide to adopt an arbitration policy this year. Will your policy be binding on existing employees, or only on new employees hired after implementation of the policy? The courts have reached conflicting answers to this question. Ask your attorney how to best ensure that your policy covers both current and future employees. The basic idea here is that new employment conditions, such as the arbitration of disputes, are not legally enforceable unless employees receive something of value (other then compensation or benefits to which they are already entitled). For example, some courts have ruled that an agreement to arbitrate future employment claims is enforceable if incorporated into current employees' annual performance reviews.[293] Other courts have allowed an arbitration policy to apply to current employees so long as they agree in writing to be bound by the policy at the time they receive a pay raise.

Case Studies

• *A federal appeals court enforced the decision of an arbitrator in an employment dispute between a church-operated school and its principal. The principal was fired from her position, and later sued the school for breach of contract and discrimination. The school asked the court to compel her to arbitrate her claims pursuant to an arbitration provision in her employment contract. The arbitrator awarded the principal $150,000 in damages. In reaching his decision, he determined that the school had wrongfully discharged the principal by failing to follow biblical precepts, as required in her employment contract; specifically, the conflict resolution process described in Matthew 18. The school asked a federal district court to vacate the arbitration on the basis of a state arbitration law which empowered the civil courts to vacate arbitration awards under narrow conditions including arbitrator bias and an arbitrator acting outside the scope of his or her authority. A federal district court ruled that none of these exceptions applied, and the school appealed. A federal appeals court agreed that none of the narrow grounds for vacating the arbitrator's award existed in this case.*[294]

• *An Illinois court upheld the validity of a church arbitration policy despite the alleged "bias" of the arbitrators. The court concluded that the arbitration policy was not rendered invalid as a result of its restricting arbitrators to members of employees of a parent denomination. It pointed out that the purpose of the arbitration procedure was to resolve disputes within the church, and that pastors consented to the procedure when they were ordained.*[295]

• *A New York court ruled that an arbitration clause in an employment contract between a synagogue and a rabbi was legally enforceable, and so the rabbi was barred from suing the synagogue in civil court for discrimination and wrongful termination. The court concluded, "We perceive no public policy reasons for not enforcing anticipatory agreements to arbitrate statutory employment discrimination claims arising under [state law]. Moreover, the broad arbitration clause in [the rabbi's] employment contract encompasses his claim of wrongful discharge based on a physical disability."*[296]

Employee Handbooks § 8-28

Key Point 8-28> *Employee handbooks can provide employees with valuable information on the terms and conditions of their employment. However, they may also expose a church to an increased risk of liability. For this reason, it is important for churches to have an attorney prepare, or review, an employee handbook before it is adopted.*

---

[293] Miller v. Public Storage Management, Inc., 121 F.3d 215 (5th Cir. 1997).

[294] Prescott v. Northlake Christian School, 141 Fed.Appx. 263 (5th Cir. 2005).

[295] Jenkins v. Trinity Evangelical Lutheran Church, 825 N.E.2d 1206 (Ill. App. 2005).

[296] South Huntington Jewish Center, Inc. v. Heyman, 723 N.Y.S.2d 511 (App. Div. 2001).

Many employers have adopted employee handbooks as a way of informing employees of various job-related policies and benefits. While handbooks can be helpful in avoiding disagreements and false expectations, they can create legal risks to the employer in some cases. Here are some important points to consider in drafting an employee handbook:

- *Legal review.* Plaintiffs' lawyers will scrutinize every word in your employee handbook, looking for language that confers rights that may or may not have been intended. As a result, it is imperative for churches to have an attorney draft, or at least review, their employee handbook.

- *Commercially available handbooks.* Employers can find sample employee handbooks at any office supply store, many discount stores, or on the Internet. While some of these handbooks may contain valuable information, they should not be used without legal review.

- *Brevity.* Keep it short. The longer it is, the more likely a court will find some unexpected "right" that was violated by the church. Also, it becomes difficult to remember and apply the provisions in employee handbooks that become excessively lengthy.

- *Essential provisions.* What should an employee handbook address? Key provisions will include: discipline and termination; compensation and fringe benefits; accrual of benefits; expense reimbursement; employee evaluations; equal opportunity statement (clarifying that the church is legally permitted to discriminate on the basis of religion in its employment decisions); vacation and other types of leave; retirement plans and contributions; work hours and breaks; overtime; employee standards; computer inspection policy; and arbitration of disputes.

- *Disclaimer.* Many employee handbooks contain a notice clarifying that the document is not a contract, and that only the church board may enter into contractual obligations on behalf of the church.

- *New hires.* Have all new hires sign a document in which they agree to be bound by the terms of the handbook.

Employee Privacy §8-29

Key Point 8-29> *Employees may have a limited right of privacy in their workspace that may extend to the contents of their desk and cabinet drawers, and employer-provided computers. This right of privacy can be superseded by a policy that clearly authorizes the employer to inspect these items.*

Do employees have a "right of privacy" in their workspace? Are the contents of their desk off limits to prying staff? Can church leaders dismiss an employee if they find pornographic files on his office computer? Or, would this amount to an invasion of the employee's privacy or a violation of wiretap laws? These were the questions addressed by a federal court in Wisconsin.[297]

A church employed a young man ("Don") as its youth pastor. By accepting this position, Don agreed "to teach faithfully the Word of God . . . in its truth and purity . . . to exemplify the Christian faith and life, to function in an atmosphere of love and order characteristic of the Body of Christ at work, and to lead others toward Christian maturity, to show a due concern for all the phases of mission and ministry."

After serving as youth pastor for a few years, Don was criticized by church board members who had received complaints about his job performance. The church personnel committee gave Don a negative performance review and advised him of areas that needed improvement.

Don opened a Microsoft Hotmail e-mail account from a computer terminal at a local public library. Hotmail accounts are Web-based, free, and reside on servers that are part of the Microsoft network. Don used his Hotmail account for personal purposes. At the time he opened his Hotmail account, he did not own a computer or subscribe to any Internet service provider. He accessed his Hotmail account from the church's computers using the church's Internet service provider, among other places.

Don arrived early at the church one morning and read the e-mail messages on his Hotmail account. He saw that he had received an e-mail message from "John Jacobsen," who asked that Don call him. Don did not recognize the name. Later that morning, Don informed the church secretary (with whom he shared an office) that he was going down the hall to the associate pastor's office. He did not tell the secretary that he was going to make a telephone call, although he often used the associate pastor's office for this purpose. The church's senior pastor had told Don to use the associate pastor's office to make personal phone calls or in any situation in which he needed privacy.

A short time later, the church secretary left her office to place schedules in the mail trays. She took along a cordless telephone because her primary job was answering calls. The church had six telecommunication lines, two for computers and four for telephones. The cordless phone tied into one line of the telephone system. Because the secretary sometimes received church-related calls at home, she tried to call home to check her answering machine for messages. Instead of hearing a dial tone, she heard two male voices involved in a sexually graphic conversation. She recognized one voice as Don's. According to Don, the other man on the telephone was "John Jacobsen," a tutor he had known in college who was having a "sexual identity crisis." The church secretary alleged that Jacobsen talked with Don about his sexual experiences and feelings, at times in graphic detail, and that Don recounted various homosexual encounters of his own. Don later insisted that he had not made any obscene or pornographic statements during this conversation. Rather, he merely listened to Jacobsen because he had been trained as a counselor to listen to people. Don, who was married and had four young children, denied being homosexual or bisexual.

The church secretary became concerned about the possibility of improper contact between Don and children participating in the church's youth programs,

---

[297] Fischer v. Mt. Olive Lutheran Church, Inc., 207 F.Supp.2d 914 (W.D. Wis. 2002).

given Don's position in the church. Shaking from fear and shock, she walked to the church business administrator's office because she believed the conversation she had overheard was an extremely serious matter that should be witnessed by another employee. She gave the administrator the cordless phone and whispered something about Don's being on the line. The administrator heard Don and Jacobsen discussing homosexual acts and making lewd noises (Don later denied this). Believing that the caller was threatening violence to Don or others in the church, the administrator instructed the church secretary to use another phone line to call the police.

The church secretary called the police, and requested that an officer be sent to the church to remove Don from the premises because she was scared and repulsed by the conversation. The administrator walked down the hallway and confronted Don about his phone conversation and asked him to leave the building. Don thought that he had been accused of participating in an obscene conversation over the Internet on the church's computer. He left the building ten minutes later.

After Don left the church, the administrator called the senior pastor and described briefly what had happened. A police detective called the church and asked the secretary and administrator to come to the police station and provide statements. Shortly after they returned to the church, Don returned as well. The senior pastor met with Don to discuss what had happened, and told Don that he was being suspended with pay pending an investigation. According to the senior pastor and business administrator, Don stated that he had told his wife "everything," that his marriage was over, that he had nothing left to live for, and that he had checked his life insurance policy to assure his family would be adequately provided for and that he was contemplating suicide. Don later claimed that he had only told the senior pastor that a suspension would ruin his reputation in the church and community and that he had told his wife of the accusations. However, because of the senior pastor's concerns that Don was suicidal, he stepped out of his office momentarily and had the church secretary contact the police again. Two police officers arrived a short time later and met with Don and the senior pastor. The officers shared the senior pastor's concern regarding suicide, and had Don committed involuntarily to a hospital for observation.

The senior pastor visited with Don's wife that evening, telling her that Don was a "sick" man, that he had had three or four gay relationships, and that he was suicidal.

In response to police recommendations, the senior pastor retained a computer technician to examine the church's computer files that Don used and to check Don's e-mail messages for any improper sexual communications with minors. Using the church's computer, the technician accessed Don's Hotmail account using a password "guessed at" by the senior pastor. The technician printed the e-mail messages that he found in Don's Hotmail account. The e-mails, from senders with male names, referred to Don as "my hot man," "my favorite stud," and "sweetie," and included the statements "miss you babe" and "as always you were a treat!" Don insisted that before June 10, 1999, there were no such e-mail messages in his account.

The next day Don accessed his Hotmail account in the presence of his wife and a neighbor and found no offensive e-mails in his account. The senior pastor claimed that nothing had been deleted from Don's Hotmail account and that no Hotmail settings or passwords had been changed. Later that day the senior pastor again accessed Don's Hotmail account to see whether any new messages had been received that would indicate improper communications with minors. He found two old e-mails which contained photographs of nude males. Don did not know how these e-mails ended up in his account. The next day the senior pastor again accessed Don's Hotmail account and found a new incoming e-mail in which the sender wrote, "Wish I were there to give you a big kiss, hug and more this morning! You take care sweetie! Yours, Bill."

A few days later the senior pastor, along with the chairman of the church's board of elders, visited Don at his home to deliver his final paycheck and to encourage him to resign in order to avoid having his misconduct brought to the attention of others. Don's wife asked what evidence the church had to support its claims. The senior pastor told her that he could provide the information only if Don signed a release. Don refused to do so.

The next day the church's board of elders unanimously approved a motion to schedule a meeting of the congregation to consider the termination of Don's employment. At the congregational meeting the church's attorney described the telephone call that had been overheard by the church secretary and business administrator, but he did not refer to any e-mails. At the meeting, Don implied that the church had no documents to support its charges. The church's attorney responded that he had copies of Don's e-mails with him and asked whether Don would consent to their being read to the congregation. Don declined to give his consent, and so the contents of the e-mails were not disclosed. The congregation voted 91 to 43 in favor of terminating Don's employment.

Don sued the church, the senior pastor, church secretary, and business administrator (the "defendants") claiming that they had all violated federal and state electronic privacy laws by intercepting his telephone conversation and by accessing his Hotmail account without his permission. He also sued each defendant for invasion of privacy and defamation. The defendants filed a motion to dismiss the case. The court's analysis of each of Don's claims is summarized below.

Electronic Communications Privacy Act

The federal Electronic Communications Privacy Act, also known as the Wiretap Act, prohibits the *intentional interception* of "wire, oral or electronic communications." The defendants conceded that Don's telephone conversation was a "wire communication." The Act defines an "interception" as "the acquisition of the contents of any wire, electronic, or oral communication through the use of any electronic, mechanical, or other device." However, the Act has a "business extension" exemption which permits employees to use company telephones in the ordinary course of business without violating the Act. The court conceded that this exemption would apply to the interception of Don's telephone call by the church secretary and business administrator if they were using the cordless phone in the ordinary course of business.

The defendants claimed that the Wiretap Act was not violated since the phone was being used for business purposes when Don's conversation with John Jacobsen was intercepted by the church secretary and business administrator. The defendants noted that Don was allegedly using the phone at the time to "counsel" John Jacobsen. Don insisted that his call was personal and that the secretary and business administrator had an obligation to stop listening as soon as they determined that the call was personal in nature, and in failing to do so they violated the Act.

The court agreed with Don, for two reasons. First, the senior pastor conceded that Don was allowed to make personal calls from the church phone. And second, it was not clear that Don's duties included conversations "with a college friend, such as Jacobsen, or an adult who is not a member of the congregation, even if the call occurred during work hours."

Defendants argued that even if the call was personal in nature, they had a legal interest in listening in because it raised concerns about (1) the safety of church personnel, and (2) possible church liability for improper contact between an employee and a minor. The court disagreed:

> First, I am uncertain how a private telephone conversation raised safety concerns for church personnel, however sexually graphic and homosexual in nature it may have been. . . . Second, the church might have a legal interest in continuing to listen to the conversation if Don were speaking to a minor. However, it is undisputed that [the secretary and business administrator] believed that Don was speaking with an adult. . . . At the point [they] determined that the call was personal and that Don was not talking to a minor, they had an obligation to cease listening and hang up. Any legal interest the church might have had in protecting itself against Don's conversation with a minor ceased to exist when [the secretary and business administrator] formed the belief that Don was talking with an adult.

Electronic Communication Storage Act

The Act specifies that "whoever (1) intentionally accesses without authorization a facility through which an electronic communication service is provided; or (2) intentionally exceeds an authorization to access that facility; and thereby obtains, alters, or prevents authorized access to a wire or electronic communication while it is in electronic storage in such system" violates the Act. "Electronic storage" is defined as "(A) any temporary, intermediate storage of a wire or electronic communication incidental to the electronic transmission thereof; and (B) any storage of such communication by an electronic communication service for purposes of backup protection of such communication."

The defendants claimed that the senior pastor did not violate the Act when he accessed Don's Hotmail account because Don's Hotmail e-mail was not in "electronic storage" as defined under the Act. The defendants argued that the Act "does not apply to the accessing of e-mail messages in a recipient's mailbox for at that point, transmission of the messages has been completed." The court disagreed. It noted that the Act defines "electronic storage" as either temporary, intermediate storage incidental to the electronic transmission or any storage of such communication by an electronic communication service for purposes of backup protection. The senior pastor accessed Don's e-mail while it was stored on a remote, Web-based server that was owned by Microsoft, an electronic communication service provider. The court concluded that Congress intended the Act to cover the exact situation in this case, as illustrated by an example provided in the Senate Report:

> For example, a computer mail facility authorizes a subscriber to access information in their portion of the facilities storage. Accessing the storage of other subscribers without specific authorization to do so would be a violation of the act. Similarly, a member of the general public authorized to access the public portion of a computer facility would violate this section by intentionally exceeding that authorization and accessing the private portions of the facility.

The court noted that accessing Don's Hotmail account intentionally was not enough to violate the act. Don also had to show that the defendants obtained, altered, or prevented his authorized access to his e-mail account. The court concluded that there was enough evidence that this requirement was met that the defendants' motion to dismiss had to be denied. It noted, in particular, that there was evidence that the church prevented Don from accessing his e-mail account by changing his password.

The defendants also claimed that it was the computer technician, not they, who accessed Don's e-mails, and so they had not violated the Act. The court disagreed. It concluded that the technician was acting as the church's agent. However, the court concluded that the church secretary and business administrator did not violate the Stored Communications Act because they never accessed Don's e-mails.

Computer Fraud and Abuse Act

Under the federal Computer Fraud and Abuse Act, anyone who "intentionally accesses a computer without authorization . . . and thereby obtains . . . information from any protected computer if the conduct involved an interstate or foreign communication" may have violated the act. However, in order to maintain a civil action under the Act, Don must have suffered "damage or loss" by reason of a violation. "Damage" is defined as "any impairment to the integrity or availability of data, a program, a system, or information that . . . causes loss aggregating at least $5,000 in value during any 1-year period to one or more individuals." Damages are limited to economic damages. The Act does not define a "loss," but the courts have interpreted it to cover "remedial expenses." The defendants argued that Don failed to produce evidence that he suffered any damage or loss as a result of their acts of copying his e-mail messages from his account. Don would have had to suffer damages or loss of at least $5,000 in order to maintain a cause of action under the Act. Although Don alleged that he could no longer access his Hotmail account because the defendants allegedly changed his password, he failed to show that he suffered any damage or loss as a result. As a result, the court granted the defendants' motion for summary judgment as to Don's claims under the Computer Fraud and Abuse Act.

Invasion of Privacy

Under Wisconsin law, an "invasion of privacy" includes "an intrusion upon the privacy of another of a nature highly offensive to a reasonable person, in a *place that a reasonable person would consider private.*" Don claimed that his right to privacy was intruded upon when (1) the church secretary and business administrator eavesdropped on his telephone conversation, and (2) the pastor and church accessed his e-mail account. The defendants argued that neither a telephone conversation nor an e-mail account is "a place" under the privacy law.

Don conceded that a telephone conversation is not "a place." He argued, however, that at the time he was on the telephone, he was in an office that the pastor had allowed him to use for private telephone calls and the door to that office was closed. Therefore, Don reasoned, the "place" was the office, not the phone conversation. The defendants replied that it was "absurd" for Don to contend that he had a right of privacy when he was located in his employer's office. The court was not convinced. It observed, "Defendants argue that it is the call that was intruded upon, not the office. However, Don was in a place (the office) where his privacy right was allegedly violated (via a phone extension). In other words, the fact that defendants used a phone extension to listen in on Don's conversation rather than pressing an ear against the door is of no consequence. . . . When A taps B's telephone wires A has invaded B's privacy."

The court conceded, however, that it was not clear that the acts of the church secretary and business administrator in eavesdropping on Don's telephone call were "highly offensive to a reasonable person" as required to be an invasion of privacy. It left these questions to the jury.

The court then addressed the question of whether the access to Don's e-mail account by the pastor and church invaded his privacy. It concluded, "On its face, the language, 'intrusion upon the privacy of another . . . in a place that a reasonable person would consider private' does not limit the intrusion to a person's immediate physical environment but rather encompasses a person's private belongings as long as the place these private belongings are intruded upon is one that a reasonable person would consider private."

The court quoted with approval from the *Restatement (Second) of Torts* (a respected legal treatise), "Intrusion on privacy of another may be by some other form of investigation or examination into his private concerns, as by opening his private and personal mail, searching his safe or his wallet, examining his private bank account, or compelling him by a forged court order to permit inspection of his personal documents." Because it was disputed whether Don's e-mail account was a place that a reasonable person would consider private, the court denied the defendants' request to dismiss the case.

Defamation

Don contended that the defendants defamed him by reporting falsely to the church's board of directors that he "was an active participant in a telephone conversation with graphic sexual content, including homosexual acts and encounters, sodomy, and other acts of depravity." The court noted that "a communication is defamatory if it tends to harm the reputation of another so as to lower that person in the estimation of the community or deter third persons from associating with him or her." However, consent to the publication is an absolute defense. The defendants argued that when Don accepted his employment, the church bylaws specified that he could be terminated by a two-thirds vote of the congregation. As a result, by accepting his employment, Don "consented" to the publication of information relating to the suitability of his continued employment with the church, which included the defendants' version of the telephone conversation. The court disagreed, noting that there was no specific evidence of consent. The bylaws "were neither part of Don's call nor incorporated" into his employment contract.

The defendants also claimed that the "common interest privilege" protected their allegedly defamatory disclosure to the church's board of directors and the voting members of the church. The court defined the common interest privilege as follows: "An occasion makes a publication conditionally privileged if the circumstances lead any one of several persons having a common interest in a particular subject matter correctly or reasonably to believe that there is information that another sharing the common interest is entitled to know. . . . The common interest privilege is based on the policy that one is entitled to learn from his associates what is being done in a matter in which he or she has an interest in common" and "is particularly germane to the employer-employee relationship."

The court again quoted from the *Restatement (Second) of Torts*, "The common interests of members of religious . . . associations . . . is recognized as sufficient to support a privilege for communications among themselves concerning the qualifications of the officers and members and their participation in the activities of the society. This is true whether the defamatory matter relates to alleged misconduct of some other member that makes him undesirable for continued membership, or the conduct of a prospective member."

The court concluded that it was clear that the defendants' allegedly defamatory statements were conditionally privileged. However, it noted that a conditional privilege may be forfeited if it is abused. It cited five conditions mentioned in the *Restatement (Second) of Torts* that may constitute an abuse of a conditional privilege: (1) a defendant knows the matter to be false or acts in reckless disregard as to its truth or falsity; (2) the defamatory matter is published for some purpose other than that for which the particular privilege is given; (3) the publication is made to some person not reasonably believed to be necessary for the accomplishment of the purpose of the particular privilege; (4) the publication includes defamatory matter not reasonably believed to be necessary to accomplish the purpose for which the occasion is privileged; or (5) the publication includes unprivileged matter as well as privileged matter.

Don contended that the defendants' conditional privilege was forfeited because the church secretary and business administrator knew that their version of the events was false. The court agreed, noting that "Don has adduced evidence that [the secretary and business administrator] made false statements to the board of directors about Don's role in the telephone conversation." The court rejected the defendants' request to dismiss Don's allegation of defamation, and sent this issue to the jury. However, the court dismissed the defamation claims against the senior pastor and church since Don had not presented evidence that the senior pastor knew that the account of the telephone conversation provided by the secretary and business administrator was false.

Relevance to church leaders

What is the relevance of this case to church leaders? While a decision by a federal district court in Wisconsin is not binding in any other state, the fact remains that this is the first court to address the liability of churches and church staff members for unauthorized access to an employee's private telephone conversations and e-mail. Therefore, this ruling may be given special consideration by other courts addressing the same issues, and it is for this reason that the case merits serious study by church leaders in every state.

1. The federal Electronic Communications Privacy Act. This Act (often referred to as the "Wiretap Act") prohibits the intentional interception of "wire, oral or electronic communications" by any "electronic, mechanical, or other device." As this case demonstrates, a telephone conversation is a "wire communication," which means that it is unlawful to intentionally intercept a telephone conversation by means of an "electronic, mechanical, or other device." However, the Act exempts

> any telephone . . . (i) furnished to the subscriber or user by a provider of wire or electronic communication service in the ordinary course of its business and being used by the subscriber or user in the ordinary course of its business or furnished by such subscriber or user for connection to the facilities of such service and used in the ordinary course of its business; or (ii) being used by a provider of wire or electronic communication service in the ordinary course of its business . . . . [298]

This exemption is called the "business extension" exemption since it applies to the use of an "extension" telephone at an employer's place of business *so long as the extension telephone is being used "in the ordinary course of business."* Note that there are two requirements for this exemption to apply: the intercepting equipment must be (1) furnished to the user by the phone company or connected to the phone line, and (2) used in the ordinary course of business. The "ordinary course of business" requirement was a central issue in this case. The court concluded that the extension telephone used by the church secretary and business administrator to eavesdrop on Don's call was *not* being used in the ordinary course of business, for two reasons:

- The senior pastor of the church conceded that Don, and other church employees, were allowed to use church telephones for personal calls.

- Don claimed that he was speaking with an old college friend when his call was intercepted by the church secretary and business administrator.

Most churches allow employees to use telephones for personal calls, even if they have a written policy strictly prohibiting such use. As this case demonstrates, allowing employees to use church telephones for personal calls will make it more difficult for the church to qualify for the business extension exemption to the Wiretap Act. To illustrate, if a church is charged with violating the Wiretap Act

---

[298] 18 U.S.C.A. 2510(5).

because of the interception of a telephone call, it cannot claim that all calls made on church premises are necessarily "business" in nature if the church permits employees to use telephones for personal calls. The church may still be able to prove that it intercepted a call while a telephone was being used in the ordinary course of business, but this will be more difficult if it allows personal calls (or has a policy prohibiting personal calls that is routinely ignored).

Key Point > *When a church employee picks up a telephone and hears another conversation in progress, he or she must immediately determine if the conversation is business or personal. If it is personal in nature, then the employee should hang up the telephone. Continuing to listen in on a personal telephone call may subject the employee, and the church, to criminal and civil liability.*

Let's see how other courts have interpreted the business extension exemption. The leading cases are summarized below.

Case Studies

• *An employee received a call from a friend who asked about a recent job interview the employee had with another company. The employee's supervisor listened in on the call and fired the employee as a result of what he learned. The employee sued the employer for violating the Act. The employer insisted that the business extension exemption applied. A federal appeals court concluded, "The general rule is if the intercepted call was a business call, then the [employer's] monitoring of it was in the ordinary course of business. If it was a personal call, the monitoring was probably, but not certainly, not in the ordinary course of business." The court concluded that the business extension exemption did not apply: "While the employer might have been curious about [the employee's] plans . . . it had no legal interest in them. . . . [The employee's] interview was thus a personal matter, neither in pursuit nor to the legal detriment of [the employer's] business." The court held that under the Wiretap Act, the employer "was obliged to cease listening as soon as [the employer] had determined the call was personal, regardless of the contents of the legitimately heard conversation."*[299]

• *A business was burglarized and nearly $20,000 was stolen. The business owner suspected that an employee was the perpetrator. Hoping to catch the employee in a confession, the owner purchased and installed a recording device on an extension phone. When turned on, the machine would automatically record all conversations made or received on either phone, with no indication to the parties using the phone that their conversation was being recorded. The owner recorded, and listened to, 22 hours of the employee's telephone conversations. While the employee never mentioned the burglary, she did admit to other indiscretions that led to her termination. She sued her former employer for violating the Wiretap Act. The owner claimed that the business extension exemption applied. A federal appeals court concluded that the business extension exemption did not apply: "We do not quarrel with the contention that the [owner] had a legitimate business reason for listening in: he suspected [the employee's] involvement in a burglary of the store and hoped she would incriminate herself in*

[299] Watkins v. L.M. Berry & Co., 704 F.2d 577 (11th Cir. 1983).

284

a conversation on the phone. Moreover, [she] was abusing her privileges by using the phone for numerous personal calls even, by her own admission, when there were customers in the store. The [owner] might legitimately have monitored [her] calls to the extent necessary to determine that the calls were personal and made or received in violation of store policy. But the [owner] recorded 22 hours of calls, and listened to all of them without regard to their relation to his business interests. Granted, [the employee] might have mentioned the burglary at any time during the conversations, but we do not believe that the [owner's] suspicions justified the extent of the intrusion. . . . We conclude that the scope of the interception in this case takes us well beyond the boundaries of the ordinary course of business." [300]

• *An employer listened in on telephone calls made by an employee to see if he was sharing trade secrets with a former employee who owned a competing business. A federal appeals court concluded that "when an employee's supervisor has particular suspicions about confidential information being disclosed to a business competitor, has warned the employee not to disclose such information, has reason to believe that the employee is continuing to disclose the information, and knows that a particular phone call is with an agent of the competitor, it is within the ordinary course of business to listen in on an extension phone for at least so long as the call involves the type of information he fears is being disclosed." The court added, "In general, it is hard to see how use of an extension telephone to intercept a call involving non-business matters could be in the ordinary course of business, since such activity is unlikely to further any legitimate business interest. However, interception of calls reasonably suspected to involve non-business matters might be justifiable by an employer who had had difficulty controlling personal use of business equipment through warnings." However, the court stressed that even these conversations could be monitored only long enough to determine if they were "personal" in nature.* [301]

2. Consent. The federal Wiretap Act provides that "consent" is a defense to criminal liability:

> It shall not be unlawful under this chapter for a person not acting under color of law to intercept a wire, oral, or electronic communication where such person is a party to the communication or where one of the parties to the communication has given prior consent to such interception unless such communication is intercepted for the purpose of committing any criminal or tortious act in violation of the Constitution or laws of the United States or of any State.[302]

According to this provision, a church will not violate the Wiretap Act when it intercepts employees' telephone conversations so long as the employees have consented to the interceptions. Can a church simply adopt a policy allowing it to intercept employee telephone calls, and require every employee to sign a form acknowledging and agreeing to the policy? Several courts have addressed the issue of consent in this context, and it is possible that a church could avoid liability under the Wiretap Act for occasional interceptions of employee telephone calls by adopting the following procedures:

---

[300] Deal v. Spears, 980 F.2d 1153 (8th Cir. 1992).

[301] Briggs v. American Air Filter Co., Inc., 630 F.2d 414 (5th Cir. 1980).

[302] 18 USCA 2511(2)(d).

(1) Adopt a written policy informing employees that their telephone calls may be monitored. It would be best to base this policy on a legitimate business purpose, such as the limitation of personal calls during office hours. It is not clear whether such a policy can apply to current employees unless they provide the church with something of value. This is a result of the basic principle of contract law that no contractual commitment is binding unless a party gives up something of value. This problem may be avoided by having current employees sign a written form (agreeing to the policy) at the time they receive a pay raise. This is an issue that should be addressed with a local attorney.

(2) Explain the policy to all new employees at the time of hiring.

(3) Have all new employees sign a statement acknowledging that they understand and agree to the policy.

(4) Attach a notice to the front cover of all telephone directories, reminding employees of the policy. While it may seem excessive to some, church leaders should also consider attaching an appropriate notice to all office telephones.

Case Studies

Summarized below are some of the leading cases addressing the issue of consent:

• *A business was burglarized and nearly $20,000 was stolen. The business owner suspected that an employee was the perpetrator. Hoping to catch the employee in a confession, the owner purchased and installed a recording device on an extension phone. When turned on, the machine would automatically record all conversations made or received on either phone, with no indication to the parties using the phone that their conversation was being recorded. The owner recorded, and listened to, 22 hours of the employee's telephone conversations. While the employee never mentioned the burglary, she did admit to other indiscretions that led to her termination. She sued her former employer for violating the Wiretap Act. The owner claimed that the employee had "consented" to the interception and recording of her personal telephone calls because he had mentioned that he might be forced to monitor calls or restrict telephone privileges if abuse of the store's telephone for personal calls continued. A federal appeals court disagreed. It conceded that consent may be implied from the circumstances, but cannot be "cavalierly implied." Further, "knowledge of the capability of monitoring alone cannot be considered implied consent." The court concluded, "We do not believe that [the employee's] consent may be implied from the circumstances. The [owner] did not inform [the employee] that he was monitoring the phone, but only told her he might do so in order to cut down on personal calls. Moreover, it seems clear that the owner anticipated the employee would not suspect that he was intercepting her calls, since he hoped to catch her making an admission about the burglary, an outcome he would not expect if she knew her calls were being recorded."* [303]

• A federal appeals court ruled that a prison inmate consented to the interception and recording of her personal telephone calls, and therefore no violation of the Wiretap Act occurred. The prison routinely monitored inmates' telephone calls. Inmates received notice of the monitoring in several forms. They were given two handbooks stating that all calls other than those to their attorneys would be monitored. They signed a consent form acknowledging that their calls might be monitored and recorded and that use of the telephones constituted consent to monitoring. They also received an orientation lesson plan stating that calls were monitored. Also, the prison reminded inmates that their calls might be monitored by placing notices of monitoring on or near the actual telephones. Calls were recorded at all times, and recordings were maintained on magnetic tapes connected to a computer that could search them. The court concluded that the inmate in this case "consented" to the interception and recording of her telephone calls.[304]

• A federal appeals court ruled that a criminal defendant "consented" to the interception and recording of a private telephone call by prison officials and therefore no violation of the Wiretap Act occurred. The court noted that prison regulations required a notice to be posted at all monitored telephones advising users that "all conversations are subject to monitoring and that use of the telephone constitutes consent to this monitoring." In addition, prison regulations require inmates to sign a form stating their awareness of and consent to this policy. The court concluded that under these facts inmates "consented" to the interception and recording of their telephone calls and therefore no violation of the Act occurred.[305]

• A federal appeals court ruled that three criminal defendants "consented" to the interception and recording of private telephone calls by prison officials and therefore no violation of the Wiretap Act occurred. The court noted that "consent is not voluntary merely because a person makes a knowing choice among alternatives; it must be an exercise of free will. The court must determine whether the actor's free will has been overborne and his capacity for self-determination critically impaired. Consent to a wire intercept is not voluntary where it is coerced, either by explicit or implicit means or by implied threat or covert force." The court concluded that the inmates consented to the interception and recording of their telephone calls by prison officials: "They had various options to choose from, since no one forced them to make these phone calls. There is not the slightest suggestion that the prison officials encouraged or lured them in to using the phone. . . . Moreover, the defendants signed forms which specifically stated that their phone calls could be recorded. . . . Inmates are provided with rules and regulations stating that the calls may be monitored and recorded. There is an intake screening with a counselor who explains the procedures and the forms to each inmate. The counselors who went over the forms with the defendants testified that they followed the procedures and explained the guidelines for making telephone calls. [The inmates] all signed forms acknowledging that they had either read the provisions themselves or had the acknowledgment read to them that their phone calls might be monitored and recorded. Absent some evidence that they were coerced or misled, the court can only conclude that the defendants knowingly and voluntarily consented to have their calls monitored and recorded. It is difficult to imagine what more the government could have done to make it clear to the defendants that the calls

---

[303] Deal v. Spears, 980 F.2d 1153 (8th Cir. 1992).

[304] U.S. v. Hammond, 286 F.3d 189 (4th Cir. 2002).

[305] United States v. Lanoue, 71 F.3d 966 (1st Cir. 1995).

*could be monitored and taped. This information was included in the guidelines given
to them, on the form they signed, and they were told of this during their interview. All
the evidence points to the conclusion that the defendants knew that their phone calls
might be recorded, and that their consent was freely given. If they did not wish to submit to recording, they had the option not to use the phones. The fact that they knew
of the recording and used the phones with such knowledge is further evidence of their
consent."* [302]

• *A federal appeals court ruled that three criminal defendants "consented" to the interception and recording of private telephone calls by prison officials and therefore no violation of the Wiretap Act occurred. The court observed: "They were on notice of the
prison's interception policy from at least four sources. [Federal law] provides public
notice of the possibility of monitoring. In addition, inmates receive actual notice. First,
upon first arriving at [the prison] and upon returning to the institution after an absence
of nine months or more, each inmate must attend an admission and orientation lecture
in which the monitoring and taping system is discussed. Second, every inmate receives
a copy of* The Inmate Informational Handbook *which contained the following notice
about the taping system: 'Telephones . . . are located in each housing unit and are
turned on every other day on a rotating basis. . . . These phones utilized by the inmates
are MONITORED and TAPED.' Third, notices were placed on each telephone, stating,
'The Bureau of Prisons reserves the authority to monitor conversations on this telephone.
Your use of institutional telephones constitutes consent to this monitoring' . . . .
Moreover, prison records indicate that a case manager presented the inmates with a form
containing the written notice of the monitoring and taping system, which they refused
to sign. Thus, the [inmates] had notice of the interception system and that their use of
the telephones therefore constituted implied consent to the monitoring."* [303]

• *A federal appeals court ruled that an employee's knowledge that her employer had the
ability to monitor employees' private telephone calls did not constitute "consent" to
such monitoring.* [304]

3. Penalties for violating the Act. A violation of the Wiretap Act can result
in both criminal and civil penalties.

criminal penalties

The Wiretap Act specifies that those who violate the Act "shall be fined under
this title or imprisoned not more than five years, or both."

civil penalties

The Wiretap Act specifies that persons whose telephone or other electronic
communications are intercepted in violation of the Act may sue the perpetrator for
money damages. Private lawsuits must be filed within two years "after the date upon
which the claimant first has a reasonable opportunity to discover the violation."

4. The Electronic Communications Storage Act. The Electronic
Communications Storage Act, also known as the Stored Communications Act,

---

[302] U.S. v. Rohlsen, 968 F.Supp. 1040 (D.V.I. 1997).

[303] U.S. v. Amen, 831 F.2d 373 (2nd Cir. 1987).

[304] Watkins v. L.M. Berry & Co., 704 F.2d 577 (11th Cir. 1983).

was added to the Wiretap Act in 1986. The Act specifies that "whoever (1) intentionally accesses without authorization a facility through which an electronic communication service is provided; or (2) intentionally exceeds an authorization to access that facility; and thereby obtains, alters, or prevents authorized access to a wire or electronic communication while it is in electronic storage in such system" violates the Act. "Electronic storage" is defined as "(A) any temporary, intermediate storage of a wire or electronic communication incidental to the electronic transmission thereof; and (B) any storage of such communication by an electronic communication service for purposes of backup protection of such communication."

The court noted that the Act defines "electronic storage" as either temporary, intermediate storage incidental to the electronic transmission or any storage of such communication by an electronic communication service for purposes of backup protection. The senior pastor accessed Don's e-mail while it was stored on a remote, Web-based server (Hotmail) that was owned by Microsoft, an "electronic communication service provider." The court concluded that Congress intended the Act to cover this very situation. However, the court also noted that Don had to prove that the defendants "obtained, altered or prevented his authorized access" to his Hotmail e-mail account. This requirement may have been met, the court concluded, if the church prevented Don from accessing his e-mail account by changing his password.

The court concluded that its conclusion that the church violated Don's rights under the Electronic Communications Storage Act by accessing his e-mail was not inconsistent with the *Fraser* case (summarized in the next example) since the church accessed Don's e-mail while it was stored on a remote, Web-based server (Hotmail) that was owned by Microsoft, an electronic communication service provider.

Case Study

• *A federal court ruled that the Electronic Communications Storage Act could be violated only by accessing e-mail that has not yet been downloaded to the recipient's hard drive. An employer accessed an employee's e-mail that was located on its server after it had been downloaded by the employee to his hard drive. The e-mail message that was accessed was not stored by an electronic communication service but was stored on the employer's server. The court concluded that the Act, which prohibits unauthorized "access" to an electronic communication while it is in "electronic storage" provides protection for private communications only during the course of transmission: "Electronic storage is defined under the Act as '(A) any temporary, intermediate storage of a wire or electronic communication incidental to the electronic transmission thereof; and (B) any storage of such communication by an electronic communication service for purposes of backup protection of such communication.' Part (A) of the definition fits [what may be called] intermediate storage. It is clear that the Stored Communications Act covers a message that is stored in intermediate storage temporarily, after the message is sent by the sender, but before it is retrieved by the intended recipient. Part (B) of the definition refers to what [may be called] back-up protection storage, which protects the communication in the event the system crashes before transmission is complete. The phrase 'for purposes of backup protection of such communication' in the definition makes clear that messages that are in post-transmission* storage, after transmission is complete, are not covered by part (B) of the definition of 'electronic storage.' Therefore, retrieval of a message from post-transmission storage is not covered by the Stored Communications Act. The Act provides protection only for messages while they are in the course of transmission." The court noted that the employer retrieved the employee's e-mail from storage after the e-mail had already been sent and received by the recipient. It acquired the employee's e-mail from post-transmission storage. Therefore, its conduct "is not prohibited under the Stored Communications Act." [309]

Very few courts have applied the Electronic Communications Storage Act to an employer's access to an employee's e-mail account. From the limited precedent, it would appear that an employer does not violate the Act by accessing e-mails on a computer after they have been downloaded by an employee to his or her hard drive. The Act is violated when an employer accesses without consent an employee's e-mail account directly on the "electronic communication service provider" (such as Hotmail) and in addition "obtains, alters, or prevents authorized access" to an electronic communication "while it is in electronic storage in such system." While a church may not violate the Act when it accesses an employee's e-mail after it has been downloaded to the employee's computer hard drive, it may invade the employee's privacy by doing so (as noted below). Church leaders should not access an employee's e-mail without first consulting with a local attorney.

5. State electronic privacy laws. Don alleged that the defendants violated the Wisconsin Communication Privacy Act. The court rejected the defendants' request to dismiss this claim. Church leaders must realize that several states have their own electronic privacy laws that may apply to the interception of telephone calls and inspection of e-mails on church computers. These laws should be consulted.

6. Invasion of privacy. The court also concluded that Don could sue the defendants for invasion of privacy. Note that this basis of liability is completely separate from federal and state electronic privacy laws. It requires proof of intrusion upon the privacy of another in a manner highly offensive to a reasonable person, in a place that a reasonable person would consider private. The court concluded that Don's privacy may have been invaded when (1) the church secretary and business administrator eavesdropped on his private telephone conversation, and (2) the pastor and church accessed his e-mail account. The court quoted with approval from the *Restatement (Second) of Torts* (a respected legal treatise): "Intrusion on privacy of another may be by some other form of investigation or examination into his private concerns, as by opening his private and personal mail, searching his safe or his wallet, examining his private bank account, or compelling him by a forged court order to permit inspection of his personal documents." Because it was disputed whether Don's e-mail account was a place that a reasonable person would consider private, the court denied the defendants' request to dismiss this claim.

This aspect of the court's decision is very important. Even if state or federal electronic privacy laws are not violated by an interception of a church employee's

---

[309] Fraser v. Nationwide Mutual Insurance Co., 135 F.Supp.2d 623 (E.D. Pa. 2001).

telephone call, or inspection of the employee's e-mail or computer, such acts may amount to an invasion of privacy for which the church may be liable.

7. Defamation. The court noted that "a communication is defamatory if it tends to harm the reputation of another so as to lower that person in the estimation of the community or deter third persons from associating with him or her." It concluded that the defendants clearly met this definition when they "falsely reported" to the church's board of directors that Don "was an active participant in a telephone conversation with graphic sexual content, including homosexual acts and encounters, sodomy, and other acts of depravity." The court then addressed two possible defenses to defamation:

> • *Consent.* The court acknowledged that consent is a defense to defamation, but it rejected the church's claim that Don "consented" to the disclosures made to the board and congregation as a result of provisions in the church bylaws. The court noted that there was simply no evidence that Don ever specifically "consented" to having the church bylaws govern his employment. In particular, the court pointed out that nowhere in Don's employment contract was there any provision incorporating the church bylaws.
>
> • *Common interest privilege.* The court acknowledged that a statement is not defamatory if it is protected by the "common interest privilege." This privilege is defined in the *Restatement (Second) of Torts* as follows:

The common interests of members of religious . . . associations . . . is recognized as sufficient to support a privilege for communications among themselves concerning the qualifications of the officers and members and their participation in the activities of the society. This is true whether the defamatory matter relates to alleged misconduct of some other member that makes him undesirable for continued membership, or the conduct of a prospective member.

However, the court noted that this privilege may be forfeited if it is "abused," and it listed the following five conditions that may constitute an abuse of the privilege: (1) a defendant knows the matter to be false or acts in reckless disregard as to its truth or falsity; (2) the defamatory matter is published for some purpose other than that for which the particular privilege is given; (3) the publication is made to some person not reasonably believed to be necessary for the accomplishment of the purpose of the particular privilege; (4) the publication includes defamatory matter not reasonably believed to be necessary to accomplish the purpose for which the occasion is privileged; or (5) the publication includes unprivileged matter as well as privileged matter.

The court concluded that the common interest privilege was forfeited because the church secretary and business administrator "made false statements to the board of directors about Don's role in the telephone conversation."

8. Other cases. Summarized below are other cases addressing the privacy rights of employees.

This case suggests that church employees should refrain from intercepting or recording employees' telephone calls or inspecting employees' private e-mail unless they are familiar with the following rules:

• The federal Electronic Communications Privacy Act (also known as the Wiretap Act) prohibits the intentional interception of telephone calls without consent. But, under the so-called "business extension exemption," an employer may listen in on an employee's telephone calls on an "extension telephone" so long as this is done in the ordinary course of business. This will be harder to prove if employees are permitted to use church telephones for personal calls (even if doing so violates a written policy).

• When a church employee picks up a telephone and hears another conversation in progress, he or she must immediately determine if the conversation is business or personal. If it is personal in nature, then the employee should hang up the telephone. Continuing to listen in on a personal telephone call may subject the employee, and the church, to criminal and civil liability.

• A church does not violate the Wiretap Act when it intercepts employees' telephone conversations if the employees have consented to the interceptions. It is possible to obtain employees' consent through appropriate policies that are explained to and acknowledged by the employees.

• The Electronic Communications Storage Act is violated when an employer accesses without consent an employee's e-mail account directly on the "electronic communication service provider" (such as Hotmail) and in addition "obtains, alters, or prevents authorized access" to an electronic communication "while it is in electronic storage in such system." While a church may not violate the Act when it accesses an employee's e-mail after it has been downloaded to the employee's computer hard drive, it may invade the employee's privacy by doing so.

• Several states have their own electronic privacy laws that may apply to the interception of telephone calls and inspection of e-mails on church computers. These laws should be consulted.

• Even if state or federal electronic privacy laws are not violated by an interception of a church employee's telephone call, or inspection of the employee's e-mail or computer, such acts could amount to an invasion of privacy for which the church may be liable.

Case Studies

• *A federal appeals court ruled that employees have a reasonable expectation of priva-cy in the contents of their desks, cabinets, and computers, but that this expectation can be reduced or eliminated by policies or practices.*[310]

• *A federal appeals court ruled that an employee did not have an expectation of privacy in his workplace computer, and therefore the police did not act improperly in accessing the computer and finding evidence of child pornography. The prosecutor conceded that the employee had a "subjective" expectation of privacy in the computer—"the use of a password on his computer and the lock on his private office door are sufficient evidence of such expectation." But, "his expectation of privacy in his workplace computer must also have been objectively reasonable." The court concluded that this requirement was not met: "Though each computer required its employee to use an individual log-in, the employer had complete administrative access to anybody's machine. It had also installed a firewall, which is a program that monitors Internet traffic from within the organization to make sure nobody is visiting any sites that might be unprofessional. Monitoring was therefore routine, and the employer reviewed the log created by the fire-wall on a regular basis, sometimes daily if Internet traffic was high enough to warrant it. Upon their hiring, employees were apprised of the company's monitoring efforts through training and an employment manual, and they were told that the computers were com-pany-owned and not to be used for activities of a personal nature. Ted, who has the bur-den of establishing a reasonable expectation of privacy, presented no evidence in con-tradiction of any of these practices. He does not assert that he was unaware of, or that he had not consented to, the Internet and computer policy." The court noted that "other courts have scrutinized searches of workplace computers in both the public and private context, and they have consistently held that an employer's policy of routine monitoring is among the factors that may preclude an objectively reasonable expectation of priva-cy." The court acknowledged that some courts had found a reasonable expectation of privacy in a workplace computer, but pointed out that in each of those cases the employ-er "failed to implement a policy limiting personal use of or the scope of privacy in the computers, or had no general practice of routinely conducting searches of the comput-ers."* [311]

• *A California court ruled that an employee who was fired for using his office computer to access pornographic websites on the Internet was barred from suing his employer for wrongful termination or invasion of privacy because he signed a "computer use agree-ment" giving his employer the right to inspect his computer and dismiss him for inap-propriate or unauthorized use of the computer.* [312]

• *A federal court in North Carolina dismissed a lawsuit brought by a pastor against his former church in which he claimed that the church had violated his rights under feder-al electronic privacy laws by searching his laptop computer for pornography, failing to follow denominational procedures in investigating him, and defaming him. The court concluded that the First Amendment guaranty of religious freedom prevented it from*

---

310 Leventhal v. Knapek, 266 F.3d 64 (2nd Cir. 2001).

311 United States v. Ziegler, 456 F.3d 1138 (9th Cir. 2006).

312 TBG Insurance Services Corporation v. Superior Court 117 Cal.Rptr.2d 155 (Cal. App. 2002).

resolving the pastor's claims: "Each allegation [in the pastor's lawsuit] relates to him in his capacity as the church's senior pastor. Thus, in deciding the issues raised in his lawsuit, the court would in essence be made to inquire into the church's decisions regarding its own internal management, and discipline of its clergy. Furthermore, if the court did not agree with the procedure used and the effects therefrom, in holding the church liable, the court would be substituting its laws and disciplinary action for that of the church." [313]

• An Ohio court ruled that a church could be sued for invasion of privacy as a result of an announcement on the church's website disclosing the music director's psychological disorder and that he was being hospitalized for it. The court observed, "The right of privacy is the right of a person to be let alone, to be free from unwarranted publicity, and to live without unwarranted interference by the public in matters with which the public is not necessarily concerned." The court concluded, "The comments made on the church's website were based purely on [the music director's] private affairs, i.e. his hospitalization for depression. While he did inform those necessary persons about his condition—the pastor and a few close friends who belonged to the church—this cannot be seen as a waiver to enter his private life. . . . While the church's publication could be based upon informing the congregation of [his] return to the church, the inclusion of the additional personal information about his bipolar illness could be viewed as offensive or objectionable to a reasonable person." [314]

▶ Churches that provide employees with computers that include Internet access should adopt a computer use policy that authorizes the inspection and monitoring of computers as well as discipline or dismissal for unauthorized or inappropriate use. Such a policy should be consented to by all employees. It is not clear whether such a policy can apply to current employees unless they provide the church with something of value. This is a result of the basic principle of contract law that no contractual commitment is binding unless a party gives up something of value. This problem may be avoided by having current employees sign a written form (agreeing to the policy) at the time they receive a pay raise. This is an issue that should be addressed with a local attorney. The policy should be explained to all new employees at the time of hiring, and they should be required to sign a statement acknowledging that they understand and agree to the policy.

Insurance

§ 8-30

Key Point 8-30> Most church general liability insurance policies exclude employment practices. This means that many churches face a potentially significant uninsured risk. Employment practices liability insurance is available to cover most employment-related claims.

Employment disputes are one of the most common sources of litigation involving churches. However, many churches are not insured against this risk,

---

[313] Jacobs v. Mallard Creek Presbyterian Church, 214 F.Supp.2d 552 (W.D.N.C. 2002).

[314] Mitnaul v. Fairmount Presbyterian Church, 778 N.E.2d 1093 (Ohio App. 2002).

often because of an assumption that the church's comprehensive general liability (CGL) policy covers these claims. In many cases, this is not the case since the typical CGL policy excludes "employment practices."

How can church leaders respond to this potentially uninsured risk? The best response is twofold:

1. Implement an effective risk management program that addresses the most common types of employer liability. This text contains many suggestions that will assist church leaders in implementing a risk management program.

2. Purchase employment practices liability insurance (EPLI). Often, EPLI insurance can be purchased as a special endorsement to a CGL policy.

▶ *Church leaders should ask their church insurance agent if the church has insurance for employment practices. If not, ask how this coverage can be obtained.*

Here are some points to consider in evaluating the need for EPLI coverage:

1. Check with the church insurance agent or company to determine if your church presently has employment practices coverage. If so, find out the amounts of coverage and determine if the coverage is adequate. As with any insurance policy, the EPLI policy should be reviewed periodically.

2. If you have EPLI coverage, or are considering the purchase of an EPLI policy, check to see who is covered under the policy. Generally, the employer and its officers, directors, and employees are covered. But, some policies exclude part-time employees and self-employed workers. Ask the church's insurance agent about covering these persons if they are excluded.

3. If you have EPLI coverage, or are considering the purchase of an EPLI policy, check the amount of coverage to be sure it is adequate. Also, note that under most EPLI policies the costs of providing a legal defense for the employer come out of the policy limits. To illustrate, assume that a church has an EPLI policy with coverage of up to $300,000. If defense costs come out of the coverage limit, and the insurer incurs defense costs of $75,000, this reduces the coverage limit to $225,000.

4. If you have EPLI coverage, or are considering the purchase of an EPLI policy, carefully examine the exclusions under the policy. Common exclusions include claims made under the Fair Labor Standards Act (for overtime pay, or the minimum wage), claims resulting from layoffs, claims under the Consolidated Omnibus Budget Reconciliation Act (COBRA); and claims under the Employee Retirement Income Security Act (ERISA). Some EPLI policies exclude punitive damages, while others do not. However, note that several states prohibit insurance policies from insuring against punitive damages.

5. Determine the amount of the deductible, or any "self-insured retention," under the policy. A self-insured retention is the amount the employer is required to pay in defense costs or settlement amounts before coverage under the policy is triggered. To illustrate, if a church's EPLI policy has a $20,000 retention, the church must pay the first $20,000 in attorneys' fees and any settlement amount. Only after the church pays this amount will the insurer be obligated to pay additional amounts under the policy, up to the coverage limit.

6. If you have EPLI coverage, or are considering the purchase of an EPLI policy, pay special attention to those persons who can bring claims that will be covered under the policy. Some policies limit coverage to claims made by current full-time employees. Others broaden the coverage to include claims made by part-time employees and self-employed workers, and former employees.

7. Most EPLI policies are "claims made" policies. A claims made policy covers injuries for which a claim is made during the policy period if the insured has continuously been insured with claims made policies with the same insurer since the injury occurred. Some insurers who offer claims made policies may agree to cover claims made during the current policy period for injuries occurring in the past when the insured carried insurance with another insurer. This is often referred to as "prior acts coverage."

8. EPLI policies will define how and when a claim must be made under the policy. It is essential for church leaders to be familiar with these provisions, since a failure to comply with the policy's claims or notice requirements may lead to a loss of coverage.

9. Most EPLI applications require the church to identify any facts or incidents that may result in an employment-related claim including wrongful dismissal, sexual harassment, or various forms of discrimination. It is important for the church to provide accurate and complete information in response to such questions. This should not be done by one person. A better practice would be for the board and staff to collectively provide input.

10. Some churches have purchased directors and officers insurance. Such policies may provide limited coverage for employment-related claims. Usually, these policies carry a large retention (deductible).

11. The need for EPLI insurance increases with the number of church employees. More employees means additional exposure to employment-related claims.

12. Most EPLI policies cover a wide variety of employment-related claims including some or all of the following: sexual harassment, discrimination, wrongful dismissal, breach of employment contract, wrongful discipline, emotional distress, negligent selection and supervision, invasion

of privacy, and defamation. Be sure to note whether an EPLI policy covers claims of discrimination filed with the EEOC or state human rights agencies are covered.

13. Many EPLI policies contain a "hammer clause." Such a clause gives the insurer the authority to recommend the settlement of a pending claim for a specified amount. If the employer disagrees, and the case proceeds, the insurer's liability under the policy cannot be more than the settlement amount it recommended. It is important for church leaders to be aware of the existence of such a provision in an existing EPLI policy, or an EPLI policy that is being considered.

14. Be sure to note whether an EPLI policy covers arbitration awards. Many churches have inserted arbitration clauses in employee handbooks or employment applications that require employment-related disputes to be resolved through binding arbitration. Churches that have adopted arbitration policies to resolve employment-related disputes should ensure that their EPLI policy will cover arbitrators' awards.

> *Churches should appoint an insurance committee composed of persons having some knowledge of insurance. This committee can evaluate insurance options and coverages, and make recommendations to the church board.*

Instructional Aids
to Chapter 8

Terms

Age Discrimination in Employment Act

Americans with Disabilities Act

"at will" employee

Civil Rights Act of 1964, Title VII

commerce

Employee Polygraph Protection Act

employer

Fair Labor Standards Act

Family and Medical Leave Act

Form I-9

good cause

hostile environment sexual harassment

minimum wage

National Labor Relations Act

Occupational Safety and Health Act

overtime pay

preschool

qualified individual with a disability

quid pro quo sexual harassment

reference letter

sexual harassment

vicarious liability

workers compensation

Learning Objectives

- Understand the meaning of workers compensation, and explain the application of workers compensation laws to religious organizations.

- Understand the application of Form I-9 to religious organizations.

- Explain the "employment at will" doctrine, and identify several exceptions to it.

- Understand the procedure employees follow when filing a discrimination claim under federal civil rights laws.

- Understand the importance of the term "commerce" in the context of federal employment and civil rights laws, and explain its meaning.

- Explain the "clergy exemption" under federal civil rights laws.

- Understand the major provisions of Title VII of the Civil Rights Act of 1964, and explain its application to religious organizations.

- Understand the major provisions of the federal Age Discrimination in Employment Act, and explain its application to religious organizations.

- Understand the major provisions of the Americans with Disabilities Act, and explain its application to religious organizations.

- Understand the major provisions of Employee Polygraph Protection Act, and explain its application to religious organizations.

- Understand the major provisions of Occupational Safety and Health Act, and explain its application to religious organizations.

- Understand the major provisions of Fair Labor Standards Act, and explain its application to religious organizations.

- Understand the major provisions of National Labor Relations Act, and explain its application to religious organizations.

- Understand the major provisions of Family and Medical Leave Act, and explain its application to religious organizations.

- Identify the legal risks associated with the use of reference letters, and explain how these risks may be reduced.

- Understand the application to religious organizations of state laws banning employment discrimination on the basis of sexual orientation.

Short-Answer Questions

1. Explain the new hire reporting requirements. Do they apply to churches?

2. Paul is a citizen of a foreign country where he is employed as a pastor. Paul is in the United States on a visitor's visa. Several churches have invited Paul to conduct worship services. Can Paul be compensated for performing these services?

3. Describe the purpose of the R-1 visa.

4. Describe the purpose for workers compensation laws, and their application to churches.

5. A church hires a full-time custodian. Several months later the pastor learns that the custodian is receiving workers compensation benefits. Is the church subject to any penalties for hiring the custodian? Explain.

6. Describe two of the main provisions of the Fair Labor Standards Act.

7. A church has 10 employees. It does not operate any commercial activity that generates revenue. Is the church subject to "enterprise coverage" under the Fair Labor Standards Act?

8. Does the Fair Labor Standards Act exempt church employees from coverage? Explain.

9. A church operates a preschool for children who are four and five years of age. The preschool incorporates a curriculum covering basic math and verbal skills, and Bible stories. Is the preschool subject to enterprise coverage under the Fair Labor Standards Act? If so, what does this mean?

10. A church operates a private school for grades K-12. Is the school subject to enterprise coverage under the Fair Labor Standards Act? What if its total annual revenue is less than $500,000?

11. A church has annual revenue of $300,000 and employs four persons (a pastor, a youth pastor, a church secretary, and a custodian). It engages in no "businesses" that compete with for-profit companies, and does not operate a preschool or school. Is the church secretary entitled to overtime pay for hours that she occasionally works in excess of 40 per week?

12. Same facts as question 11 except that the secretary purchases office supplies from a local office supply store two or three times each year.

13. Same facts as question 11, except that for the past three years the church secretary has purchased office supplies about 12 times each year over the Internet from various out-of-state office supply stores. These purchases included computers, computer software, office equipment, and office supplies, and averaged $4,000 per year. Do these purchases satisfy the individual coverage provisions of the FLSA, entitling the secretary to overtime pay for hours worked in excess of 40 each week?

14. Same facts as question 11, except that the secretary places or receives between 5 and 10 long-distance calls each month involving persons in other states. Do these calls satisfy the individual coverage provisions of the FLSA, entitling the secretary to overtime pay for hours worked in excess of 40 each week?

15. Same facts as question 11, except that the secretary sends and receives several e-mail messages each week from a computer in her church office. Many of these e-mails are sent to, and received from, persons in other states. Do these e-mails satisfy the individual coverage provisions of the FLSA, entitling the secretary to overtime pay for hours worked in excess of 40 each week?

16. Can church employees be protected by the overtime and minimum wage requirements of the Fair Labor Standards Act if their employing church is not subject to enterprise coverage under the Act?

17. A church wants to avoid the FLSA overtime pay requirements for its custodian (who often works more than 40 hours per week) and so it pays him an annual salary of $25,000 instead of an hourly wage. Will this plan work?

18. A church treasurer would like the church secretary to be an exempt employee because she works so many hours of overtime. He tells the senior pastor that if the secretary is paid a salary of $25,000 then the church can treat the secretary as an exempt administrative employee and avoid having to pay overtime. Is this advice correct?

19. A church pays it pastor on an hourly basis of $15 per hour. Is the pastor entitled to overtime pay?

20. A church pays its senior pastor an annual salary of $45,000. The pastor frequently works 60 hours or more per week, and asks the church treasurer if he is entitled to overtime pay. Is he?

21. Lisa works for two hours on one Sunday each month in her church's nursery. If the church decides to pay Lisa for her services, must it pay her no less than the federal or state minimum wage (whichever is greater)?

22. All federal laws prohibiting discrimination in employment apply only to those employers that are engaged in interstate commerce. What is the reason for this requirement?

23. A church is accused of engaging in sex discrimination in violation of Title VII of the Civil Rights Act of 1964. The church insists that it is not covered by Title VII. What is the most likely outcome?

24. A church with 10 employees is accused of violating the federal age discrimination law by not hiring a job applicant who is 60 years old. Is the church subject to the federal age discrimination law? Explain.

25. A church has 16 employees. It has an opening for an associate pastoral position. A disabled minister applies for the position, but is rejected. The rejected applicant sues the church for violating the federal Americans with Disabilities Act. What is the most likely outcome?

26. Same facts as question 15 except that the church has eight full-time and five part-time employees.

27. A woman was employed by a church as its music director. She was not a credentialed minister. She suffered from a variety of disabilities, including chemical allergies. She claimed that the church refused to modify her work schedule to allow full recovery from injuries she suffered as a result of inhaling fumes from chemicals used by church custodians for cleaning purposes. She sued the church for violating the Americans with Disabilities Act. Assuming that the Act applies to the church, what is the most likely disposition of this case?

28. A black female sued her religious denomination, claiming both sex and race discrimination in violation of Title VII of the Civil Rights Act of 1964 when her application for appointment as a member of the clergy was denied. What is the most likely result of this case? Explain.

29. The following questions pertain to Title VII of the Civil Rights Act of 1964:

  A. Who enacted this legislation?

  B. Describe the main provisions of Title VII.

  C. Who is subject to the provisions of Title VII?

  D. Explain the application of Title VII to churches.

  E. Does Title VII prohibit sexual harassment?

  F. Does Title VII prohibit discrimination in employment based on age?

  G. Does Title VII prohibit discrimination in employment based on violation of a church's moral teachings?

30. A pastor learns that an unmarried female secretary employed by the church is pregnant. Since extramarital sexual relations violate the church's moral

teachings, the pastor terminates the secretary's employment. Assuming that the church is subject to Title VII, has it committed unlawful discrimination? Explain.

31. Same facts as question 30. The church employed a male associate pastor 10 years ago who engaged in an extramarital affair. The associate pastor was reprimanded, but was "forgiven" and allowed to retain his job. Would this be relevant in the secretary's case? If so, how?

32. Describe each of the two main types of sexual harassment.

33. An associate pastor threatens to terminate a church employee's job if she does not engage in an extramarital affair with him. Answer the following questions:

A. Is this an example of sexual harassment? If so, which kind?

B. Is the church subject to liability for sexual harassment? Explain.

C. The pastor insists that the affair was consensual. Is this is an effective defense to sexual harassment?

34. A nonsupervisory church employee engages in frequent behavior of a sexual nature that offends other employees. His behavior includes sexually suggestive touching and language. Employees repeatedly ask him to stop, but to no avail. If one of the offended employees sues the church for violating Title VII's ban on sexual harassment, what is the most likely outcome? Assume the church is subject to Title VII.

35. The United States Supreme Court has recognized an "affirmative defense" that will provide employers with some protection from sexual harassment claims. Describe this affirmative defense.

36. Should a church have a sexual harassment policy? If so, what are the most important provisions to include in the policy?

37. A church has six employees. A female employee believes that she has been subjected to sexual harassment, and she contacts the EEOC. What is the most likely result? Explain.

38. A church is subject to Title VII. It adopts a written sexual harassment policy that defines harassment, encourages employees to report harassing behavior, and assures employees that they will not suffer retaliation for reporting harassment. A male supervisory employee engages in frequent offensive remarks and physical contact of a sexual nature with a female employee. The female employee is greatly disturbed by this behavior, and considers it inappropriate in a church. In fact, she had sought church employment because she considered it a safe environment and her job would be a ministry. The supervisor eventually dis-

misses the employee because of her refusal to "go along" with his offensive behavior. Throughout her employment, the employee never informed church leadership of the supervisor's behavior. Several months after her termination, the employee files a sexual harassment complaint with the EEOC. Will the church be liable for the supervisor's behavior under these circumstances? Explain.

39. Same facts as the previous question, except that the employee was not dismissed and suffered no "tangible employment decision" (firing, failing to promote, reassignment with significantly different responsibilities, or a decision causing a significant change in benefits).

40. A church is subject to Title VII. It has not adopted a written sexual harassment policy. A female employee files a complaint with the EEOC, claiming that a supervisor has engaged in hostile environment sexual harassment. She never informed church leadership of the supervisor's behavior before filing her complaint with the EEOC. Will the church qualify for the "affirmative defense" to sexual harassment claims?

41. A church is opposed, on the basis of its interpretation of the Bible, to hiring homosexuals. B and C are homosexual men. B applies for a volunteer position as a Sunday School teacher, and C applies for a paid staff position as a business administrator. The church rejects both applications because B and C are homosexuals. B and C retain an attorney who threatens to sue the church. Answer the following questions:

A. Has the church violated B's rights under Title VII of the Civil Rights Act of 1964? Explain.

B. Assume that the church is in a state with a civil rights law that bans discrimination in employment on the basis of sexual orientation. Has the church violated B's rights under this law? Explain.

C. Has the church violated C's rights under Title VII of the Civil Rights Act of 1964? Explain.

D. Assume that the church is in a state with a civil rights law that bans discrimination in employment on the basis of sexual orientation. Has the church violated C's rights under this law? Explain.

42. A church has 18 employees. Is it subject to the federal Age Discrimination in Employment Act? Explain.

43. Explain the "ministerial exception." To whom does this exception apply?

44. A church that is subject to the Americans with Disabilities Act (ADA) has an opening for an accountant. The job description requires that the individual be a college graduate with a degree in accounting. A blind applicant satisfies

these requirements. She can perform all the essential functions of the job if she is provided with a part-time reader. If the church decides not to hire the applicant because of the cost of a part-time reader, has it violated the ADA? Explain.

45. A church is building a new sanctuary. A member insists that the Americans with Disabilities Act requires the church to install an elevator in the new building. Is this correct?

46. A church has nine employees. Is it subject to the provisions of the federal Family and Medical Leave Act?

47. A youth pastor is accused of inappropriate conduct with a member of the church's youth group. The youth pastor denies any wrongdoing. The senior pastor suggests that the youth pastor take a polygraph test in order to establish his innocence. Are there any legal consequences to this recommendation? Explain.

48. Same facts as question 47, except that the church has only four employees.

49. A church uses a small orchestra during worship services twice each week. The orchestra practices for two hours each week in addition to performing in worship services. Members of the orchestra are exposed to decibel levels exceeding the permissible levels specified by the Occupational Safety and Health Act (OSHA). Is the church liable for exceeding these limits?

50. Helen is a church organist. She plays the organ several times each week at worship services, choir rehearsals, funerals, weddings, and other special functions. She is frequently exposed to decibel levels exceeding the permissible levels specified by OSHA. Is the church liable for exceeding these limits?

51. Summarize the application of federal workplace poster requirements to churches.

52. Explain the "at will" employment rule.

53. A church hires a clerical worker. Nothing is said regarding the term of employment. Answer the following questions:

A. This type of employment relationship is often referred to by what term?

B. Historically, an employer could terminate such a relationship on the basis of what grounds?

C. Historically, did an employer have any recourse against an employee who terminated such a relationship?

D. Do the courts still recognize this rule in most states?

E. Are there any exceptions to the historical rule that are commonly recognized by the courts today?

54. T is a church employee who has been hired for an indefinite period. The church terminates T's employment because of a "personality conflict" with the pastor. T sues the church for wrongful termination. What is the likely outcome of this case?

55. Same facts as question 54, except that T was hired for a three-year term, and is terminated after only one year on the job.

56. The church board failed to designate a housing allowance for Pastor B this year. At the end of the year, Pastor B instructs the church bookkeeper to prepare and "backdate" a fraudulent board resolution designating in advance a housing allowance for the entire year. The employee refuses to do so, and is dismissed. The employee sues the church for wrongful termination. The church insists that the worker was an at will employee who could be terminated for any reason. What is the likely outcome of this case?

57. What is a severance agreement? Give an example of how such an agreement can reduce a church's risk of legal liability when dismissing an employee.

58. J has served as a bookkeeper at his church for more than 20 years. Pastor H learns that J has embezzled over $10,000 of church funds. Pastor H confronts J and obtains a full confession. J's employment is immediately terminated. Members of the staff and congregation immediately notice that J is missing. She no longer shows up at work, and has quit attending the church. People begin asking questions about the reasons for J's sudden departure. Rumors spread that J was fired. In order to respond to these questions, Pastor H informs the staff (at a weekly staff meeting) that J was dismissed because of embezzlement. Pastor H makes a similar disclosure to the congregation following a morning worship service. J learns of these disclosures, and sues Pastor H and the church. Answer the following questions:

A. What is the likely outcome of this case?

B. What precautions could Pastor H have taken to reduce the risk of litigation?

59. A church dismisses Pastor K, its senior pastor. Pastor K, who is 68 years of age, believes that the church dismissed him because of his age. He retains an attorney who writes the church a letter threatening to sue for unlawful age discrimination unless the church settles with her client for $1 million. Answer the following questions:

A. Has the church committed unlawful age discrimination? Assume that the main reason it dismissed Pastor K was that it wanted a younger, more dynamic minister.

B. How should the church respond to the attorney's letter?

C. How could the church have minimized the risk of this dispute?

60. Pastor V has served as senior pastor of a church for several years. He has a stroke that permanently affects his speech, making it very slow and unintelligible. The church reluctantly dismisses him. Pastor V retains an attorney who threatens to sue the church for violating the Americans with Disabilities Act. List four defenses that may be available to the church.

61. A church has 20 employees, and is engaged in commerce. It is looking for a new youth pastor, and receives an application from an ordained minister of a different religious denomination. The church refuses to consider this application. Answer the following questions:

A. Has the church committed religious discrimination?

B. If the church has committed religious discrimination, has it violated Title VII of the Civil Rights Act of 1964? Explain.

62. A church needs a new custodian. It refuses to consider E, a qualified applicant, because E is a member of a different faith. Answer the following questions:

A. Has the church committed religious discrimination?

B. If the church has committed religious discrimination, has it violated Title VII of the Civil Rights Act of 1964?

C. Is a church permitted by Title VII to engage in religious discrimination with respect to custodial positions, or other positions not involving "ministerial" duties? Explain.

63. A church operates a preschool. The pastor learns that an unmarried female employee at the preschool is pregnant. The employee is dismissed because of "pregnancy, out of wedlock." The former employee sues the church for sex discrimination. Answer the following questions:

A. What is the likely outcome of this case?

B. What precautions could the church have taken to reduce the risk of litigation?

64. Same facts as question 63, except that the church dismissed the employee for "extramarital sexual relations in violation of the chu"s religious teachings." The former employee sues the church for sex discrimination, claiming that the church discriminates against women because male employees who were guilty of extramarital sexual relations in the past were not dismissed but rather were warned to discontinue such behavior. Answer the following questions:

A. What is the likely outcome of this case?

B. What precautions could the church have taken to reduce the risk of litigation?

65. A 75-year-old person applies for a secretarial position at a local church. The church hires a 35-year-old person (because of better typing skills and familiarity with computers). The 75-year-old person believes that the church practiced illegal age discrimination in not offering her the job. Answer the following questions:

A. Does the Age Discrimination in Employment Act apply to the church? Assume that it has five employees.

B. Does the Age Discrimination in Employment Act apply to the church? Assume that it has 30 employees.

C. Assume that the Age Discrimination in Employment Act does apply to the church. Did the church violate it?

D. Assume that instead of applying to a local church for a secretarial position, the 75-year-old applied to a denominational agency. What difference would this make? Assume that the agency engages in the publication and distribution of literature.

66. A church has at least 15 employees and is engaged in commerce. It needs to hire a new custodian, and two persons apply. One is a nondisabled member of the church, and the other is a disabled nonmember who could perform the essential functions of the job with reasonable accommodations by the church. The church hires the nondisabled member. Has it violated the Americans with Disabilities Act? Explain.

67. Same facts as question 66, except that the church has only five employees.

68. A church has at least 15 employees and is engaged in commerce. It needs to hire a custodian. One of the essential functions of the position is the ability to lift boxes weighing up to 50 pounds. This requirement is noted in a job description for the position. T, who suffers from multiple sclerosis, applies for the job. T is not able to lift 50-pound boxes. The church decides not to hire T. Has it violated the Americans with Disabilities Act?

69. A church decides to pay its entire staff, including custodians, bookkeeper, and secretaries, a salary in order to avoid the overtime pay requirements. Will this arrangement work?

70. A 10-year-old child informs her mother that a volunteer Sunday School teacher improperly touched her. The mother informs her pastor, who confronts the teacher. The teacher adamantly denies any wrongdoing. The church board is not sure how to proceed. One member suggests that the teacher be asked to take a polygraph exam. The board agrees that this would be a good idea. Answer the following questions:

    A. The church has only three employees. Is it subject to the Employee Polygraph Protection Act?

    B. Assume that the church is subject to the Employee Polygraph Protection Act. Would it violate the Act by requiring that the teacher "pr"" his innocence by taking a polygraph exam?

    C. Assume that the church is subject to the Employee Polygraph Protection Act. Would it violate the Act by suggesting that the teacher take a polygraph exam?

    D. Assume that the church is subject to the Employee Polygraph Protection Act. Would your answers be different if the teacher were a paid employee of the church? Why?

71. A former member sues a church, alleging that the pastor seduced her in the course of a counseling relationship a few years ago. The pastor adamantly denies any wrongdoing. The woman's attorney has her submit to a polygraph exam, which indicates that the woman is telling the truth. The woman's attorney says that she will drop the lawsuit if the pastor is tested by the same polygraph examiner and is found to be telling the truth. The pastor refuses to do so, insisting that he does not need a test to prove that he is telling the truth. The church board urges the pastor to reconsider, and to take the exam. Assuming that the church is subject to the Employee Polygraph Protection Act, has the church violated the Act? Explain.

72. A church board suspects the church's volunteer treasurer of embezzling several thousands of dollars of church funds. The treasurer is called into a board meeting, and is told "you can clear your name if you submit to a polygraph exam." Does this conduct violate the Employee Polygraph Protection Act? Explain.

73. Same facts as the previous example, except that the church suspects a full-time secretary of embezzlement. What steps can the church take to qualify for the "ongoing investigation" exception under the Employee Polygraph Protection Act?

74. What are four ways that a church can reduce its risk of liability when providing references about current or former employees?

75. Explain the concept of "qualified privilege."

76. G worked as a volunteer children's worker at First Church. After parents complained to the senior pastor about G's inappropriate touching of a number of children, G is removed from his position. A few months later G leaves First Church and begins attending Second Church. When he applies as a children's worker, Second Church contacts First Church for a reference. First Church sends a letter containing a strong and unqualified recommendation of G. Nothing is disclosed regarding G's inappropriate touching of several children. G later molests a child at Second Church. When the child's parents learn of First Church's recommendation, they sue the church. Is it possible for First Church to be legally responsible for G's acts of molestation occurring at Second Church? Explain.

77. Same facts as the previous example, except that First Church refused to respond to Second Church's request for a reference regarding G.

78. Church staff inspect a church-owned computer in the youth pastor's office at the church, and discover persistent use of the Internet to view and download pornographic images. The church has no policy addressing access to staff computers. The church dismisses the youth pastor on the basis of this evidence. If the dismissed youth pastor sues the church, what is the most likely result?

79. Same facts as question 78. What steps could the church have taken to reduce its risk of liability?

Discussion Questions

1. *Some local churches are not covered by the federal minimum wage and overtime compensation requirements, and they rely on this exemption to pay less than the minimum wage to their workers and avoid overtime pay for hours worked in excess of 40 each week. Other churches feel strongly that they have a moral duty to honor the minimum wage and overtime compensation rules. What is your opinion? Would you, as a senior pastor, be willing to pay less than the minimum wage to church workers? Why or why not?*

2. *Many Americans are opposed to the "enforcement of morality" by the government. Yet, is not this what federal civil rights and employment laws seek to do? To illustrate, are federal laws that prohibit discrimination in employment on the basis of race, ethnicity, religion, sex, age, or disability examples of the enforcement of morality by government? And, could it not be argued that such laws are enforcing religious values as well?*

3. *Some church leaders sincerely believe that the government should not have the authority to force churches to comply with employment and civil rights laws. Do you believe that the government should, or should not, have this authority? Why? What if a law violates a church's religious tenets, such as a law prohibiting employers (including churches) from discriminating in employment decisions on the basis of sexual orientation?*

Index

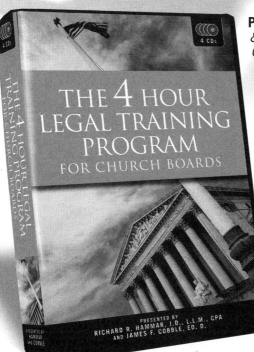

Is Your Church Prepared for the Business Side of Ministry?

YOUR CHURCH RESOURCES

Visit us today at:
www.ChurchLawCatalog.com

Trusted resources for your ministries' financial, legal, tax and risk needs.